BOWL GAMES

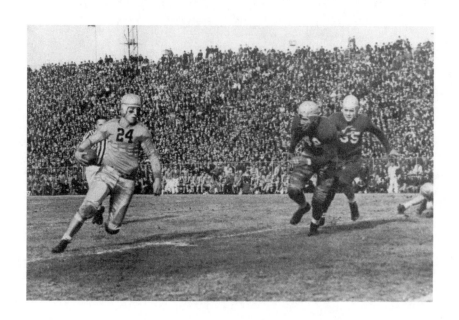

BOWL GAMES

College Football's Greatest Tradition

ROBERT M. OURS

WESTHOLME

Yardley

First Printing
10 9 8 7 6 5 4 3 2 1

ISBN 1-59416-001-5

www.westholmepublishing.com

Printed in Canada on acid-free paper.

Frontispiece: Colorado tailback (and future Supreme Court Justice) Byron "Whizzer"
White (24) returns a pass interception 47 yards for a touchdown against Rice to give
his team a 14–0 lead in the first quarter of the 1938 Cotton Bowl.

CONTENTS

INTRODUCTION:
AN AMERICAN TRADITION

GREAT TEAMS AND GREAT GAMES, MEMORABLE plays and memorable players are all part of the story of college football bowl games. In the more than one hundred years since the first one was played in Pasadena, California, on New Year's Day, 1902, these games have become ingrained as an American tradition and have helped establish college football as a sport of national interest. In addition, postseason games have played important roles as fundraisers and as morale boosters during the Great Depression and both world wars, and have temporarily diverted attention from other serious world and national events to provide entertainment and escapism for millions of Americans. Even in years without a major crisis, they provide the basis for regional and conference bragging rights and the determination of a national champion—or more fuel for the debates on which was the best college football team in a given season. Bowl games feature halftime pageantry beyond that normally enjoyed during regular season, and several include parades or other associated events, often lasting for days or even weeks preceding the big games. Millions of persons attend the contests, watch them on television, or listen to them on radio or the internet.

Team and individual performances take on a special luster with so much attention focused on the postseason games. Since January 4, 1970, when the final national rankings poll of the Associated Press was moved permanently from the end of the regular season to after the bowl season, highly rated teams have used bowl games either to reinforce their claims to national titles or to show that their postseason performance entitles them to a No. 1 ranking. Prior to 1969, the national champion was chosen at the end of the regular season, but between New Year's Day, 1937 (the 1936 regular season was the first in which the AP began its national rankings) and New Year's Day, 1969, five No. 1 teams in the wire service poll were defeated in bowl games, yet remained national champion for that season.

An informal playoff system using existing bowl games, instituted with a Bowl Coalition in 1992, has been used for a dozen years to try to determine a single national champion. But neither the coalition, the succeeding Bowl Alliance of 1995–1997, nor the Bowl Championship Series (BCS) begun in 1998 has been fully effective. Each system has had major flaws that led to increased controversy over how selections are made and which teams are eligible. Controversy peaked during the 2003 postseason when Southern California was ranked No.1 in both the AP and USA Today/ESPN polls at the end of the regular season—yet was not selected for the BCS championship game in the Nokia Sugar Bowl. Members of conferences and other schools virtually left out of the BCS playoff structure also increased the crescendo of criticism, and even Congress began looking into the situation during the 2003 season.

Discussion and scrutiny of the BCS system began in earnest well before the start of the 2004 regular season. BCS commissioners, the NCAA, and ABC-TV, in meetings between February and July, agreed on several adjustments, including a change in the selection formula that would have chosen No. 2 Oregon instead of No. 4 Nebraska for the title game after the 2001 season and No. 1 USC rather than No. 3 Oklahoma for last year's title contest. In addition, there was agreement to schedule a fifth BCS game in 2006, adding two more slots for teams from conferences not tied in automatically to the BCS. Proposals also were being considered for guaranteeing inclusion of members of all Division I-A conferences in the BCS system in the future.

Meanwhile, sparkling bowl performances continue to solidify reputations of some players as great clutch performers, and in other cases engrave the names of future stars into the minds of All-America selectors for the ensuing season or scouts for the professional draft. Bowl games also have contributed to the lore of college football's famous goofs, such as Roy Riegels's wrong-way run in the 1929 Rose Bowl and Tommy Lewis's off-the-bench tackle in the 1954 Cotton Bowl.

But the history of bowl games is much more than the winners and losers, or who reigns as national champion for a particular year. Bowl games reveal how the sport of football has changed over the decades and how college football has become a multimillion-dollar industry. Bowl games helped bring racial integration to the forefront in sports, forcing athletes and spectators to face that social crisis in the immediate post–World War II decade. Bowl games also challenged the relationship between athletics and education as many leading universities, such as Notre Dame and the Ivy League schools, refused to participate in postseason play for decades, leaving an opportunity for smaller or lesser known colleges to shine in the national football spotlight for a while.

Perhaps nothing illustrates the popularity of bowl games among current college football fans more than the proliferation of the postseason contests over the past two decades. Nine postseason games were played following the 1959 regular season, and a dozen following the 1976 season. The number increased to eighteen by the end of the 1984 season and totaled twenty-five at the end of the century. Upon completion of the 2002 season, the number of bowls had reached a record of twenty-eight, a number maintained in the 2003 postseason as well, involving fifty-six of the nation's 117 Division I-A teams. In other words, nearly half of the schools playing major-college football were rewarded at the end of the season with an opportunity to enhance their records with a victory against a reputable opponent from another section of the country and, in the process, add to their financial coffers.

The NCAA in April recertified twenty-eight bowls for postseason 2004, with the San Francisco Bowl changing its name to the Emerald Bowl and the Humanitarian Bowl renamed the MPC Computers Bowl. A few were recertified with "conditions" or "concerns" by the NCAA's Football Certification subcommittee. Bids for certification for new bowls following the 2005 season, to be acted upon in spring 2005, were submitted by Denver, Seattle, and South Florida.

The prospect of financial gain from bowl participation over the years has become a major factor, including budget planning in university athletic departments.

Bowl payouts following the 2003 season ranged from a $750,000 minimum per team for the smaller bowls to $13.5 million for each team invited to participate in the four BCS games. Several of the middle-range bowls paid each team between $1.8 and $5 million. That's a far cry from the turn of the twentieth century, when hotel owners and other businessmen in the quiet community of Pasadena, California, offered Michigan players $3 each for meal money as compensation to play a postseason football game against Stanford to top off the town's annual Tournament of Roses festival.

The fact that the vast majority of the bowls following the 2003 season had corporate sponsorship, with corporate names often attached to the name of the event, also differs from the early days of bowl games, when the names typically signified a natural product of the area in which the bowl was played. For example: Rose in California, Orange in Florida, Cotton in Texas, Sugar in Louisiana—even the Sun Bowl for the west Texas city of El Paso, where the sun shines more than three hundred days of the year on average. Before the late 1980s, the names of bowl games were easy to remember. In the past decade and a half, however, a number of bowls have changed names or sponsors. Even the venerable Rose Bowl, while retaining its original name unadorned, has had a "presenting sponsor" since 1999, most recently Citi, a division of Citigroup.

The Pasadena football experiment of New Year's Day, 1902 was not repeated until 1916, and no other postseason games appeared on the scene until the 1920s. With the construction of a new stadium based on the Yale Bowl design, the game in Pasadena received its familiar name, Rose Bowl, first used for the Southern California–Penn State contest in 1923. As postseason games grew in number and popularity, promoters picked up on the name "bowl" to distinguish these contests. Four additional bowls were inaugurated during the 1920s, but none lasted more than two or three games. Although a number of postseason games were played in the early 1930s, they were special charity contests to raise money for the relief of persons hard hit by the Great Depression. It was not until the mid-1930s that other postseason games were launched to join the Rose Bowl. Four of them—the Orange, Sugar, Sun, and Cotton—still are with us and are the basis for the tradition of postseason college football play.

These early bowl games, for the most part, were played on January 1, or on January 2 when New Year's Day fell on a Sunday, although a few attempts were made to schedule games on another day, usually around Christmas. Following the 2003 season, 18 of the bowls were played before New Year's Day, and five more took place between January 2 and January 4. Only five were played on the traditional New Year's Day, and because ABC television has exclusive broadcast rights to the four BCS bowls, it is no longer possible to have the games all appear on New Year's Day, as they had for decades. The Nokia Sugar Bowl, matching the top-ranked teams of the BCS system, closed the season the night of January 4, 2004, with Louisiana State defeating Oklahoma 21–14.

Another big difference between the early bowl games and those of the present concerns the records of the teams participating. In the earlier days, the majority of postseason participants earned their invitations either by going undefeated or by losing no more than two or three games. Following the 2003 season, given the large number of bowl games, fifteen of the participants had lost five or six games in the regular season, with four of them only breaking even with 6–6 records. Three of those subsequently lost in the bowls to finish the season with losing records.

Theoretically, for at least the first half of the twentieth century, any of the more than 650 teams that played college football annually could be considered possible participants in postseason play. In practice, however, bids were offered to the schools that played in major conferences that allowed postseason competition or that played a schedule consisting of games mostly against "big college" opponents. The latter included a number of small schools that regularly played many major teams. Several little-known universities or institutions known only through their academic reputations were at one time football powerhouses. In the 1920s, Centre, Gonzaga, Washington and Jefferson, and West Virginia Wesleyan fielded some outstanding teams, while in the 1930s and 1940s a host of small schools had football success, including Bucknell, Carnegie Tech, College of Pacific, Drake, Fordham, Georgetown, Hardin-Simmons, Manhattan, St. Mary's, San Francisco, Santa Clara, and Wichita. Most of these schools were placed in classifications below Division I-A when the National Collegiate Athletic Association (NCAA) split its members formally into different classifications in the 1970s.

What follows is the rich history of people, teams, and games that have made college football what it is today. In fact, a history of bowl games is largely a history of college football itself. At the end of each season the best teams square off and, as each year goes by, new tactics, new coaching methods, and amazing athletes appear. For when the whistle blows and the game gets under way, the action on the field obliterates, at least temporarily, the big business and big money aspects that have become such an important part of bowl games. Instead, the attention is focused, as it has been for generations, on the action between the white lines.

Postseason games played on New Year's Day or the days immediately following belong to the season just completed in the previous calendar year.

All national rankings listed are those of the Associated Press final regular season except as indicated otherwise. The AP rankings, begun during the 1936 regular season as a poll of sportswriters and sports broadcasters, is the oldest of the various nationwide rankings.

National champions mentioned in the text before 1936 are those recognized by a variety of rankings, some concurrent and some retrospective, including major newspapers and individuals who developed their own formulas or "power" systems.

Changes in school names are indicated at the first mention of that school in the text.

The Big 10 Conference was formed in 1896 as the Intercollegiate Conference of Faculty Representatives, often called the Western Conference. It was informally called the Big 10 Conference until 1988, when that name was formally adopted upon being organized as a not-for-profit organization. Thus, teams from this conference are referred to as Big 10 members throughout the text.

1 FIRST, THE ROSE

AT THE TURN OF THE TWENTIETH CENTURY, college football, which started with a game between Rutgers and Princeton in 1869, had spread to schools across the country and its popularity was beginning to rival that of other spectator sports. Pasadena at that time was a quiet little southern California town located at the foot of the San Gabriel Mountains about seven miles northeast of Los Angeles. Pasadena was known primarily as a place where wealthy persons, many of them from the East, spent their winters in the sunshine and clean air. Since 1890, to celebrate the contrast between the area's pleasant winter weather and the frigid temperatures in the major cities of the Midwest and Northeast, the town had hosted an annual New Year's Day parade of carriages covered with poinsettias and roses, and horses decked out with hibiscus and other flowers. After the parade, spectators gathered down the street at the town lot to watch games and stunts, such as footraces, polo, tug-of-war matches, and an old Spanish event called the "tourney of rings," in which speeding horseback riders with long lances tried to spear hanging rings. The latter event gave the Tournament of Roses its name.

In 1900 the Tournament of Roses not only received increased newspaper coverage but also was filmed by the Vitascope Company, allowing cinema audiences throughout the United States to enjoy the celebration for the first time. An estimated 50,000 visitors thronged Pasadena for the end-of-the-century parade that year. Resort and hotel owners along with other businessmen of the community decided it might be to their advantage to supplement the parade with some other event that would catch national attention. So, in 1901, the Tournament of Roses Association, under the prodding of James B. Wagner, agreed upon a New Year's Day football game to be played at the town lot, now known as Tournament Park, between a representative West Coast team and one from east of the Mississippi River.

At the turn of the century, the college football powerhouses were primarily Eastern schools such as Harvard, Yale, Princeton, Pennsylvania, and

Cornell—teams that had been competing in the game for nearly three decades and had developed the sport's rules. Harvard finished another outstanding season in 1901, winning all twelve of its contests. But a team from the Midwest that finished 10–0 had beaten its opponents so thoroughly that most sportswriters believed it deserved to be called the national champion. That team was Michigan, coached by a colorful young West Virginian, Fielding H. "Hurry Up" Yost. The Wolverines' victories ranged from merely 21–0 over Ohio State to 128–0 over the University of Buffalo. In fact, Yost's team, behind sensational freshman running back Willie Heston, a speedy halfback from Grants Pass, Oregon, blanked its opponents 501–0, becoming the first of a series of "point-a-minute" teams coached by Yost at Michigan. The Wolverines gained 8,000 yards in their ten games, and no opponent even crossed the Michigan 35-yard line. The invitation for the visiting team, therefore, went to Michigan. But who would be a worthy opponent to represent the West Coast?

The closest school to Pasadena that competed in football at the time was the University of Southern California in nearby Los Angeles. But the Trojans had scheduled mostly high school and regional athletic club teams annually since beginning competition in 1888. And in 1901 they played only one game, a 6–0 loss to Pomona. The University of California, some 400 miles to the north, had an outstanding season in 1901, finishing 9–0–1. But only two of the Bears' victories were against college teams, 12–0 over Nevada and 2–0 over northern California rival Stanford. All of Michigan's games had been with college opponents.

Stanford, like California, played mostly athletic club teams and ones representing military units and bases in 1901—its two ties that year were against club teams—but it lost only that close contest to California in its final game, finishing with a 3–1–2 record. What made the Indians (the Stanford nickname until 1972) a natural to be invited as the "home" team, however, was the fact that Yost had coached Stanford the previous year. A number of those who had played under Yost in 1900 were still on the Stanford team in 1901, and perhaps well versed enough in their former coach's tactics to stymie the team from the East.

The match was set for New Year's Day, 1902, but only after Tournament officials agreed to give Michigan players $3 a day in meal money while they were in California. Michigan made the entire trip by rail (the Santa Fe Railroad had been running through Pasadena since the early 1880s), and after a journey that lasted nearly a week, the team arrived in southern California. Stanford's trip from Palo Alto, though arduous enough, took considerably less time, and both teams were in Pasadena on January 1. The game was delayed by thirty minutes, however, because the players rode to Tournament Park on parade floats. Fans waited impatiently in temperatures nearing ninety degrees as the Wolverines went through a brief pre-game workout. When the game started, Michigan looked like anything but a national champion in the early stages. Stanford could gain little yardage against the Wolverines, but neither did Michigan threaten the Stanford goal.

In those early years of college football, the forward pass was not yet legal, and teams generally relied on brute force to gain yardage, either plunges up the middle of the line or sweeps around the ends. About ten minutes into the New Year's Day contest, Michigan started a sweep around right end with Willie Heston carrying the ball. Suddenly the chunky halfback stopped and sped back around left end, while his teammates continued running to the right. By the time the Stanford players had adjusted to this trickery—later known as a "naked reverse"—Heston had raced more than 40 yards before being knocked out of bounds. Moments later All-America fullback Neil Snow smashed through the center of the Stanford line for the first score of the game. After that, the contest turned into a rout. With six minutes left in the game, Michigan had stormed to a 49–0 lead behind Heston's 170 yards rushing and Snow's five touchdowns and 107 yards rushing. At that point the captain of the Stanford team admitted that his team, which had used few substitutes, was exhausted and wanted to concede the game. Stanford guard W. K. Roosevelt, a second cousin of the President, had played at least fifteen minutes with a fractured leg before finally leaving after also fracturing his ribs. Michigan played the entire game in the oppressive heat without a substitution, but the Wolverines acceded to the Stanford request. The game was declared at an end with Michigan the victor, 49–0.

The football game earned a profit of $3,161.86 for the Tournament of Roses Association and, as successful as it may have been in drawing national attention to the Rose Festival—an estimated 8,500 persons had turned out to see the game—it was a shambles as far as competition was concerned. So, over the next decade and a half, the Rose Festival was topped off by other events. Polo was the attraction in 1903, but drew only about 2,000 spectators. From 1904 through 1915, the big attraction was Roman-style chariot races, based on the novel *Ben-Hur*, which drew up to 25,000 spectators. In addition,

1902 Rose Bowl—The first postseason game was limited to running plays, as the forward pass was illegal at the time. Wolverine fullback Neil Snow, far right, begins one of his numerous runs, five of which were touchdowns. Willie Heston, who carried 18 times for 170 yards, is in the center leading the blockers. National champion Michigan had little trouble running over Stanford in a game shortened by six minutes at the request of the exhausted Stanford team. (*Pasadena Tournament of Roses*)

an airplane dropped rose petals over the parade route in 1912, ostrich races and a race between an elephant and a camel (won by the elephant) highlighted the games in 1913, and cities from San Diego to Portland, Oregon, entered floats in the 1914 parade with prizes being awarded for the most attractive ones. The chariot races, which had become highly dangerous to life and limb, were last held in 1915.

Special notice should be made of a series of postseason games played in Havana, Cuba, involving American college football teams between 1907 and 1912. None of these Bacardi Bowl games matched American teams and the contests are not recognized as true bowl games by the NCAA. In the first, on Christmas Day, 1907, Louisiana State University, a team that had finished its season with a 6–3 record, whipped Havana University 56–0. In the next, on New Year's Day, 1910, the Havana Athletic Club beat Tulane 11–0, which should have surprised no one. Tulane had lost all seven of its games in the regular season. On New Year's Day, 1912, Mississippi State defeated the Havana Athletic Club 12–0. And on Christmas Day, 1912, Florida beat the Vedado Athletic Club of Havana 28–0. The Bacardi Bowl would not be played again for twenty-five years.

In 1915 the Tournament of Roses Association decided to return to a New Year's Day football game, "so Pasadena can give the newspapermen from coast to coast something exciting to write about." Because of the popularity of the chariot races, Tournament Park already was equipped with wooden stands seating 25,000, capable of accommodating spectators for a football game.

Thus, the Tournament of Roses Association began to consider possible teams to invite for a contest on New Year's Day, 1916. The powerhouses of the Ivies—unbeaten national champion Cornell, once-beaten Harvard and Dartmouth, and twice-beaten Princeton—were not interested in an expensive trip westward to play a game weeks after the regular season had ended. Nor was a very good Syracuse team, which the committee considered for awhile. The association finally landed Brown, an Ivy team that had won five games behind backfield star and future All-American Fritz Pollard, who became the first African-American to play in a postseason game and later the first African-American coach in the National Football League. An obvious selection for the West Coast representative seemed to be Washington, which had gone unbeaten for eight consecutive seasons. But in the 1915 season, two of its games had been against noncollegiate foes. Instead, to represent the West Coast the committee selected rival Washington State, unbeaten for the first time since 1908 and having outscored opponents 190–10 while winning its six games, all against collegiate opposition.

The Brown players, admitting afterward that they had taken the game "as a lark," held only a few light practices on the West Coast and attended the Rose Parade before going to Tournament Park. Uncharacteristically for New Year's Day in Pasadena, a heavy rain fell, and only 7,000 showed up for the match. Game organizers took a heavy loss because of a $5,000 guarantee to each school. What the cold, wet spectators witnessed was complete domination by Washington State on the muddy field, as Pollard was held to 40 yards rushing, while Cougar halfback Ralph Boone and fullback Carl Dietz each scored in the second half for a 14–0 Washington State win.

Brown's train trip home may have been a mellow one despite the defeat. Barrels that had been filled with drinking water at Providence, Rhode Island, for the trip west were refilled with California wine before setting out for the trip back east. The Washington State players made out all right, too. While practicing in the Los Angeles area prior to the game, each player earned $100 a day—a fabulous amount at the time—as extras in the football segments of a Hollywood film, *Tom Brown of Harvard*. It was rumored that they pooled their earnings to bet on themselves in the Rose game. If so, they returned to Pullman with a considerable amount of loot.

Football was now set as the climactic event of the Tournament of Roses activities. For the next New Year, had the selectors been willing to wait until the end of the 1916 regular season, they might have landed unbeaten national champion Pittsburgh or perhaps unbeaten Ohio State as the visiting team. But the mindset of the committee was that the most prestigious opponent would be an Ivy team, a name applied to those Eastern schools even before they were formally organized as a conference in 1956. So a representative of the Tournament of Roses selection committee traveled east in the middle of the season to try to secure one of the better-known Ivy squads for the New Year's Day contest. Unable to land Yale or Harvard, he finally got an acceptance from Pennsylvania. Aside from early losses to Swarthmore and Pittsburgh, Pennsylvania won seven games behind All-America fullback Howard Berry and quarterback Bert Bell, future long-time commissioner of the National Football League. The West Coast invitation went to undefeated Oregon, which won six games, tied the Washington Huskies 0–0, and had been scored on by only one foe. Washington was unbeaten once again, but had been scored on by three opponents.

Under warm, sunny skies, an excellent turnout of 26,000 spectators packed Tournament Park to see the contest between the underdog Oregon team and the highly touted Pennsylvania squad. Penn spent much of the afternoon in Oregon territory, advancing once to the 3-yard line, but could not score. The Quakers missed three field goal attempts, two of them by Berry. Passing, which was legalized in 1906, had become an important weapon in the arsenal of a few college football teams by this time, and Oregon was one of them. Late in the game, the Ducks scored on a 15-yard pass from quarterback C. A. "Shy" Huntington to end Lloyd Tergurt. Huntington scored again on a 1-yard run to give Oregon a 14–0 upset win. On the day, Huntington also intercepted three passes, for in the first half of the twentieth century almost all players played both offense and defense. A number, in fact, played entire games without substitution. In the defensive formations of the time, the center and fullback often lined up as linebackers, with the halfbacks and quarterback as defensive backs.

Patriotism was a big factor in selecting the teams for the 1918 New Year's Day game, even though a number of unbeaten college teams might have been available. These included consensus national champion Georgia Tech,

1917 Rose Bowl—Behind a rugbylike scrum, Oregon's "Shy" Huntington catches a lateral and prepares to follow his blockers down the field. The Ducks made their first post-season contest a success, completing an unbeaten season with an upset victory over Pennsylvania on two late touchdowns in the second half. (*Pasadena Tournament of Roses*)

as well as Pittsburgh and Ohio State. With the United States now involved in World War I, Pasadena officials offered to call off the Rose parade, but President Woodrow Wilson said he could not see how such a celebration would hurt the war effort. Martial floats and marching units representing patriotic groups dominated the parade, and the Tournament of Roses Association decided to pit two outstanding service teams against each other in the football contest.

Dating back to the latter part of the nineteenth century, military posts often fielded football teams, playing games against nearby college and semi-professional or club teams. With a large number of men flocking to the colors during World War I, even temporary camps frequently formed football teams to play other military units as well as college teams as schedules would permit. Chosen for the 1918 Rose contest were the unbeaten Mare Island Marines from the San Francisco area and the Camp Lewis Army team from Washington state, losers of only one game. Hollis Huntington, who had played for Oregon in the Rose contest the previous year along with his brother "Shy," rushed for 111 yards and a touchdown against Camp Lewis in a 19–7 victory for the Marines. The Mare Island team played the entire game with only one substitute, the starting right end having gone out with a broken ankle on the first play.

Service teams also were chosen for the 1919 contest, although the war had ended with an armistice on November 11, 1918. The Great Flu epidemic and travel restrictions imposed by the war affected the entire football season, however, with most teams playing reduced schedules or no games at all that year. Mare Island, with its star player, Hollis Huntington, was invited back after compiling an impressive 10–0 record, while a Great Lakes Navy team from Illinois, which had two losses in an eight-game schedule, was selected as the opposition. Great Lakes was led by L. J. "Paddy" Driscoll, who had captained the impressive 1916 Northwestern team to six victories and a single loss. In the Rose game, Driscoll drop-kicked a 30-yard field goal, returned nine punts for 115 yards, averaged 43.5 yards on six punts, and threw a 45-yard touchdown pass to George Halas, future owner and long-time coach of the Chicago Bears. Halas scored both Great Lakes touchdowns, one on a 77-yard return of an intercepted pass, as Great Lakes shocked the unbeaten Marines, 17-0.

By 1920 the Tournament of Roses game had become popular enough nationally through newspaper accounts and word of mouth that an undefeated national champion Harvard team was willing to participate, despite some reluctance by a number of Harvard officials. It was felt that showing the Harvard colors on the West Coast might help with the university's $15 million endowment campaign. And there may have been a tinge of jealousy that Ivy teams from Brown and Pennsylvania had appeared in earlier Rose contests, while Harvard sat on the sidelines back East. The Crimson, behind half-back Edward Casey, had won eight games, with only a 10–10 tie with Princeton marring the record. Selected to represent the West Coast was Oregon (5–1), coached by alumnus and former Rose star "Shy" Huntington. It was the second trip to Pasadena in three years for Oregon, and the third straight Rose appearance as a player by Hollis Huntington.

Harvard made the trip west by train, stopping to be feted by alumni in Chicago and for quick practices at North Platte, Nebraska, and Green River, Wyoming. Unlike previous Ivy teams, Harvard's players took the postseason game seriously, holding the first Sunday practice in Harvard history and consenting to wear numbers on their jerseys for the first time. The players still had time to meet such celebrities as heavyweight boxing champion Jack Dempsey and film stars Douglas Fairbanks and Charlie Chaplin. The latter two accepted invitations to sit on the Harvard bench during the game, and Dempsey sat in the Harvard rooting section. On game day, about 2,500

Harvard supporters were in the stands, some of them probably having paid scalpers $25 for prime $5 seats. General admission tickets were only 65 cents.

The 1920 Rose parade, witnessed by 200,000 people, included a single float still drawn by a team of horses—everything else was mechanized. The Salvation Army Band made its first appearance, the start of the longest record of continuous participation in the parade by any unit. A biplane buzzed the playing field shortly before kickoff, dropping a football decorated with the colors of the competing teams.

Thirty thousand spectators watched a hard-fought game, with all of the scoring occurring in the second quarter. After two fine pass catches by Casey, Harvard reserve back Fred Church, substituting for injured starter Ralph Horween, ran 12 yards to cross the goal line. Arnold Horween, Ralph's brother, kicked the all-important extra point. Hollis Huntington rushed for 122 yards for Oregon, which scored on drop-kicked field goals by quarterback Bill Steers (25 yards) and C. R. "Skeets" Manerud (30 yards). But Harvard's extra point kept them ahead, 7–6. In the last few minutes of the game, the 128-pound Manerud tried a 25-yard field goal that could have given Oregon an upset win. It missed by inches.

Drop-kicking, incidentally, was a key weapon from the early days of football through the early part of the twentieth century. No holder was used, so it depended on the skill of the kicker, who dropped the football vertically and kicked it with his toe as the ball touched the ground. The kicker also had the option of running or passing at the last moment. Drop-kicking was seen less and less after 1927, when the goal posts were moved from the goal line to the back of the end zone, increasing the distance for successful field goals by 10 yards. By the 1940s, drop-kicking was almost a lost skill.

In the 1920s and throughout the 1930s, most college football teams used the single wing formation with its many variations for their offensive plays. Developed by Glenn "Pop" Warner, the single wing was good for both power and deception, using either a balanced or unbalanced line on various plays. By lining up more men on one side of the center than on the other, the formation could be used for power football with the ball carrier following the maximum number of linemen running interference. The formation also lent itself to a variety of deceptive plays, as the ball could be centered back to the tailback who stood farthest from the line of scrimmage, or the fullback who was slightly to the front and left of the tailback, or even to the quarterback, who was closest to the line of scrimmage but at a considerable angle

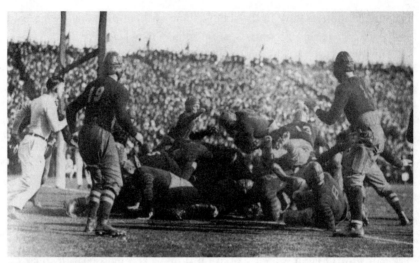

1920 Rose Bowl—National champion Harvard made its first trip to the West Coast a triumphant one by edging Oregon to finish undefeated. Fred Church (10) bullies his way into the end zone for the only touchdown of the game. Arnold Horween's extra point ended up being the game winner. It was the first game in which Harvard players wore identification numbers. (*Pasadena Tournament of Roses*)

for the center snap. The formation required a center who was a consistently good backward passer. The ideal tailback was a "triple threat"—an outstanding runner, a good passer, and a good kicker. The fullback also was expected to be strong runner and good passer. Both tailback and fullback were schooled to be adept at fakes and spinner plays with much crisscrossing by potential ball carriers to confuse the defense. The quarterback was essentially a blocking back who also could run for short yardage or drop back and pass on occasion. The other back, the wingback, would line up behind the end or tackle on either the left or right side of the line. He was primarily a pass receiver and blocker, although he could sweep back on a reverse, taking a handoff from the tailback or fullback.

Similar offensive formations in vogue at the time included the double wing, the short punt formation, and the Notre Dame box. All included some trick plays, including the popular "flea flicker" pass, often combined with a lateral. The double wing, also developed by Warner, was particularly good for reverses and other deceptive plays, but required precise timing and intricate maneuvering. For maximum effectiveness, this formation required an exceptional fullback. The short punt formation relied on speed and deception. It was excellent for passing and punting, especially quick kicks, but was not as good as the other formations for power running. It also worked best with an outstanding "triple threat" deep back.

The standard defense at the time was the 6–2–2–1, in which the ends, tackles, and guards made up the front line, the fullback and center played the linebacker positions, and the remaining backs (quarterbacks, wingbacks, tailbacks) lined up as defensive backs, with the tailback normally in the safety position. Other popular defensive lineups were the 6–3–2, the 7–2–2, and the 7–1–2–1. In the seven-man lines, the center usually was positioned in the center of the line as he normally was on offense.

New Year's Day, 1921, marked the first Tournament of Roses game matching two unbeaten teams, and plenty were available following the 1920 season. Selection of the West Coast representative was easy. The University of California's "Wonder Team" had become the first Pacific Coast team to win a national championship, hardly breaking a sweat in defeating eight opponents en route to a Pacific Coast Conference title. California had outscored opponents 482–14 in its first unbeaten season since 1910. Selection of the visiting team was more complex. Harvard had finished 8–0–1, but officials there were against their team making the trip. Princeton finished 6–0–1, but officials at the New Jersey school also frowned on a postseason game. Pittsburgh and Penn State were both unbeaten, but each had been twice tied. And Notre Dame, despite a second straight 9–0 season, still did not have the reputation of some of the Eastern or Big 10 schools. So the selectors turned to Ohio State, which had won all seven of its games and its third Big 10 championship. The Buckeyes were led by All-America back Gaylord Stinchcomb and All-America guard Iolas Huffman.

A sell-out crowd of 42,000 turned out to see the titans battle, but if they expected a close game they were disappointed. California lived up to its "Wonder Team" nickname, scoring first on a trick play, as back Albert "Pesky" Sprott flipped the ball back to sophomore end Harold "Brick" Muller, who then tossed it to Brodie Stephens for a 53-yard touchdown. That opened the floodgates, and California went on to score three more touchdowns for an easy 28–0 win. Sprott ran for 90 yards in the game, out-rushing the Buckeyes' star back, Stinchcomb, by 8 yards.

By this time it was obvious that Tournament Park seating was becoming insufficient to fulfill the demand for tickets for the game. The 1920 president of the Tournament of Roses Association, William L. Leishman, proposed plans for a stadium similar to the famous Yale Bowl to be constructed in Pasadena's Arroyo Seco area. Architects and builders were soon at work on the new stadium, but it would not be ready until the 1923 contest.

With the Tournament of Roses matchup becoming an established tradition, it was only a matter of time before other cities got into the act. Another postseason football contest, in addition to the Tournament of Roses game, was first played in Texas. In what was billed as the Fort Worth Classic, some 9,000 turned out on that first day of 1921 to see unbeaten Texas Christian University take on Centre College, a tiny Kentucky school of fewer than five hundred students. The Praying Colonels, led by All-America back Bo McMillin, had lost two games during the season, and were considerable underdogs. Things didn't look good for Centre, as TCU scored first on a 90-yard pass interception return by G. P. Jackson, but then McMillin exploded, leading Centre to 63 consecutive points, including eight rushing touchdowns—a bowl game record that still stands—in a 63–7 humiliation of the Horned Frogs. The Fort Worth Classic was not renewed. Praying Colonel center James Weaver kicked seven extra points, another record that still stands. It was a rarity for the center to handle the kicking duties; usually the place kicker was a back or occasionally a guard, tackle, or end.

The 1921 regular season saw a huge surge in the popularity of college football, particularly following two back-to-back games. On October 22, Amos Alonzo Stagg's University of Chicago team traveled east and defeated Princeton, 9–0, for the first victory by a "western" team over any of the big three—Harvard, Princeton, or Yale. On October 29, in a game the *New York Times* later labeled the greatest football upset in the first half of the twentieth century, the Praying Colonels of Centre pulled off a stunning 6–0 upset of Harvard at the Crimson's home field. These games garnered the sport national attention that would continue to swell.

Following the season, San Diego stole a march on its neighbor to the north by sponsoring the San Diego East-West Christmas Classic on December 26, a week before the Tournament of Roses contest. Centre, again led by McMillin, was the visitor in this game, having been invited on the basis of its impressive 9–0 record, and would face Arizona, winner of seven games and loser only to Texas A&M, 17–13. The Wildcats put up a better battle against Centre than had TCU the year before, but still lost 38–0.

A week later, unbeaten California returned to the Tournament of Roses game to represent the West Coast, while tiny Washington & Jefferson College from Pennsylvania, on the basis of a 10–0 season, was invited to represent the East when national champion Cornell declined an invitation. For the most

1921 San Diego East-West Christmas Classic—The first postseason contest played on a date other than New Year's Day matched unbeaten Centre against Arizona on December 26. In this rare photograph of an early bowl game, Centre All-American Red Roberts, readily identified by his trademark white headband, is moving to defend against an Arizona run. Although helmets were becoming standard football equipment at this time, they were not required. It is clear from this picture that the game was played under miserable weather conditions. (*Centre College Archives*)

part, Washington & Jefferson was looked upon with disdain by West Coast writers, who figured the game would be a runaway in favor of California. In fact, one newspaper reported that California Coach Andy Smith had joked, "Afraid of Washington and Jefferson? Who ever heard of them? They've been dead for a hundred years." This was just the kind of comment appreciated by Washington & Jefferson Coach Earle "Greasy" Neale, a wily native of Parkersburg, West Virginia. Neale, who in the late 1940s would coach successive NFL champion Philadelphia Eagles teams, told his squad: "They say Washington and Jefferson have been dead for a hundred years. You boys don't look dead to me. I hope you convince California of that." In a steady downpour, Washington & Jefferson played the entire game without a substitution, yet California could gain little yardage in the mud against the fired-up Presidents led by All-America tackles Wilbur "Fats" Henry and Russell Stein. In fact, Washington & Jefferson had 137 total yards to 49 for California and eight first downs to two for the Golden Bears—and scored the only touchdown that day, only to have it called back on an offside penalty. The game ended 0–0, the first scoreless postseason contest, but it was a moral victory for the Presidents. Despite the rain, the final Tournament of Roses game to be played at Tournament Park was a sell-out, leading to a profit of $17,000.

For the second consecutive year another game was played on the same day as the Rose contest. On January 2, 1922, Texans inaugurated their second postseason football contest, the Dixie Classic at Dallas. Texas A&M was chosen as the home team, while the visitors' invitation went to the same Centre team that had whipped Arizona just a week earlier at San Diego. Centre, no doubt worn down by its long season and holiday travels, finally tasted defeat, losing to Texas A&M 22–14 before 12,000 fans. Aggies end T. F. "Puny" Wilson scored on a 15-yard pass and a 5-yard run while teammate W. E. Winn returned a pass interception 45 yards for a touchdown. Despite the victory for the home team, it would be two years before the Dixie Classic was played again.

During the 1922 season, Princeton made the trip west to play Chicago and avenged its loss the year before, defeating the Maroons 21–18. Chicago received more than 100,000 ticket requests for the game, a gauge of football's immense popularity. Also that year, the American Professional Football Association, which was formed in 1920, changed its name to the National Football League.

San Diego kept the East-West Christmas Classic going for one more year at the end of the 1922 season, inviting unbeaten West Virginia to take on Washington state's Gonzaga in the first football game played on Christmas Day. The Mountaineers rolled to a 21–0 lead behind halfback Nick Nardacci, who rushed for 120 yards and a score and threw a touchdown pass to halfback Jack Simons, and tackle Russ Meredith, who scored on an 80-yard pass interception return. Tiring in the heat on the sandy field, the Mountaineers hung on for a 21–13 win. The crowd once again numbered only about 5,000, and it would be twenty-five years before San Diego attempted another postseason game.

Fanfare greeted the 1923 Tournament of Roses game, the first to be played in the 57,000-seat stadium in Pasadena. Although still open on the south end at the time, plans called for the $272,000 facility to eventually be closed into a bowl shape. That occurred a few years later, with further enlargements taking place in 1932, 1949 and 1972. Even so, reporter Harlan "Dusty" Hall of the *Pasadena Star-News* suggested that the new stadium be called the "Rose Bowl," and the name stuck. Also for the first time, the Rose contest would feature a truly local squad as the home team. Tournament of Roses representatives had invited Penn State to the New Year's game back in the spring preceding the 1922 season following two straight undefeated

1922 Rose Bowl—Heavily favored California tries to move the ball against a tough Washington & Jefferson defense in a clash of unbeaten teams. The Golden Bears gained only 49 total yards in the first scoreless postseason contest. (*Pasadena Tournament of Roses*)

Nittany Lion seasons. But in 1922 Penn State lost three games, and California, which had gone unbeaten for the third straight season, refused to play a "mediocre" squad in the Rose Bowl. So the West Coast invitation went to the University of Southern California, which had won nine games and lost only to California.

Unbeaten national champion Cornell would have been a natural selection as the visiting team, but by this time presidents of most Ivy schools, and those in the Western Conference—better known as the Big 10 by this time—as well as the superintendent at West Point, had decided that postseason football games interfered too much with academic schedules and frowned on such participation. Most of the unbeaten teams in 1922, including Army, Princeton, and Michigan, were among those schools whose administrators prohibited postseason play, so Penn State's April invitation as visiting team was confirmed. Coach of the Nittany Lions was Hugo Bezdek, who had coached Rose Bowl winners in 1917 and 1918 at Oregon and Mare Island.

On New Year's Day, Penn State players rode on parade floats and arrived fifteen minutes after the game was supposed to begin following dedication ceremonies for the new stadium. USC Coach "Gloomy Gus" Henderson was infuriated and he and Bezdek nearly engaged in pre-game fisticuffs. When the game finally got under way at 3:05 P.M., more than an hour after its scheduled start, it was the Trojans who made the most noise before a substantial crowd of 43,000. After spotting Penn State an early 3–0 lead on a 20-yard field goal, USC scored touchdowns by Roy "Bullet" Baker and Gordon Campbell, winning the game 14–3. It was so dark by the end of the contest that sports writers in the unlighted press box were finishing their stories by striking matches for illumination.

Following the 1923 season, the Rose Bowl was the only football game to be played, as there were no new attempts at hosting a postseason game. By this time, Tournament of Roses officials had decided to turn over the responsibility for game invitations to the Pacific Coast Conference. The PCC would select one of its members as the home team, and that school would have a say in which team would be invited from elsewhere. The Tournament of Roses Committee already had invited Navy before the 1923 season began, however, and, unlike the superintendent at Army, the headman at the Naval Academy decided to allow the team to play. The choice of Navy looked like a good one, since the Midshipmen had finished the season with only one loss, while neither of the two undefeated Ivy schools, Cornell and Yale, nor the two unbeaten Big 10 teams, national champion Illinois and Michigan, was available because of postseason bans.

California had finished unbeaten for the fourth consecutive season, but because the Bears had turned down the Rose Bowl invitation the previous year, the PCC decided to go with Washington, which won nine and lost only to California. The game day crowd of 40,000 would have been larger, but Navy had taken its game share in tickets, then had distributed thousands of them among sailors in the fleet harbored nearby—only to have the fleet admiral order the ships to sea the day before New Year's. Despite losing many of its supporters before the start of the contest, Navy outgained Washington 362 yards to 202 and made fifteen first downs to Washington's nine. The Midshipmen took a 14–0 lead as quarterback Ira "Pete" McKee threw two touchdown passes to halfback Carl Cullen. Washington rallied, however, on a 14-yard touchdown run by sophomore halfback George Wilson, a 12-yard scoring pass from quarterback Fred Abel to James Bryan, and two extra points by Les Sherman—who kicked both despite a broken toe. The game ended in a 14–14 tie. As it turned out, it was Navy's one chance at postseason glory for thirty years. Following the contest, the superintendent at Navy decided to go along with the postseason ban.

Three bowl games were on tap for the 1924 postseason. Taking over where San Diego left off, Los Angeles decided to have its own Christmas Day contest. Missouri Valley Conference champion Missouri was invited to play hometown Southern California and, before a huge crowd of 47,000, the Trojans won easily, 20–7. Despite the excellent turnout, the Los Angeles Christmas Festival football contest turned out to be a one-time affair.

The 1925 Rose Bowl game a week later was an intriguing contest between two unbeaten teams, Notre Dame with its fabled "Four Horsemen" and Stanford with powerful fullback Ernie Nevers, a future All-America choice and professional football star. Knute Rockne's third unbeaten Notre Dame team had rolled through a nine-game schedule unscathed to win its first national championship, while Glenn "Pop" Warner's Stanford team had stumbled only once in an eight-game schedule—a 20–20 tie with unbeaten California. All-American Elmer Layden was the most visible "Horseman" that day, scoring three touchdowns, two on pass interception returns of 78 and 70 yards and the other on a run. He also got off an 80-yard punt. Another All-American "Horseman," Jim Crowley, rushed for 59 yards, caught a 30-yard pass, and kicked three extra points. A fourth Irish touchdown was scored by end Ed Hunsinger on a 20-yard fumble return. Nevers rushed for 117 yards despite heavily taped injured ankles, and Stanford had a total yardage edge of 298 to 179, but the Fighting Irish won 27–10. It was a bittersweet victory, perhaps, because this was to be the last bowl appearance for Notre Dame for nearly half a century, as Notre Dame, like Navy the year before, decided to adopt the ban on postseason play following the game. The game also featured the first wire transmission of a bowl game photo, sent to newspapers throughout the country by the Associated Press.

The Dixie Classic in Dallas returned on New Year's Day after a two-year hiatus. The game featured an interesting match-up of two Methodist-supported colleges, unbeaten Southern Methodist University and West Virginia Wesleyan College from Buckhannon, West Virginia, which, despite being a very small school had defeated Navy, a strong Syracuse team, and Kentucky in an 8–2 season. The Bobcats began the new year on a winning note, as they upset SMU 9–7. Only 7,000 fans turned out to see the Dixie Classic, however, and it would be the last official postseason game to be played other than the Rose Bowl for the next nine years.

The 1926 contest saw the first Southern football team to compete in the Rose Bowl when Wallace Wade's Alabama squad was invited to play PCC champion Washington. Alabama had outscored opponents 277–7 in its first unbeaten season since 1897, and had been proclaimed national champion along with undefeated Dartmouth. The Ivy school declined the Rose Bowl bid, as expected, opening the way for Alabama. Washington won ten games in its first unbeaten season since 1916 but had been tied by Nebraska. The New Year's Day contest was broadcast locally on radio for the first time by Pasadena station KPSN, with former Olympic sprint star Charles Paddock as the announcer, possibly the first instance of a former athlete turning to the broadcast booth. Part of Paddock's Olympic story appeared in the 1981 movie *Chariots of Fire.*

The game was one of the more dramatic contests in Rose Bowl history. Washington took a 12–0 halftime lead behind All-America backfield ace George Wilson, but during a twenty-two-minute stretch in the second half, while Wilson sat out with injuries, Alabama rallied for 20 points behind halfback—and future Hollywood cowboy movie star—Johnny Mack Brown and fullback A. T. S. "Pooley" Hubert. Washington scored again when Wilson re-entered the game midway through the fourth quarter, but Alabama held on to win, 20–19. There were stars aplenty. Brown caught touchdown passes of 30 yards from Hubert and 59 yards from quarterback Grant Gillis. Hubert rushed for 97 yards and scored the other Alabama touchdown. For Washington, Wilson rushed for 139 yards and passed for two touchdowns. Halfback Harold Patton scored the other Washington touchdown on a 1-yard run.

The 1927 game attracted even more interest when Alabama was invited back after another undefeated season. What was intriguing was the fact that the Crimson Tide had been proclaimed national co-champion again, this time with unbeaten Stanford—and Stanford would be Alabama's Rose Bowl opponent. The contest drew so much attention that it became the second sporting event to be broadcast nationwide (the 1926 World Series was first), on NBC radio with Graham MacNamee and Bill Munday as announcers. A capacity crowd jammed the stadium in anticipation of a close game that would really decide the national champion. In the first quarter, the Indians scored on a 20-yard pass from George Bogue to Ed Walker, with Bogue kicking the extra point. Stanford continued to dominate the game but neither team could score. Despite both offensive and defensive heroics by star end Ted Shipkey, Stanford clung to the lead until the final minutes of the game when sophomore tackle Clarke "Babe" Pearce blocked a Stanford punt. Alabama halfback Jimmy Johnson scored on a short run soon after, and

Herschel Caldwell kicked the all-important extra point. Stanford ended the game with a huge 305–98 margin in total yardage but had to settle for a 7–7 tie.

All-star bowl games are beyond the purview of this book, but mention should be made of the first one that took place at the end of the 1927 season. This was the inauguration of the East-West charity game in San Francisco sponsored by the Shriners. The West won that first contest 7–0.

Thanks to completion of the south end of the Rose stadium, it was now a true "bowl" and played host to 65,000 spectators for the 1928 game. Stanford returned to represent the West Coast, this time against Jock Sutherland's undefeated Pittsburgh team, making its first postseason appearance. The game was a defensive battle in which fumbles played a key part. After a scoreless first half, Pittsburgh scored in the third quarter when Jimmy Hagan picked up a fumble and ran 20 yards for a touchdown. Stanford sophomore Walt Heinicke blocked the extra point try. Later, Frankie Wilton scooped up a Pittsburgh fumble on the 2-yard line and scored the tying touchdown. Clifford "Biff" Hoffman then kicked the extra point for a 7–6 Stanford victory.

A year later, The logical choice for the "home team" would have appeared to be Southern California, which shared national championship laurels with Georgia Tech. But the one blemish on the USC record was a 0–0 tie with California, so the PCC named the Golden Bears to meet Georgia Tech on January 1, 1929, California's first appearance in the game since 1922. The fans that packed the bowl were treated to one of the most famous and strangest plays in football history. During the second quarter of the hard-fought game, outstanding center/linebacker Roy Riegels of California picked up a Georgia Tech fumble near midfield and set off for the goal line. Unfortunately, he became confused when hit and spun around by a Georgia Tech lineman, and he ran in the wrong direction. California halfback Benny Lom, running behind Riegels, yelled, "Turn around! Turn around!" But the crowd drowned out his voice. By the time Lom was able to catch Riegels and start to pull him back in the right direction, Riegels was tackled on California's own 1-yard line by Georgia Tech's Frank Waddey. Moments later, Tech sophomore tackle Vance Maree blocked a punt through the end zone for a safety, giving Georgia Tech a 2–0 lead.

Each team later scored a touchdown—back J. G. "Stumpy" Thomason on a 15-yard run for Tech and All-America end Irv Phillips on a short pass from

Lom for California—but the winning margin in Tech's 8–7 win resulted from Riegels's "wrong-way run." California had little luck that day. A 60-yard return of a fumble recovery for an apparent touchdown by Lom was nullified when the referee said that he had blown his whistle to stop the play before the fumble. And on one California punt the impact of the kicker's foot ruptured the ball and the deflated pigskin flopped to the ground, giving the ball to Georgia Tech near the original line of scrimmage. The $270,000 gate for the football game allowed the Tournament of Roses Committee to pay off the mortgage for the Rose Bowl stadium.

In 1930, Jock Sutherland brought another unbeaten Pittsburgh powerhouse to the Rose Bowl to take on a strong Southern California team coached by Howard Jones. The crowd was treated to a forward pass display like none seen before in the traditional classic. The Panthers scored twice through the air, 28 yards from Tony Uansa to William Wallinchus and 36 yards from Thomas Parkinson to sophomore Paul Collins. But USC scored on three touchdown passes, two thrown by sophomore tailback Gaius "Gus" Shaver—a 55-yarder to Harry Edelson and 28 yards to sophomore back Erny Pinckert—and a 13-yarder from "Racehorse" Russ Saunders to Edelson. The Trojans also had little trouble scoring on the ground, with Saunders reaching the end zone on a 13-yard run and Marshall Duffield running in two more for a 47–14 USC victory—one of the worst defeats in Sutherland's illustrious coaching career.

The escalation of Rose Bowl crowds during the decade, from 42,000 in 1921 to 72,000 in 1930, reflected a golden age of sports in America. Sports sections in newspapers expanded greatly throughout this period, while the emergence of tabloids, particularly in big cities such as New York, Chicago, and Los Angeles, and radio broadcasts contributed to an explosion in sports coverage. Horse racing already had seen a boost in such publicity, which had led to the virtual deification of Man O' War. Major league baseball was a huge beneficiary of media interest in the1920s, leading to the worship of such stars as Babe Ruth and helping fans forget the Black Sox scandal following the 1919 World Series. Boxing was heavily covered both in the newspapers and on radio, with Jack Dempsey becoming a household name. The first live coverage of boxing on radio came in 1921, and radio also began covering baseball's World Series in 1921 with nationwide coverage by 1926.

In this atmosphere, college football reached new heights of popularity through such sportswriters as Grantland Rice, Ring Lardner, Heywood

1929 Rose Bowl—Roy Riegels of California sets out on his famous "wrong-way" run against unbeaten Georgia Tech. His error, following a fumble recovery, set up a safety that proved to be the winning points for the national champion Yellow Jackets. (*Pasadena Tournament of Roses*)

Broun, and Damon Runyon. During the decade most Americans, sports fans or not, became familiar with Notre Dame's "Four Horsemen," the feats of Illinois running back Harold "Red" Grange, known as the "Galloping Ghost," and the teams selected for the holiday postseason games. KDKA of Pittsburgh in 1921 became the first commercial radio station to broadcast play-by-play coverage of a regular-season college football game, Pittsburgh's 21–13 win over West Virginia. Radio station WGN of Chicago began covering Big 10 football games in 1924, even airing some games from Nebraska, Pennsylvania, and Southern California during the decade. But with the collapse of the stock market, the Rose Bowl would be joined by other postseason games that took on a special social function as a way to raise money for charity.

2 ORANGE, SUGAR, SUN, AND COTTON

IN 1930 THE UNITED STATES, A NATION of 123 million persons, saw its unemployment rate rise to 8.9 percent—a result of the stock market crash in October 1929—and continue to increase until 10 million persons were out of work by early 1932. Banks had closed by the thousands, and there was as yet no Social Security or any New Deal programs. In an effort to raise money for relief of the unemployed, two postseason football games were played in New York City's Yankee Stadium in December 1930. On December 6, before 20,000 spectators, Colgate, which had lost only to Michigan State in a nine-game season, won a hard-fought 7–6 game over intrastate rival New York University, and on December 13, Army met Navy. The two service academies had severed athletic relations in 1928 after fights between the two had flared up on the playing fields and in the stands. The two agreed to meet following the 1930 season, however, for this charity game. Army had lost only to unbeaten national champion Notre Dame in the season, while Navy had lost four games, but in front of 70,000 the Midshipmen gave the Cadets all they could handle before losing 6–0.

On New Year's Day, 1931, the third unbeaten Alabama team to be invited to the Rose Bowl faced a Washington State team with an identical 9–0 record. Amidst thousands of empty seats in the stadium, which recently had been expanded to a capacity of nearly 84,000, the crowd watched Alabama coast to a 24–0 victory. Although Washington State Coach "Babe" Hollingberry attempted to intimidate the Crimson Tide by dressing his players totally in red—from helmets to shoes—it was the Alabama team that turned Hollingberry red by putting the game away in the second quarter with three quick touchdowns, two by quarterback John "Monk" Campbell, including a spectacular 43-yard run, and the other on a 61-yard trick pass play from end Jimmy Moore to halfback John Henry "Flash" Suther.

Benefit games around the country continued following the 1931 season, some of them featuring doubleheader tournaments in which four teams were paired to play halves or modified quarters. Of the regular type of football games played for charity, at least seventeen involved major college teams. Some notable games included a match-up in Chicago on November 28 between Purdue and Big 10 co-champions Northwestern. The two teams had not met during the regular season, and the Boilermakers won, 7–0. An undefeated Tennessee team traveled to New York on December 5 and defeated New York University, 13–0, at Yankee Stadium. A week later, on December 12, Yankee Stadium hosted Army and Navy again, and before 75,000, Army beat Navy 17–7. In this case, the charitable feelings spread beyond the game, as the service academies agreed to resume normal athletic relations and have met on the gridiron every year since.

Bernie Bierman's last Tulane squad before he went on to coach several national champions at Minnesota had the best record of any major team in 1931 at 11–0, and was invited to play in the 1932 Rose Bowl. The Green Wave's opponent, Southern California, despite having suffered one loss, had been tabbed the national champion at the end of the regular season because of its tougher schedule, including an away game at Notre Dame, where the Trojans ended the Fighting Irish's twenty-six-game unbeaten string with a 16–14 win. USC had six players who had made various All-America teams that season, and they proved their abilities in the New Year's Day contest. One of the All-Americans, halfback Ernie Pinckert, scored two touchdowns on runs of 25 and 30 yards, and end Ray Sparling scored on an end-around play from the 6-yard line as the Trojans prevailed 21–12. Harry Glover starred for Tulane, rushing for 139 yards and a touchdown. During the game USC captain Stan Williamson displayed a bit of sportsmanship that would probably not occur these days. Tulane's All-America end, Jerry Dalrymple, had bruised a kidney in an earlier game and wore protective padding that required frequent adjustments. When Dalrymple needed extra time to make a readjustment, Williamson told referee Herb Dana, "Let him have all the time he needs."

By the time of the 1933 Rose Bowl, the effects of the Great Depression in America were so severe that there was talk of not having a parade before the game. But a *Los Angeles Times* writer pointed out that "there is no depression in the world of flowers, nor in the spirit of Pasadenans and their neighbors in other Southern California cities who have contributed entries for the dazzling pageant." So the parade continued with movie star Mary Pickford, "America's Sweetheart," serving as the first female grand marshal. Dressed in white, she rode at the head of the parade in a coach drawn by four white horses.

With the Rose Bowl nearly filled to capacity, undefeated teams from Southern California and Pittsburgh met for the second time in the classic. Unbeaten and untied USC shared the national title with Michigan, but since the Wolverines were prohibited from playing postseason games, the bid went to Jock Sutherland's Panthers, winners of eight games in a tough schedule along with 0–0 ties with Ohio State and Nebraska. It was the third year Sutherland had taken an unbeaten team to the Rose Bowl, still looking for a win, but in this case the third time was not a charm. Southern California built up a 14–0 lead going into the fourth quarter, then broke open the game with three touchdowns for a surprising 35–0 victory. Ford Palmer scored the first Trojan touchdown on a 50-yard pass from back Homer Griffith, who later scored a touchdown of his own. Behind the powerful USC line, 145-pound sophomore back Irvine "Cotton" Warburton rushed for 87 yards and two touchdowns.

That same day, January 2, 1933, the forerunner of the Orange Bowl was launched in Florida in imitation of the Rose Bowl. George E. Hussey, an official at Florida Power & Light who served as Miami's official greeter, was looking for a way to attract tourists to the southern Florida city. Miami, with a population of just over 100,000 in 1930, had suffered from the collapse of the Florida land boom in the 1920s and a powerful 1926 hurricane preceding the beginnings of the Depression in 1929. The Hialeah Race Course had become the winter home for many of racing's leading thoroughbreds by the late 1920s, and Hussey wondered how sports might help bring in a larger tourist industry to boost the local economy. He noticed the media attention generated by the Tournament of Roses parade and Rose Bowl football game in California and figured that since Miami had a climate similar to Pasadena's, it too could host a postseason football game.

Hussey was a friend of Manhattan coach Chick Meehan, and he inquired as to whether Meehan would bring his team down from New York to play the University of Miami on January 2. Meehan agreed, and thus was launched the Palm Festival game. Henry L. Doherty, owner of the Miami Biltmore and other Miami real estate, agreed to underwrite $5,000 of the game's expenses and to lodge the Manhattan team at his hotel. Manhattan's team arrived after a three-day trip down the coast by ocean liner but would not take the field until the festival committee's $3,000 guarantee was paid. Only half of the guarantee had been raised, but one of the Palm Festival organizers (who was also the sheriff) made arrangements with local bookies to make up the missing half. The organizers had one request of Meehan: hold down the score if the margin got to be as high as three touchdowns. They were fearful because Miami had only a 3–3–1 record in 1932 and had played no one of Manhattan's status. Meehan agreed, but as it turned out he did not have to work that angle. The game was played before 6,000 fans on a field at Moore Park that was six inches deep in sand, and although Manhattan mounted several threats, all were stopped by the Hurricanes, including one drive that ended inside their 1-yard line. Finally, in the fourth quarter, Miami freshman Cecil Cook scored on a 3-yard run, giving the Hurricanes a 7–0 upset victory. The Palm Festival games ultimately were not recognized by the National Collegiate Athletic Association as legitimate bowl games, because they simply matched the local University of Miami team, regardless of record, against an invited foe. But they did set the machinery in motion for the Orange Bowl two years later.

By the 1930s the NCAA had become the governing force in supervising the rules, regulations, and eligibility requirements under which college sports were played. Created in 1906 as the Intercollegiate Athletic Association of the United States to foster reforms to reduce football injuries and deaths, it was renamed the National Collegiate Athletic Association in 1910. For several years the NCAA was primarily a discussion group and rules-making body, but over the years its authority in supervising football—as well as other collegiate sports—was strengthened, and in 1937 it began compiling individual and team statistics of members on an annual basis. It would keep an increasingly watchful eye on postseason football contests in an attempt to protect the amateur athletes from being exploited by commercial interests.

The planning for the 1934 Rose Bowl offered a rare chance for the selection committee when they learned that administrators at one Ivy school, Columbia University, would allow the football team to compete in postseason play. The Lions had an outstanding regular season, losing only to unbeaten Princeton 20–0, and the Tigers and national champion Michigan were still prohibited from postseason play. The tournament invitation went to Columbia to meet Stanford. Columbia's student newspaper was aghast, claiming the university "repudiated its own standards" by accepting the Rose Bowl bid. Stanford was a heavy favorite, and one Los Angeles sportswriter wrote, "This Columbia outfit is just Pomona High School in light blue jerseys."

The train trip westward for Columbia was a leisurely one, the Lions taking a week off in Tucson, Arizona, for practice. When they arrived in Pasadena on New Year's Eve, they found the Rose Bowl playing field under

1934 Rose Bowl—One of the big upsets in bowl history occurred when Columbia scored on this trick play to defeat solid favorite Stanford. Rain held the crowd to 35,000, smallest at the Rose Bowl in fifteen years. (*Pasadena Tournament of Roses*)

eight inches of water as a result of an unprecedented storm. Twelve inches of rain had fallen on Pasadena over the previous forty-eight hours, the first holiday rainfall of any significance there since 1922. Local firetrucks pumped out water overnight, and although the field remained soggy, it was playable. A light, sporadic drizzle continued to fall on game day, and before a half-empty stadium, Stanford racked up 272 total yards to 114 for Columbia, with Indian fullback Bobby Grayson rushing for 152 yards despite the difficult conditions. But Stanford could not push the ball across the goal line. Three times the Lions stopped Stanford inside their 1-yard line. In the second quarter, after a pass advanced the ball to the Stanford 17-yard line, the Lions decided to try a trick play they had practiced in Tucson—a version of the old hidden ball play. Quarterback Cliff Montgomery took the snap and, with his back to the Stanford line, slipped the ball to left halfback Al Barabas, quickly faked to right halfback Ed Brominski heading in the other direction, then turned and plunged into the line as if he still had the ball. The Stanford defense, hesitating to determine who the real ball carrier was, did not even touch Barabas as he hid the football against his hip, ran to his left and sauntered into the end zone. That was enough to give Columbia a 7–0 victory, one of the biggest upsets in Rose Bowl history.

Also on New Year's Day 1934, the Dixie Classic was revived in Dallas for one last time, the first officially recognized postseason game other than the

Rose Bowl in nine years. The Classic had been briefly renewed five years earlier as a benefit game for the Texas Scottish Rite Hospital for Crippled
Children, but those games were all-star contests, pitting Southwest
Conference stars against the Big 6 in 1929 and against Big 10 stars in 1930
and 1931. The final Dixie Classic matched Arkansas against unbeaten
Centenary of Louisiana. Centenary, behind All-America end Paul Geisler,
had won eight games and tied three, and its propensity for tie games showed
up again in Dallas as the teams battled to a 7–7 draw.

In the second Palm Festival game, Duquesne beat Miami 33–7. An additional postseason game was played on the first day of 1934, although this
one, like the Palm Festival, was not recognized by the NCAA for similar rea-
sons. This was the first New Year's Classic in Honolulu, later named the Poi
Bowl in 1936, and the Pineapple Bowl in 1940. The bowl always featured
Hawaii as the home team. It was interrupted by World War II and resumed
in 1947, but was finally discontinued after the New Year's 1952 game.

As 1934 moved toward 1935, the Great Depression, now worldwide, entered   **1934**
its sixth year. Germany was in its second year under the political control of
Adolf Hitler, who would repudiate the Treaty of Versailles while marching
inexorably toward a war that would rage around the globe. But over the past
twelve months, America had been struggling with its own problems, with
gangland violence in the cities and raging dust storms in the Great Plains
that ruined farms and forced hundreds of thousands to abandon their
homes and migrate to the North and West. As diversions, people flocked to
movies, listened to the radio, and read comic books and pulps. In sports, basketball was becoming popular as a collegiate game and postseason play in
college football took a dramatic turn. In addition to the Rose Bowl, which
already had twenty games in the record book, the Orange Bowl would be
inaugurated in Miami and the Sugar Bowl introduced in New Orleans.
College football and bowl games were now linked, and with the steady
growth and interest in postseason play from this point on, the bowls were on
their way to ultimately deciding the national champion.

During 1934 in Miami, Chamber of Commerce president W. Keith
Phillips had formed a group, including Palm Festival veterans, to put on
another postseason football game to be identified with Florida and particularly with the city of Miami. Under direction of Earnie Seiler, Miami's recre-
ation director, a game was organized for January 1, 1935, under the name
Orange Bowl, suggested by Phillips and local radio announcer Dinty Dennis.

Unlike the Palm Festival contest, the Orange Bowl subsequently would be recognized by the NCAA as legitimate because the University of Miami would not automatically be selected annually as the home team, although the Hurricanes were invited for the first game, to face Bucknell. Each team was paid $12,500 for appearing in the game, to be played at a small baseball stadium adjacent to Miami Field. Bucknell spent $3,000, including meals, for its twenty-two-man team to travel to Miami from Pennsylvania by a special train. Miami had only fifteen players on its squad. Bucknell had played a tougher schedule and had little difficulty in whipping Miami on a rainy New Year's Day. The Bisons held the Hurricanes to 38 total yards for the game and scored on a 23-yard pass from Henry Jenkins to William Wilkinson, a 4-yard run by Phillip Miller, an 8-yard run by Stuart Smith, a 10-yard run by Joe Reznichak, and two extra points kicked by Walter Dobie for a 26–0 victory. Only 5,134 attended this first Orange Bowl game, but it laid the groundwork for the illustrious Orange Bowl of the future.

Meanwhile, the New Orleans Mid-Winter Sports Association in late October 1934 announced that it had the money to promote the inaugural Sugar Bowl Football Classic to be played on January 1, 1935. The idea of such a contest dated to 1927, when publisher James M. Thomson and sports editor Fred Digby of the *New Orleans Item* suggested the idea of a postseason football game in New Orleans. Digby came up with the Sugar Bowl name, as New Orleans was near the heart of Louisiana's sugar cane industry. Civic and political leaders began discussing the idea and by February 1934 had formed the New Orleans Mid-Winter Sports Association, a "voluntary, non-profit civic organization." The game would be played in the stadium of Tulane University, itself located on the site of an old sugar plantation.

In December, the association's executive committee discussed eligible teams to play in the first classic. They decided to pair the most evenly matched teams possible from anywhere in the nation, although area teams, especially from the Southeastern Conference, would be given special consideration if deserving. Unlike the Rose Bowl, however, the local team would have no say in selecting the opponent. Tulane was a natural as the home team for the first Sugar Bowl contest, having earned a share of its first SEC title. Initially, the Tulane players turned down the bid, only to be persuaded by their coaches to accept. Chosen as the Green Wave's opponent was unbeaten Temple, coached by the famous Glenn "Pop" Warner, who previously had coached the Carlisle Indians, Pittsburgh, and Stanford. Temple's

1935 Orange Bowl—Bucknell back John Sitarsky, returning a punt in the inaugural Orange Bowl, is collared by one Miami player while another grasps his foot. Despite the heat and a bright "tropical" sun, the northern team won the game handily. (*Bucknell University Archives*)

Owls, the only bowl-eligible undefeated major team outside of the Rose Bowl selections, had won seven games in 1934 while tying Indiana 6–6 and Bucknell 0–0.

The Sugar Bowl guaranteed $15,000 to the visiting team, an excellent sum in the midst of the Great Depression, with the "home" team assured of $12,500. Within two days after advance tickets went on sale, more than $20,000 worth of Sugar Bowl tickets had been sold, at $3.50 and $1.50.

On a cool, cloudy afternoon with more than 22,000 fans in attendance, the inaugural Sugar Bowl game turned out to be a thriller. Temple took a 14–0 lead on a pass from quarterback Glenn Frey to Danny Testa and a 25-yard touchdown run by sophomore fullback Dave Smukler, described by a Sugar Bowl official as "212 pounds of speed and power." Smukler also kicked both extra points. Then Tulane halfback Claude "Monk" Simons, who was wearing a special pad to protect a shoulder fractured a month earlier in a game with LSU, scored on an 85-yard kickoff return to close the score to 14–7 at halftime. End Dick Hardy caught two touchdown passes, 4 yards from sophomore Howard "Bucky" Bryan in the third quarter and 42 yards from Barney Mintz in the fourth quarter, as the Green Wave rallied for a 20–14 win. After the game, each school was presented with a check of $20,759.20, considerably more than they had been guaranteed. The Sugar Bowl was off to an auspicious start.

In Pasadena, the original postseason bowl matched yet another unbeaten Alabama team, this time coached by Frank Howard, with undefeated Stanford. The Crimson Tide, Southeastern Conference co-champions and winners of a national title that it shared with unbeaten Minnesota, was led by All-America halfback Millard "Dixie" Howell and fabulous pass-catching All-America end Don Hutson, a future professional star. Stanford, in its first unbeaten season since 1926, was paced by All-America fullback Bobby Grayson and All-America tackle Bob Reynolds. With the additions to Rose Bowl seating in recent years, a crowd more than 84,000 was able to marvel at the abilities of Howell and Hutson. The slim, 161-pound Howell completed nine of twelve passes for 160 yards and a touchdown, scored on runs of 5 and 67 yards, returned four kicks for 74 yards, and averaged 43.8 yards on six punts. Hutson, a 6-foot, 1-inch, 185-pounder, caught six passes for 165 yards and two touchdowns—a 59-yarder from Howell and a 54-yarder from sophomore halfback Joe Riley. Quarterback Riley Smith kicked a 22-yard field goal for good measure and Alabama triumphed 29–13. The Indians scored on a 1-yard run by Grayson and a 12-yard run by Elzo "Buck" Van Dellen.

1935 In addition to the two new bowl games that debuted on January 1, the year 1935 also saw the start of the most important individual award in college football. The Downtown Athletic Club in New York City created an annual award for the outstanding college football player that was to be announced at the end of the regular season. The first trophy was awarded to halfback Jay Berwanger of the University of Chicago, and in its second year it was named in honor of John W. Heisman, the club's first president and a college football legend. Due to prohibitions on postseason play for many football programs, a Heisman Trophy winner did not appear in a bowl game until 1939, when quarterback Davey O'Brien led Texas Christian to a victory in the Sugar Bowl. Until 1970, only eleven Heisman winners played in the postseason, but with the lifting of bans against accepting bowl bids and the increase in the number of postseason games, Heisman winners have been regular participants in every bowl season since, except 1989, when André Ware's Houston team was on NCAA probation.

The New Year's Day, 1936, lineup included an additional bowl game that would carry forward to today: the Sun Bowl in El Paso, Texas. The idea for such a game had grown out of a suggestion by Dr. Brice Schuller at a meeting of the local Kiwanis club on October 18, 1934, that a football game between El Paso high school all-stars and a worthy opponent be played as a fund-raising event to benefit underprivileged children and to finance improvements to the El Paso High School Stadium. That contest took place on January 1, 1935, with the all-stars defeating Ranger, Texas, 25–21. Dr. C. M. Hendricks suggested the Sun Bowl name, and over the next year, with the additional backing of four more El Paso service clubs, plans were expanded to include a week-long series of "Sun Carnival" events leading to a New Year's game matching two college opponents. Thus, the first intercollegiate Sun Bowl contest took place on January 1, 1936, at El Paso High School Stadium between Hardin-Simmons and New Mexico A&M (now New Mexico State). Eleven thousand attended the game, which featured twenty-nine punts and ended in a 14–14 tie. The bowl was a success and was destined for great games in the future.

In the Rose Bowl, Stanford's "Vow Boys" were back for a third straight year. Most of the Stanford starters were seniors who, as sophomores in 1933, had vowed never to lose to Southern California after the Indians had lost to the Trojans for six straight years. And they had kept that promise, beating USC all three years they had been on the varsity. Now they vowed not to lose again in the Rose Bowl, where they had suffered two straight defeats. They made it back to Pasadena behind two All-Americans, fullback Bobby Grayson and end James "Monk" Moscrip. This second vow would not be an easy one to fulfill, for Stanford's opponent on January 1 would be undefeated national co-champion Southern Methodist University, led by All-America back Bobby Wilson and All-America guard J. C. Wetsel. There would be no worry about filling the Rose Bowl for the contest, for an estimated 200,000 Texans made inquiries about tickets. A capacity crowd, many of them from Texas, watched as Stanford scored in the first quarter on a 1-yard run by sophomore quarterback Bill Paulman to take a 7–0 lead. After that, the Mustangs outgained the Indians, but fumbled away their best scoring opportunity. Paulman also intercepted three SMU passes. The Indians' second vow was fulfilled, as Stanford won 7–0.

After Bucknell's easy win over Miami in the initial Orange Bowl in 1935, the Orange Bowl Committee decided that the 1936 game should pair two outstanding out-of-state teams, figuring that such a matchup would double nationwide interest. Mississippi was selected to represent the South and Catholic University was chosen to represent the North. The first King

Orange Jamboree Parade was held before the game, honoring Florida's citrus industry, and CBS radio broadcast the game to a regional audience. The Orange Bowl paid the network $500 to carry the contest. Compare that to today, when the networks pay the bowls millions of dollars to broadcast their games, and most income in postseason games comes from selling broadcasting rights. Attendance was only a bit higher than in the previous year, but the game was an exciting one. Catholic built a 14-point lead on two Pete Dranginis touchdown passes and a 24-yard return of a blocked kick. Entering the fourth quarter and trailing 20–6, Mississippi rallied for two touchdowns, a 1-yard run by fullback Dave Bernard and a 24-yard pass from sophomore quarterback Herb Baumsten to end James "Buster" Poole, but missed extra points cost the Rebels the game, 20–19, despite out-gaining Catholic University in yardage 300–153.

Until the late 1950s, a number of games each season were lost on missed extra points because the kicker rarely was a specialist and the goal posts were nearly five feet closer together than in the modern game. The kicker usually was a first stringer at some offensive position, back or lineman, who had minimal time to kick during regular team practices. Also, after a long run or late in the game, tiredness could have an effect on his efficiency and accuracy, as well as on that of the holder.

The Sugar Bowl, featuring local favorite Louisiana State University and Texas Christian University, led by ace tailback "Slingin' Sammy" Baugh, reached an agreement with NBC for a national radio broadcast of the 1936 game, immediately preceding airing of the Rose Bowl contest, which would reach approximately 15 million fans. Tickets were priced slightly higher than for the first game a year earlier, but only a few hundred remained three weeks before the contest. Although it had not rained on New Year's Day in New Orleans in twenty-five years, it poured during the last three days of 1935. It looked like the rain would stop for the game, but it started again shortly before kickoff. The muddy field and heavy, soaked woolen jerseys and leather pads and helmets stifled the offenses of both teams. After falling behind on a safety 2–0, TCU managed to score in the second quarter on a 26-yard field goal by Taldon Manton, and that was enough for a 3–2 Horned Frog victory. Baugh's excellent punting (44.6 yards average on fourteen punts) and two pass interceptions kept the Tigers away from the TCU goal line for most of the game. Afterward, Baugh could remember little about the contest. He had been dazed by a blow to the head in the second quarter and played the rest of the game largely by instinct. Each school received $30,041 for participation. The first two Sugar Bowl contests already had proved that a postseason game in New Orleans would prove highly popular, and plans were laid for an enlarged stadium in the future.

In 1936, the Associated Press rankings, a poll of sportswriters and sports **1936** broadcasters, began to determine the national champion. Discussions of what teams deserved to be national champions date back to the nineteenth century and were hot and heavy among fans—particularly of Ivy teams—in the early days. And sportswriters and sports sections in big city newspapers often printed their own selections. In the late 1920s, mathematical systems similar to today's "power ratings" began to appear, such as the Dickinson, Houlgate, and Dunkel systems. These were often syndicated in newspapers and magazines and have been used to determine the national champions. The number and popularity of these systems varied over the years, but the AP has remained the most widely circulated poll since its inception and is a major part of the current Bowl Championship System formula.

Pittsburgh, which finished No. 3 in the new AP poll, came back to the Rose Bowl once more, but this time the Panthers were not undefeated. They had lost 7–0 to crosstown rival Duquesne and played a 0–0 tie with Fordham, but won seven games. The Panthers would face No. 5 Washington, loser only to national champion Minnesota in its opener. What was expected to be a close intersectional battle turned out to be all Pittsburgh. Embarrassed by their earlier Rose Bowl showings, the Panthers had spent two weeks at nearby San Bernardino preparing for the game and becoming acclimated to their surroundings. The plan paid off. Sutherland finally got a Rose Bowl win when his squad pounded Washington 21–0. Fullback Frank Patrick scored two touchdowns on short runs and sophomore end Bill Daddio scored on a 71-yard lateral interception return, while halfback Bobby LaRue rushed for 199 yards on fifteen carries. The Huskies gained only 153 total yards.

Pittsburgh's regular-season record enabled it to take the initial Lambert Trophy as the best Eastern team. The East was the only region with no major football conference at the time, so two prominent college football boosters, brothers Victor and Henry Lambert of a distinguished Madison Avenue jewelry establishment in New York, instituted a trophy to be awarded annually to the region's outstanding team. Awarded every year since 1936, the trophy is named after the founders' father, August V. Lambert. The trophy is still awarded each year, but it does not carry the prestige it had when the major Eastern teams were independents. With Penn State's entrance into the Big 10 and the formation of the Big East Conference in the early 1990s—and raiding of the Big East members by the Atlantic Coast Conference in 2003— the Eastern teams are no longer clustered in one group for clear supremacy.

The Orange Bowl landed 14th-ranked Duquesne to play unranked Mississippi State, which was making its first postseason appearance. This time the Orange Bowl convinced CBS radio to broadcast the game nationwide at its own expense with primary announcer Ted Husing at the microphone. The Maroons, as Mississippi State teams were known at the time, built up a 12–7 lead on a 10-yard run by fullback Ike Pickle and a 40-yard pass from tailback Charles "Pee Wee" Armstrong to Fred Walters. But Duquesne pulled out a 13–12 victory on a 72-yard scoring pass from Boyd Brumbaugh to Earnie Hefferle in the final two minutes of the game. Brumbaugh, who had been hospitalized with a severe sore throat earlier during the holidays, had notched the first Duquesne touchdown on a 1-yard run, then had kicked the extra point that turned out to be the winner.

Undefeated SEC champion Louisiana State, ranked No. 2, returned to the Sugar Bowl to meet No. 6 Santa Clara, which had won eight straight and accepted the Sugar Bowl bid before losing to Texas Christian 9–0 in its final game. An additional 5,000 temporary seats were installed in Tulane Stadium so that 41,000 people could enjoy the game. In the first eleven minutes of the game, Santa Clara jumped to a 14–0 lead on a 29-yard pass from halfback Don DeRosa to halfback Manuel Gomez followed by another 29-yard touchdown pass from Bruno Pellegrini to Norm Finney. LSU did not make a first down until only five minutes were left in the half, but then scored on a 50-yard pass from Bill Crass to All-America end Gaynell "Gus" Tinsley, cutting the margin to 14–7 at halftime. Santa Clara scored again early in the third quarter on a fumble recovery by quarterback Nello Falaschi, one of ten fumbles the two teams had on the muddy field. LSU made it close in the final quarter, scoring on a 12-yard pass from Crass to Rocky Reed, but the Broncos upset the Tigers 21–14. Santa Clara fans back in northern California were frustrated when NBC radio cut to the Rose Bowl with two minutes left in the Sugar Bowl contest. It was some time before it was announced that Santa Clara had, indeed, won the game.

On New Year's Day, 1937, the Cotton Bowl at Dallas, Texas, joined the other four bowls. The new postseason event owed its existence directly to the

Tulane Stadium—Seating capacity for the 1935 Sugar Bowl (top) consisted of two side concrete stands for 21,000 and wooden seats at each end zone that held an additional 3,000 spectators. By the 1937 game (middle) a bowl shape began to emerge, as seating capacity had been raised to nearly 40,000 with the addition of steel stands in the north end for 14,000 and an increase in seating along the sides. By 1940 (bottom), a true "bowl" design was achieved with permanent stands built on the south end of the field; an additional deck was added to the side stands for a capacity of 69,000. (*R. M. Ours*)

Rose Bowl. J. Curtis Sanford, a Dallas oilman, attended the 1936 Rose Bowl and was so impressed with the pageantry surrounding SMU's appearance there that he returned home and immediately got to work creating a New Year's Day game of his own. Advisers insisted his plan would never work in the Depression and war-clouded years of the 1930s, but he pursued his vision by financing the first four games out of his own pocket. He received a copyright for the name Cotton Bowl and arranged to rent Fair Park Stadium in Dallas from the State Fair of Texas, later urging city leaders to rename it the Cotton Bowl.

The brand-new Cotton Bowl had an excellent match-up for its first game, pitting No. 16 Texas Christian against No. 20 Marquette, and featuring two of the nation's top passers, Baugh of TCU and All-American Ray "Buzz" Buivid of Marquette. Sanford put up $6,000 of his own money to cover the minimum guarantee for the visiting Marquette team. TCU received a $10,000 guarantee. A crowd of 17,000 showed up at Fair Park Stadium and watched Baugh live up to his reputation, as he threw a 50-yard touchdown pass to end L. D. "Little Dutch" Meyer, nephew of TCU Coach "Dutch" Meyer, and also kicked a 33-yard field goal and an extra point. Meyer scored the other TCU touchdown on an 18-yard pass from Vic Montgomery as the Horned Frogs won 16–6.

Hardin-Simmons was invited back to the Sun Bowl to meet the hometown Texas College of Mines (Texas–El Paso), but the game was no contest. The Cowboys' Si Addington started the rout with a 13-yard scoring run in the first quarter. Halfback Pete Tyler scored twice on short runs, while fullback Ed Cherry and Paul White added one each of their own. The Miners' only tally came on a 45-yard pass from O. P. May to Boyd Arnold, for a final score of 34–6.

For 1937 only, a unique postseason game would be played in Havana, Cuba. Officials of the Cuban National Sports Festival at Havana, with the backing of Bacardi Rum, decided to get in on the American postseason football craze in 1936 and arranged for a game to be played on New Year's Day, 1937, between Alabama Polytechnic Institute—better known as Auburn— and Villanova. Unlike the earlier Barcardi Bowls, this one matched American college teams and was recognized by the NCAA as a legitimate bowl. This Bacardi Bowl became the first instance of corporate naming of an official bowl and was the first one played outside the United States. The highlight of the game, which ended in a 7–7 tie, was a 40-yard touchdown run by Auburn halfback Billy Hitchcock. Although 12,000 spectators turned out for the contest, the Bacardi Bowl turned out to be a one-shot affair.

For the next eight years, from 1938 through 1945, postseason football games would consist of the same five bowls: Rose, Orange, Sugar, Sun, and Cotton. They would all be played on New Year's Day, except in 1939 when January 1 fell on Sunday and the games were played the following Monday.

On New Year's Day, 1938, No. 4 Alabama, shut out of the bowls the previous **1937** year, took an unbeaten team to the Rose Bowl for the fifth time with its bowl record still unblemished. Yet the SEC champion was not assured an invitation until No. 7 Dartmouth made it clear that it would not accept a bid. Alabama was matched with No. 2 California, which was named national champion by some selectors. The game, before a huge crowd of 90,000, was a disaster for the Crimson Tide, which lost four fumbles and had four passes intercepted. California halfback Vic Bottari rushed for 137 yards and scored on two short runs to give the Golden Bears a 13–0 win and snap Alabama's four-game Rose Bowl victory string.

The Orange Bowl, still working on the principle of inviting out-of-state teams, remained too small in stadium capacity, despite a larger $325,000 facility that seated 22,000, to attract such unbeaten teams as national champion Pittsburgh. So it matched Michigan State with Auburn. Michigan State, still an independent at the time, had lost only to Manhattan 3–0 while winning eight times. Auburn had won five games while losing two close ones (to Rice 13–7 and LSU 9–7), but had played three scoreless ties during the season. That tough defense was to be a key in the New Year's Day game.

The brand-new stadium allowed 18,972 fans—nearly double any previous Orange Bowl crowd—to watch as Auburn's Tigers ran up a 312–57 margin in total yardage and held the Spartans to just two first downs. Ralph O'Gwynne scored the only touchdown of the game on a short run following a 60-yard punt return by sophomore George Kenmore and a 32-yard pass from Kenmore to O'Gwynne, to give Auburn a 6–0 victory. At halftime, the crowd was entertained by twelve bands and five drill teams—a far cry from the first halftime show just three years earlier when the entertainment consisted of the University of Miami band followed by coeds tossing oranges and tangerines to the crowd.

No. 8 Louisiana State returned to the Sugar Bowl for the third year in a row and faced its opponent from the previous year, No. 9 Santa Clara.

Although it was drizzling at kickoff time, the field was in excellent shape, having been covered several days in advance as a precaution. In a defensive battle, each team punted fourteen times. Santa Clara again upended LSU. The only score came in the second quarter on a 4-yard pass from Santa Clara's Bruno Pellegrini to end Jimmy Coughlan, who was hit by three Tigers but held onto the ball as he struggled into the end zone for a 6–0 victory. LSU outgained Santa Clara by a wide margin, but suffered its first shutout since 1933.

Two ranked teams also met in the Cotton Bowl that year, No. 17 Colorado, behind fabulous All-America tailback, Rhodes Scholar, and future U.S. Supreme Court Justice Byron "Whizzer" White, and No. 18 Rice. The crowd watched in awe during the first quarter as White threw an 8-yard touchdown pass to Joe Antonio, scored on a 47-yard pass interception return, and kicked both extra points to give Colorado a quick 14–0 lead. But that was it for the Buffaloes. Rice sophomore tailback Ernie Lain then took over the game, passing for three scores and running one in himself as the Owls came back for a 28–14 victory.

Border Conference champion Texas Tech was selected as the home team in the Sun Bowl to take on a strong West Virginia team from the East. The Red Raiders had lost three consecutive games early in the season, but had finished 8–3, while West Virginia had lost only to unbeaten national champion Pittsburgh 20–0 and tied Georgetown 6–6 in a nine-game schedule.

The Sun Bowl was a tough defensive battle between the Miners and the Mountaineers. The game was decided in the second quarter when West Virginia recovered a fumble on the Texas Tech 3-yard line and converted it into a score on a 1-yard run by Davey Isaac. Quarterback Emmett "Kelly" Moan then kicked the extra point. The Red Raiders scored shortly before halftime on a 4-yard run by sophomore Charlie Calhoun, but the Mountaineers blocked the extra point try and went on to win 7–6. Halfback Harry "Flash" Clarke, who would eventually star for the Chicago Bears, paced West Virginia with 132 yards rushing.

1938   Unbeaten, untied, and unscored-on Duke, ranked No. 3 in the nation, was the heavy favorite over No. 7 Southern California in the 1939 Rose Bowl. But both teams were unable to score for three quarters. In the fourth, the Blue Devils finally took the lead on a 24-yard field goal by sophomore tackle Tony Ruffa. Since Duke had not given up a point all season, that appeared to be enough. But with time running out, USC quickly moved down the field

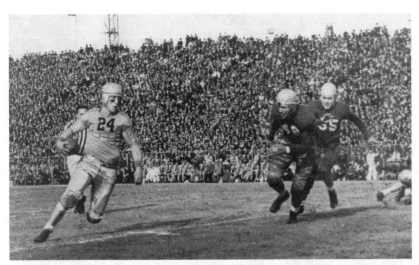

1938 Cotton Bowl—In his last college football game, future Rhodes Scholar Byron "Whizzer" White (24) scored one touchdown and passed for another against Rice. White led the nation in scoring, total offense, and rushing yardage in the regular season. (*Collegiate Images*)

against a tiring Duke team with a passing attack orchestrated by a fourth-team tailback and a second-team end. Tailback Doyle Nave completed four straight passes to "Antelope" Al Krueger, the final one a 19-yarder for a touchdown with less than a minute to play, and Southern California had pulled off a dramatic 7–3 upset victory.

The Orange Bowl had its first marquee match-up, landing unbeaten No. 2 Tennessee, selected as national champion in some listings, to face unbeaten No. 4 Oklahoma. The contest was the result of a media blitz that Orange Bowl officials made to woo the Sooners away from the Sugar and Cotton bowls, which were offering more guarantee money. "On to Miami" was chalked on sidewalks at the Norman campus in the dead of night, and promoter Earnie Seiler gave a morning lecture that featured large posters of girls on Miami Beach, clad in the skimpiest bathing suits allowed in the 1930s. A request by Oklahoma coach Tom Stidham that his friend, Tennessee coach Robert R. Neyland, be asked to bring his Volunteers to Miami to be Oklahoma's foe also was happily acceded to by Orange Bowl officials. However, two Sooner backfield starters, tailback Howard "Red" McCarty and wingback Bill Jennings, were injured and would not play in the bowl game, a huge blow to Oklahoma's chances. Five thousand temporary bleacher seats were erected in each end zone, allowing more than 32,000 fans to see the match of unbeaten, but another 10,000 still had to be turned

1939 Rose Bowl—Duke, unscored on in the regular season, collared Southern California runners throughout the game as illustrated here, but the Blue Devils yielded a touchdown pass in the final minute of play to lose a heartbreaker to the Trojans. (*Pasadena Tournament of Roses*)

away, leading to future enlargement of the stadium. But those in attendance did not see the close game expected. Instead, Tennessee held the Sooners to just 116 yards of total offense and scored on touchdown runs by sophomore Bob Foxx and Walter "Babe" Wood, and a 22-yard field goal by All-America end and future coach Bowden Wyatt for a 17–0 Tennessee victory.

The contest was marked by fights and rough play. Tennessee was penalized 157 yards and Oklahoma 85 yards, with officials ejecting players from both sides. Injuries took more players out of the contest, including Tennessee All-America guard Bob Suffridge. Even a Tennessee cheerleader was knocked unconscious when a Volunteer receiver ran into her while he was going out of bounds. But fans were entertained by the halftime show if not by a close football game. By the late 1930s the Orange Bowl already was known for halftime extravaganzas arranged by Earnie Seiler, a founding member of the Orange Bowl Committee who became general manager in 1939. "Halftime shows are shows," he said, "not something just to link the two halves of football games." In the 1939 contest, more than a dozen bands and drill teams took the field at halftime. By the late twentieth century, guest performers included such organizations as the Royal Philharmonic Orchestra of London.

The Sugar Bowl landed the No. 1 team in the nation, Texas Christian University, led by the nation's leading passer, Heisman Trophy winner Davey O'Brien. This was the first appearance of a Heisman Trophy winner in the postseason. The Horned Frogs' opponent was No. 6 Carnegie Tech (Carnegie Mellon), a team made up of forty-two engineering students and one music major. Carnegie Tech lost quarterback Ray Carnelly with a severe ankle injury in the first quarter, but the Skibos (a nickname taken from founder Andrew Carnegie's Skibo Castle in Scotland) took a 7–6 lead just before the end of the first half on a 37-yard pass from halfback Pete Moroz to George Muha, who then kicked the extra point. O'Brien did not disappoint his supporters, though. Just five plays into the second half, the tailback—who passed for 224 yards in the game—threw a touchdown pass that put the Horned Frogs back into the lead for good. He later added a 20-yard field goal to guide the Horned Frogs to a 15–7 win.

Before the 1939 Cotton Bowl game, founder J. Curtis Sanford turned the classic over to the Cotton Bowl Athletic Association, although he still played a part in staging the contest. The Cotton Bowl invited a ranked team for its "home" team, unbeaten No. 11 Texas Tech, to play unranked St. Mary's of California. Forty thousand turned out expecting an easy Texas Tech victory, but Red Raider fans went away with a disappointing 20–13 defeat as Galloping Gaels backs Andy Marefos, Ed Heffernan, and Mike Klotovich starred for St. Mary's. In El Paso, Utah and New Mexico squared up for the Sun Bowl contest, but it was not much of a contest. Utah won easily, 26–0.

Early in the 1939 regular college football season, the stunning news of **1939** Germany's invasion of Poland on September 1 splashed across the front pages of the nation's papers. And although Europe was plunged into another brutal war, it would be more than two years before American life, including intercollegiate football programs, would suffer major effects from the growing worldwide conflict.

The 1940 Rose Bowl hosted an unbeaten, untied, and unscored-on team for the second successive year, No. 2 Tennessee, after the president of Cornell University declined a bid for his school's team. (The undefeated Big Red finished with a No. 4 national ranking and recorded only two shut-outs, but the desire to have an Ivy team in the Rose Bowl died hard.) Going against the Volunteers would be the nation's No. 3 team, undefeated Southern California. USC coach Howard Jones had the opportunity to seek his fifth straight Rose Bowl win in the contest against Bob Neyland's seventh unbeaten Tennessee team. Unfortunately for Tennessee, All-America back George Cafego sat out the game with a knee injury. A sold-out Rose Bowl of 92,200 spectators were on hand to see if the Trojans could do what they had done a year earlier—defeat an unscored-on team. They could and did. USC back Ambrose "Amby" Schindler ran in a touchdown in the second quarter and passed to end Al Krueger, one of the heroes of the previous year's Rose Bowl, for another in the fourth as the Trojans prevailed 14–0, breaking Tennessee's twenty-one-game win streak. The Vols became the tenth team to lose in the Rose Bowl after compiling a perfect record during the regular season.

No. 6 Missouri was invited to the Orange Bowl to face No. 16 Georgia Tech. Tech scored first on a 1-yard run by fullback Howard Ector. The Tigers' All-American, Paul Christman, answered with a 1-yard run of his own to tie the game. But after that it was all Georgia Tech. The Yellow Jackets rolled to a 21–7 victory highlighted by touchdowns by end Rob Ison and Earl Wheby for the biggest upset of the 1940 postseason.

Thanks to the financial boon the Sugar Bowl festivities provided to the New Orleans economy, a new addition had been added to Tulane Stadium in time for the 1940 contest. The TCU and Carnegie Tech followers of 1939 had spent more money in the four-day period leading up to the game than at any other event or convention in New Orleans for the year, including Mardi Gras. The drive for subscriptions for the stadium addition began on March 7, and the goal was reached in forty days. The first piling was driven in June, and contractors succeeded in having a complete double-deck stadium that could now seat more than 70,000 ready in time for the January 1 contest.

For the second straight year, the top-ranked team once again appeared in the Sugar Bowl, where unbeaten No. 1 Texas A&M, the nation's leader in total defense, faced unbeaten No. 5 Tulane, the first time two undefeated teams were paired in the game. Once again, the Tulane players were reluctant to play in the Sugar Bowl—hoping vainly for a Rose Bowl bid—but their coaches and Tulane's president, Dr. Rufus Harris, persuaded them to accept the Sugar Bowl invitation. The game was all that the capacity crowd could wish for in a contest between two unbeaten, highly ranked teams. Back Bob "Jitterbug" Kellogg scored for the Green Wave on a 75-yard punt return and, with the game tied early in the fourth quarter, Monette Butler put the Green Wave ahead 13–7 on a 2-yard run. But Texas A&M end Herb Smith, the smallest man on the field, shot across the line to block the second Tulane extra point try. All-America fullback John Kimbrough, a 210-pounder who had played all sixty minutes in every Aggie game that year, rushed for 152 yards in the game, and his second touchdown and the extra points by half-back Jim Thomason gave Texas A&M a 14–13 win. The bowl was carried to the nation by the colorful and popular announcer Walter "Red" Barber on NBC radio.

Cotton Bowl fans also expected a close game in a match-up of No. 11 Boston College and No. 12 Clemson. With no area team involved, the crowd was the smallest yet for the game, but if they liked defense, the fans who did show up got their money's worth. Clemson edged the Eagles 6–3 as sophomore fullback Charlie Timmons rushed for 115 yards and scored the game's only touchdown on a 2-yard run. End Alex Lukachik kicked a 24-yard field goal for the Eagles. Clemson All-America back Banks McFadden knocked down two Boston College passes in the end zone and punted for an average of 42.6 yards. In the Sun Bowl, fumbles and interceptions negated a big statistical edge by Arizona State over Catholic University, and the game ended in a 0–0 tie. Only three passes were completed during the game, all by Catholic.

Going into the 1940 season, the war news was grave; France had surrendered to Germany, and as college games across the United States were played that autumn, Great Britain came under siege from the air and in the water. In the Far East, Japan was waging a war in mainland China. The United State remained neutral, but it was difficult to focus on anything but what was happening abroad. In the midst of the turmoil, college football was played as usual, but a change in the game would mark the difference between early football and the modern game.

3 FROM BATTLES TO A BOWL BOOM

BY THE 1940 SEASON, A FEW TEAMS had begun to return to the T formation after decades of using either the single-wing and double-wing formations developed by Coach Glenn "Pop" Warner or the Notre Dame box utilized by Knute Rockne. The T formation, dating to the early years of the game, now was based primarily on finesse and deception, however, not on brute strength. It required a quarterback with passing skills, ball-handling ability, and play-calling intelligence, because the rules of the day required plays to be called by a player on the field, not sent in by the coach. This fundamental change that emphasized the quarterback would sweep the country and set the sport on course to its modern form.

No one in the college ranks in 1940 demonstrated the new formation better than Stanford coach Clark Shaughnessy and his left-handed quarterback, All-American Frankie Albert. Stanford, which had won only one game in 1939, won all nine games in Shaughnessy's first year at Palo Alto and captured its seventh Pacific Coast Conference title. The surprising Indians ended up ranked No. 2 in the nation and were invited to the Rose Bowl to meet No. 7 Nebraska. The Cornhuskers lost their opening game 13–7 to undefeated national co-champion Minnesota, but won their next eight games to capture their ninth Big 6 title. It would be the first of many bowl appearances for Nebraska.

Nebraska's powerful single-wing attack grabbed a 13–7 lead on a 2-yard run by fullback Vike Francis and a 33-yard pass from halfback Herman Rohrig to sophomore halfback Allen Zikmund. Stanford soon proved the efficiency of the T formation, however, as halfback Hugh Gallarneau scored on a 9-yard run and the Indians took a 14–13 lead on a 41-yard touchdown pass from Albert to Gallarneau. Halfback Pete Kmetovic, who rushed for 141 yards in the game, clinched Stanford's 21–13 victory with a 39-yard punt return for a touchdown in the third quarter. Albert kicked all three extra points.

In the Orange Bowl, No. 9 Mississippi State was invited to meet No. 13 Georgetown. Only a 7–7 tie with Auburn marred the Mississippi State record in its first unbeaten season since 1903. Georgetown's only loss was a late-season heartbreaker to unbeaten Boston College, 19–18, which ended the Hoyas' twenty-three-game winning string. In the Orange Bowl, Mississippi State's Hunter Corhern blocked a punt and tackle John Tripson recovered it in the end zone for one Bulldog touchdown, and tailback Billy Jefferson later scored on a 2-yard run. After a touchdown by the Hoyas' Jim Castiglia, Mississippi State stopped a late Georgetown drive on the 6-yard line to preserve a 14–7 conquest.

The 1941 Sugar Bowl came up with another top match, pitting undefeated No. 4 Tennessee against unbeaten No. 5 Boston College, coached by thirty-two-year-old Frank Leahy. After the bowl game, Leahy would accept the head coaching job at Notre Dame, where he would develop six unbeaten teams and five national champions. Tennessee, which led the nation in scoring defense (2.6-point average), was considered the nation's top team in some rankings. Boston College, winner of its first Lambert Trophy as the East's best team, led the nation in scoring, averaging 32 points a game. This Sugar Bowl contest raised the question of what happens when an irresistible force meets an immovable object on the football field. There also was some question about Boston College's ability to win on the road, since nine of the Eagles' games had been at home.

On January 1, more than 73,000 packed the Sugar Bowl to learn the answers. Tennessee scored first on a short run by Van Thompson and led 7–0 at the half. Following a blocked punt in the third quarter, Boston College tied it on a run by Harry Connolly. The Vols went back ahead 13–7, but the Eagles tied the game again on a short run by sophomore fullback Mike Holovak. With two minutes left in the game, 147-pound "Chuckin'" Charlie O'Rourke ran 24 yards for a score giving Boston College a 19–13 win. The winning touchdown, ironically, was on a Tennessee fake pass play that Coach Leahy adopted for his own offense during practice leading up to the game.

The tie-in of the Cotton Bowl with the Southwest Conference began with the 1941 contest, so No. 6 Texas A&M was on hand to defend its Cotton Bowl championship of the previous year. Selected to face the Aggies was No. 12 Fordham. The Rams allowed double figures just once, a 24–12 win over Pittsburgh. Fordham put up a good battle, but Texas A&M won 13–12 on a 62-yard pass from quarterback Marion Pugh to Earl "Bama" Smith, a 1-yard run by All-America fullback John Kimbrough, and Pugh's extra point, the only successful one in the game. In the Sun Bowl, Western Reserve (Case Reserve) defeated Arizona State 26–13. The outstanding play of the game, however, was a spectacular 94-yard touchdown run by Arizona State halfback Hascall Henshaw.

Attendance at NCAA-sanctioned bowl games topped a quarter million for the first time. Clearly, postseason football was among the most popular sporting events in the country. But January 1, 1941, would be the last peacetime New Year's Day in the United States for four years.

1941   Between the end of the 1941 football season and the playing of the regular New Year's Day bowl games Japan attacked Pearl Harbor. The United States now entered directly into World War II. The national response was rapid and the sport of college football, similar to many other aspects of the American scene, would be interrupted and, in other ways, changed forever. Some of the schools that fielded teams that had appeared in bowl games over the previous twenty years would suspend or reduce their support of football for the duration of the war. Several of those failed to resume their former football status at war's end and faded from national recognition. After the tremendous Allied victory in 1945, the country tried to put the long years of war behind and return to normal life and, in the American quest for peacetime diversions, before the decade was out, more bowls would be played on New Year's Day than in any other time in postseason history.

Fears of a Japanese attack on the West Coast raised doubts of whether a Rose Bowl game should be played at all that year, and the Tournament of Roses parade was immediately discontinued until the end of the war. It was decided that the annual football game would be played as usual on New Year's Day—but not in Pasadena. Instead, the contest was transferred to Durham, North Carolina, home of the second-ranked team in the country, the Duke Blue Devils. Duke, winner of its fifth Southern Conference title, led the nation in total offense, while its defense ensured that no opponent had come closer than thirteen points. Instead of simply traveling down the West Coast, the Blue Devils' opponent, the PCC champion Oregon State Beavers, ranked No. 12, would have to cross the country for the only Rose Bowl game ever played outside of Pasadena. Officials at Duke used temporary seats to increase the capacity of the stadium from 35,000 to 56,000, but it was still the smallest Rose Bowl crowd since 1934.

1942 Rose Bowl—Freshman halfback Tom Davis (30) of Duke carries the ball against Oregon State at Durham, North Carolina, in the only Rose Bowl played outside of Pasadena. The game was moved from the West Coast because of the Japanese attack less than a month earlier at Pearl Harbor. (*Pasadena Tournament of Roses*)

The packed stadium witnessed a shocking 20–16 victory by Oregon State. The Beavers scored on a 15-yard run by halfback Don Durdan, a 31-yard pass from Bob Dethman to George Zellick, and a 68-yard pass from Dethman to Gene Gray. Halfback Steve Lach was outstanding for Duke, rushing for 129 yards, including a touchdown, and averaging 47.3 yards on eight punts, but it was not enough to avert the upset.

The Orange Bowl chose No. 14 Georgia, led by the nation's leading rusher, All-America tailback Frank Sinkwich, and unranked Texas Christian University for its New Year's Day match-up. The game turned out to be one of the highest scoring games in bowl history up to that time. Georgia dominated much of the game and Sinkwich was sensational. Despite a broken jaw, partially protected by a special mask, he passed for 243 yards and three touchdowns, including ones of 61 and 60 yards, and rushed for 139 yards and a score. Georgia rolled to a 40–7 lead before TCU began a furious charge in the third quarter. Bruce Alford caught two touchdown passes for the Horned Frogs, but the final score was Georgia 40, TCU 26.

Two teams with similar records were lined up for the 1942 Sugar Bowl, No. 7 Missouri and No. 6 Fordham, winner of its first Lambert Trophy. It began to drizzle just before the kickoff in New Orleans, and the expected offensive show turned into a fierce defensive battle, with neither team able to cross the opponent's goal line or even kick one through the goal posts as a driving rain drenched the field. Fordham blocked a Missouri punt for a safety in the first quarter, and that held up for a victory—the only 2–0 game in bowl history. A 45-yard field goal attempt by halfback Bob Steuber in the closing minutes would have won the game for Missouri, but it fell just short. Fordham, normally a passing team, won the contest without completing a single pass. A United Press reporter wrote that by the end of the game, "the field was ready for stocking with trout and bream, and tarpon were reported to be leaping in the end zone."

In the Cotton Bowl, No. 9 Texas A&M, winner of its third straight Southwest Conference title, faced No. 20 Alabama, which had just wrapped up its thirtieth consecutive winning season. Texas A&M outgained Alabama 309–75 in total yardage and racked up thirteen first downs to just one for the Crimson Tide, yet lost the game 29–21. The Aggies had seven passes intercepted and lost the ball five more times on fumbles. Alabama halfback Jimmy Nelson paced the Crimson Tide with two interceptions, a 72-yard punt return for a touchdown, and a 21-yard scoring run from scrimmage.

In the only other bowl game played on January 1, 1942, Tulsa met Texas Tech in the Sun Bowl, where the Golden Hurricanes beat the Red Raiders 6–0 as Tulsa fullback Glenn Dobbs passed for 239 yards, including the game's only score, a 32-yard touchdown strike to end Saxon Judd.

Left on the outside looking in on New Year's Day, 1942 were three major unbeaten teams. National champion Minnesota and No. 3 Notre Dame still were operating under self-imposed postseason bans, while No. 8 Duquesne (8–0), had only two victories over major teams with winning records.

1942   By the time New Year's Day, 1943 rolled around, college football had undergone drastic changes as a result of America's entry into World War II. Many prospective college football players had either voluntarily joined or had been drafted into the armed forces before the 1942 season got under way, and more entered service during the season itself. And not only players, but coaches, too, flocked to the colors, including such luminaries as Robert Neyland of Tennessee, Wallace Wade of Duke, Bernie Bierman of Minnesota, Jim Crowley of Fordham, and "Tex" Oliver of Oregon. The manpower shortage was such that a number of schools considered dropping varsity football.

Uncertainty as to which schools would actually field teams, and the fact that a number of service teams were interested in playing football against collegiate opposition, caused numerous schedule changes throughout the war years. As the war progressed and rationing of gasoline and other essentials became common, travel restrictions also forced frequent schedule changes. Many intersectional games, in particular, had to be cancelled. And several schools played each other twice—usually on a home and home basis—for the first time since the early part of the century.

Yet, with all of the difficulties in maintaining football programs during the war, there was never any serious consideration of canceling the bowl games. Like major league baseball, which President Franklin Roosevelt encouraged to continue, college football was considered a morale booster not only for people on the home front but also for persons serving in the armed forces. And the bowl games were the climax of each season.

In fact, bowl games were so much a part of the American sports scene by World War II that wherever service personnel were stationed, makeshift bowl games (complete with local hype) were played by members of the armed forces, even in far-ranging areas overseas. These included such games as the Lily Bowl at Hamilton, Bermuda; the Arab Bowl at Oran, North Africa; the Potato Bowl at Belfast, Ireland; the Tea Bowl in London; the Riviera Bowl at Marseille, France; and the Coconut Bowl in New Guinea. The most intriguing game involving overseas personnel may have been the Atom Bowl on January 1, 1946, at Nagasaki, Japan, site of the second atomic bomb explosion not quite five months previously, played between two teams from the U.S. Marine Second Division.

Military personnel, especially those in the Navy and Marines, became prominent in the football programs at several universities that had V-12 or other officer training programs located on their campuses. Many of the servicemen were allowed to play varsity football where they were stationed to encourage them to stay physically fit. NCAA regulations requiring players to sit out a year if they transferred were put on hold for the duration, which meant that an all-conference player at Wisconsin one year might be a star at Michigan the following season. Rosters could also change as a result of mid-season military orders, and a player who was an important part of a team in September might be gone before November. The schools that had no military training programs on campus were at a disadvantage when it came to fielding a football team of experienced players.

Eventually, many college football squads would consist of a mixture of 4-F athletes, fuzzy-cheeked freshmen, and players enrolled in on-campus military programs. A number of other schools determined that a varsity squad simply could not be supported and dropped the sport for one or more years.

Navy pre-flight programs at the universities of Iowa, St. Mary's, North Carolina, and Georgia developed powerful football teams of their own. The Naval Training Station at Great Lakes also became a power, and there were good teams at Naval training facilities at Pensacola, Jacksonville, and Corpus Christi, among others. A number of Army and Air Force facilities also fielded strong teams, notably at March Field in California and Randolph Field in Texas, as well as the Second Air Force base located at McChord Field, Washington, and later at Colorado Springs, Colorado. Many service teams included former All-Americans and other ex-college players, and even some from the professional ranks.

The biggest beneficiaries of the upheaval at the university level were West Point and Annapolis. Both service academies not only could hold onto top recruits who made the grade, but also had a number of outstanding football players transfer in from other colleges and universities after being accepted into the Army or Navy.

On New Year's Day, 1943, bowl games in the United States returned to normal as much as they could under wartime circumstances. The Rose Bowl was once again back in Pasadena, where No. 13 UCLA made its first postseason appearance after winning its first outright PCC title. Once-beaten Ohio State was ranked No. 1 in the nation but could not be invited to the game, so No. 2 Georgia, the nation's leader in total offense and national champion in some selections, was chosen instead. Georgia also boasted the Heisman Trophy winner, "Fireball Frankie" Sinkwich, star of the 1942 Orange Bowl, but unfortunately his Rose Bowl action would be limited because of badly injured ankles.

A crowd of 93,000, the largest bowl attendance during the war years, turned out to see what Georgia could do without the full abilities of Sinkwich. His replacement, tailback Charley Trippi, played most of the game, rushing for 115 yards, throwing for 88 yards, and intercepting a pass on defense. But at the end of three quarters, the score remained 0–0. Then, in the final period of play, substitute tackle Willard "Red" Boyd blocked a UCLA punt through the end zone to give Georgia a 2–0 lead. Later, Sinkwich (who had 71 yards of total offense despite restricted playing time) reentered the game and scored from one yard out to clinch a 9–0 victory for the Bulldogs.

No. 10 Alabama was invited to the Orange Bowl to take on No. 8 Boston College. The Eagles had beaten eight straight opponents before suffering a shocking 55–12 defeat to Holy Cross in their final game. That loss, however, may have saved the lives of many of the BC players. A celebration party scheduled for the Cocoanut Grove nightclub in Boston was cancelled after the unexpected loss, and a fire at the nightclub that evening killed nearly five hundred persons.

In the Orange Bowl game All-America back Mike Holovak was outstanding for BC, rushing for 158 yards and scoring touchdowns on runs of 65, 34, and 2 yards. But Alabama overcame a 14–0 first-quarter deficit to whip the Eagles 37–21, icing the game with 15 second-half points as the Boston College team wilted in the Miami heat. For the Crimson Tide, fullback Tom "Bobby" Jenkins scored two touchdowns, one on a 40-yard run, while sophomore halfback Johnny August ran in a 15-yard score and passed 17 yards to freshman end Ted Cook for another.

The Sugar Bowl had its usual outstanding match-up, with unbeaten No. 4 Tulsa facing No. 7 Tennessee. Tulsa led the nation in both scoring (42.7 points per game) and scoring defense (3.2-point average). Tulsa appeared on track in the second quarter when tailback Glenn Dobbs completed seven straight passes, the last a 9-yarder to back Cal Purdin in the back of the end zone for the game's first touchdown. Tennessee came right back but missed the extra point and trailed 7–6 at halftime. Early in the third period, sophomore tackle Denver Crawford blocked a punt for a safety, giving Tennessee an 8–7 lead. An interception a short time later led to a 1-yard touchdown run by Clyde Fuson that clinched the game for the Vols, 14–7, ruining Tulsa's unblemished record.

Southwest Conference champion Texas earned its first ever postseason appearance and faced No. 5 Georgia Tech in the Cotton Bowl. The No. 11 Longhorns, who led the nation in total defense, made their postseason debut a successful one with a 14–7 upset victory. The Longhorns built a 14–0 lead before Davey Eldredge scored for Tech on a fourth-down "Statue of Liberty" play—a play in which a back stands cocking his arm as if to pass (looking somewhat like the statue) as another player sweeps around, grabs the ball from the "passer's" hand, and runs up field while the defense is still expecting a pass. Texas preserved its victory by halting Georgia Tech at the

Texas 3-yard line in the game's waning moments. At halftime, thirty-one men from Texas, Oklahoma, and Alabama took the oath of enlistment in the Navy's air arm.

The Sun Bowl invited unbeaten Second Air Force, the first service team to participate in a New Year's Day contest since World War I, to play unbeaten Hardin-Simmons. The Second Air Force squad included players who lettered at such schools as Minnesota, Northwestern, Ohio State, Stanford, and Washington State. Hardin-Simmons, champion of the Border Conference, led the nation in rushing behind Rudy "Doc" Mobley, the country's top rusher. The seasoned Second Air Force team won 13–7 as the Bombers held Mobley to 44 yards rushing. Mobley did score the Cowboys' lone touchdown, however, on a 69-yard pass interception return.

1943 Two of the 1943 bowl participants, Alabama and Hardin-Simmons, were among the many schools that decided not to field teams in the following autumn. Other former postseason participants that suspended the sport in 1943 were Arizona, Arizona State, Auburn, Carnegie Tech, Duquesne, Fordham, Georgetown, Manhattan, Michigan State, Mississippi, Mississippi State, New Mexico A&M, Oregon, Oregon State, St. Mary's, Santa Clara, Stanford, Tennessee, Texas Mines, Washington State, and Western Reserve. Former bowl contestant Catholic University had dropped the sport in 1941, not to play again until 1947.

Some schools—Alabama, Auburn, Michigan State, Mississippi, Mississippi State, and Tennessee—stayed out for only one year. Others stayed out for two years or for the duration of the war, and a handful of these teams, including Carnegie Tech, Catholic University, Duquesne, Manhattan, and Western Reserve, would never achieve their former gridiron glories on the major college level.

With many schools not participating in the sport in 1943, and with rationing and wartime travel restrictions in effect, the bowls had to scramble to find satisfactory match-ups for the New Year's Day contests. For the Rose Bowl, the two most attractive teams east of the Mississippi River were prohibited from postseason play, despite any travel restrictions, national champion Notre Dame and Big 10 champion Purdue. The Rose Bowl resorted to matching two West Coast teams, No. 12 Washington and unranked USC. With most of the teams in the Pacific Northwest not fielding a team that season, Washington found itself playing only one collegiate foe, Whitman, beating the Missionaries easily, 35–6, and sweeping three other games against service teams—and that was the extent of its schedule. USC was considered an underdog since it lost to March Field, 35–0, while Washington whipped the same team, 27–7.

A token Rose parade moved down the parade route on January 1, 1944, consisting of three decorated automobiles carrying the tournament president, the Rose queen, and grand marshal Amos Alonzo Stagg. Known as "the Grand Old Man of Football," Stagg, long-time coach at the University of Chicago, had just been named national coach of the year for directing College of Pacific to a record of 7–2—at age eighty-one.

To the surprise of most, USC had little trouble dismantling Washington, 29–0. Trojan quarterback Jim Hardy threw three touchdown passes and the defense held Washington to only five pass completions while intercepting three. George Callanan and freshman end Gordon Gray each caught two touchdown passes for USC.

The Orange Bowl was unable to come up with ranked teams, and settled on a rematch between LSU and Texas A&M's "Kiddie Corps," made up predominantly of freshmen and sophomores. During the regular season, the Aggies beat the Tigers 28–13. The nation's scoring leader and future professional star tailback Steve Van Buren made the difference, as the LSU Tigers upset the Aggies 19–14. Despite a sprained ankle, the 6-foot, 205-pounder ran for 172 yards and two scores (one on a 63-yard run), threw a 21-yard touchdown pass to end Burton Goode, and kicked an extra point. Van Buren also stood out on defense and kicked off for the Tigers. LSU made it to the Orange Bowl with the help of fuel stamps donated by Tiger fans.

The Sugar Bowl was able to match ranked teams, although not as highly ranked as usual for the classic in New Orleans. The bowl committee wanted a powerful No. 2 Iowa Pre-Flight team, which had lost only to national champion Notre Dame, 14–13. But the Navy had a forty-eight-hour limit on furloughs, making it impossible for the Seahawks to participate in a bowl. So the Sugar Bowl committee chose No. 13 Georgia Tech and undefeated No. 15 Tulsa.

For Georgia Tech and coach William A. Alexander, the invitation completed a remarkable cycle of participating in all four major bowls—the first school to do so. The Yellow Jackets competed in the Rose Bowl in 1929, the Orange Bowl in 1940, the Cotton Bowl in 1943, and now the Sugar Bowl. Although Tulsa was making a repeat trip to the Sugar Bowl, it included only six returning members from the previous year's team. Of the forty squad members, twenty-four were classified 4-F or had medical discharges from the military, and nine others were eighteen years of age or younger. Included on the squad were one-armed guard Ellis Jones (an all-conference player nonetheless), a player with only one lung, another with only one kidney, and a player (back Camp Wilson) who had to wear a special shoe because of a severed Achilles tendon.

Tulsa took an 18–7 halftime lead that featured a touchdown pass on a fake field goal play. In the second half, Georgia Tech rallied for two touchdowns to pull out a 20–18 victory, with successful extra points kicked by end Phil Tinsley being the margin of victory. Eddie Prokop had 199 yards rushing and threw a 46-yard touchdown pass to Tinsley for the winners.

No. 14 Texas, bolstered with Marine and Navy trainees, repeated as Southwest Conference champion to earn a Cotton Bowl berth again. Chosen to oppose the Longhorns was a powerful service team, Randolph Field from San Antonio, Texas, led by former Tulsa All-American Glenn Dobbs. Only 15,000 spectators, the smallest Cotton Bowl crowd in history, turned out in a steady downpour to watch Texas and Randolph battle to a 7–7 tie, as neither team could mount much of an offense on the slippery field. Randolph Field had a slight edge in the game—150 total yards to 110 for the Longhorns and seven first downs to three for Texas.

Southwestern, its team bolstered with a wealth of military personnel, was chosen for the Sun Bowl to meet a New Mexico team that had played only four games. New Mexico put up a good fight before a crowd of 18,000, but lost 7–0.

1944 At the end of the 1944 season, the Associated Press named a "G.I. All-American Team" of players who had starred for the various military squads. With their college teams in parentheses, named first team were: ends Jack Russell, 25, of Randolph Field (Baylor) and Nick Susoeff, 23, of Second Air Force (Washington State), tackles Joe Stydahar, 32, of Fleet City Navy (West Virginia and the Chicago Bears) and John Woudenberg, 26, of St. Mary's Pre-Flight (Colorado College), guards Garrard Ramsey, 23, of Bainbridge Navy (William & Mary) and Russell Letlow, 30, of Camp Peary (San Francisco), center George Strohmeyer, 20, of Iowa Pre-Flight (Texas A&M and future Notre Dame star), backs Otto Graham, 22, of North Carolina Pre-Flight (Northwestern and future Cleveland Browns star), Charles Trippi, 23, of Third Air Force (Georgia), William "Bullet Bill" Dudley, 23, of Randolph Field (Virginia and the Pittsburgh Steelers), and Leonard Eshmont, 27, of

Norman Navy (Fordham). Among those selected on the second team were Glenn Dobbs of Second Air Force, star of Tulsa's Sugar Bowl team two years earlier and of the Second Air Force Cotton Bowl team the previous year, and Charles "Choo Choo" Justice of Bainbridge Navy, a high school player from Asheville, North Carolina, who would gain fame after the war at the University of North Carolina.

By New Year's Day, 1945, wartime travel restrictions had eased enough to allow a more normal selection of bowl teams. Unbeaten Tennessee, ranked No. 12, was able to make the trip to the Rose Bowl to play unbeaten No. 7 Southern California in the first match of undefeated teams in Pasadena in five years. The only other undefeated major teams that season, Army's powerhouse national champion, Ohio State, and Yale, were not eligible for postseason play. The Rose Bowl ended up not being much of a game as Trojan quarterback Jim Hardy, one of the stars in USC's win over Washington in the previous year's contest, led his team to a surprisingly lopsided 25–0 victory.

At the Orange Bowl, in a rematch of the 1944 Sugar Bowl, No. 13 Georgia Tech faced No. 17 Tulsa, the nation's leader in total offense and passing. Tulsa took a 14–0 first quarter lead on two touchdowns by wingback Ed Shedlosky, and made it 20–0 in the third quarter on a 65-yard pass/lateral play from Perry Moss to Shedlosky to Barney White. This time Georgia Tech was unable to come from behind to win, despite the heroics of future coach, athletic director, and TV commentator Frank Broyles, who passed for 304 yards, including a 51-yard touchdown pass to Johnny McIntosh to close the gap to 20–6. Fullback Camp Wilson returned the ensuing kickoff 90 yards for a score, sealing a 26–12 victory for Tulsa.

The Sugar Bowl selected Duke to play an Alabama team just back from a year's layoff from football. Duke, fortified with Navy V-12 trainees, was ranked No. 11 in the nation. Unranked Alabama's young civilian contingent included only one 200-pounder, All-America center Vaughn Mancha, and the offense was guided by eighteen-year-old freshman tailback Harry Gilmer. Duke was a solid two-touchdown favorite.

What ensued was a game considered to be among the most exciting bowl match-ups of all time. Duke started the scoring early in the game as freshman halfback George Clark ran the ball in from 14 yards out. The Crimson Tide scored a bit later on a short run by freshman fullback Norwood Hodges but missed the extra point. Late in the first quarter Alabama struck again when Gilmer set up another short touchdown plunge by Hodges with a 40-

yard jump pass to the 1-yard line on third down and 27 to go. The extra point was blocked, but the Crimson Tide led 12–7. In the second quarter Gilmer set up another score with his jump passes, climaxed with a 10-yard touchdown toss to end Ralph Jones, who had four receptions that day for 136 yards. This time Gilmer kicked the point and Alabama led 19–7. Just before halftime, Duke cut the margin to 19–13 on a 1-yard run by halfback Tom Davis. Early in the third period Davis carried the ball on ten consecutive plays, again scoring from the 1-yard line, and end Harold Raether kicked the second of his three extra points to put the Blue Devils in front, 20–19. In the fourth quarter freshman Hugh Morrow returned a pass interception 75 yards for a touchdown to put Alabama back in the lead, 26–20. Deep in its own territory late in the game, Alabama took an intentional safety, cutting the margin to 26–22. Alabama kicked the ball back to Duke and in the next series, with time running out, Clark burst off tackle through the Alabama line and raced 20 yards for his second score of the day—putting Duke ahead 29–26. On the last play of the game, Gilmer hit Jones with a pass at the Duke 30-yard line, and for a moment it appeared the Alabama end might go all the way, the crowd standing, roaring, as he turned toward the end zone. The Duke safety, Blue Devil captain Gordon Carver, caught Jones and dragged him down at the 24-yard line as the final gun went off.

Texas Christian won the Southwest Conference title to break Texas' two-year hold on the Cotton Bowl berth. Chosen to face TCU was Oklahoma A&M (Oklahoma State), winner of the Missouri Valley Conference title behind All-America tailback Bob Fenimore, the nation's leader in total offense. Fenimore passed for 137 yards and scored two touchdowns on short runs, and freshman fullback Jim Spavital rushed for 119 yards, including a 52-yard touchdown run, as A&M, in its first postseason appearance, rolled over TCU 34–0.

The Sun Bowl that year had an unusual match-up. Another good Southwestern team was invited back to play the University of Mexico, the only time a team from outside the United States has been chosen for an American bowl game. Before 13,000, Southwestern won the international contest easily, 35–0. Mexico finished with minus 21 total yards.

1945   By the time New Year's Day, 1946 arrived, World War II had been over for four months. Despite the fact that most of the schools that had dropped football in 1943 and 1944 began competition again in 1945, the 1945 season was played largely under the conditions of the previous three seasons, including

1945 Sugar Bowl—Duke halfback Tom Davis fights his way toward the goal line against an Alabama defense featuring Tom Whitley (55), All-America center/linebacker Vaughn Mancha (41), and Buddy Edwards (46). The lead changed hands four times before Duke won in one of the more exciting games in bowl history. (*R. M. Ours*)

the fact that many players still were being drafted into the armed forces. In addition, few schools now had the luxury of adding on-campus military personnel to their football squads as V-12 and similar programs were being phased out. On balance, a number of football lettermen from the 1941–43 period were returning to finish their degrees after being discharged from the various military branches. As a result, most squads were made up of an unusual mixture of older, experienced players trying to regain their football form along with some talented but very young squad members, many of them freshmen. The 1945 postseason also kicked off an expansion of new bowl games, an expansion that would continue for the rest of the century. Three new bowls debuted on January 1, 1946—the Gator Bowl at Jacksonville, Florida, the Raisin Bowl at Fresno, California, and the Oil Bowl at Houston, Texas—bringing the total number of New Year's games to eight. The Oil Bowl appeared to be the most promising at the time.

During the 1945 season, Army was undefeated going into its final game, against Navy, and there were rumors that the Cadets might finally break their bowl ban for a Rose Bowl trip. Army would not commit itself before the end of the season, however, and the PCC selectors decided they could not take a chance of missing out on an unbeaten team that definitely was available: No. 2 Alabama, the nation's leader in rushing defense and total defense. Representing the PCC was the nation's No. 11 team, Southern California, which had yet to lose a Rose Bowl game. Army, incidentally, finished its season with a 32–13 win over Navy and was crowned national champion.

The Rose parade resumed in 1946 in full glory under the theme "Victory, Unity and Peace" with Admiral William F. "Bull" Halsey as grand marshal, but there was no celebration for USC. Instead of extending its eight-game winning string in the Rose Bowl, the Trojans gave up more points in this contest than in all their previous appearances combined, losing to Alabama 34–14. The Crimson Tide outgained USC 351–41 in total yards and had eighteen first downs to three for the Trojans. Alabama tailback Harry Gilmer rushed for 116 yards and a touchdown and threw a 24-yard touchdown pass to quarterback Hal Self, while fullbacks Lowell Tew and Norwood Hodges each added scores on short runs.

In the Orange Bowl, hometown Miami, making its first appearance since the inaugural game of 1935, faced No. 16 Holy Cross. Although Miami was unranked, the game remained close, and with time running out and the score 6–6, Holy Cross was driving toward the Hurricane goal line. But then a Crusader pass was snared on a leaping grab by reserve sophomore halfback Al Hudson of Miami, who returned the interception 89 yards, crossing the goal line after the final gun sounded for a stunning 13–6 Miami victory, one of the most dramatic endings that has taken place in a bowl game.

The Sugar Bowl selectors considered inviting Army's unbeaten national champions, but seeing that Army was involved in drawn-out discussions with the Rose Bowl (which ultimately led to nothing), the Sugar Bowl officials decided they could not wait to see what happened there. So the invitations went to unbeaten No. 5 Oklahoma A&M and No. 7 St. Mary's, a tiny Christian Brothers school from northern California with an enrollment of fewer than three hundred. The game would match two All-America backs, Bob Fenimore of the Aggies and Herman Wedemeyer of St. Mary's, who finished as the top two rushers in the nation in 1945. Oklahoma A&M's starting lineup included seven war veterans (fullback Jim Reynolds flew fifty-two combat missions over Germany and tackle Bert Cole had been shot down over Yugoslavia), while St. Mary's had seven starters only seventeen years of age and was outweighed by the Aggies fifteen pounds per man.

St. Mary's struck first on a 46-yard touchdown pass from Wedemeyer to Dennis O'Connor, but the Aggies responded in just five plays, scoring on a 28-yard pass from Fenimore to Cecil Haskins. In the second quarter, Fenimore scored on a 1-yard run, but the Gaels came back with a touchdown

1946 Cotton Bowl—Texas sophomore tailback Bobby Layne follows a wall of blockers for a big gain against Missouri, but is finally dragged down by Missouri's Fred Riddle. In one of the great performances in bowl history, Layne ran for three touchdowns, passed for two, caught a touchdown pass, and kicked four extra points in accounting for every point in the Longhorn victory. (*Collegiate Images*)

on a 44-yard lateral play from Wedemeyer to guard Carl DeSalvo. Wedemeyer missed the extra point, leaving underdog St. Mary's trailing 14–13 at the half. The second half was all Oklahoma A&M, as the Aggies scored 19 unanswered points for a 33–13 victory. For the day, Fenimore ran and passed for 206 yards, scored two touchdowns, passed for another, and averaged 53.2 yards on four punts.

No. 10 Texas returned to the Cotton Bowl to face unranked Big 6 champion Missouri. The game would be a record-setting showcase for Texas sophomore tailback Bobby Layne. Layne, who returned from military service in time to play four games in the regular season, had the most productive game in bowl history, accounting for every Texas point in a 40–27 victory. In an extraordinary performance, Layne ran for three touchdowns, passed for two more, caught a 50-yard touchdown pass from Ralph Ellsworth, and kicked four extra points.

In the Sun Bowl, New Mexico defeated Denver 34–24 as Don Rumley threw three touchdown passes for the Lobos.

The inaugural Gator Bowl in Jacksonville was not indicative of the quality of teams the bowl would attract in the future. Having decided that Florida could support another bowl game in addition to the Orange Bowl, the Gator

Bowl Committee headed by businessman W. E. "Ted" Arnold had to settle for a re-match between No. 19 Wake Forest and unranked South Carolina, which had tied 13–13 in a regular season game. Neither school had been in a bowl game previously. The participating teams received $20,000 each. A small crowd of 7,362 turned out to see Richard "Rock" Brinkley lead Wake Forest to a 26–14 victory.

The first Raisin Bowl selected hometown Fresno State to meet Drake from Des Moines, Iowa, but the local team lost a heartbreaker, 13–12, as Drake intercepted six Fresno State passes and recovered three fumbles.

The Oil Bowl got off to a great start, featuring two nationally ranked teams, No. 17 Tulsa and No. 18 Georgia, in an exciting game won by Georgia, 20–6, as tailback Charley Trippi scored on a 68-yard punt return and threw a 64-yard touchdown pass to halfback John Donaldson.

1946 Things were still not quite normal in 1946 in the first full peacetime football season in five years. Military veterans were returning to the college campuses in droves, many with the help of the G.I. Bill, and were battling talented youngsters for starting positions on the football squads. Most schools in 1946 were playing fully collegiate schedules once more, and in the postseason three more bowls were added to the schedule, the Tangerine Bowl at Orlando, Florida, the Alamo Bowl at San Antonio, Texas, and the Harbor Bowl at San Diego, California, bringing the total number of games to eleven.

As New Year's Day, 1947 approached there was a major change concerning teams eligible for the Rose Bowl. After decades of prohibiting postseason play, the Big 10 had a change of heart under Kenneth L. "Tug" Wilson, who became Big 10 commissioner in 1944. Negotiations with representatives of the PCC and Tournament of Roses were completed, and on September 1, 1946, the ban on postseason play was partially lifted, with administrators of the Big 10 agreeing that a conference team could go to the Rose Bowl for the next five years, starting on January 1, 1947, to face a Pacific Coast Conference opponent. Normally, the Big 10 representative would be the conference champion, but conference officials would determine which team would go, and they were not in favor of any team going two years in succession, champion or not. The pact also called for the Big 10 and the PCC each to receive 42.5 percent of the net revenue from the game, with the Tournament of Roses receiving the other 15 percent. Wilson, former Northwestern athletic director, was able to assure faculties of Big 10 schools

1946 Oil Bowl—Halfback Charles "Rabbit" Smith (18) scores the first Georgia touchdown in the inaugural Oil Bowl at Houston. The Bulldogs defeated Tulsa, making its fifth bowl appearance in as many years. (*R. M. Ours*)

that there would be no time lost from classes. This agreement, with modifications, subsequently would be periodically renewed for more than fifty years until it was superseded by the Bowl Championship Series agreement in 1998.

The new pact almost guaranteed that the annual visitor to the Rose Bowl would be a top-quality team, quite possibly the national champion, as a Big 10 team had won at least a share of the national title eight times since 1932. The opportunity to see a Big 10 team in the Rose Bowl for the first time since 1921 was intriguing. But the monopoly meant there would not be a variety of top teams selected from the South or the East, no chance to see top individual players from those areas, no waiting in anticipation at the end of a season to see whether the visitor would be an outstanding team from Tennessee, Alabama, Oklahoma, Duke, or Pittsburgh.

There was another reason the agreement initially was not received with much enthusiasm on the West Coast. Many fans wanted the pact to be postponed a year so that Army, wrapping up a third straight undefeated season, might appear in the bowl. All-America halfback Glenn Davis, from Claremont, California, was one of the big stars of the unbeaten Cadet teams of 1944–1946, and he wanted nothing more than to return to southern California to play in the Rose Bowl. There had been talk that the winner of the November 9, 1946, game between undefeated Army and unbeaten Notre

Dame might be allowed by school administrators to participate in the Rose Bowl. But that classic contest ended in a 0–0 tie, and the Big 10–PCC pact was put into effect.

The first beneficiary of the new agreement was No. 5 Illinois, which would make its first postseason appearance against an impressive unbeaten UCLA team, ranked No. 4. The launching of the Big 10–PCC pact was not the close game expected, however, as the Fighting Illini romped over the Bruins 45–14, with halfback Claude "Buddy" Young rushing for two touchdowns and two Illini interceptions returned for scores, one of 68 yards by linebacker Russ Steger. UCLA's only bright spot was a 103-yard kickoff return (officially 100 yards in NCAA records) by 139-pound halfback Al Hoisch, the first kickoff return for a touchdown in Rose Bowl history.

The Orange Bowl featured two conference champions, No. 7 Tennessee from the Southeastern Conference and No. 10 Rice, co-champion of the Southwest Conference. The game was a defensive battle, with all scoring taking place in the first quarter. The only touchdown of the game came on a 50-yard play in which Rice fullback Carl "Buddy" Russ ran for 23 yards, then lateraled to sophomore halfback Huey Keeney, who completed the journey to the end zone. Freshman tackle Ralph "Goose" Murphy later blocked a Tennessee punt through the end zone for a safety, and the 8–0 score held up for the rest of the game.

The Sugar Bowl selectors had considered unbeaten Army for an invitation, but in the long run Army stuck to its postseason ban when no Rose Bowl bid came through. The Sugar Bowl still got an outstanding team in unbeaten No. 3 Georgia, the nation's scoring leader (37.2-point average) featuring Maxwell Award–winning tailback Charley Trippi. The Bulldogs went into the game a fourteen-point favorite over No. 9 North Carolina, making its first postseason appearance behind freshman tailback sensation Charlie "Choo Choo" Justice. Both star tailbacks played the full sixty minutes of the game. But, while Trippi did throw a 67-yard touchdown pass to sophomore end Dan Edwards and had 54 yards rushing in the Bulldogs' 20–10 victory, it was Georgia's defense that earned top honors, holding Justice to just 37 yards rushing. UNC came closer than expected and might have done even better had it not been for two obviously bad calls by officials, one of which robbed the Tar Heels of a score in the last quarter.

The Cotton Bowl lined up No. 8 Louisiana State and Southwest Conference co-champion No. 16 Arkansas. In rain, sleet, and snow the teams battled on a cold, muddy field. Led by future NFL star Y. A. Tittle, LSU had a 271–54 margin in total yardage and its defense held the Razorbacks to a single first down, yet the Tigers had to settle for a demoralizing 0–0 tie.

The second installment of the Gator Bowl saw an interesting intersectional match-up between No. 14 Oklahoma and No. 18 North Carolina State, making its first postseason appearance. Oklahoma fullback Tommy "Eddy" Davis scored three touchdowns to lead the Sooners to an easy 34–13 victory.

The Sun Bowl experimented with matching two teams from east of the Mississippi River, Cincinnati and Virginia Tech, neither of which had ever appeared in a bowl before. Only 10,000 spectators, the lowest Sun Bowl number since 1937, turned out as Cincinnati rolled to an 18–6 win.

In the second Raisin Bowl, San Jose State, champion of the California Collegiate Athletic Association, shut out Utah State, co-champion of the Mountain States Conference, 20–0.

The second, and last, Oil Bowl matched No. 11 Georgia Tech against unranked St. Mary's of California. In rainy, frigid weather the Yellow Jackets beat the Gaels 41–19. Four of Tech's touchdowns were set up by pass interceptions, one returned 73 yards for a score by Pat McHugh, and another by a fumble.

The first Harbor Bowl saw a scrappy game between New Mexico and Montana State that ended in a 13–13 tie. It was a remarkable comeback for Montana State's Golden Bobcats, who lost their entire 1940 starting team as casualties during World War II, and had just returned to varsity competition in 1946 after a four-year layoff.

The Tangerine Bowl made no pretense of being a "major" bowl for a decade and a half. In fact, no teams classified as major participated in the game until 1962. But it eventually would develop into a first-rate bowl. The Tangerine Bowl's inaugural match-up featured Catawba, the North Carolina State Intercollegiate Conference champion, and Maryville of Tennessee. Catawba won the game easily, 31–6.

The Alamo Bowl would have played its first contest on New Year's Day, but the field was covered with two inches of ice. The game was postponed to January 4, with unbeaten Hardin-Simmons facing Denver. A three-year layoff during the war seemed not to have hurt Hardin-Simmons. The Cowboys outscored opponents 302–48 during their first season back and swept ten games while taking the Border Conference title for the second time. Denver finished 5–4–1 and earned a share of the Mountain States Conference title. The temperature still was below freezing at game time, but Hardin-Simmons remained unbeaten by whipping Denver 20–0 as Rudy "Doc" Mobley, the nation's rushing leader, scored two touchdowns. San Antonio did not try another postseason game for nearly fifty years.

1947   The postwar boom in bowl games continued apace following the 1947 regular season. Three new ones were set for January 1, 1948, the Salad Bowl at Phoenix, Arizona, the Delta Bowl at Memphis, Tennessee, and the Dixie Bowl at Birmingham, Alabama, bringing the total number of games played on New Year's Day to an all-time high of twelve. The following New Year's would also have twelve games, and then the number would steadily drop. Part of the reason was the fact that bowls were beginning to compete nationally for media attention as radio and ultimately television audiences were demonstrating the immense popularity of these contests. With so many games and a crowded schedule, only a few could anticipate benefiting from national coverage, making dates other than New Year's Day more attractive.

In the meantime, however, another new bowl was attempted in early December at Cleveland, Ohio, a surprising location for a winter football game. Nonetheless, the backers lined up Kentucky and Villanova for the first—and only NCAA-sanctioned—Great Lakes Bowl on December 6. Kentucky, in its second year under Paul "Bear" Bryant, beat Villanova 24–14 behind sophomore halfback Bill Boller, who scored on a 15-yard run and a 49-yard pass interception return, and quarterback George Blanda, who kicked a 27-yard field goal and three extra points. Blanda would go on to a long professional football career as both a quarterback and a kicker. The Great Lakes Bowl was played once again the following season, on December 5, 1948, when John Carroll beat Canisius 14–13, but the second edition was not sanctioned by the NCAA as an official bowl.

In the 1948 Rose Bowl, the Big 10–PCC pact produced what looked like a good match-up between No. 2 Michigan, considered national co-champion along with unbeaten Notre Dame in some rankings, and No. 8 Southern California. Michigan would be making its first trip to the Rose Bowl since the inaugural Rose contest of 1902.

The 93,000 who jammed the stadium—some of whom paid as much as $25 just to park their cars in Pasadena parking lots—and the fans who watched the contest locally on Los Angeles television station KTLA (the first college football game televised in the city), saw a game eerily reminiscent of

Michigan's first trip to Pasadena. USC crossed the midfield stripe only twice in the whole game, and the 49–0 final score was exactly the same as that Michigan victory in 1902. All-America tailback Bob Chappuis, an Army Air Force combat veteran, passed for two touchdowns, while fullback Jack Weisenburger rushed for 91 yards and three scores, and center Jim Brieske kicked seven extra points.

The Michigan victory was so impressive that the Associated Press took an informal poll following the New Year's games, and Michigan edged Notre Dame for the national championship. The official poll, however, remained the one at the end of the regular season that placed Notre Dame first. It would be twenty-one years before postseason games would be recognized in the final national rankings.

No. 10 Georgia Tech and No. 12 Kansas, in its first postseason appearance, were selected for the Orange Bowl contest. Additional seats in a second deck allowed for the largest Orange Bowl crowd yet, 59,578, and those fans—some of whom paid scalpers $50 for a ticket—were treated to an exciting game. Quarterback Jim Still passed for 129 yards and all three Yellow Jacket touchdowns, but it was his 5-foot, 8-inch, 185-pound teammate, guard Rollo Phillips, who preserved a 20–14 victory by securing a Jayhawk fumble in the closing minutes just inches from the Georgia Tech goal line.

In the Sugar Bowl, No. 5 Texas rolled to a surprisingly easy 27–7 victory over No. 6 Alabama, following a 7–7 standoff in the first half. All-America tailback Bobby Layne passed for a touchdown and ran in another for the Longhorns. Texas also scored on a blocked punt that was recovered in the end zone by Vic Vasicek.

The Cotton Bowl came up with an outstanding match-up with undefeated No. 3 Southern Methodist, led by Maxwell Award-winning tailback Doak Walker, facing undefeated No. 4 Penn State, the nation's leader in total defense, scoring defense (three-point average), and a rushing defense that yielded only 17 yards a game, a record that still stands.

Selection of Penn State caused a problem not directly connected with the game. The Nittany Lions had two African-American players, reserve end Dennie Hogard and reserve wingback Wally Triplett, and no black player had yet participated in the Cotton Bowl. Dallas at the time had segregated hotels and restaurants. When Boston College played in the 1940 Cotton Bowl, the Eagles left African-American reserve back Louis Montgomery at home. In 1946 Penn State canceled a game at Miami when the Nittany Lions were requested to come without their black players, but no such request was

made by Cotton Bowl or SMU officials for the 1947 contest. "I think you have
to give a lot of credit to the whole SMU ball club," Penn State center/line-
backer John "Shag" Wolosky said some years later. "Dennie and Wally were
two gentlemen, and I think the team never wanted to put any pressure on
them. We would not have gone down if SMU had requested us to leave them
behind."

The problem of housing was solved when the Naval Air Station near
Dallas made its barracks, mess hall, and other facilities available for Penn
State's use, although many of the Penn State players, especially the World
War II veterans, were not happy about being quartered at a military installa-
tion. There were no serious incidents in the game. "Other than the accom-
modations, SMU and the city of Dallas treated us very well," Hoggard
recalled in later years. "SMU played a hard, tough game but there was no
name calling." There were, however, some boos from the spectators when
Hoggard and Triplett took the field.

Doak Walker was as good as advertised, throwing a 53-yard touchdown
pass to wingback Paul Page, rushing for another touchdown, and kicking an
extra point in the first half. With only ninety seconds left in the second quarter, Penn State got back into the game, scoring on a 38-yard pass from pint-
sized tailback Elwood Petchel to halfback Larry Cooney, and trailed 13–7 at
halftime. Penn State dominated the third quarter and finally scored late in
the period, on a 6-yard pass from Petchel to Triplett, but missed the extra
point. On the game's last play, Petchel threw a 37-yard pass into the end
zone, where Hoggard just missed making a leaping catch, and the game
ended in a 13–13 tie.

The Gator Bowl selected Georgia and Maryland, making its first postseason appearance. The Terps were paced by halfback Lu Gambino, the
nation's leading scorer. The two teams battled to a 20–20 tie. Gambino
rushed for 165 yards and scored all three Maryland touchdowns on two runs
and a pass reception. Georgia quarterback John Rauch passed for a touchdown and scored on a 1-yard run, while halfback Joe Geri scored on another run and kicked two extra points for the Bulldogs.

The Raisin Bowl matched College of Pacific and Wichita. Pacific already
had defeated Utah State 35–21 on December 13 in the inaugural Grape
Bowl, in Lodi, California, a contest not officially recognized by the NCAA.
Pacific won its second bowl game of the season—the first time a school had
played two postseason games since Centre did it following the 1921 season—
defeating Wichita 26–14, as 5-foot, 7-inch quarterback Eddie LeBaron passed

1948 Raisin Bowl—College of the Pacific halfback Don Brown (42) tries to shake a tackler as the Tigers beat Wichita for their second bowl victory of the season. COP had defeated Utah State in the inaugural Grape Bowl on December 13. (*R. M. Ours*)

for 118 yards and two touchdowns, averaged 48.5 yards on three punts, and had a 36-yard pass interception return.

In San Diego, the Harbor Bowl selected hometown San Diego State to take on Hardin-Simmons. A crowd of 12,000 turned out on New Year's Day, but there was no contest. Hardin-Simmons rolled to a 28–0 halftime lead and crushed the Aztecs 53–0. Among the stars for the Cowboys was freshman Wilton "Hook" Davis, who led the nation in rushing during the regular season. In the Sun Bowl unbeaten Mid-American Conference champion Miami (Ohio) squeezed past Border Conference champion Texas Tech 13–12.

The first Salad Bowl game at Phoenix matched Nevada against North Texas State, with Nevada winning 13–6, highlighted by a 93-yard touchdown pass from quarterback Stan Heath to back Tommy Kalminar. The name Salad Bowl may appear to be a poor pun, but it actually fit with the origins of most other bowls up to that time, as the contest was designed to promote lettuce and other agricultural products that were important to Arizona's economy.

The inaugural Delta Bowl at Memphis came up with a plum in SEC champion No. 13 Mississippi (8–2), guided by All-America tailback Charles Conerly, the nation's passing leader, and end Barney Poole, the nation's leader in pass receptions. In cold, windy weather, unranked opponent TCU took a surprising 9–0 lead in the first half when sophomore quarterback/safety Lindy Berry scored on a 30-yard pass interception return and tackle Weldon "Scratch" Edwards blocked a punt out of the end zone for a safety. Mississippi finally rallied in the fourth quarter as Conerly threw two touchdown passes for a 13–9 victory.

The other new bowl, the Dixie Bowl in Birmingham, also hosted a nationally ranked team, No. 14 William & Mary, which faced unranked Arkansas. Local businessman Leo Burson underwrote the game, dividing profits with the city of Birmingham and the American Legion. His share came to $20,000. In an exciting game, Arkansas pulled off a 21–19 upset, highlighted by a 59-yard touchdown pass from quarterback Ken Holland to sophomore wingback Ross Pritchard and a 70-yard pass interception return for a score by Melvin McGaha, while tailback Aubrey Fowler kicked three important extra points. Fullback "Flyin'" Jack Cloud scored twice for William & Mary.

The Tangerine Bowl invited an outstanding Catawba team back to take on Marshall. Catawba had the only score, winning 7–0.

1948   Postseason 1948 had fourteen officially sanctioned bowl games, including two new ones played in December, the Shrine Bowl (sponsored for charity by the Shriners, as was the all-star game in San Francisco) at Little Rock, Arkansas, and the Camellia Bowl at Lafayette, Louisiana. Neither lasted beyond one year. Also that year, three New Year's Day contests, the Harbor, Delta, and Dixie Bowls, were played for the last time. But it would be thirty years—the postseason of 1978—until this number of NCAA-recognized bowls would be played again. The NCAA, concerned with the exploitation of athletes and athletic programs, already had a committee surveying the bowl situation to determine the degree of participation by commercial promoters. Some fifty bowls were included in the 1948 postseason, most not officially recognized by the NCAA. Sponsors of these games included charity organizations, chambers of commerce, stadium proprietors, civic committees, and city councils. Beneficiaries included hospitals, scouting, veterans, underprivileged children, welfare projects, and scholarship funds as well as civic treasuries and stadium expansion.

The tiny school of Hardin-Simmons played an integral part in the 1948 postseason and had one of the more remarkable records in college football in the decade beginning in 1939. The Cowboys won thirty-two games, tied three, and lost only five in the 1939–42 period before dropping football for the remainder of World War II. Two of those Hardin-Simmons teams were unbeaten, although the 1942 club tasted defeat in the Sun Bowl, the first postseason contest for the Cowboys, against a "stacked" service team. When Hardin-Simmons resumed the sport in 1946, it went unbeaten in ten games, followed by a win in the Alamo Bowl. The Cowboys won the Harbor Bowl easily following the 1947 season. In 1948, Hardin-Simmons was only 4–4–2 in the regular season, but the popular Cowboys were invited to a total of three bowl games. On December 4, in the second annual Grape Bowl, they played a 35–35 tie with College of Pacific. In that one, they had taken a 21–0 lead into the second half, but diminutive Pacific quarterback Eddie LeBaron passed the Tigers into a 35–28 lead with less than five minutes left in the game. The tying score for Hardin-Simmons was set up by a long punt return by Wilton "Hook" Davis, but LeBaron had Pacific back on the Cowboys' 1-yard line when the game ended.

The Shrine Bowl, played on December 18, 1948, matched Hardin-Simmons against Ouachita College. By the date of the Shrine Bowl, Ouachita had won the Texoma Bowl at Denison, Texas, on December 10, beating Southeastern Oklahoma 7–0. On December 18, Hardin-Simmons continued its unusual bowl odyssey, rolling past Ouachita 40–12 before 5,000 fans in a warm-up for its final bowl game of the season.

On December 30 the Cowboys completed their three-game bowl season undefeated in the brand-new Camellia Bowl, whipping Wichita 49–12. It was a good game for thirty minutes, but the Cowboys scored 35 unanswered points in the second half and finished with 634 yards of total offense. Bob McChesney had eight pass receptions for 200 yards and four touchdowns for Hardin-Simmons, while teammate Pat Bailey rushed for 163 yards and two scores. The Cowboys' defense forced six turnovers.

Rose Bowl fans may have felt cheated in the Big 10 selection for the 1949 contest. Undefeated national champion Michigan was the conference champion, but because the Wolverines had appeared in the Rose Bowl the previous year, the Big 10 representatives selected runner-up No. 7 Northwestern to make the trip to Pasadena to play undefeated California, ranked No. 4.

The 93,000 on hand got their money's worth—and more. Northwestern scored a disputed touchdown by fullback Art Murakowski, whose goal-line fumble on a 2-yard plunge appeared to have occurred before the ball crossed the goal (photographic evidence later appeared to support this claim). Despite the apparent bad call on Murakowski's touchdown, California took a 14–13 lead in the second half and, with only six minutes left in the game, an apparent California recovery of a Wildcat fumble on the Northwestern 12-yard line would have given the Bears a chance to clinch the victory. But, in another controversial call, officials ruled that the whistle had blown before the Northwestern halfback lost the ball. The Wildcats then drove 88 yards, the last 43 yards on a run by 165-pound Ed Tunnicliff, for a score, giving Northwestern a 20–14 upset victory.

In the Orange Bowl, No. 8 Georgia squared off against unranked Texas. The Longhorns were motivated by a string of stories in Miami newspapers criticizing the selection of an "inferior" Texas team. What was expected to be an easy win for Georgia turned out to be a Longhorn rout with Texas backs running for five touchdowns, including one by future pro football star and long-time Dallas Cowboys coach Tom Landry for a 41–28 win and Georgia's first bowl loss in six games under coach Wallace "Wally" Butts.

The Sugar Bowl was set for a great game, pitting No. 3 North Carolina in its first unbeaten season since 1898 and led by All-America tailback Charlie "Choo Choo" Justice against No. 5 Oklahoma guided by thirty-three-year-old coaching sensation Charles "Bud" Wilkinson. North Carolina's chances suffered a blow when Justice came down with the flu three days before the game and could eat nothing until a small meal on game day.

Anticipation of the showdown was such that additional seating was added to Tulane Stadium to accommodate a huge Sugar Bowl crowd of 82,000. North Carolina opened the game moving the ball quickly downfield with its single wing offense, but a 69-yard pass interception return by linebacker Myrle Greathouse led to Oklahoma's first touchdown and turned things around. In the second half Oklahoma dominated the game with its split-T offense and rugged defense, finally clinching the game on an 8-yard touchdown run by halfback Lindell Pearson to pull off a 14–6 upset. Despite his weakened condition, Justice had 84 yards rushing and 54 yards passing for the Tar Heels.

Getting special permission from the Pacific Coast Conference to compete in the Cotton Bowl, No. 9 Oregon faced No. 10 Southern Methodist, featuring Heisman Trophy winner Doak Walker. Thanks to completion of an upper section on the west side of the Cotton Bowl, the stadium was able to accommodate 69,000 for the game. Walker rushed for 66 yards and a touchdown, passed for 79 yards, kicked two extra points and got off a 79-yard quick kick, while his teammate, sophomore halfback Kyle Rote, rushed for 93 yards and a touchdown, caught four passes for 55 yards, and got off an 84-yard quick kick—the longest punt in bowl history—leading the Mustangs to a 21–13 victory. Oregon's quarterback, future NFL Hall of Famer Norm Van Brocklin, passed for 145 yards and a touchdown in a losing effort. Although the quick kick, a surprise punt on any down preceding fourth down, was still a com-

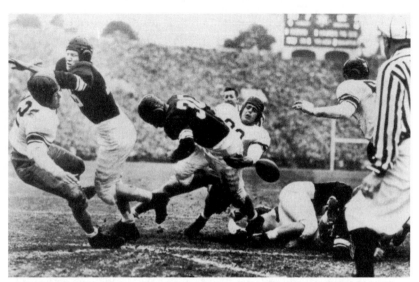

1949 Rose Bowl—In one of the more controversial plays in bowl history, Northwestern fullback Art Murakowski lost the ball when tackled by California end Norm Pressley at the goal line, but officials ruled he had scored first. That touchdown was the margin of victory for the Wildcats. (*Pasadena Tournament of Roses*)

mon weapon in the late 1940s, it was unusual to see two by one team in a single game that covered such long distances as those by Walker and Rote in the 1949 Cotton Bowl. Such punts were used to gain field advantage by catching the defensive team by surprise with no one in position to field the ball after it was kicked. The quick kick is rarely used in today's game.

West Virginia was selected to play in the Sun Bowl for the first time since 1938 after an 8–3 record highlighted by a season-ending 16–14 upset of Maryland, the winning points coming on a drop-kicked field goal by tiny kicker Gene Simmons—one of the last drop-kicking specialists in the college game. The host team was hometown Texas College of Mines, led by back Fred Wendt, the nation's leader in both rushing and scoring. On New Year's Day 1949, Texas College of Mines officially became Texas Western University, but the name change did not lead to a victory on the football field. West Virginia spotted the Miners a 6–0 lead, then charged back for a 21–12 win, led by quarterback Jimmy Walthall's 25-yard touchdown pass to Clarence Cox and halfback Jim Devonshire's two scoring runs. Wendt did score on a spectacular 60-yard run, but the West Virginia defense held him in check for most of the game.

The Gator Bowl landed the nation's No. 11 team, unbeaten Clemson, to play Missouri. The game was a thriller, with Clemson winning 24–23 on a Jack Miller 32-yard field goal late in the fourth quarter. Lined up for the fourth Raisin Bowl contest were Colorado A&M (Colorado State) and the unbeaten Occidental Tigers of California. The Tigers remained unbeaten with a 21–20 victory, despite touchdown runs of 71 and 79 yards by Rams halfback Eddie Hanna. In the Salad Bowl, Drake edged the Arizona Wildcats 14–13.

This postseason saw the final games for three bowls, the Harbor, Delta, and Dixie Bowls on New Year's Day. The Harbor Bowl bowed out with a match between Villanova and Nevada, the nation's leader in passing, total offense, and scoring (44.4-point average). But Villanova, behind diminutive quarterback Billy Doherty and a tough defense, had little trouble in upending Nevada 27–7 after Wolf Pack quarterback Stan Heath left with an injury early in the game. The last Delta Bowl featured No. 17 William & Mary and Oklahoma A&M. William & Mary upheld its national ranking, whipping Oklahoma A&M 20–0 with tailback Tommy Korczowski passing for two touchdowns and tackle Lou Creekmur scoring on a 70-yard pass interception return. The last of the three bowls to disappear after January 1, 1949, was the Dixie Bowl, which pitched No. 20 Wake Forest against unranked Baylor, making its first postseason appearance. A good turnout of 20,000 fans saw Baylor take a 20–0 lead in the first half that held up for a 20–7 upset victory.

In the Tangerine Bowl, still selecting "small college" teams at this time, Murray State of Kentucky and Sul Ross State of Texas played to a 21–21 tie. As early as 1946 the NCAA began to expand its annual football statistics to the smaller colleges and universities in addition to covering the 125 schools whose teams either were members of the principal college conferences or played most of their games against "major" opposition. By 1948 the NCAA classified about 120 college football teams as "major college" and the remainder as "small college" based on class of competition. The actual splitting into Division I, Division II, and Division III did not take place until 1973, with the formation of Division I-AA (splitting off from Division I-A) following in 1978.

One other minor bowl deserves mention for New Year's Day, 1949. That was the Ice Bowl at Fairbanks, Alaska, where the University of Alaska met the Ladd Field Army post. Before five hundred brave fans on a windy, snowy, twenty-five-below-zero day, the two teams battled to a 0–0 tie, finishing at 1 P.M. as the sun went down behind an ice-swathed goal post.

Before the 1949 football regular season got under way, the NCAA decided to
take steps to stop the proliferation of bowl games—or at least to bring them
under stricter quality controls. New regulations discouraged overenthusias-
tic promoters and civic boosters by requiring that 80 percent of gross bowl
receipts go to the competing colleges. The following year that provision was
changed to 75 percent of the gross receipts, including ancillary revenue such
as broadcast and concession money, to go to the participating teams. Also,
competing schools were to receive between one-sixth and one-third of the
seats in the stadium, and the postseason contest had to be certified by the
NCAA's Extra Events Committee. The new rules had an immediate effect.
From fourteen recognized "major" bowl games following the 1948 season,
the number dropped to nine following the 1949 season. It would further
drop to eight for the 1952 postseason and then to seven for the 1953 bowl
season, where it would hold steady for six years.

Thus, the only major bowls that would continue following the 1949 season would be the Rose, Orange, Sugar, Sun, Cotton, Gator, Tangerine, Salad,
and Raisin. And this would be the last year for the Raisin Bowl.

The Raisin contest pitted San Jose State against Texas Tech. San Jose, winner of the California Collegiate Athletic Association title, had an 8–4 record,
including a 103–0 win over the University of Mexico to start the season
(because Mexico is not a member of the NCAA, the modern scoring record
recognized by the NCAA remains Houston's 100–6 win over Tulsa in 1968).
In the last Raisin Bowl, San Jose State beat the Red Raiders 20–13.

New Year's Day fell on Sunday in 1950, so most of the postseason games
were played on January 2. An exception was the Salad Bowl, which did take
place on January 1, and saw Xavier (Ohio) defeat Arizona State, 33–21,
despite four pass interceptions by the Sun Devils' defensive back Manuel Aja.

Unbeaten No. 3 California returned to the Rose Bowl to face No. 6 Ohio
State. The two teams first met in the 1921 Rose Bowl, which California won
handily, 28–0. Recent enlarging of the Rose Bowl stadium led to the first
100,000 attendance for a bowl game. A crowd of 100,963 saw a closely con-
tested game, not decided until the final minutes. Late in the fourth quarter,
with the score tied 14–14 and California backed up deep in its own territory,
quarterback Bob Celeri was unable to get off a punt because of a bad snap
from a substitute center, and Ohio State took over at the 13-yard line. Even
then, the Buckeyes were stopped short of a first down. With only about two
minutes left to play, end Jimmy Hague kicked a 17-yard field goal to give

Ohio State a 17–14 victory, the first time a Rose Bowl game had been decided by a field goal.

In the Orange Bowl, Paul "Bear" Bryant's No. 11 Kentucky, the nation's leader in total defense and scoring defense (4.8 points per game), was selected to meet No. 15 Santa Clara. While Bryant put his Wildcats through heavy workouts at a high school practice field at Cocoa Beach, Santa Clara Coach Len Casanova followed the advice of a greyhound trainer, the father of one of Casanova's assistant coaches, who warned against working the players too hard in southern Florida's heat and humidity. Casanova gave his squad only light workouts in the three days following a four-day train ride from the West Coast. The advice worked as the Wildcat defense yielded the most points it had all season, and Santa Clara won, 21–13, capped by a 17-yard touchdown run by Bernie Vogel in the fourth quarter.

The nation's No. 2 team, unbeaten Oklahoma, and No. 9 Louisiana State were set to meet in the Sugar Bowl. Oklahoma led the nation in rushing defense while Sooner halfback George Thomas was the nation's leading scorer with 117 points. LSU, coached by Gaynell "Gus" Tinsley, one-time LSU All-America end, defeated three conference champions during the course of the season—Rice, North Carolina, and Tulane. But what was expected to be a close game was not. LSU gained only 38 yards rushing against the outstanding Oklahoma defense, and the Sooners rolled to a 35–0 victory. Oklahoma rushed for 286 yards, 170 of them by fullback Leon Heath, who scored touchdowns on runs of 86 and 34 yards.

The Cotton Bowl hosted No. 5 Rice and No. 16 North Carolina, led by tailback Charlie "Choo Choo" Justice and All-America end Art Weiner, the nation's leading pass receiver. Justice still did not get a bowl victory, as Rice quarterback Tobin Rote passed for 140 yards and two touchdowns to lead the Owls to a 27–13 win. Both Tar Heel scores came in the last eight minutes of the game.

The Gator Bowl lined up two top twenty teams for its January 2 contest, No. 14 Maryland and No. 20 Missouri. The Terrapins jumped to a 20–0 lead by halftime, as Bob Shemonski scored two touchdowns, and held on for a 20–7 win. In the Sun Bowl, hometown Texas Western, the nation's rushing leader, defeated Georgetown 33–20 as halfback Harvey "Pug" Gabriel scored two touchdowns and center Wayne Hansen scored on a 51-yard run.

Two unbeaten teams faced off in the Tangerine Bowl, St. Vincent of Pennsylvania, which outscored opponents 227–6 in a 9–0 season, and undefeated Emory & Henry of Virginia, champion of the Smoky Mountain Athletic Conference. Emory & Henry already had beaten Hanover of Indiana 32–0 on November 24 in the unsanctioned Burley Bowl at Johnson City, Tennessee, but lost to St. Vincent 7–6 in its second bowl game.

Left out of 1950's major bowl games were three major unbeaten teams— national champion Notre Dame (10–0), No. 4 Army (9–0), and No. 10 Pacific (11–0). Notre Dame and Army both were still under postseason bans by their administrators. Although Pacific, sparked by quarterback Eddie LeBaron, made the top ten rankings, it was considered to have played a small college schedule overall. The Tigers, however, did outscore opponents 575–66, including wins over Loyola (California) 52–0, Portland 75–20, San Diego State 62–14, California Poly 88–0, and Hawaii 75–0.

At the end of the first half of the twentieth century, bowl games already had become a tradition in the minds and hearts of college football players, coaches, and fans, even though most postseason games had been on the scene only fifteen years or so. The exception was the Rose Bowl, which would see its thirty-seventh contest on New Year's Day, 1951. The other fixtures from the 1930s (Orange, Sun, Sugar, and Cotton) had been joined by the Gator and Tangerine bowls in the immediate post–World War II period, along with a number of others that would not stand the test of time. The glamour and popularity of the postseason contests would only grow stronger over the second half of the century.

4 NEW YEAR'S DAY MEANS FOOTBALL

THE 1950 REGULAR SEASON BEGAN WITH the country at war again, fighting Communist North Korea as part of a United Nations "police action" to defend democratic South Korea. After early setbacks following the North Korean aggression of June 25, it appeared the UN forces would sweep to victory throughout the Korean peninsula. By the time selections for the postseason bowls were under way, however, the picture had dramatically changed. On November 26, Chinese Communist forces opened a massive counteroffensive. Three years of deadly stalemate followed before an armistice was signed, halting major actions on June 26, 1953. Also in 1950, United Press (later to become United Press International) began its own college football rankings poll to rival that of its wire service competitor, the Associated Press. The new rankings were determined by a board of coaches, whereas the older AP poll used a panel of sportswriters and sports broadcasters. The bowls were not always able to secure the top teams, however; in 1950, No. 2 Army (8–1) and No. 6 Princeton (9–0), were still prohibited from postseason appearances.

Beginning with the 1950 postseason, a set schedule of seven bowls was established for most of the following decade. These bowls—the Rose, Orange, Sugar, Sun, Cotton, Tangerine, and Gator—were played on New Year's Day each year (although the Gator Bowl ended up shifting to late December during this period) and were joined on occasion by a few new bowls that appeared—then quickly disappeared.

One of the new events was the Presidential Cup at College Park, Maryland, following the 1950 regular season. Although it was sanctioned by the NCAA as a "major" bowl, it lasted only one year. The game, set for December 9, 1950, matched Georgia against Texas A&M, neither of which was nationally ranked. A crowd of 12,245 showed up for what turned out to be a Texas A&M runaway. Aggie fullback Bob Smith returned the game's opening kickoff 100 yards for a touchdown, later ran 81 yards for another score, returned punts for 121 yards, and finished with 160 yards rushing. Texas A&M led 33–0 at halftime. The second half was mostly Georgia's as halfback Anthony "Zippy" Morocco scored two touchdowns (one on a 65-yard punt return), but it was too little, too late. The final score was Texas A&M 40, Georgia 20.

In the Rose Bowl on New Year's Day, 1951, California's coach, Lynn "Pappy" Waldorf, was hoping for better luck than he had had in his previous two outings there, having lost to Northwestern and Ohio State in the 1949 and 1950 contests. This year the No. 5 Golden Bears' opponent would be Michigan, the nation's No. 9 team. The third time for Waldorf was not a charm. California led 6–0 on a 39-yard pass from Jim Marinos to Bob Cummings for most of the game, but in the last ten minutes Michigan came back with two touchdowns by fullback Don Dufek for a 14–6 win. That gave the Big 10 victories in all five Rose Bowls since the pact with the PCC had gone into effect in 1947.

Unbeaten No. 15 Miami was the host team in the Orange Bowl, where it would meet another unbeaten team, No. 10 Clemson. The contest was one of the most exciting in Orange Bowl history. Early in the third quarter, Clemson held a 13–0 lead, but Miami's offense finally took off and scored two quick touchdowns to go up 14–13. The score remained the same until the final few minutes of the game, when a penalty wiped out a 79-yard Hurricane touchdown run, and then a series of subsequent penalties put Miami back on its 1-yard line. Trying a sweep around end, Miami blew a blocking assignment and a Clemson lineman, Sterling Smith, got into the backfield untouched and tackled the runner, Frank Smith, for a safety to give the Tigers a thrilling 15–14 victory.

The nation's No. 1 team and winner of thirty-one consecutive games, Bud Wilkinson's undefeated Oklahoma Sooners, were invited to the Sugar Bowl to meet Bear Bryant's Kentucky Wildcats, ranked No. 7. Both teams had ten victories, but Kentucky stumbled trying to attain its eleventh, losing to Tennessee 7–0 in the final game of the regular season. This Sugar Bowl match was a defensive battle. Kentucky recovered a fumble on the Oklahoma 23-yard line three minutes into the game and, on the next play, All-America quarterback Vito "Babe" Parilli passed to back Wilbur Jamerson for a touchdown. Jamerson scored for Kentucky again in the second quarter, and with six minutes left in the game the Sooners finally got into the end zone on a

1951 Sugar Bowl—Fullback Leon Heath (40) of national champion Oklahoma eludes the grasp of Kentucky tackle Walt Yowarsky (74) on this play. But Yowarsky was named the Player of the Game as the Wildcats upset the Sooners and ended Oklahoma's thirty-one-game winning string. (*R. M. Ours*)

17-yard pass from sophomore halfback Billy Vessels to Merrill Green. But that was it. Kentucky pulled off a big 13–7 upset win. The defeat did not affect Oklahoma's national championship, of course, as the final rankings had been determined by the polls at the end of the regular season, but a number of fans and some sportswriters had been calling for post–bowl game polls since Michigan's rout of Southern California in the 1948 Rose Bowl, and this game added to the clamor.

The Cotton Bowl had what promised to be an ideal match-up with No. 3 Texas and No. 4 Tennessee. Tennessee opened the scoring on a 75-yard touchdown run by tailback Hank Lauricella, but Texas answered with two touchdowns, taking a 14–7 halftime lead on a 35-yard scoring toss from Ben Tompkins to sophomore back Gilbert "Gib" Dawson. Texas still held the lead when the Vols missed the extra point after a fourth quarter touchdown but, with less than three minutes left, Tennessee was able to put the ball into the end zone once more on a 12-yard run by sophomore fullback Andy Kozar, giving Tennessee a 20–14 victory.

In the Gator Bowl, unbeaten No. 12 Wyoming was invited to play Southern Conference champion No. 18 Washington & Lee. Wyoming, behind tailback Eddie Talboom, won its second successive Skyline 6 title in its first unbeaten season since 1902. The Skyline 6 grew out of the old Rocky Mountain Conference when Brigham Young, Colorado A&M (Colorado State), Denver, Utah, Utah State, and Wyoming formed the new conference in 1949. It became the Skyline 8 with the addition of New Mexico and Montana in 1951 but was dissolved after the 1961 season. Talboom scored two touchdowns in the Gator Bowl, passed for another, and kicked two extra points as Wyoming won easily, 20–7.

Arizona State was invited to the Salad Bowl to play a team from the Buckeye State for the second year in a row, this time Mid-American Conference champion Miami (Ohio). The result was the same as the Redskins defeated the Sun Devils, 34–21, despite an outstanding perform-ance by Arizona State halfback Wilford "Whizzer" White, the nation's leader in rushing and all-purpose yards. In the Sun Bowl, Border Conference cham-pion West Texas State (now West Texas A&M) edged Cincinnati 14–13, high-lighted by a 62-yard touchdown pass from Gene Mayfield to Bill Cross.

The Tangerine Bowl again invited Emory & Henry of Virginia, this time to face Morris Harvey (now University of Charleston) of West Virginia. Emory & Henry was coming off a victory over unbeaten Appalachian State, 26–6, in the unsanctioned Burley Bowl on November 23 at Johnson City, Tennessee. But Emory & Henry was no match for a tough Morris Harvey team, which upended the Wasps 35–14.

During the Korean War period of 1950–1953, some schools scheduled games **1951** with service teams, but the military's impact on college sports was nothing like it had been during World War II. A number of schools, partly because of military demands but mostly because of rising costs, however, gave up foot-ball. Some would resume competition later, often playing at a less visible level, while a few never fielded teams again. Among those disbanding their football programs were former postseason participants Catholic University, Duquesne, Georgetown, St. Mary's, Santa Clara, Southwestern (Texas), and West Virginia Wesleyan. Although most of these schools eventually participat-ed in football again, none resumed competition at the top level.

By the end of the 1951 football season, only seven NCAA-recognized bowls remained that invited major teams and one of those, the Salad Bowl, would have its last contest on New Year's Day, 1952. The Pineapple Bowl, which was never recognized by the NCAA, also would see its last game on

1951 Salad Bowl—Arizona State halfback Wilford "Whizzer" White led the nation in scoring and rushing in the regular season, but he was sandwiched by George Acus (30) and another Miami (Ohio) defender on this attempted pass reception as Miami won a high-scoring game. (*R. M. Ours*)

January 1. Of the minor bowls still surviving at the end of the 1951 season, only the Tangerine would eventually grow into a major bowl.

An important factor in bowl selections for the 1951 postseason was that the Big 7, the conference of powerhouses Oklahoma and Nebraska, and the Southern Conference, which included major teams such as Maryland and Duke, joined the Ivy schools in banning bowl games for members, a ban that still was in effect for Notre Dame and the service academies and for Big 10 teams other than the one selected by conference representatives for the Rose Bowl. The banning of postseason play would erode quickly over the next few years, though, except for the Ivy schools. For the New Year's Day games of 1952, the bans affected four top-ten teams: No. 2 Michigan State, recently admitted to the Big 10 and not eligible for a Rose Bowl berth for another two years, No. 3 Maryland, and No. 6 Princeton (these three being undefeated), and No. 10 Oklahoma. There would be no problem in lining up quality teams for the top New Year's Day contests despite the bans, but some of the secondary bowls would find slimmer pickings.

Ending California's three-year string of hosting the Rose Bowl, No. 7 Stanford squared off against undefeated Illinois, ranked No. 4 in the nation. No matter what the outcome was, this bowl had a great distinction: it was the first nationally televised college football game. Those in attendance and those watching the NBC telecast saw Stanford put up a battle for three quarters—it led 7–6 at the half—only to succumb 40–7 as the Illini exploded for 34 unanswered points, 27 in the fourth quarter. Fullback Bill Tate rushed for 150 yards and two touchdowns for the winners, and sophomore linebacker Stan Wallace set up two Illini scores with pass interceptions.

Television eventually would become the largest medium for enjoying college football despite strict NCAA rules beginning with the 1952 regular season that limited each NCAA school to no more than one TV appearance per season, ostensibly as a way to safeguard home attendance. The rules, however, did not include bowl games, which remained free to televise their contests no matter who played. Over time, the NCAA slowly eased restrictions, yet kept tight controls on the televising of college games for more than thirty years, until the U.S. Supreme Court in 1984 ruled 7–2 in the case of *National Collegiate Athletic Association v. Board of Regents of the University of Oklahoma et al.* that the NCAA's television policy violated the nation's antitrust laws. The case grew out of a challenge of the NCAA's television policy by the Universities of Oklahoma and Georgia in 1981. The 1984 ruling in effect made the televising of college games a free market.

The most exciting game of the 1951 post season was the Orange Bowl, where No. 5 Georgia Tech faced No. 9 Baylor. The game was covered by CBS radio, as usual, but also was carried on local closed circuit television. With six minutes left in the game and Baylor leading 14–7, Georgia Tech tied the score on a 22-yard pass from quarterback Darrell Crawford to end Buck Martin. Shortly after Baylor received the ensuing kickoff, the Yellow Jackets' Pete Ferris intercepted a pass and returned it 46 yards. That set up a 16-yard field goal try for sophomore Franklin "Pepper" Rodgers, who kicked the ball through the uprights for a 17–14 win.

Despite the new ban on postseason play, No. 3 Maryland defied its conference and accepted an enticing Sugar Bowl bid to meet No. 1-ranked Tennessee. The Terps, unbeaten for the first time since 1893, were the nation's scoring leader with an average of 39.2 points per game. Maryland's actions got the school suspended from the Southern Conference for a year and led to the Terps taking an active part in helping to form the Atlantic Coast Conference late in 1953. The game did not go as Volunteer fans expected. Maryland scored three touchdowns in a seven-minute span in the first half, two of them set up by fumbles. Maryland scored again in the third quarter on a 46-yard pass interception return by halfback Bob Shemonski. In the fourth quarter Tennessee got its second touchdown, but it was already too late. Maryland chalked up a 28–13 upset victory. It was the second straight year the national champion fell at New Orleans; still, Tennessee remained the No. 1 team despite the embarrassing loss.

Texas Christian earned its way into the Cotton Bowl for the first time since 1945 by winning its fifth Southwest Conference title. The Horned Frogs had only a 6–4 record, but were ranked No. 11 in the nation. Selected to play TCU were the 7–4 Kentucky Wildcats, ranked No. 15.

At the Cotton Bowl, a crowd of 75,347 turned out to see how Bear Bryant's No. 15 Kentucky team would fare against Leo "Dutch" Meyer's TCU team. Playing his final college game, Kentucky quarterback Babe Parilli passed for two touchdowns to Emery Clark to lead the underdog Wildcats to a 20–7 victory. This, too, was Bryant's final bowl game as the Kentucky coach. He would move to Texas A&M in 1954 and then on to Alabama.

The Gator Bowl came up with a Florida team for the first time, picking Miami to meet No. 20 Clemson in a rematch of the previous year's Orange Bowl game. Clemson, like Maryland, defied the new Southern Conference ban against postseason games and as a result was not allowed to play any conference teams during the 1952 regular season. The Tigers ended up joining the new ACC in 1953. Selection of a Florida team seems to have paid off, as a large home crowd cheered Miami to a 14–0 upset over Clemson, avenging the Orange Bowl defeat. The Hurricanes stymied the Tigers' offense with four pass interceptions by Jim Dooley, three of them inside the Miami 20-yard line, while back Harry Mallios ran for both Hurricane touchdowns.

In the Sun Bowl, Texas Tech, loser of all five of its previous postseason games, finally got a victory, defeating College of Pacific 25–14.

The Salad Bowl's final official contest matched Houston against Dayton, with Houston winning 26–21 on an outstanding performance by Cougars back Gene Shannon, who rushed for 175 yards and all four Houston touchdowns. The Salad Bowl was played four more times before disappearing, but instead of collegiate competition, the bowl hosted service teams twice and served as a regional all-star game on two more occasions.

With only seven major postseason games, such unbeaten teams as Michigan State (9–0), Princeton (9–0), San Diego State (10–0–1), San Francisco (9–0), and Xavier (Ohio) (9–0–1) were left out of the bowl picture. Of course, Michigan State and Princeton were not bowl eligible because of conference prohibitions. The other three quite possibly were not invited because their schedules were considered weaker than most other bowl-eligible contenders. There were rumors that San Francisco, ranked No. 14 by both wire service polls, may have been left out because its All-America backfield ace, future professional star Ollie Matson, and star lineman/linebacker Burl Toler (who in 1965 became the first black official in the National Football League), were African-Americans. No black player had yet participated in two of the major bowl games, the Orange and Sugar, which were located in segregated Southern cities. Late in the season the Orange Bowl had publicly announced that it was considering San Francisco as a participant, but subsequently selected Georgia Tech and Baylor, both higher ranked nationally than the San Francisco Dons. The Salad Bowl, too, had some interest in lining up San Francisco for its postseason game, but after the disappointment of not landing the Orange Bowl bid, San Francisco did not respond. The small Jesuit school on the Bay ended up dropping football after the highly successful 1951 season, stating that the game had become "too much a part of the entertainment world, too great and costly a spectacle, to be maintained."

During the summer before the 1952 regular season, the Ivy schools—still try- **1952** ing to agree on regulations that would tie them together into a formal conference—adopted an "Ivy Group Agreement" that reiterated the long-standing policy against postseason play. It also did away with spring practice. Altogether, the agreement helped lead to the establishment of formal Ivy League competition in 1956. But a direct byproduct of the prohibition of spring drills and other parts of the agreement, such as elimination of scholarships for playing football, was that Ivy League squads in the future would gradually fall from the ranks of the nation's elite teams in the sport. The last Ivy League teams to finish nationally ranked were Princeton again in 1952 (No. 19 by AP and No. 14 by UP), Yale in 1956 (No. 17 by UP), Yale in 1960 (No. 14 by AP and No. 18 by UPI), Princeton in 1964 (No. 13 by UPI), and Dartmouth in 1970 (No. 14 by AP and No. 13 by UPI). The final appearance of an Ivy team in a bowl game would remain Columbia's remarkable upset of Stanford in the 1934 Rose Bowl. Brown, Pennsylvania, and Harvard also appeared in Rose Bowls, with Harvard the only other winner, while great teams fielded by Princeton, Yale, Dartmouth, and Cornell over the years never experienced the magic of a bowl game.

On New Year's Day, 1953, the nation's football fans had an opportunity for the first time to watch all four of the biggest bowl games—Rose, Sugar,

Orange, and Cotton—on national television. The starting times were staggered enough, especially with the different time zones, that the avid fan could see much of each game. Bowl attendance averaged 61,050 per game, the highest since multiple bowls had begun being played in a single postseason.

No. 5 Southern California, the nation's leader in scoring defense (4.7-point average), made it back to the Rose Bowl for the first time in five years to play No. 11 Wisconsin. Unbeaten national champion Michigan State was the best of the Big 10 teams, but was not yet eligible for the title, so the trip to Pasadena was awarded to the Badgers. The game was a defensive struggle and neither team could manage to score until the third quarter when USC completed a 22-yard touchdown pass from Rudy Bukich (who had replaced Jim Sears, the Trojan All-America quarterback forced out of action with a broken leg early in the game) to halfback Al "Hoagy" Carmichael. That single touchdown stood up for a 7–0 Southern California win.

CBS purchased the rights to televise the Orange Bowl nationally for the first time. But the game between No. 9 Alabama and No. 14 Syracuse would turn out to be one of the biggest mismatches in bowl history. The game was a contest for only a few minutes. Alabama scored first on a 27-yard touchdown pass, and Syracuse came right back with a 78-yard drive culminating in a 15-yard scoring pass. But the Orangemen missed the extra point, and after that it was "Roll Tide." Alabama scored on the ground and through the air, including an 80-yard punt return by Cecil "Hootie" Ingram, a 60-yard pass interception return by Marvin "Buster" Hill, and a touchdown pass by freshman quarterback and future Green Bay Packers sensation Bart Starr. The result was a 61–6 Alabama win, the largest margin ever in a bowl game.

Two of the three major teams that had gone unbeaten in the 1952 season, No. 2 Georgia Tech and No. 7 Mississippi, were matched up in the Sugar Bowl. ABC paid $100,000 to carry the game nationally in a combined television-radio package. The game would decide who really deserved to be SEC champion. Mississippi started out quickly to make its case, scoring a touchdown in the first quarter. Following a Yellow Jacket fumble, Ole Miss might have had a second touchdown, but officials ruled the runner was inches short of scoring on fourth down. Early in the second half, with Georgia Tech leading 10–7, Tech recovered a fumble on the Mississippi 18-yard line and the Yellow Jackets were able to run the ball in for another score, although Mississippi players swore that the runner's knee touched the ground on the

1953 Orange Bowl—Syracuse runners had trouble all day against a powerful Alabama defense as the Crimson Tide rolled to a 61–6 win, the biggest margin of victory in bowl history. (*Collegiate Images*)

3-yard line. Still another controversial call in the third quarter deprived Mississippi of the ball at the Georgia Tech 21-yard line on an apparent Yellow Jacket muff of a punt catch. Georgia Tech put the game away in the fourth quarter with a 28-yard touchdown pass from quarterback Franklin "Pepper" Rodgers to Jeff Knox. The Yellow Jackets won, 24–7, but some of the victory's luster was dimmed by the controversial officiating. The sports editor of the *New Orleans Times-Picayune,* Bill Keefe, noted that three of the four game officials lived in Georgia, two of them from Georgia Tech's Atlanta home. And Mississippi Governor Hugh White wrote letters to the president of the SEC Officials' Association and to SEC Commissioner Bernie Moore saying it was "the worst officiating I have ever seen."

No. 8 Tennessee, the nation's leader in total defense, was invited to meet No. 10 Texas in the Cotton Bowl. It was understandable if the 75,504 who packed the stadium thought Texas, not Tennessee, had led the nation in defense. For the game, Texas held the Volunteers to minus 14 yards rushing and only 46 yards passing. And Tennessee fumbles led to both Texas touchdowns (short runs by "Gib" Dawson and sophomore Billy Quinn) and a safety as the Longhorns won, 16–0.

The Gator Bowl again invited a Sunshine State team, this time the No. 15 Florida Gators, making their first postseason appearance, to face No. 12

Tulsa, the nation's leader in total offense. Florida jumped to a 14–0 lead on scores by fullback Rick Casares and John "Papa" Hall and two extra points by Casares. Tulsa came back on short touchdown runs by Willie Roberts and Howie Waugh, but missed an extra point and lost 14–13. College of Pacific returned to the Sun Bowl for the second year in a row, this time to face Mississippi Southern (now Southern Mississippi), and won easily, 26–7. In the Tangerine Bowl, East Texas State (now Texas A&M–Commerce) shut out Tennessee Tech, 33–0, for its nineteenth straight win.

1953   Following the 1952 season, partly to cut down on the costs of football programs, the NCAA put an end to the two-platoon system that had become popular with college coaches during the latter stages of World War II. Instead of playing specialists (offense, defense, special teams), as had become common in the past decade, coaches now had to find the best eleven men to play all aspects of the game, largely as it had been for much of the previous history of college football. It would be another decade before specialization began to creep in again, and in the mid-1960s, the NCAA would rescind this requirement and the game would become more specialized than ever.

Also by the beginning of the 1953 season, the Big 7 and Southern Conference dropped their short-lived bans against postseason participation, so the bowl selectors had more quality teams to consider. There was an additional major conference to consider, as seven Southern Conference schools, including Maryland and Clemson, which had been suspended for defying the conference's regulation against playing in bowl games following the 1951 season, formed the Atlantic Coast Conference. In fact, the new ACC agreed to a pact with the Orange Bowl to play a Big 7 representative, but not necessarily the champion. Both conferences were allowed to designate their representatives, although the Big 7 would not allow a team to go to the bowl two years in a row.

No. 3 Michigan State got a share of the Big 10 title in its first year of eligibility and faced No. 5 UCLA in the Rose Bowl. UCLA jumped to a 14–0 lead as All-America tailback Paul Cameron passed for one touchdown and scored another, but Michigan State end Ellis Duckett blocked a punt and returned it 16 yards for a touchdown to close the gap to 14–7 at halftime. In the third quarter Michigan State made two long drives for touchdowns; UCLA then countered with a 28-yard touchdown pass from Cameron to sophomore end Rommie Loudd, but the kick failed. In the fourth quarter, with the score 21–20, a 62-yard punt return by Michigan State halfback Billy Wells clinched the game for the Spartans, 28–20. In defeat, Cameron passed for 152 yards, had punts of 59 and 52 yards, intercepted two passes, and returned five kicks for 95 yards. Newspaper reports afterward praised both teams for playing an exceptionally clean and hard game.

Maryland, which two years earlier had upset national champion Tennessee in the Sugar Bowl, went into the 1954 Orange Bowl with a national championship of its own. The No. 1 Terps led the nation in rushing defense and scoring defense (3.1-point average) while sweeping ten opponents and earning a share of the initial Atlantic Coast Conference title. Challenging Maryland would be Big 7 champion No. 4 Oklahoma, the nation's rushing leader. Maryland drove deep into Oklahoma territory twice in the first half, only to be stopped on downs each time inside the Oklahoma 10-yard line. In the second quarter, Oklahoma drove 80 yards, scoring on a 25-yard run by Larry Grigg. And that score held up for a 7–0 Sooner win, the first time in fifty-one games that Maryland had been shut out.

No. 8 Georgia Tech, declining a Cotton Bowl bid, returned to the Sugar Bowl for the second year in a row to take on Southern Conference champion No. 10 West Virginia. Speedy Georgia Tech opened up a passing attack to defeat the Mountaineers 42–19 for its fifth straight bowl victory. Tech quarterback "Pepper" Rodgers, who had thrown only fifty-nine passes all season, was 16–26 for 195 yards and three touchdowns against West Virginia. He also kicked an 18-yard field goal and two extra points. After the Yellow Jackets scored on their first possession of the game, the Mountaineers came right back with a 60-yard touchdown run by fullback Tommy Allman, but it was nullified by a controversial holding penalty—the first of several calls in favor of Georgia Tech. West Virginia was hurt all day by penalties and miscues, losing five fumbles in the game.

No. 6 Rice won the Cotton Bowl easily, defeating No. 13 Alabama 28–6 behind halfback Dicky Moegle (spelled that way at the time, but now listed as Maegle in the Rice record books), who had a sensational day. But the game is remembered for one of the most unusual plays ever in college football. Moegle rushed for 265 yards and three touchdowns on runs of 79, 95 and 34 yards, although he actually ran only 53 yards on the longest score. Moegle appeared to be in the clear on the Alabama 42-yard line on that carry when he was hit and dropped by Crimson Tide fullback Tommy Lewis—who came off the bench to make the tackle. Referee Cliff Shaw ruled the play a touchdown, nonetheless. Lewis had scored Alabama's only touchdown on a

1-yard plunge early in the game. Following the contest, he explained how his tackle off the bench occurred. "I'm too emotional," he said. "I kept telling myself, 'I didn't do it. I didn't do it.' I was just too full of Alabama. He [Moegle] just ran too close."

One of the stronger teams in Texas Tech history was invited to the Gator Bowl to play No. 17 Auburn. The No. 12 Red Raiders led the nation in scoring (38.9-point average) and nearly hit that mark in their 35–13 bowl victory, as halfback Bobby Cavazos rushed for 141 yards and two touchdowns and caught a 30-yard scoring pass from sophomore quarterback Jack Kirkpatrick. Another Texas team, Texas Western (Texas–El Paso), played Mississippi Southern in front of 9,500, the smallest crowd in Sun Bowl history. Texas Western rolled to a 30–7 halftime lead and ultimately a 37–14 victory. For the Miners, quarterback Dick Shinaut passed for two touchdowns and kicked a 25-yard field goal along with four extra points. Even the Tangerine Bowl hosted a team from Texas, as undefeated East Texas State battled Arkansas State, which also had an undefeated season, to a 7–7 tie.

1954 By the end of the 1954 season, a number of bowl slots were automatically filled by conference tie-ins. The Rose Bowl had been matching Pacific Coast Conference and Big 10 teams since 1947, and the Orange Bowl pact that matched a team from the new Atlantic Coast Conference with a Big 7 representative was in effect in time for the January 1, 1954, contest. The Southwest Conference supplied the host team for the Cotton Bowl, unofficially since 1941 and officially starting with the 1954 contest. But both spots still were open in the Sugar Bowl and the Gator Bowl, along with one spot in the Cotton Bowl. This would be important in picking teams for the games of New Year's Day, 1955, because Navy dropped its ban on postseason participation. The most glaring of the bowl omissions that year was No. 16 Virginia Tech, which finished 8–0–1 for its first unbeaten season since 1918.

The Gator Bowl experimented with a New Year's Eve game following the 1954 season, and kicked off the postseason activity. No. 13 Auburn was chosen to return for the second year in a row to play No. 18 Baylor. Auburn, which had been soundly beaten the year before, turned things around this time and whipped Baylor 33–13. Fullback Joe Childress rushed for 134 yards and two touchdowns, halfback Fob James scored on a 43-yard run, and quarterback Bobby Freeman ran for one score and passed for another.

A big disappointment was in store for Rose Bowl fans because the PCC adopted the Big 10 stance of not allowing a team to appear in the game two

1954 Cotton Bowl—Alabama fullback Tommy Lewis (42) prepares to leave the sideline for the famous "off-the-bench" tackle of Rice halfback Dicky Maegle. Officials gave Maegle credit for a 93-yard touchdown run, anyway—one of three long scoring runs by the Rice star that day. (*Collegiate Images*)

years in a row, champion or not. That meant that there would not be a show-down between national co-champions UCLA, ranked No. 1 by UP, and Ohio State, ranked No. 1 by AP. Instead, Ohio State would face No. 17 Southern California.

A steady rain held throughout the day, and on the muddy field Buckeye quarterback Bill Leggett scored the first Ohio State touchdown on a 3-yard run and passed 21 yards to Bobby Watkins for another. Despite 123 yards rushing on just nine carries by Trojan halfback Jon Arnett, USC managed to score only on an 86-yard punt return by Aramis Dandoy, losing the game 20–7. This was the first Rose Bowl appearance for controversial long-time Buckeye coach Woody Hayes.

The second year of the Orange Bowl pact saw a disappointment for fans of that bowl, too. Big 7 conference champion, unbeaten No. 3 Oklahoma, could not appear because of the no-repeat rule. Instead, unranked Nebraska would face No. 14 Duke, in its first postseason contest since the 1945 Sugar Bowl. Duke took a 14–0 lead into halftime on touchdowns by halfback Bob Pascal and end Jerry Kocourek, but Nebraska closed it to 14–7 midway through the third quarter. That was it for the Cornhuskers, however. The Blue Devils broke the game open with three unanswered touchdowns, winning 34–7. Nebraska finished with only 110 yards of total offense.

The Sugar Bowl landed Navy for its first postseason appearance since the 1924 Rose Bowl, as the Midshipmen were given permission by Naval Academy authorities to participate in postseason play. Navy, which finished with a No. 5 ranking, would face No. 6 Mississippi. The changing American social scene was reflected in the seating at the 1955 Sugar Bowl. Navy had distributed its allotment of 13,000 tickets without regard to racial restrictions, and Sugar Bowl officials assured ticket holders that they would be honored. African-Americans had attended Sugar Bowl games since the first contest, but until this game they had been seated in segregated areas.

Navy took complete command of the game. The Midshipmen scored on their opening drive on a short run by fullback Joe Gattuso. In the second quarter, in another controversial Sugar Bowl call, Navy was denied a score when Maxwell Award–winning end Ron Beagle was ruled out of the end zone on a fourth-down pass reception. (Films indicated he had made a legitimate catch.) Navy scored again early in the third quarter when halfback Jack Weaver caught a 16-yard pass from quarterback (and future Navy and Virginia coach) George Welsh. Gattuso put the game out of reach with another short scoring run in the fourth quarter, for a 21–0 victory. Navy outgained Mississippi 442–121 in total yards.

In the Cotton Bowl, No. 10 Arkansas was favored over a Georgia Tech team that was not ranked by the AP, but Yellow Jackets Coach Bobby Dodd made it six victories in as many bowl appearances. His team, trailing 6–0 at halftime, stressed its running game in the second half, scoring touchdowns by sophomore halfback Paul Rotenberry and sophomore quarterback Wade Mitchell to give the Yellow Jackets a 14–6 upset victory.

Texas Western made its second straight appearance in the Sun Bowl, this time facing Florida State. The Miners raced to a 34–7 halftime lead en route to a 47–20 victory. Quarterback Jesse Whittenton was nearly unstoppable for the Miners. He passed for three touchdowns, including a 56-yarder to freshman Rany Rutledge, ran for two more scores, and kicked six extra points.

The Tangerine Bowl selected unbeaten University of Omaha (now Nebraska–Omaha) to face unbeaten Eastern Kentucky State. The Omaha Indians, behind star sophomore back Bill Engelhardt, outscored opponents 353–61 in winning ten games, but this game was a defensive battle won by Omaha, 7–6.

1955   At the end of the 1955 season the Gator Bowl once again opened the official postseason play with a New Year's Eve game featuring No. 8 Auburn—its third straight appearance in the bowl—and fellow SEC member, unranked Vanderbilt, making its first bowl appearance. Auburn's offense was hampered by five lost fumbles, while quarterback Don Orr led Vanderbilt with a 7-yard touchdown pass and a 3-yard keeper for another score in a surprising 25–13 victory.

No. 4 UCLA was eligible to appear in the 1956 Rose Bowl, but since Ohio State repeated as Big 10 champions and had appeared in the game the previous year, Michigan State was the conference's choice. This was no disappointment. The Spartans actually had a better overall record than the Buckeyes and were ranked No. 2. The game was an exciting seesaw battle. UCLA took a 7–0 lead on a short plunge by fullback Bob Davenport, but Michigan State tied the game on a 13-yard pass from All-America quarterback Earl Morrall to sophomore halfback Clarence Peaks. The Spartans then took the lead on a 67-yard touchdown pass from Peaks to end John Lewis before the Bruins tied it on a short run by halfback Doug Peters. With only seven seconds left in the game, end Dave Kaiser kicked a 41-yard field goal to give Michigan State a 17–14 victory. These three points were something of a miracle. Kaiser had not practiced field goals for two months prior to the game because of a leg injury, and because he had lost his contact lenses, he could barely see the goal posts and had to look for the referee's signal to see whether he made the kick. The win was the ninth in ten games for the Big 10 since the Rose Bowl pact had gone into effect.

Oklahoma had been prohibited from playing in the previous year's Orange Bowl because of the conference no-repeat rule, but the Sooners were even better this time around, and they were eligible. In defeating ten straight opponents, No. 1 Oklahoma led the nation in total offense, rushing, and scoring (36.5-point average). It would face ACC co-champion No. 3 Maryland, also unbeaten in ten games, which led the nation in rushing defense. The Sooners were riding a twenty-nine-game winning string, while Maryland had won sixteen straight heading into the game. More than 76,000 packed the newly enlarged Orange Bowl stadium to see which team would falter. Oklahoma proved to be as good as advertised. Maryland scored first in the second quarter on a 15-yard run by halfback Ed Vereb. But Bud Wilkinson's Sooners came back in the second half with short touchdown runs by halfback Tommy McDonald and Jay O'Neal and an 82-yard pass interception return by Carl Dodd to take a 20–6 win. The statistics were more even than the score, though, with Oklahoma finishing with 254 total yards against Maryland's 245.

The Sugar Bowl lined up No. 7 Georgia Tech, the nation's leader in scoring defense (4.6-point average), and No. 11 Pittsburgh, making its first post-season appearance since winning the 1936 Rose Bowl. The selection of Pittsburgh caused a storm, however, and not just because the Panthers had lost three games—the most of any Sugar Bowl participant since 1945. The problem was that a part-time starter on the Pittsburgh roster, Bobby Grier, was African-American, and no black player had yet participated in the Sugar Bowl. Boston College in 1939 and 1940 had a black player on its team, reserve running back Louis Montgomery. But the Sugar Bowl committee had made it plain that "a Negro would not be allowed to play" in the 1941 game. The previous year, Montgomery had stayed at home when Boston College played in the Cotton Bowl, but in 1941 he at least had been allowed to watch his teammates in the game—working as a spotter for reporters in the press box.

Times were changing by 1956, but not without protest. When Pittsburgh was selected, Georgia Governor Marvin Griffin requested that no team in Georgia's university system "be permitted to engage in contests with other teams where the races are mixed." But Pittsburgh made it clear that Grier would "travel, eat, live, practice, and play with the team." A Georgia Tech spokesman said, "Our boys voted to play in the Sugar Bowl, and we will not break our contract, especially since [both] Georgia and [Georgia] Tech have played against Negroes before and there has been no criticism." Georgia Tech quarterback Wade Mitchell added, "I personally have no objection to playing a team with a Negro member on it, and, as far as I know, the rest of the boys feel the same way." So Grier would play in the game—leading to further controversy.

The crowd of 80,175 got their money's worth if they liked defense. The game was decided in the first quarter on a pass interference call on Grier in the end zone. Grier later claimed that he was pushed by Georgia Tech end Don Ellis, and that he was lying flat on the ground when the ball sailed over both his and Ellis' heads—along with a penalty flag from the back judge. Ellis claimed that Grier shoved him in the stomach, knocking him off stride. Game films were inconclusive. The penalty set up a 1-yard touchdown run by quarterback Wade Mitchell that put the Yellow Jackets ahead 7–0. Pitt drove to the Georgia Tech 1-yard line just before the end of the first half, but quarterback "Corny" Salvaterra was stopped inches short of the goal on fourth down. The Panthers drove inside the Tech 20-yard line twice in the third

1956 Sugar Bowl—Pittsburgh back Bobby Grier, first African-American to play in the Sugar Bowl, picks up yardage against Georgia Tech. But a controversial pass interference call against Grier in the first quarter led to the only touchdown of the game. (*Collegiate Images*)

quarter but failed to score. Time ran out with the Panthers inside the Tech 5-yard line at the end of the game. Even then, Pitt players claimed that officials had told them more time remained than was apparently the case. (The stadium clock had not been functioning properly throughout the contest, so time was being kept on the field by the officials.) With the 7–0 victory, coach Bobby Dodd had his seventh straight postseason win.

In the Cotton Bowl, No. 6 Texas Christian and its All-America halfback Jim Swink, the nation's leader in scoring and all-purpose yards, were matched with SEC champion No. 10 Mississippi in what would be remembered as a classic game. Swink led the Horned Frogs to a 13–7 halftime lead with touchdown runs of 1 and 39 yards. But with just 4:22 left in the contest, Mississippi sophomore halfback Billy Lott scored on a 5-yard run and fullback Paige Cothren, who had scored the Rebels' first half touchdown, kicked his second extra point of the day to give Mississippi a 14–13 win.

The Sun Bowl saw Wyoming beating Texas Tech 21–14 on touchdowns by wingback John Watts, Hank Marshall, and fullback Ova Stapleton.

The Tangerine Bowl again came up with an undefeated team for one of its slots. Juniata of Pennsylvania swept through an eight-game schedule, giving up only 32 points while scoring 240. Chosen to meet the Indians was

Missouri Valley College, which had already rolled over Hastings 31–7 in the Mineral Water Bowl (one of the minor bowls not officially recognized by the NCAA) at Excelsior Springs, Missouri, on November 24. In Orlando, Juniata and Missouri Valley battled to a 6–6 tie, the second time in three years that the Tangerine Bowl contest had ended in a tie.

1956 Following the 1956 season, the Gator Bowl kicked off bowl play for the third straight year, this time on December 29 rather than on New Year's Eve. Selected as participants were No. 4 Georgia Tech and No. 13 Pittsburgh, which had met in the controversial Sugar Bowl contest a year earlier. Georgia Tech was the highest ranked team yet to appear in the Gator Bowl, and led the nation in scoring defense (3.3-point average). Georgia Tech jumped to a 14–0 lead in the first half, but Pittsburgh closed the gap to 14–7 just before halftime on a 42-yard touchdown pass from quarterback "Corny" Salvaterra to Dick Bowen. The Panthers tied the game on a Salvaterra 1-yard run in the second half, but Georgia Tech scored the clinching touchdown in a 21–14 victory in the third quarter on a 5-yard run by halfback Paul Rotenberry.

The best team in the country, No. 1 Oklahoma, was riding a forty-game winning string and rampaged through the 1956 season. But because of the no-repeat rule, the Sooners could not return to the Orange Bowl. That left the door open for No. 20 Colorado to meet No. 19 Clemson in a contest that was a battle to the wire. Colorado scored three touchdowns in the second quarter to take a 20–0 lead, the last two scores set up by a blocked punt and an intercepted pass. And the Buffaloes might have scored again had they not fumbled at the Clemson goal line on the last play of the first half. During halftime, Clemson coach Frank Howard tongue-lashed his players and threatened to quit on the spot if they continued to embarrass him. Duly chastised, Clemson surged back to take a 21–20 lead with two touchdowns in the third period by halfback Joel Wells (one on a 58-yard run) and another score in the fourth. But Colorado recovered an ill-conceived onside kick by Clemson and drove 53 yards, capped by a 2-yard run by fullback John "The Beast" Bayuk, to give the Buffalos a 27–21 victory.

No. 10 Oregon State lost to No. 3 Iowa 14–13 in the regular season, but since both teams won their conferences, the Beavers got another crack at Iowa in the Rose Bowl. Oregon State was able to win the conference crown partly because the PCC in 1956 barred California, Southern California, UCLA, and Washington from Rose Bowl consideration for infractions of conference rules. But Iowa, in its first postseason appearance, proved its victory over Oregon State in the regular season had been no fluke, winning 35–19 as quarterback Kenneth Ploen scored on a 49-yard run in the first five minutes of the game and later threw a 16-yard touchdown pass to end Jim Gibbons. Collins Hagler scored two touchdowns for Iowa, including a 66-yard run.

Much attention on New Year's Day was on the Sugar Bowl, where unbeaten Tennessee, ranked No. 2, squared off with No. 11 Baylor. No. 6 Miami probably would have been the choice to play Tennessee had not the Hurricanes been on NCAA probation for recruiting violations. Baylor dominated the first quarter, its line outweighing Tennessee's by fourteen pounds per man, and took a 6–0 lead in the second period on a 12-yard touchdown pass from quarterback Bobby Jones to end Jerry Marcontell. Tennessee's offense was stymied by four pass interceptions, but the Volunteers went ahead 7–6 in the third quarter on a 1-yard plunge by All-America tailback (and future coach) Johnny Majors, who carried the ball nine times on a 39-yard drive. With about five minutes left in the game, Tennessee gave up the ball on a muffed punt reception on its own 15-yard line, and moments later, sophomore quarterback Buddy Humphrey plunged over the goal line from a foot out to give Baylor a 13–7 upset victory. Tennessee almost pulled out a win in the final moments of the game, when a fourth down Majors pass barely eluded the reach of a receiver in the end zone.

Unranked Texas Christian finished second to unbeaten Texas A&M in the Southwest Conference, but returned to the Cotton Bowl because the Aggies were on NCAA probation for recruiting violations. Its opponent was No. 8 Syracuse, led by All-America halfback Jim Brown. The Orangemen were making their first postseason appearance since the humiliating loss to Alabama in the 1953 Orange Bowl. It was an exciting game, as TCU scored a touchdown in every quarter while Syracuse answered with a pair of touchdowns in the second and fourth periods. Brown led the Orange with 132 yards and three touchdowns rushing and kicked three extra points. Charles Curtis passed for 176 yards and two touchdowns and scored on a 7-yard run for TCU, but it was Chico Mendoza's block of a Syracuse extra point try that gave the Horned Frogs a 28–27 victory and ended TCU's bowl-losing string at five. Harold Pollard kicked four extra points for the winners.

The Tangerine Bowl began taking steps toward greater status by lining up West Texas State and Mississippi Southern. Mississippi Southern took a 13–0 lead in the second quarter on a statue of liberty play that saw sophomore J. C. Arban run 51 yards for a touchdown and a 53-yard pass from Bobby Hughes to Jerry Taylor. But West Texas State came back in the second half to win, 20–13. In the Sun Bowl, George Washington shut out Texas Western 13–0.

This year's glaring bowl omission was unbeaten No. 16 Wyoming, which won the Skyline 8 championship behind halfback Jim Crawford, the nation's rushing leader.

1957   The Gator Bowl continued its role as the official start the following postseason, this time on December 28, 1957, when No. 9 Texas A&M, led by Heisman Trophy-winning halfback John David Crow, faced No. 13 Tennessee. This was the first bowl game appearance for a team coached by Bear Bryant since Kentucky's 1952 Cotton Bowl victory, but it would be the only one with the Aggies, as he accepted the head coach position at his alma mater, Alabama, in 1958. On a wet, muddy field, the defenses dominated the contest until Tennessee finally began to move the ball late in the final quarter. The Aggies stiffened at their goal line, however, and on fourth down, with 5:30 left in the game, Sammy Burklow kicked a 17-yard field goal—the only field goal by the Volunteers all season—to give Tennessee a 3–0 victory.

The 1958 Rose Bowl match-up looked like it would be a runaway victory for No. 2 Ohio State, which was a three-touchdown favorite over Oregon, unranked by the AP but No. 17 in the UP poll. Ohio State took the opening kickoff and drove 79 yards for a score, quarterback Frank Kremblas going over from a yard out and then kicking the extra point. But in the second quarter Oregon drove 80 yards to score, the touchdown coming on a 5-yard run by Jim Shanley. In the fourth quarter, with the game tied 7–7, Ohio State pulled out a 10–7 victory on a 34-yard field goal by Don Sutherin. A number of Midwestern sportswriters after the game praised the Oregon team's heart and desire, saying the Ducks had deserved to win. They actually edged the Buckeyes in total yardage and first downs.

No. 4 Oklahoma finally tasted defeat in 1957, in a late-season loss to Notre Dame, 7–0, that ended the Sooners' remarkable 47-game winning string, a record that still stands today. But the Sooners were eligible for the Orange Bowl and would face No. 16 Duke, which finished second to No. 15 North Carolina State in the ACC but still received the Orange Bowl bid. The game was closer than expected—at least for a while. Oklahoma led 21–14 at

1958 Rose Bowl—Ohio State sophomore fullback Bob White runs for some of his 82 yards in a hard-fought victory over Oregon. The Ducks outgained the national co-champions in total yardage and first downs. (*Pasadena Tournament of Roses*)

the start of the fourth quarter, but then won going away, 48–21. Starring for Oklahoma was quarterback/safety David Baker, who scored on a 94-yard pass interception return and a 29-yard pass from quarterback Brewster Hobby and also threw a 9-yard touchdown pass to Hobby. Sophomore Dick Carpenter scored another Sooner touchdown on a 73-yard return of an intercepted lateral.

Undefeated national co-champion Auburn (10–0) would have received a Sugar Bowl bid had the Tigers not been on NCAA probation for recruiting violations, so the invitation went to No. 7 Mississippi to face No. 11 Texas. Fans were surprised by the dominance of the Mississippi team. In an incredible performance reminiscent of Bobby Layne's in the 1946 Cotton Bowl, Rebel quarterback Raymond Brown rushed for 157 yards and two touchdowns—including a 92-yard run when, back to punt, he took off to avoid a hard-charging Texas lineman—threw a touchdown pass, and set up another Mississippi score by intercepting a pass, one of three he picked off that day, en route to a 39–7 Rebel victory.

In the Cotton Bowl, No. 5 Navy handed No. 8 Rice its first bowl loss ever in five appearances. Navy ran for three touchdowns and recovered five Rice fumbles in a 20–7 win. Quarterback Tom Forrestal passed for 153 yards for the winners, while fullback Ned Oldham ran 19 yards for a score and kicked two extra points.

In its last New Year's Day game before going to a December contest, the Sun Bowl was without a Texas team for the first time in five years when it matched Drake and Louisville. Louisville, behind Lenny Lyles, the nation's leading scorer among "small colleges," outscored opponents 316–86 in an 8-1 season. Although Louisville lost Lyles to an injury in the first quarter, his replacement, sophomore Ken Porco, rushed for 119 yards and a touchdown as the Cardinals won 34–20. Mississippi Southern returned to the Tangerine Bowl, but lost to East Texas State 10–9.

Two unbeaten teams considered for bowl berths but not selected were No. 12 Arizona State (10–0), the nation's leader in scoring (39.7-point average), and No. 20 Virginia Military Institute (9–0–1), winner of the Southern Conference title.

1958   Several innovations came onto the college football scene before the start of the 1958 regular season. One was a major rule change that allowed the team scoring a touchdown to try for a two-point conversion instead of the traditional one-point try. If a team successfully passed or ran the ball across the goal line, it would be worth two points, while the successful kick through the uprights still was worth one point. The Rules Committee also decided to bring the foot back into football by widening the goal posts from 18 feet, 6 inches to 23 feet, 4 inches, thus increasing the likelihood of making field goals and extra points.

Another big adjustment involved the Pacific Coast Conference, which had been in existence since December 1915. The 1958 season would be the last one for the venerable conference, as it was to be dissolved on June 30, 1959 because of serious disagreements by members on a number of conference rules. The Rose Bowl would have only one more year to have the host team selected by the PCC. Also that year, United Press merged with International News Service to become United Press International, and retained the coaches poll under the UPI logo.

Meanwhile, the Sun Bowl and Tangerine Bowl joined the Gator Bowl in playing their annual postseason contests in December rather than on the traditional New Year's Day date. The Sun Bowl decided on a New Year's Eve contest while the Gator Bowl moved its date back still another day from the previous year, settling on December 27—the date also selected by the Tangerine Bowl.

There was a new bowl on the scene, the first new postseason game in nearly a decade. This was the Bluegrass Bowl, to be played at Lexington, Kentucky. And it was the earliest, with the game scheduled for December 13. Invited to the Bluegrass Bowl were two teams located a considerable distance from Kentucky—unranked Florida State and, as somewhat of a plum for a new bowl, a ranked team, No. 19 Oklahoma State. Only 7,000 braved the ten-degree weather to watch the Cowboys' Forrest Campbell rush for 130 yards and halfback Duane Wood score two touchdowns to lead Oklahoma State to a 15–6 victory. Wood also caught a two-point conversion pass, the first ever in postseason play, from quarterback Dick Soergel. The weather and small crowd would be major factors in ending this Kentucky attempt at postseason play after a single contest.

The Gator Bowl definitely was "big time" now, as it was able again to land top-twenty teams for its postseason contest. Selected were two Southeastern Conference teams that had not met in the regular season for ten years—No. 11 Mississippi and No. 14 Florida. An impressive crowd of more than 41,000 turned out, but any late arrivals missed all of the scoring. Mississippi drove 70 yards on its first possession for a 7–0 lead on a short run by sophomore fullback Jim Anderson. Florida's Jimmy Dunn returned the ensuing kickoff 56 yards and the Gators drove to the Mississippi 11-yard line before settling for a field goal. And that was it for the scoring, the final tally being 7–3. Florida did reach the Mississippi 2-yard line in the fourth quarter, but failed to score. That same day, East Texas State had little trouble in defeating Missouri Valley 26–7 in the Tangerine Bowl.

The Sun Bowl's first New Year's Eve contest was a battle of Cowboys—from Hardin-Simmons and Wyoming. Hardin-Simmons, coached by Sammy Baugh, was making its first bowl appearance since playing in three bowl contests following the 1948 season. Wyoming scored two second-quarter touchdowns behind a pair of sophomores, fullback Mark Smolinski and halfback Clifford "Buddy" Snyder, to win 14–6.

In the Rose Bowl, No. 16 California hosted No. 2 Iowa, the nation's leader in total offense behind All-America quarterback Randy Duncan, the nation's passing leader. The Hawkeyes surprised California by utilizing the run more than the pass, rushing for 429 yards and scoring five touchdowns on the ground. Halfback Bob Jeter ran for 194 yards, including an 81-yard touchdown, while halfback Willie Fleming scored twice on short runs for the Hawkeyes in a 38–12 romp. It was the twelfth win in thirteen games for the

Big 10 since the pact with the PCC had first gone into effect in 1947. But the table was about to turn for a long time in the Western teams' favor.

The five-year Orange Bowl pact between the Big 7 and the Atlantic Coast Conference expired before the 1958 season, so selectors were able to invite No. 5 Oklahoma back without a year off between appearances. Chosen to challenge Bud Wilkinson's team was No. 9 Syracuse. The Sooners got off to a quick start, scoring on the second play of the game on a 42-yard run by fullback Prentice Gautt, followed soon after by a 79-yard touchdown pass from quarterback Brewster Hobby to end Ross Coyle. Hobby scored himself in the third quarter on a 40-yard punt return for a 21–6 victory.

National champion Louisiana State was chosen for the Sugar Bowl, its first bowl bid in nearly a decade, and would face No. 12 Clemson, winner of the ACC title. But most of the fans and press in New Orleans derided the choice of Clemson, preferring a match-up with Southern Methodist, ranked only No. 18 in the nation but led by spectacular quarterback Don Meredith. LSU was a solid fourteen-point favorite, but it was a much closer game than anyone expected. The Bayou Bengals dominated the first half, three times approaching the Clemson goal line but failing to score. The final threat ended when fullback J. W. "Red" Brodnax fumbled into the end zone and Clemson's Doug Cline recovered for a touchback. Brodnax felt he had crossed the goal before the fumble, but the officials disagreed. LSU also was handicapped by the loss of quarterback Warren Rabb, who left the game with a broken hand in the second quarter. In the third quarter LSU recovered a fumbled snap from center at the Clemson 11-yard line and scored moments later on a 9-yard pass from All-America halfback Billy Cannon to sophomore end Mickey Mangham. A final Clemson threat died inside the LSU 25-yard line with less than two minutes left, and LSU came away with a 7–0 victory, the first national champion to win the Sugar Bowl contest since 1940.

No. 10 Texas Christian returned to the Cotton Bowl for the third time in four years to host No. 6 Air Force, which completed an unbeaten season in only its third year of varsity competition and would be making its first post-season appearance. Despite cold, wet weather, both teams had opportunities to score, as Air Force missed three field goal tries, TCU missed two, and each team lost three fumbles. The game ended in a 0–0 tie, the first scoreless bowl game since the 1947 Cotton Bowl. TCU fullback Jack Spikes rushed for 108 yards to top all runners. Another service academy team, No. 3 Army, also went unbeaten in 1958, but Earl Blaik's sixth and last undefeated team was still barred from postseason play by West Point's administration.

By the end of the 1959 regular season, two new bowls were approved by the NCAA, the Liberty Bowl at Philadelphia, and the Bluebonnet Bowl at Houston, increasing to nine the number of postseason games set for the bowl season, the highest number since the 1950 postseason. Unlike the Bluegrass Bowl, which expired after a single game in 1958, these bowls had multiple contests in their futures. Both set their initial contests for December 19, 1959.

The new bowls got off to a good start with nationally ranked teams. Invited to participate in the inaugural Liberty Bowl at Philadelphia, a game which had been instituted partly to give more postseason opportunities to Eastern teams, were No. 12 Penn State, led by Maxwell Award–winning quarterback Richie Lucas, and No. 10 Alabama. A crowd of 36,211 gathered in cavernous Municipal Stadium in Philadelphia to watch the first of many memorable Alabama and Penn State match-ups. Lucas was injured in the second quarter and had to leave the game, but Penn State pulled out a 7–0 victory on a fake field goal play later in the same period when Lucas's replacement, sophomore quarterback Galen Hall, threw an 18-yard touchdown pass to sophomore halfback Roger Kochman.

On the same day, No. 7 Texas Christian and No. 11 Clemson met in the first Bluebonnet Bowl, which with a crowd of 55,000 on hand got off to a more auspicious start than the Liberty Bowl. Going into the fourth quarter, TCU led 7–3, but then Clemson rallied for 20 points and a 23–7 upset victory, highlighted by a 68-yard touchdown pass from quarterback Harvey White to sophomore end Gary Barnes.

When the Pacific Coast Conference dissolved before the 1959 season began, Rose Bowl officials signed an agreement with the five schools that formed the Athletic Association of Western Universities (California, Southern California, Stanford, UCLA, and Washington) to supply the Western team for the Rose Bowl and to invite a Big 10 opponent. The Big 10 at the time left it up to its individual membership whether to accept the AAWU bid, and this arrangement remained in effect until the formation of the Pacific-8 Conference in 1964, when a new agreement, similar to the one in effect before the PCC dissolved, was instituted. Washington State was added to the AAWU in 1962 and, in 1964, with the inclusion of Oregon and Oregon State, the Pacific-8 name was adopted.

No. 8 Washington, the only non-California school in the original AAWU, was selected for the 1960 Rose Bowl over co-champions Southern California and UCLA, because of the Huskies' better overall record, to face No. 6

Wisconsin. The biggest Rose Bowl crowd in four years, 100,809, probably found it hard to believe what they witnessed on New Year's Day. Washington not only broke a six-game Rose Bowl winning string by the Big 10, but did it by a shocking 44–8 score. One-eyed quarterback Bob Schloredt led the Huskies to a 17–0 lead before Wisconsin even had a first down. In the game, Schloredt passed for 102 yards, including a 23-yard touchdown strike to Lee Folkins, and rushed for 81 yards and another score. Schloredt's teammate, halfback George Fleming, scored on a 53-yard punt return, kicked a 36-yard field goal and five extra points, and had 122 yards on three punt returns.

The Orange Bowl began annual match-ups of Southeastern Conference and Big 8 teams with No. 5 Georgia against No. 18 Missouri. The Bulldogs would be making the last of their eight bowl appearances under coach Wally Butts, while Missouri made the trip because Big 8 champion Oklahoma had appeared in the Orange Bowl the previous two years. Missouri gave the SEC champion a battle. Three times Missouri drove inside the Georgia 20-yard line as quarterback Phil Snowden passed for 152 yards, but the Tigers could not score. Georgia won 14–0, scoring in the first and third quarters on passes of 20 yards to sophomore halfback Bill McKenny and 33 yards to end Aaron Box by scrambling quarterback and future NFL Hall-of-Famer Fran Tarkenton.

The Sugar Bowl came up with an intriguing pairing for its New Year's Day contest, a rematch of two of the most bitter rivals in the Southeastern Conference: No. 2 Mississippi, the nation's leader in scoring defense (2.1-point average), and No. 2 Louisiana State. In the regular season LSU handed Mississippi its only loss, 7–3, on Halloween night, which cost the Rebels not only an SEC title but quite possibly a national championship. The Sugar Bowl received an estimated quarter of a million inquiries about tickets to the game. LSU faced the psychological barrier of having to defeat an outstanding team for the second time in one season and, in addition, lost halfback Jimmy Robinson with a broken hand in practice on December 22. Mississippi wanted to prove—as its followers claimed—that LSU's regular-season win had been a fluke. And prove it the Rebels did on the cold, damp, muddy field. LSU halfback Billy Cannon, the Heisman Trophy–winner who scored the key touchdown in the Tigers' regular-season victory on a spectacular 89-yard punt return, was held to just eight yards rushing in six carries. And LSU never got past the Mississippi 38-yard line. Meanwhile, the Mississippi quarterbacks shone. With less than a minute left in the first half, Jerry "Jake"

Gibbs threw a 43-yard touchdown pass to wide open halfback James Lee "Cowboy" Woodruff, giving Ole Miss a 7–0 halftime lead. In its first possession of the second half, Mississippi scored again on an 18-yard pass from quarterback Bobby Ray Franklin to end Larry Grantham. And in the fourth quarter, the Rebels clinched the game on a 9-yard pass from Franklin to halfback George Blair for a 21–0 victory. Prior to this game, LSU had not yielded a touchdown pass in fourteen games. Mississippi's dominance was shown in its total yardage edge of 373 to 74.

National champion Syracuse, which led the nation in total offense, rushing, scoring (39-point average), total defense, and rushing defense, played No. 4 Texas in the Cotton Bowl. Leading the Syracuse attack, sophomore halfback Ernie Davis scored on an 87-yard pass from halfback Gerhard Schwedes, scored again on a 1-yard run, and caught two two-point conversion passes from sophomore quarterback Dave Sarette. Texas countered with a 69-yard touchdown pass from quarterback Bobby Lackey to sophomore halfback Jack Collins, who also scored on a 1-yard run, but the hard-fought game was ultimately won by the national champions, 23–14.

On New Year's Day, the Tangerine Bowl, which had been played in December as an experiment following the 1958 season, saw unbeaten Middle Tennessee State defeat Presbyterian 21–12 in what turned out to be the last New Year's Day contest for that bowl. Following the 1960 regular season, the Tangerine would change permanently to a December playing date. In the Sun Bowl, New Mexico State rolled to a 28–8 victory over North Texas State, as quarterback Charley Johnson threw two touchdown passes.

The January 2, 1960, Gator Bowl matched unranked Georgia Tech and No. 9 Arkansas. An interesting sidelight of the contest was that Arkansas was coached by Frank Broyles, who had been a star quarterback under Georgia Tech coach Bobby Dodd. Following a 51-yard touchdown run by Tech quarterback Marvin Tibbetts, Arkansas responded with two scores, including a 19-yard run by halfback Jim Mooty, and that held up for a 14–7 Razorback victory, snapping Georgia Tech's eight-game bowl-winning string.

After the 1959 season, as more and more postseason games were added to the schedule, the trend would be for more contests to be played in December than on New Year's Day or the days after, and this has been true for every bowl season since, except 1964 and 1992.

5 PEACH AND FIESTA ARRIVE

AFTER SIX DECADES OF POSTSEASON COLLEGE football games, the pattern seemed to be set. There would be a half-dozen or so New Year's Day contests, along with a growing number of December games sanctioned by the NCAA. Lining up for postseason play following the 1960 season would be the granddaddy of them all, the Rose Bowl in Pasadena, California, with antecedents to 1902, plus the other well-established contests: the Orange Bowl in Miami, Florida, and the Sugar Bowl in New Orleans, Louisiana, both dating to 1935, the Sun Bowl at El Paso, Texas, dating to 1936, and the Cotton Bowl at Dallas, Texas, dating to 1937. The schedule also would include newer bowls that managed to survive long enough to become set for the foreseeable future: the Gator Bowl at Jacksonville, Florida, dating to 1946, and the Tangerine Bowl at Orlando, Florida, dating to 1947. The upstart Bluebonnet Bowl at Houston, Texas, and the Liberty Bowl at Philadelphia, Pennsylvania, would eventually establish themselves as long-standing bowls, but other bowls came and went, such as the Aviation Bowl at Dayton, Ohio, and the Gotham Bowl in New York City, both of which would begin play following the 1961 season. The Aviation Bowl would be played one time only, and the Gotham Bowl would not make it past two contests. Among a half-dozen bowls—some ultimately successful, some not—that sprang up in the 1960s and 1970s, the two that would end up joining the elite bowls were the Peach Bowl at Atlanta, Georgia, which would have its start in December 1968, and the Fiesta Bowl—now one of the Bowl Championship Series anchors—at Tempe, Arizona, that would first be played in December 1971.

During this period, changes deeply affecting the American people took place off the field, and some important changes took place on the playing field as well. The Cold War deepened with the building of the Berlin Wall in 1961 and the Cuban missile crisis in 1962, while the United States became heavily involved in the Vietnam War for most of the 1960s and into the mid-

1970s. Students protesting the Vietnam War and various aspects of American society also decried the role of football and other varsity sports on many college campuses. Still, football remained highly popular, with total home attendance during the regular season rising to nearly 33 million in 1977, over 12.5 million more than in 1960.

On the field, teams were going back to multi-platoon football as the NCAA loosened the substitution rules in the late 1950s and early 1960s. And virtual free substitution was once again in effect by the mid-1960s.

Following the 1960 season, No. 1 Minnesota was the heavy favorite against No. 6 Washington in the Rose Bowl. But Huskies quarterback Bob Schloredt, who passed for one touchdown and scored another, and halfback George Fleming, who added a 44-yard field goal and two extra points, starred in the bowl for the second straight year, handing the Gophers a stunning 17–7 loss. Minnesota retained its national title, however, because there were no post-bowl wire service polls.

In the Sugar Bowl, unranked Rice outgained No. 2 Mississippi 281–186 in total yardage, but could score only on a short run by halfback Butch Blume. All-America quarterback Jake Gibbs ran in both Rebel touchdowns for a 14–6 win.

The Orange Bowl invited the nation's No. 5 team, Big 8 champion Missouri, to meet No. 4 Navy. The Midshipmen scored on a 98-yard return of an intercepted lateral by end Greg Mather and on a sensational 27-yard pass reception by halfback Joe Bellino, winner of the Heisman Trophy and the Maxwell Award. Bellino, however, was held to just 4 yards rushing, while Missouri scored twice on the ground and Norm Beal returned a pass interception 90 yards for a touchdown, giving the Tigers a 21–14 victory, the school's first bowl win ever in eight tries. The Navy players had not really wanted to play over the holiday break, one of the rare times Midshipmen had time away from the academy. Coach Wayne Hardin said his squad voted overwhelmingly against going to any bowl, but added, "then the brass said we needed the money and had to go."

In the Cotton Bowl, halfback and future professional star Lance Alworth scored on a 49-yard punt return for the No. 7 Arkansas Razorbacks, and those six points held up until the last three minutes of the game, when No. 10 Duke upset the Southwest Conference champion 7–6 with a 9-yard pass from quarterback Don Altman to end Claude "Tee" Moorman, and an extra point kicked by guard Art Browning, for a 7–6 Blue Devil victory.

Among other postseason games, No. 17 New Mexico State remained undefeated by edging Utah State 20–13 in the Sun Bowl, No. 18 Florida edged No. 12 Baylor 13–12 in the Gator Bowl, and on December 17, 1960, No. 9 Alabama battled unranked Texas to a 3–3 tie before an all-time record Bluebonnet Bowl crowd of 68,000.

1961   The 1961 postseason got off to an early start with a charity game on November 23 at Fresno, California, aimed at raising money for widows and children of twenty-two Cal Poly football players, staff, and supporters killed in a plane crash the previous year while returning from a game with Bowling Green in Ohio. More than 33,000 turned out for what was termed the Mercy Bowl contest between unbeaten California Collegiate champion Fresno State and Mid-American Conference champion Bowling Green. Fresno State won easily, 36–6, as sophomore quarterback Beau Carter passed for 246 yards and two touchdowns and scored twice himself. The bowl raised $200,000.

In the Sugar Bowl, unbeaten SEC co-champion Alabama, the nation's scoring defense leader (2.2-point average) and ranked No. 1, met No. 9 Arkansas. The only touchdown in the game came on a 12-yard run by Alabama quarterback Pat Trammell, and the Crimson Tide defeated the Razorbacks, 10–3, to solidify claims to a fourth national championship.

In the Cotton Bowl, No. 4 Texas broke Mississippi's five-bowl winning string. The No. 5 Rebels scored on a 20-yard pass from quarterback Glynn Griffing to sophomore end Reed Davis, but Texas scored touchdowns on a 16-yard pass from Mike Cotton to Jack Collins and a 1-yard run by All-America back James Saxton to win the game 12–7.

No. 3 LSU rolled over No. 6 Colorado in the Orange Bowl. LSU completely shut down the Colorado offense—the Buffaloes' only touchdown came on a 59-yard pass interception return by Loren Schweninger—while scoring two rushing touchdowns and another on a blocked punt by end Gene Sykes, who recovered the ball in the end zone, for a 25–7 win.

In the first Rose Bowl game to be telecast in color coast-to-coast, No. 7 Minnesota, the first Big 10 team to play in successive Rose Bowl contests, met unranked UCLA. After the termination of the Pacific Coast Conference and the formation of the American Association of Western Universities, the Big 10 and the AAWU renewed the Rose Bowl pact, but the no-repeat rule was not retained by either conference. So despite the better record of conference champion No. 2 Ohio State, conference representatives selected

Minnesota. The Bruins took an early 3–0 lead on a 28-yard field goal by half-back Bobby Smith, but Minnesota came back to win 21–3 as All-America quarterback Sandy Stephens scored two touchdowns on short runs and half-back Bill Munsey scored on a 3-yard run.

No. 14 Syracuse met unranked Miami in the Liberty Bowl. Miami scored two touchdowns, including a 60-yard punt return by sophomore Nick Spinelli, and led at the half, 14–0. But the Orange came back as quarterback Dave Sarette passed for a score and a two-point conversion and Heisman Trophy–winning halfback Ernie Davis rushed for 140 yards and a touchdown for an exciting 15–14 Syracuse victory.

On December 9, the first Gotham Bowl was played in Manhattan's Polo Grounds. New York City promoters had decided that if the Liberty Bowl founded in 1959 could be successful in the City of Brotherly Love, an annual postseason game could be successful in the Big Apple. After invitations were turned down by Oregon State, Holy Cross, and Colorado, undefeated but unranked Utah State and Baylor agreed to play. In the game, Utah State lost the ball eight times on turnovers, while sophomore quarterback Don Trull and halfback Ronnie Bull starred for Baylor in a 24–9 upset victory. The turnout for the bowl was poor and the investors lost $100,000. Even so, one more Gotham Bowl would be attempted.

The other new bowl that year was the Aviation Bowl, also played on December 9, at Dayton, Ohio, home of the Wright brothers. There, New Mexico beat Western Michigan 28–12 before a disappointing crowd of only 3,694. The Aviation Bowl was not played again.

The 1963 Rose Bowl hosted No. 1 Southern California and No. 2 **1962** Wisconsin, in the first postseason meeting of the top two teams since the AP poll began in 1936, and it featured one of the wildest fourth quarter rallies in bowl game history. Wisconsin, the nation's leader in scoring (31.7 average), trailed 42–14 going into the last period, but Badger quarterback Ron VanderKelen engineered three touchdown drives, throwing for two scores and running 17 yards for another that, along with a safety, left Wisconsin trailing by only 42–37 when time ran out as hazy darkness descended on the field. Both quarterbacks had spectacular games, VanderKelen passing for 401 yards, 163 of them on eleven receptions by All-America tight end Pat Richter, and USC quarterback Pete Beathard passing for four touchdowns, including a 57-yarder to All-America end Hal Bedsole.

In the Sugar Bowl, unbeaten No. 3 Mississippi kept its perfect season intact as quarterback Glynn Griffing passed for 242 yards and a touchdown and scored another himself to edge No. 6 Arkansas 17–13. No. 4 Texas entered the Cotton Bowl with a single tie to mar its otherwise undefeated season, but it was shut out by No. 7 Louisiana State, 13–0, as the Tigers never allowed Texas to get inside their 25-yard line.

President John F. Kennedy attended the Orange Bowl between No. 5 Alabama and No. 8 Oklahoma, where he did the pre-game coin toss. The President also spoke to the Sooner team before the game but did not address the Alabama squad, something coach Bear Bryant used as a psychological ploy to fire up the Crimson Tide. Sophomore quarterback Joe Namath engineered three Alabama scoring drives, including a 25-yard touchdown pass to split end Richard Williamson, while All-America center/linebacker Lee Roy Jordan tallied an incredible thirty-one tackles in a 17–0 win. Jordan also left Miami with a special souvenir. As team captain, Jordan won the pre-game toss for the Crimson Tide and kept the coin flipped by the President.

No. 9 Penn State was upset by unranked Florida, 17–7, in the Gator Bowl on December 29 as sophomore quarterback Tom Shannon passed for two touchdowns. The Associated Press ranked only the top ten teams from 1962 through 1967, but two teams ranked in the top twenty by UPI clashed in the Bluebonnet Bowl on December 22, No. 11 Georgia Tech and No. 12 Missouri. Missouri won 14–10 as back Bill Tobin scored on a 77-yard run and end Jim Johnson scored on a 21-yard run.

Other 1962 postseason games included a thrilling win by Nebraska over No. 18 (UPI) Miami in the second Gotham Bowl on December 15. Nebraska's Willie Ross returned a kickoff 92 yards for a touchdown, and fullback Bill "Thunder" Thornton ran in two touchdowns and a 2-point conversion, while Miami quarterback George Mira passed for 321 yards, two touchdowns, and a 2-point conversion, but Miami lost, 36-34, despite a 34–12 edge in first downs. The promoters managed to arrange for the game to be played in Yankee Stadium, but only 6,166 fans turned out in freezing weather, and the bowl was not played again.

The same day, before 17,048 fans at the cold, snowy Liberty Bowl in Philadelphia, No. 16 (UPI) Oregon State came out the 6–0 winner over Villanova on a 99-yard touchdown run by Heisman Trophy–winning quarterback Terry Baker, who finished the game with 137 yards rushing and 123 yards passing. It was the longest touchdown run from scrimmage during the entire season and remains the longest ever in a bowl game.

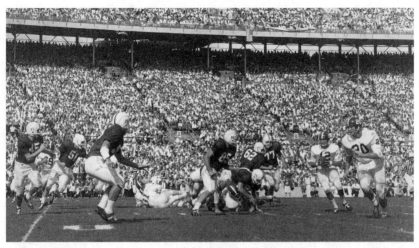

1963 Orange Bowl—Sophomore quarterback Joe Namath (12) engineered three scoring drives to lead Alabama to victory over Oklahoma before 73,380 fans, including President John F. Kennedy. (*Collegiate Images*)

Just as bowl bids were being considered following the 1963 regular season, America underwent a national trauma with the assassination of President Kennedy in Dallas on November 22. Most college football games that weekend were cancelled or postponed. When possible, the games were rescheduled for the weekends of November 30 or December 7. Since bowls wished to have top teams lined up as soon as possible, putting off games at this point meant that a deserving team could be left out entirely. A prime example was Pittsburgh, a top ten team with a 7–1 record at the time of the Kennedy assassination. The Panthers postponed important contests with Miami and Penn State to November 30 and December 7, and they won those games, 31–20 over Miami and 22–21 over Penn State, to finish with a No. 4 national ranking. But by then all of the bowl berths were filled, and Pittsburgh players spent the holidays at home.

1963

The nation's top two teams met in postseason for the second year in a row, this time in the Cotton Bowl, where No. 1 undefeated Texas hosted No. 2 Navy. The sellout crowd watched the Longhorns completely dominate the game as quarterback Emmett "Duke" Carlisle passed for touchdowns of 58 and 63 yards to sophomore wingback Phil Harris. Outland Trophy–winning tackle Scott Appleton sparked a Texas defense that held Navy quarterback Roger Staubach, winner of the Heisman Trophy and Maxwell Award, to minus 47 yards rushing, although Staubach did have 228 yards passing. The

28–6 victory clinched the first national championship for the Longhorns in their first perfect season since 1920.

The only other unbeaten team in a major bowl game, No. 7 Mississippi, the nation's leader in scoring defense (3.7-point average), faced No. 9 Alabama in the Sugar Bowl, their first meeting since 1944. On a clear, cold day with the field surrounded by snow from a rare New Year's Eve snowstorm in New Orleans, the Rebels turned the ball over six times on fumbles and three times on pass interceptions. Crimson Tide kicker Tim Davis booted four field goals, including kicks of 46 and 48 yards for a 12-7 victory.

In the Orange Bowl, No. 6 Nebraska defeated No. 5 Auburn 13–7. Quarterback Dennis Claridge scored on a 68-yard run and Dave Theisen kicked two field goals for Nebraska. No. 3 Illinois met No. 15 (UPI) Washington in the Rose Bowl. The Illini trailed 7–3 at halftime, but rallied behind sophomore fullback Jim Grabowski in the second half to win 17–7.

The Tangerine Bowl on December 28 matched two unbeaten teams for the first time since 1955, with Western Kentucky rolling over the Coast Guard Academy 27–0. On the same day, No. 19 (UPI) North Carolina flattened Air Force 35–0 in the Gator Bowl.

1964   In the first Orange Bowl game played under the lights, undefeated No. 2 Alabama (10–0) met No. 5 Texas on January 1, 1965. The Longhorns jumped to a 21–7 halftime lead as back Ernie Koy scored two touchdowns, one on a spectacular 79-yard run, while teammate George Sauer was on the receiving end of a 69-yard scoring pass from quarterback James Hudson. The Longhorns hung on to win 21–17 despite the efforts of Alabama quarterback Joe Namath, who passed for 255 yards and two touchdowns despite a knee injury that kept him from starting. Before the game, Texas coach Darrell Royal told his squad: "Listen, men. I always ask you to play hard. But I want to make sure nobody goes after Namath's knee. That's not the way we play football." The most successful coach in Texas football history, Royal compiled a record of 167–47–5 with the Longhorns in 1957–1976, including three national championships.

Meanwhile, the Cotton Bowl saw unbeaten No. 3 Arkansas rally in the fourth quarter for a 10–7 win over No. 7 Nebraska as tailback Bobby Burnett scored on a short run and kicker Tom McKnelly added a 31-yard field goal.

In the 1965 Sugar Bowl, No. 6 Louisiana State faced No. 12 (UPI) Syracuse, the first Northern team to appear in that bowl since Pittsburgh nine years earlier. Because Pittsburgh had played an African-American,

Louisiana had passed a statute immediately after that game requiring racial segregation at public entertainment and athletic events, effectively limiting the bowl's selection of teams for nearly a decade. This was the first Sugar Bowl contest played since the U.S. Supreme Court ruled that the statute was unconstitutional. The smallest Sugar Bowl crowd since 1939 turned out to see LSU win a close game as the Tigers scored on a safety, a 28-yard field goal by flanker Doug Moreau, a 57-yard touchdown pass from quarterback Billy Ezell to Moreau, and a 2-point conversion for a 13–10 win. Syracuse's touchdown came on a 28-yard return of a blocked punt by Brad Clarke.

In a clash of top-ten teams in the Rose Bowl, No. 4 Michigan rolled to an easy 34–7 win over No. 8 Oregon State as fullback Mel Anthony rushed for three touchdowns, including an 84-yarder, and quarterback Bob Timberlake scored on a 24-yard run, ran for a 2-point conversion, and kicked two extra points.

The Liberty Bowl became the first bowl ever played indoors, on December 19, when executive director Bud Dudley accepted an offer to avoid possible bad weather in Philadelphia and instead play the game inside the Atlantic City Convention Hall in New Jersey. Astroturf had not yet been invented, so sod installed for the game was maintained by constant lighting. Players later said the footing was acceptable, but that the field was very hard. The game had some appeal for an ABC national television audience, but just over 6,000 $10 tickets were sold, enough to fill about half of the convention hall seats. Selected for the unusual game were No. 14 (UPI) Utah and West Virginia, fresh off a big upset of Syracuse. In the game, Utah jumped to a 19–0 halftime lead and cruised to a 32–6 win. Utah touchdowns included a 53-yard run by halfback Ron Coleman, a 47-yard run by Andy Ireland, and a 33-yard pass from quarterback Richard Groth to sophomore William Morley. The following season, Dudley moved the bowl to Memphis, Tennessee, where it has been played since.

The Gator Bowl, which was not played until January 2, 1965, lined up No. 11 (UPI) Florida State and unranked Oklahoma. The Seminoles had little trouble whipping the Sooners 36–19 behind the passing duo of quarterback Steve Tensi, who threw for 303 yards and 5 touchdowns, and flanker Fred Biletnikoff, a future All-Pro player, who caught four of those touchdowns on thirteen catches for 192 yards in the game.

Three teams went into the 1965 postseason undefeated: Michigan State, **1965** Nebraska, and Arkansas. No. 1 Michigan State, the nation's leader in scoring defense (6.2-point average) faced No. 5 UCLA in the Rose Bowl, a team it beat in the regular season opener, 13–3. The Spartans fell behind 14–0 by halftime as Bruin sophomore quarterback Gary Beban scored twice on short runs with Kurt Zimmerman adding the extra points. Michigan State rallied for two fourth quarter touchdowns, one on a 38-yard run by fullback Robert Apisa, but both tries for 2-point conversions failed, giving UCLA a 14–12 upset victory, its first in the Rose Bowl after six tries.

In the Orange Bowl, No. 3 Nebraska played No. 4 Alabama and, like Michigan State, the favored Cornhuskers fell behind 24–7 by halftime. Crimson Tide quarterback Steve Sloan threw two touchdown passes to end Ray Perkins, while fullback Steve Bowman scored twice on short runs. Husker quarterback Bob Churchich passed for 232 yards and three touchdowns and scored on a 1-yard run, but it was not enough to avert a 39–28 loss.

The final undefeated team, No. 7 Arkansas, the nation's scoring leader (32.4-point average), faced No. 14 (UPI) Louisiana State in the Cotton Bowl. The Razorbacks took an early 7–0 lead on a 19-yard pass from quarterback Jon Brittenum to end Bobby Crockett, but had their twenty-two-game winning string snapped when they could not score again. LSU halfback Joe Labruzzo scored two touchdowns on short runs for the upset 14–7 win. It was the first time all season that Arkansas was held below twenty points.

Because the three unbeaten teams that appeared in major bowl games all went down to defeat, a special Associated Press poll after the postseason was called to name a national champion. Michigan State still held onto a share of its second national title through its UPI ranking at the end of the regular season, while Alabama jumped from No. 4 to a No. 1 ranking and a share of its sixth national crown in the January 4 special AP poll.

No. 6 Missouri pulled out a 20–18 win over No. 12 (UPI) Florida in the Sugar Bowl, despite an outstanding performance by Steve Spurrier. The Florida quarterback passed for 352 yards and two touchdowns and scored on a 2-yard run. Missouri won behind halfback Charlie Brown, who rushed for 120 yards and a touchdown, All-America defensive back Johnny Roland, who threw an 11-yard scoring pass, and kicker Bill Bates, who had two field goals and a pair of extra points.

The Bluebonnet Bowl had an intriguing match-up of No. 7 Tennessee and No. 16 (UPI) Tulsa for their first postseason meeting since the 1942 Sugar Bowl. Tennessee won easily, however, 27–6, as Tulsa turned over the

ball seven times in a pouring rain and Vols sophomore quarterback Dewey
Warren scored two touchdowns and passed for another.

Notre Dame and Michigan State finished ranked No. 1 and No. 2 in both **1966**
wire service polls at the end of the 1966 season with identical 9–0–1 records,
an epic 10–10 face-to-face meeting accounting for the one tie. Neither was
involved in postseason play, however; Notre Dame still prohibited postseason
play, and the Big 10 picked Purdue, not Michigan State, to represent the conference in the Rose Bowl. The highest ranked team that was able to play in
a bowl, undefeated and untied No. 3 Alabama, the nation's scoring defense
leader (3.7-point average), faced No. 6 Nebraska in the Sugar Bowl. Rain fell
in New Orleans for two days preceding the January 2 contest, and a steady,
light rain on game day finally stopped about an hour and a half before the
afternoon kickoff. Alabama disposed of the Cornhuskers easily as left-handed quarterback Kenny Stabler, destined for an outstanding professional
career, passed for 218 yards, including a 45-yard touchdown to All-America
end Ray Perkins, and scored on a 14-yard run. Alabama's convincing 34–7
win showed that the Crimson Tide were at least as deserving of the national
title as the Fighting Irish. But there was no poll after the bowl games this season.

In the only Cotton Bowl contest ever played on New Year's Eve, No. 4
Georgia came out an easy winner over No. 10 Southern Methodist, 24–9,
highlighted by a 74-yard touchdown run by Bulldog sophomore halfback
Kent Lawrence. In the Orange Bowl, No. 11 (UPI) Florida pulled off a
27–12 upset of No. 8 Georgia Tech behind Heisman Trophy–winning quarterback Steve Spurrier, sophomore running back Larry Smith—who rushed
for 187 yards, including a 94-yard touchdown run—and fullback Graham
McKeel, who scored twice on short runs.

In the Rose Bowl, No. 7 Purdue won its first bowl appearance ever,
against No. 18 (UPI) Southern California. Boilermaker sophomore fullback
Perry Williams scored twice on short runs with quarterback Bob Griese kicking both extra points. Defensive back George Catavolos preserved the lead
by intercepting USC's 2-point conversion pass attempt following a Trojan
touchdown with less than three minutes left in the game. Purdue hung on to
win, 14–13.

The Liberty Bowl came up with a strong pair of teams for its December
10 game, when No. 9 Miami took on No. 20 (UPI) Virginia Tech. Tech

scored following a blocked punt to take a 7–0 halftime lead, but Miami won 14–7 with two second-half touchdowns. And in the Gator Bowl, on December 31, No. 14 (UPI) Tennessee defeated No. 16 (UPI) Syracuse 18–12.

1967   Bowl games continued to increase in popularity, with average attendance per bowl game reaching an all-time high of 65,178 in the 1967 postseason. That year there was only one major unbeaten team, No. 7 Wyoming. On a rainy, chilly New Year's Day in the Sugar Bowl, Wyoming took a 13–0 halftime lead over unranked Louisiana State as running back Jim Kiick scored a touchdown and kicker Jerry DePoyster added an extra point and two field goals. But the Tigers came back on two scoring passes by quarterback Nelson Stokley to split end Tommy Morel and a 1-yard touchdown run by sophomore tailback Glenn Smith, a New Orleans resident, to win 20–13. It was Wyoming's first postseason loss after four victories.

In the first satellite television broadcast to Europe of an American college football game, No. 1 Southern California faced No. 4 Indiana, making its first bowl appearance, in the Rose Bowl. All-America tailback O. J. Simpson, the nation's rushing leader, ran for 128 yards and both Trojan touchdowns as USC clinched its fifth national title, defeating the Hoosiers 14–3.

The Orange Bowl matched No. 5 Oklahoma and No. 2 Tennessee. The Sooners jumped to a 19–0 lead in the first half, then had to hang on for an exciting 26–24 win when a last-second field goal attempt by the Volunteers went wide. Quarterback Bobby Warmack led the Sooners with a 7-yard touchdown run and a 20-yard scoring pass to wingback Eddie Hinton, while Bob Stephenson added a score on a 23-yard pass interception return. Tennessee's second half comeback was sparked by a 36-yard pass interception return for a touchdown by Jimmy Glover.

In cold, drizzly weather in the Cotton Bowl, which returned to New Year's Day, unranked Texas A&M came up with five turnovers that led to a 20–16 upset of No. 9 Alabama. Aggie quarterback Edd Hargett threw two touchdown passes and fullback Wendell Housley scored on a 20-yard run. Quarterback Kenny Stabler scored both 'Bama touchdowns on short runs. After the game, losing coach Bear Bryant helped Texas A&M players carry winning coach Gene Stallings off the field in triumph. Bryant had coached Stallings at A&M in the mid-1950s.

Good matchups also were made for the Liberty, Bluebonnet, and Gator bowls in the 1967 postseason. The December 16 Liberty Bowl pitted No. 17

(UPI) North Carolina State against No. 18 (UPI) Georgia. The Wolfpack won 14–7 behind two great goal-line stands in the fourth quarter. In the Bluebonnet Bowl on December 23, No. 13 (UPI) Colorado outscored No. 16 (UPI) Miami 31–21. In the Gator Bowl, on December 30, Lambert Trophy winner No. 11 (UPI) Penn State took a 17–0 halftime lead over No. 15 (UPI) Florida State as quarterback Tom Sherman passed for two touchdowns, kicked a 27-yard field goal, and added two extra points. But the Seminoles came back in the second half as quarterback Kim Hammond passed for one touchdown and scored another, and sophomore kicker Grant Guthrie tied the game, 17-17, with a 26-yard field goal with seventeen seconds left.

Postseason 1968 saw five undefeated teams in action, and no team with more **1968** than one defeat played in the four biggest bowls. The city of Atlanta debuted its first bowl game, the Peach Bowl, which was successful, unlike a number of postseason experiments of the previous decade. Also, the Associated Press decided on a permanent policy to conduct its final rankings poll after the bowl games were completed; it also returned to ranking twenty teams instead of just the top ten.

The Peach Bowl idea developed in the late 1960s when George Crumbley, past director of the Georgia Lions Lighthouse Foundation, headed a committee to discuss a postseason football game in Atlanta with the NCAA. The game's original goal was to help raise funds for the foundation, which donated money, guide dogs, and equipment to aid those with sight problems. After obtaining NCAA validation, the first Peach Bowl was scheduled for December 30, 1968, at Georgia Tech's Grant Field. Selected for the inaugural game were Louisiana State and Florida State, both unranked. Rainy weather kept the crowd to 35,545, leaving some 24,000 empty seats, but the fans saw an exciting game as back Maurice LeBlanc scored on a short run with 2:39 left in the game to give LSU a 31–27 victory. The win moved LSU up to No. 19 in the new postseason AP poll.

Within three years the Peach Bowl became so successful that Crumbley and his committee turned it over to the Atlanta Chamber of Commerce, and the game was moved to Atlanta/Fulton County Stadium for the next twenty years. Since 1993 it has avoided the vagaries of Atlanta's winter weather by being played indoors at the Georgia Dome. Today, the Peach Bowl ranks first in average attendance among all non-BCS bowl games.

1968 Orange Bowl—Tennessee kept hammering at the Oklahoma defense after falling behind 19–0 in the first half, but came up two points short at the end of the game. The Vols still scored the most points all season against the nation's scoring defense leader. (*Collegiate Images*)

In the most important bowl game following the 1968 season, undefeated Ohio State, ranked No. 1 in the nation, met No. 2 Southern California, which had won the inaugural Pacific-8 title and whose record was marred only by a 21–21 tie with Notre Dame in its season finale. Ohio State sophomore quarterback Rex Kern passed for two touchdowns, and fullback Jim Otis had 101 yards and a touchdown rushing. Heisman Trophy– and Maxwell Award–winning tailback O. J. Simpson rushed for 171 yards, including an 80-yard touchdown run, and had eight pass receptions for 85 yards for USC, but also lost two fumbles and threw a pass interception. Ohio State clinched its fourth national crown with a convincing 27–16 Rose Bowl win.

One of the most exciting games in the history of the Orange Bowl was played between Lambert Trophy winner No. 3 Penn State and Big 8 co-champion No. 6 Kansas. The Nittany Lions, down 14–7 with just fifteen seconds remaining in the game, scored a touchdown on a 3-yard run by quarterback Chuck Burkhart. Instead of settling for a tie, coach Joe Paterno decided to go for the win. Kansas stopped Penn State's first try at a 2-point conversion, but was penalized for having twelve men on the field. Given a second chance, the Nittany Lions scored the 2-pointer on a run by Bob

Campbell, who had 101 yards rushing in the game, for a gutsy 15–14 victory.

In the Sugar Bowl, undefeated SEC champion Georgia, ranked No. 4, lost five fumbles and had three passes intercepted while being upended 16–2 by No. 9 Arkansas. Sophomore end Chuck Dicus caught 12 passes for 169 yards, including a touchdown from sophomore quarterback Bill Montgomery, for the Razorbacks. In the Cotton Bowl, No. 5 Texas rolled to a 28–0 halftime lead over No. 8 Tennessee and went on to win, 36–13. The Texas combination of quarterback James Street and sophomore end Charles "Cotton" Speyrer hooked up on two 79-yard pass plays for touchdowns as well as on a 2-point conversion.

Another undefeated team in a bowl game, MAC champion No. 15 Ohio University, was upset 49–42 by Southern Conference champion Richmond in the Tangerine Bowl on December 27. Ohio quarterback Cleve Bryant threw four touchdown passes, but Richmond quarterback Buster O'Brien passed for 447 yards and four scores of his own, while Walker Gillette had 20 pass receptions for 242 yards for the Spiders.

Two other unbeaten teams in 1968 were Ivy League co-champions Harvard and Yale, which played to a dramatic 29–29 tie in the season finale. Harvard fell behind 22–0 but came back, and, as the student newspaper recorded, "Harvard Wins 29–29."

1969

Five undefeated teams again saw action in postseason play after the 1969 season, and this time the story was different. Undefeated Texas, the nation's No. 1 team, played host in the Cotton Bowl as Southwest Conference champion, but the game had added interest. The Longhorns' opponent was No. 9 Notre Dame, making its first bowl appearance since the days of Knute Rockne and the Four Horsemen. After a forty-five-year postseason absence, the Fighting Irish began well, leading Texas 10–0 in the second quarter, as the three surviving Horsemen looked on among the 73,000 spectators. But the Longhorns spoiled Notre Dame's return, coming back for a 21–17 victory on three rushing touchdowns. Irish quarterback Joe Theismann passed for 231 yards and two touchdowns, including a 54-yarder to sophomore split end Tom Gatewood.

No. 2 Penn State could have gone to the Cotton Bowl for a showdown with Texas, but the players enjoyed the Orange Bowl atmosphere the previous year and voted to return to Miami instead. On January 1, coach Joe Paterno's second straight unbeaten team remained perfect with a 10–3 win over No. 6 Missouri. Penn State quarterback Chuck Burkhart passed for 187 yards, including a 28-yard touchdown to sophomore halfback Lydell Mitchell. But it was the Nittany Lion defense that dominated the game, intercepting seven Missouri passes and recovering two fumbles.

In the Rose Bowl, No. 5 Southern California took on No. 7 Michigan. In a hard-fought game, the Trojans won 10–3 on a third quarter touchdown pass from quarterback Jim Jones to Bobby Chandler, giving the Wolverines their first postseason defeat ever in five Rose Bowl appearances. Glenn "Bo" Schembechler, in his first year coaching Michigan, suffered a heart attack on the eve of the contest and had to turn game direction over to assistant coach Jim Young.

The other victorious unbeaten teams in the postseason were MAC champion No. 20 Toledo, which beat Davidson 56–33 in the Tangerine Bowl, and Don Coryell's San Diego State team, the nation's scoring leader with a 46.4-point average, which beat Boston University 28–7 in the Pasadena Bowl. The Pasadena Bowl had started as the Junior Rose Bowl in the 1967 postseason, then was renamed the Pasadena Bowl when it was resumed in the 1969 postseason. It would host two more games, one in the 1970 postseason, a 24–24 tie between Louisville and Long Beach State, and the final contest in 1971, when San Jose State beat Texas Tech 20–13.

The 1970 Sugar Bowl matched No. 3 Arkansas and No. 13 Mississippi. Razorbacks quarterback Bill Montgomery passed for 338 yards and two touchdowns, including a 47-yarder to end Chuck Dicus, and ran for 103 yards. But Mississippi quarterback Archie Manning led the Rebels to a 27–22 upset victory, passing for 273 yards and a touchdown and scoring himself on an 18-yard run. Fullback John "Bo" Bowen added a 69-yard touchdown run for Ole Miss and sophomore kicker Cloyce Hinton had two field goals, one of 52 yards. In the five years up through this season under the direction of coach Frank Broyles, the Razorbacks had a remarkable record of two undefeated and three one-loss seasons, yet were able to manage only two victories in five bowl appearances during this time.

In other notable games following the 1969 season, No. 14 Florida edged No. 15 Tennessee 14–13 on sophomore Richard Franco's two extra points in the Gator Bowl, No. 17 West Virginia beat South Carolina 14–3 in the muddy Peach Bowl as fullback Eddie Williams ran for 208 yards, and No. 12 Houston rolled past No. 20 Auburn 36–7 in the Bluebonnet Bowl as running back Jim Strong had 184 yards and two touchdowns rushing.

Texas, the nation's scoring leader (41.2-point average), went into the 1971 Cotton Bowl ranked No. 1 in the final regular season AP poll, and was guaranteed at least a share of the national championship as No. 1 in the final UPI poll. But in the first Cotton Bowl played on artificial turf, the Longhorns' thirty-game winning streak and five-bowl winning string came to an end as No. 6 Notre Dame avenged its loss to Texas the year before. All of the scoring took place in the first half as Irish quarterback Joe Theismann scored two touchdowns and Notre Dame recovered five Texas fumbles in a 24–11 victory. Texas quarterback Eddie Phillips passed for 199 yards and had 164 yards rushing in a losing effort.

In the Orange Bowl, No. 3 Nebraska and No. 5 LSU fought a close game, with Husker quarterback Jerry Tagge, who passed for 153 yards, scoring a touchdown on a 1-yard run in the fourth quarter for a 17–12 Nebraska win. The victory lifted Nebraska to a share of its first national title with a No. 1 ranking in the final AP poll.

Evangelist Billy Graham served as parade grand marshal in the Tournament of Roses Festival, and what followed in the Rose Bowl later on that warm, sunny day might well have been considered a miracle. During the season, only one team had come within six points of unbeaten No. 2 Ohio State, but Heisman Trophy– and Maxwell Award–winning quarterback Jim Plunkett led No. 12 Stanford to a stunning 27–17 upset victory, passing for 265 yards and a 10-yard touchdown to speedy little flanker Randy Vataha. But the key play occurred in the fourth quarter, with Ohio State leading 17–13, when Stanford linebacker Ron Kadziel tackled Buckeye fullback John Brockington, who had already scored twice on short runs, for a yard loss on a fourth and inches play on the Stanford 19-yard line. Stanford went on to score two unanswered touchdowns. The Ohio State defeat marked the fifteenth time a team with a perfect record fell in the Rose Bowl.

In the Sugar Bowl, heavily favored No. 4 Tennessee jumped to a 24–7 first quarter lead and rolled to a 34–13 win over No. 11 Air Force behind Don McCleary's two rushing touchdowns and defensive back Bobby Majors's 57-yard punt return for a score.

Two more unbeaten teams were successful in their bowl games. WAC champion No. 8 Arizona State bested unranked North Carolina 48–26 in blizzard-like conditions in the Peach Bowl. It was the first bowl victory in five appearances for the Sun Devils. Fullback Bob Thomas scored three touchdowns for the winners, while split end J. D. Hill scored on a 67-yard pass from quarterback Joe Spagnola. All-America running back Don McCauley had 143 yards and three touchdowns rushing for the Tar Heels. And in the Tangerine Bowl, MAC champion No. 15 Toledo rolled over Southern Conference champion William & Mary 40–12.

In other notable bowls after the 1970 season, Tulane made its first bowl appearance in thirty years, beating Colorado 17–3 in the Liberty Bowl as tailback David Abercrombie ran for 128 yards and two touchdowns, earning the Green Wave a final ranking of No. 17. No. 13 Georgia Tech took a 10–0 halftime lead and defeated No. 19 Texas Tech 17–9 in the Sun Bowl. No. 20 Oklahoma was surprised by unranked Alabama with a 24–24 tie in the Bluebonnet Bowl despite Sooner sophomore running back Greg Pruitt scoring on runs of 58 and 25 yards. And in the Gator Bowl, No. 10 Auburn outscored Mississippi 35–28 as quarterback Pat Sullivan passed for 351 yards and two touchdowns and scored on a 37-yard run for the Tigers, while Ole Miss quarterback Archie Manning, despite a broken arm, passed for 180 yards and a touchdown and ran for 95 yards and another score.

1971   The 1971 postseason welcomed a new bowl game, the Fiesta. The idea for this bowl had begun in 1968 when former Arizona State president G. Homer Durham proposed that the area host a postseason game. *Arizona Republic* sports editor Verne Boatner wrote a column supporting the idea, and several "Valley of the Sun" businessmen got behind the plan. Glenn Hawkins called a meeting of the area's community leaders, who ultimately put together a package to go before the NCAA's Special Events Committee. Jack Stewart was head of the executive committee that worked out a contract with the Western Athletic Conference, with a portion of the proceeds going to charity. And on April 26, 1971, the Fiesta Bowl gained the approval of the NCAA Council. Today the Fiesta Bowl is one of the four bowls included in the Bowl Championship Series, the only relative newcomer to achieve the status of the four major historical bowls.

More than 50,000 turned out for its inaugural game on December 27 in Sun Devil Stadium at Tempe, Arizona, between No. 8 Arizona State and unranked Florida State. It was a high-scoring game, as Sun Devils' sophomore quarterback Danny White passed for 250 yards and two touchdowns, including a 55-yarder to wingback Steve Holden, who also scored on a 68-yard punt return, and sophomore halfback Woody Green ran for 101 yards and three scores, the last a 2-yard run with 34 seconds left to win the game,

1971 Rose Bowl—Heisman Trophy-winning quarterback Jim Plunkett (16) of Stanford is stopped after a short gain against Ohio State. Stanford pulled off a stunning upset as Plunkett passed for 265 yards and a touchdown. (*Pasadena Tournament of Roses*)

45–38. Quarterback Gary Huff passed for 347 yards, three scores, and a two-point conversion for the Seminoles.

In the Orange Bowl, No. 1 Nebraska defended its national championship against No. 2 Alabama. The Cornhuskers had earned the right to play Alabama by winning the conference title on Thanksgiving with a win over previously unbeaten Oklahoma 35–31 in one of those periodic "game of the century" contests. Cornhusker quarterback Jerry Tagge, nation's passing efficiency leader, threw for 159 yards in the Orange Bowl and scored on a 1-yard run while teammate Jeff Kinney rushed for 99 yards and a touchdown, and All-America wingback Johnny Rodgers scored on a 77-yard punt return in a crushing 38–6 Nebraska victory.

The only other unbeaten team with a chance at the national title going into the bowl games was No. 4 Michigan, in its first unbeaten season since 1948. The Wolverines faced No. 16 Stanford in the Rose Bowl, but with twelve seconds left, Rob Garcia kicked a 31-yard field goal, his second of the game, to give Stanford an upset 13–12 victory.

In another major bowl, No. 3 Oklahoma, the nation's scoring leader (44.9-point average), rolled to a 31–0 halftime lead en route to a 40–22 win over No. 5 Auburn before a standing-room-only Sugar Bowl crowd. Quarterback Jack Mildren ran for 149 yards and three touchdowns, Joe Wylie scored on a 71-yard punt return, and sophomore kicker John Carroll booted a 53-yard field goal for the Sooners, while Auburn's Heisman Trophy–winning quarterback, Pat Sullivan, passed for 250 yards and a touchdown.

In the Cotton Bowl, with No. 12 Texas leading No. 10 Penn State 6–3 at the half on field goals of 29 and 40 yards by kicker Steve Valek, the Nittany Lions exploded in the second half for a 30–6 win. Nittany Lions halfback Lydell Mitchell rushed for 146 yards and a touchdown and quarterback John Hufnagel threw a 65-yard scoring pass to Scott Skarzynski.

An undefeated team appeared in the Tangerine Bowl for the sixth straight season, as No. 14 Toledo beat Southern Conference champion Richmond 28–3.

Several other nationally ranked teams participated in bowl games following the 1971 season. No. 6 Georgia got by unranked North Carolina 7–3 in the Gator Bowl as sophomore back Jimmy Poulos ran for 161 yards and scored the winning touchdown. No. 7 Colorado beat No. 15 Houston 29–17 in the Bluebonnet Bowl as sophomore tailback Charlie Davis ran for 202 yards and two touchdowns. No. 9 Tennessee edged No. 18 Arkansas 14–13 in the Liberty Bowl with fullback Curt Watson scoring the tying touchdown on a 17-yard run late in the final quarter and kicker George Hunt adding the winning extra point. The Sun Bowl saw No. 11 Louisiana State defeat unranked Iowa State 33–15 as quarterback Bert Jones passed for 227 yards and three touchdowns and scored on a 6-yard run. And No. 17 Mississippi rolled past unranked Georgia Tech 41–18 in the Peach Bowl.

1972 One major rule change for the 1972 season that had little immediate effect, but would eventually have a large impact on college football was the restoration of freshman eligibility for varsity competition. The prohibition on freshmen playing varsity had been put into effect early in the twentieth century, but had been waived during World War II and again temporarily during the Korean War in 1951. Since 1972, players who competed in high school one year might find themselves starring on a highly ranked bowl team the following season.

The only undefeated team to appear in a postseason game following the 1972 season was No. 1 Southern California. Before an all-time record Rose Bowl crowd of 106,869—crammed into a stadium recently enlarged to officially seat nearly 105,000—the Trojans met No. 3 Ohio State. The game was all USC as the Trojans wrapped up their sixth national title behind quarterback Mike Rae, who threw for 229 yards and kicked 6 extra points. Flanker Lynn Swann had 6 pass receptions for 108 yards and a touchdown for the Trojans, while sophomore tailback Anthony Davis rushed for 157 yards and a score, and fullback Sam "Bam" Cunningham scored four times on short plunges. Freshman tailback Archie Griffin had 95 yards rushing for Ohio State, but the Buckeyes were overcome 42–17.

The Sugar Bowl on New Year's Eve matched No. 2 Oklahoma and No. 5 Penn State. This was the first December contest, first night game, and first Sunday game in that bowl's history—all decisions dictated by ABC-TV. On the day of the game, Nittany Lion coach Joe Paterno learned he would be without his ace running back, John Cappelletti, who had the flu and a fever of 102 degrees. Paterno also had the virus but refused to have his temperature taken so he could be assured of being on the sidelines. What he saw that night did not improve his health. Oklahoma held Penn State to just 49 yards rushing and claimed a 14–0 victory, Oklahoma's second Sugar Bowl victory in the same calendar year. The win kept the Sooners at No. 2 in the final wire service polls. Oklahoma was led by freshman split end Tinker Owens, who started in the place of injured regular John Carroll and had 5 pass receptions for 127 yards and a touchdown.

In the Cotton Bowl, No. 7 Texas faced No. 4 Alabama. After trailing 13–3 at halftime, the Longhorns rallied to win 17–13 behind quarterback Alan Lowry, who had touchdown runs of 3 and 34 yards. In the Orange Bowl, Bob Devaney's last Nebraska team, ranked No. 9, clobbered No. 12 Notre Dame 40–6. In one of the great performances in bowl history, Heisman Trophy winner Johnny Rodgers ran for three touchdowns, scored on a 50-yard pass from sophomore quarterback David Humm, and threw a 52-yard touchdown pass to split end Frosty Anderson. Devaney moved Rodgers from his normal wingback position to I back for this contest—with obvious success.

In other bowls, No. 15 Arizona State, the nation's scoring leader with a 46.6-point average, outscored Missouri 49–35 in the Fiesta Bowl as All-America halfback Woody Green ran for 202 yards and four touchdowns and quarterback Danny White passed for 266 yards and two scores. In the Peach Bowl, unranked North Carolina State demolished No. 18 West Virginia, 49–13, as freshman quarterback Dave Buckey passed for two touchdowns and ran for another, and fullback Stan Fritts scored three times on short runs. In the Gator Bowl, No. 6 Auburn beat No. 13 Colorado 24–3. No. 10 LSU fell to No. 11 Tennessee 24–17 in the Bluebonnet Bowl as Vols sophomore quarterback Condredge Holloway ran for two touchdowns and passed for another. No. 16 North Carolina beat unranked Texas Tech 32–28 in the Sun Bowl as quarterback Nick Vidnovic passed for 215 yards, two touchdowns—including a 62-yarder to Ted Leverenz—and a two-point conversion.

1973   Postseason 1973 had one of the most exciting bowl games ever in the Sugar Bowl. Again played on New Year's Eve, the game featured No. 1 and undefeated Alabama and No. 3 Notre Dame. No opponent had come closer than fourteen points to the Crimson Tide all season. In a see-saw battle before an all-time Sugar Bowl record crowd of 85,161, Irish quarterback Tom Clements threw for 169 yards and rushed for 74 yards, while teammates Wayne Bullock and Eric Penick each scored on the ground and Al Hunter returned a kickoff 93 yards for a touchdown. Alabama countered with scores that included a 25-yard pass from sophomore halfback Mike Stock to sophomore quarterback Richard Todd and short runs by halfbacks Randy Billingsley and Wilbur Jackson. But with 4:26 left in the game, Notre Dame kicker Bob Thomas booted a 19-yard field goal to give Notre Dame a 24–23 victory. The win boosted Notre Dame to its eleventh national title in the final AP poll on January 3, while Alabama hung onto a share of its seventh national crown with its No. 1 ranking in the UPI poll at the end of the regular season.

Only three bowl games were played on New Year's Day, and two of them had unbeaten teams as participants. Unbeaten No. 4 Ohio State had tied No. 5 Michigan, which also remained undefeated, in the regular-season finale for both teams. They shared the Big 10 crown, but as the higher ranked team nationally, the Buckeyes received the Rose Bowl bid. Ohio State stayed unbeaten with a convincing 42–21 win over No. 7 Southern California. For the Buckeyes, sophomore tailback Archie Griffin ran for 149 yards, including a 47-yard touchdown gallop, while fullback Pete Johnson had 94 yards and three touchdowns rushing. Quarterback Pat Haden led USC with 229 yards passing. The win moved Ohio State into No. 2 in the final AP rankings.

In the Orange Bowl, No. 6 Penn State had running back John Cappelletti in the lineup this time for the game against No. 13 Louisiana State. Despite being held to only 50 yards rushing, Cappelletti, the Heisman Trophy and Maxwell Award winner, scored the winning touchdown on a 1-yard run for a 16–9 victory. Quarterback Tom Shuman passed for 157 yards for Penn State, including a 72-yard touchdown pass to Chuck Herd, and

1973 Sugar Bowl—Quarterback Tom Clements (2) of Notre Dame runs for short yardage in Notre Dame's exciting win over Alabama in a New Year's Eve contest. The two teams, unbeaten in the regular season, finished as national co-champions. (*Collegiate Images*)

sophomore kicker Chris Bahr added a 44-yard field goal. LSU's lone touchdown came on a 3-yard run by tailback Steve Rogers.

In the other New Year's game, No. 12 Nebraska in its first year under Tom Osborne came up with a 19–3 win over No. 8 Texas in the Cotton Bowl. Texas took an early lead on a 22-yard field goal by kicker Billy "Sure" Schott, but the Cornhuskers came back behind sophomore fullback Tony Davis, who rushed for 106 yards and a touchdown, and back Rich Bahe, who ran in a score from 12 yards out.

The Tangerine Bowl had an undefeated team for the seventh time in eight years, with MAC champion No. 15 Miami (Ohio) defeating unranked Florida 16–7 before a sell-out crowd.

Three 10–1 teams were victorious in bowl games, No. 11 Texas Tech in the Gator Bowl, No. 10 Arizona State in the Fiesta Bowl, and No. 14 Houston in the Bluebonnet Bowl. In the Fiesta Bowl, Arizona State, the nation's scoring leader (44.6 points per game), beat Pittsburgh 28–7 as quarterback Danny White passed for 269 yards and a touchdown and All-America running back Woody Green rushed for 131 yards and three scores. In the Gator Bowl, Texas Tech beat No. 20 Tennessee 28–19 to break a five-bowl losing string as Red Raider quarterback Joe Barnes threw two touchdown passes, including a 79-yarder to end Larry Williams, and scored on a 7-yard run. Houston whipped No. 17 Tulane 47–7 in the Bluebonnet Bowl. Sophomore running back Donnie McGraw and fullback Leonard Parker each had two rushing touchdowns for the winners.

In other notable bowls following the 1973 season, No. 16 North Carolina State beat No. 19 Kansas 31–18 in the Liberty Bowl, and No. 18 Maryland was upset by Georgia 17–16 in the Peach Bowl as quarterback Andy Johnson scored one touchdown and threw a 62-yard touchdown pass to Jimmy Poulos for the Bulldogs.

In addition to Michigan, one other major unbeaten team was left out of the bowl picture. No. 2 Oklahoma, in its first year under Barry Switzer, had only a 7–7 tie with USC to mar its record in its first undefeated season since 1956, but the Sooners were on NCAA probation for recruiting violations and were ineligible for postseason play.

1974   In 1974, Oklahoma finished unbeaten again and led the nation in scoring with a 43-point average, but still was on NCAA probation and was bowl ineligible. The Sooners were named to their fourth national championship by sportswriters and broadcasters in the AP poll both before and after the bowl games. But UPI did not recognize teams on probation and selected Pac-8 champion No. 5 Southern California as its No. 1 team, giving the Trojans a share of their seventh national title.

Southern California solidified that claim on New Year's Day against No. 3 Ohio State in the Rose Bowl. Although Heisman Trophy–winning halfback Archie Griffin had only 75 yards rushing, the Buckeyes led 17–10 late in the game. But with 2:03 left quarterback Pat Haden connected on a 38-yard pass to flanker J. K. McKay, coach John McKay's son, for a touchdown, then— going for the win—tossed a two-point conversion pass to sophomore flanker Shelton Diggs for a thrilling 18–17 victory, giving coach McKay his fifth Rose Bowl win in his final appearance at Pasadena.

Undefeated No. 2 Alabama had a chance to overtake Oklahoma in the AP poll with a postseason win. But Alabama, which won three games by margins of less than a touchdown, was upset 13–11 in the Orange Bowl by No. 9 Notre Dame in Ara Parseghian's last year. Notre Dame took a 13–0 lead behind rushing touchdowns by fullback Wayne Bullock and sophomore halfback Mark McLane. Alabama quarterback Richard Todd passed for 194 yards, a touchdown, and a two-point conversion. The loss marked the eighth straight bowl without a victory for Bear Bryant's Crimson Tide.

In the Sugar Bowl on New Year's Eve, No. 8 Nebraska overcame a 10–0 deficit in the fourth quarter to beat No. 18 Florida, 13–10. Fullback Tony Davis led the Cornhuskers with 126 yards rushing, freshman running back Monte Anthony scored on a 2-yard run, and kicker Mike Coyle made field goals of 37 and 39 yards.

In the Cotton Bowl, No. 7 Penn State broke open a close game in the fourth quarter for a runaway 41–20 win over No. 12 Baylor, winner of its first Southwest Conference title in fifty years. Baylor led 17–14 after three quarters behind the passing of quarterback Neal Jeffrey and the receiving of end Ricky Thompson, who caught two touchdown passes. But Penn State rolled to victory as quarterback Tom Shuman threw for 226 yards and a touchdown—a 49-yarder to freshman wide receiver Jim Cefalo—and scored on a 2-yard run, Joe Jackson scored on 50-yard kickoff return, and kicker Chris Bahr had two field goals.

The string of undefeated teams continued in the Tangerine Bowl, where MAC champion No. 15 Miami (Ohio) beat Georgia, 21–10. In one of the more exciting December games, No. 13 North Carolina State and Houston played to a 31–31 tie in the Bluebonnet Bowl. Quarterback Dave Buckey paced the Wolfpack with 200 yards and a touchdown passing, while running backs Roland Hooks and Tommy London each rushed for scores. Houston's sophomore quarterback, Bubba McGallion, threw a 73-yard touchdown pass to sophomore Eddie Foster and sophomore running back John Housman ran for 134 yards and two scores.

In other notable bowls after the 1974 season, ACC champion No. 10 Maryland was upset 7–3 in a defensive game in the Liberty Bowl by Tennessee. And in the Gator Bowl, No. 6 Auburn rolled over No. 11 Texas 27–3.

In 1975, Woody Hayes' sixth unbeaten Ohio State team, Big 10 champs for **1975** the fourth straight year, and the nation's scoring leader with a 34-point average per game, had been ranked No. 1 in the nation since October 7 in the AP poll. By beating No. 11 UCLA in the Rose Bowl, a team the Buckeyes had beaten 41–20 in regular season, the Buckeyes would be national champion. Ohio State dominated the first half, holding the Bruins without a first down for 26 minutes, but four drives inside the UCLA 35-yard line led only to a single 42-yard field goal by Tom Klaban. The Bruins then took over, shocking the Buckeyes 23–10 as All-America quarterback John Sciarra passed for 212 yards and two touchdowns, both to flanker Wally Henry, including a 67-

yarder, while running back Wendell Tyler had 172 yards rushing, including a spectacular 54-yard touchdown run. For Ohio State, Heisman Trophy– and Maxwell Award–winning halfback Archie Griffin rushed for 95 yards and fullback Pete Johnson, the nation's scoring leader, scored the only Buckeye touchdown. Perhaps Ohio State should have been forewarned: a 4.2 magnitude earthquake struck Pasadena during the Tournament of Roses parade earlier in the day.

The Ohio State defeat opened the way for No. 3 Oklahoma to repeat as national champion with a win in the Orange Bowl against No. 5 Michigan, and the Sooners did not let the opportunity pass. Oklahoma defeated the Wolverines 14–6 as split end Billy Brooks scored on a 39-yard run, quarterback Steve Davis scored on a 9-yard run, and the Selmon brothers, All-America defensive tackle Lee Roy and All-America middle guard Dewey, led a tough defense. Running back Gordon Bell scored Michigan's only touchdown on a 2-yard run. By this time UPI had joined the AP in conducting its final rankings after the conclusion of the bowl games, and Oklahoma gained the No. 1 ranking in both polls.

In the Cotton Bowl, No. 18 Arkansas overcame an early 10–0 deficit against No. 12 Georgia, and entered the fourth quarter tied at 10–10. The Razorbacks then exploded for three touchdowns and won, 31–10. Running back Ike Forte ran for 119 yards and two touchdowns for Arkansas, Rolland Fuchs and freshman Michael Forrest scored on short runs, kicker Steve Little had a 39-yard field goal and four extra points, and linebacker Hal McAfee had twelve tackles, two fumble recoveries, and a pass interception.

Unbeaten No. 7 Arizona State nailed down the No. 2 position in both final wire service polls with a thrilling 17–14 win over No. 6 Nebraska in the Fiesta Bowl. The Sun Devils trailed 14–6 entering the fourth quarter, but pulled out a victory on a 10-yard touchdown pass from quarterback Fred Mortensen to wide receiver John Jefferson, a two-point conversion pass from Mortensen to wingback Larry Mucker, and a game-winning 29-yard field goal by Danny Kush, son of Arizona State coach Frank Kush.

In the Sugar Bowl, SEC champion No. 4 Alabama finally broke its bowl-victory drought of eight straight games with a 13–6 New Year's Eve victory over No. 8 Penn State. Crimson Tide quarterback Richard Todd, playing with a bandaged finger on his throwing hand from a Christmas Day accident, passed for 210 yards, halfback Mike Stock scored on an 11-yard run, and kicker Danny Ridgeway had two field goals. Penn State scored on field goals

1975 Peach Bowl—West Virginia wide receiver Scott MacDonald (84), a former basketball star, leaps for a pass in front of North Carolina State's Ralph Stringer (9). MacDonald later scored the winning touchdown on a 50-yard pass play. (*R. M. Ours*)

of 42 and 37 yards by kicker Chris Bahr. This was the first Sugar Bowl in which the combined payout to the participants reached $1 million. After the game, Alabama coach Bear Bryant made a plea to do away with conference tie-ins for bowl games and also opposed polls determining a national champion after postseason play. "If we are going to stay with the polls," he said, "take it out of the bowls. It puts too much pressure when bowls are used for it. It takes all the fun out of the bowls." Bryant's statement, however, had little support among fans, players, or other coaches.

The Tangerine Bowl this time did not have an unbeaten team, but No. 16 Miami (Ohio) won its third straight contest in Orlando with a 20–7 victory over South Carolina. Another 10–1 team, No. 2 Texas A&M, was upset by unranked Southern California, 20–0, at the Liberty Bowl. The highlight was a 76-yard touchdown run by sophomore fullback Mosi Tatupu on a screen pass.

In the Bluebonnet Bowl, No. 9 Texas defeated No. 10 Colorado 38–21 after trailing 21–7 at halftime, as six different Longhorns scored. ACC champion No. 17 Maryland upset No. 13 Florida 13–0 in the Gator Bowl with freshman tailback Steve Atkins running for 127 yards. No. 20 Pittsburgh beat No. 19 Kansas 33–19 in the Sun Bowl, led by running back Tony Dorsett's 142 yards and two touchdowns rushing. And West Virginia, in Bobby Bowden's last year, moved into the top twenty in the final rankings with a dramatic 13–10 Peach Bowl win over Lou Holtz's North Carolina State. Trailing 10–0, the Mountaineers scored at the end of the first half on a 39-yard pass from sophomore quarterback Dan Kendra to running back Artie Owens, then won the game in the final seven minutes on a 50-yard scoring pass from Kendra to flanker Scott MacDonald.

1976 Bicentennial celebrations in 1976 included special pre-game and halftime patriotic shows during the regular season and at several bowl games as well. No team celebrated the year more on the football field than No. 1 Pittsburgh, winner of its first Lambert Trophy since 1955. The Panthers had only one close game, a 24–16 win over West Virginia, in their first unbeaten season since 1937 and first perfect season since 1929. Both the Sugar and Sun bowls returned to January playing dates following the regular season— making the most new year contests in five years—and Pittsburgh would be in the Sugar Bowl's first day game in five years, facing No. 5 Georgia. Pittsburgh jumped to a 21–0 halftime lead and rolled over Georgia 27–3. Dorsett ran for 202 yards and a touchdown, and quarterback Matt Cavanaugh passed for one score, a 59-yarder to split end Gordon Jones, and ran for another to lead the Panthers to their fourth national crown, and first since 1937. Pittsburgh became the first team to claim the national championship, the Heisman Trophy winner—running back Tony Dorsett, who also won the Maxwell Award—and national coach of the year—Johnny Majors— in the same season.

The other major undefeated team to appear in a postseason game, No. 4 Maryland, in its first unbeaten season since 1955, was upset by No. 6 Houston in the Cotton Bowl. The Cougars jumped to a 21–0 first-quarter lead and hung on for a 30–21 win. Running back Alois Blackwell contributed 149 yards and two touchdowns for Houston, while quarterback Mark Manges passed for 179 yards and a touchdown and scored on a 6-yard run for Maryland.

Rain fell in Pasadena for several days preceding January 1, but the skies cleared and the sun came out for the parade and game. No. 3 Southern California, in its first year under John Robinson, finished as the nation's No. 2 team in the final rankings with a 14–6 win over No. 2 Michigan. USC quar-

1977 Sugar Bowl—Quarterback Matt Cavanaugh (12) of Pittsburgh launches a pass against Georgia as the Panthers wrap up an undefeated national championship season with a convincing win over the Bulldogs. Heisman Trophy–winning tailback Tony Dorsett ran for 202 yards. (*Collegiate Images*)

terback Vince Evans passed for 181 yards and scored on a 1-yard run, while freshman tailback Charles White, replacing injured All-American Ricky Bell, ran for 114 yards and a touchdown. USC's quarterback was not the only Evans in the spotlight that day. Western movie stars Dale Evans and husband Roy Rogers served as grand marshals of the Rose parade. Afterward, asked why he and his wife rode the parade route in an antique Stutz Bearcat instead of astride horses, Roy replied: "Did you ever try riding a horse and smiling for five miles?"

In the other New Year's Day game, No. 11 Ohio State came back for a 27–10 win over No. 12 Colorado in the Orange Bowl after dropping behind 10–0 early in the game. Four Buckeyes had a hand in the scoring, and sophomore linebacker Tom Cousineau had thirteen tackles for the winners.

The Sun Bowl, which had been played in December since 1958, returned to a January contest, but on January 2 rather than on New Year's Day. The largest Sun Bowl crowd in five years saw No. 10 Texas A&M clobber Florida 37–14 as fullback George Woodard ran for 124 yards, two touchdowns, and a 2-point conversion, and also caught a 15-yard scoring pass from quarterback David Walker. All-America kicker Tony Franklin added field goals of 39, 62, and 33 yards.

In the Bluebonnet Bowl, No. 9 Texas Tech lost a close 27–24 game to No. 13 Nebraska as Cornhusker quarterback Vince Ferragamo passed for 183 yards and two touchdowns and sophomore halfback Rick Berns ran for 118 yards and two scores. Quarterback Rodney Allison threw two touchdown passes to fullback Billy Taylor for the Red Raiders.

No. 7 UCLA was upset 36–6 by No. 16 Alabama in the Liberty Bowl as five Crimson Tide players scored. Big 8 co-champion No. 8 Oklahoma had little trouble disposing of Wyoming 41–7 in the Fiesta Bowl. In the Tangerine Bowl, No. 14 Oklahoma State beat Brigham Young 49–21 as running back Terry Miller ran for 173 yards and four touchdowns, including a 78-yarder. In their first meeting since 1928, No. 15 Notre Dame beat No. 20 Penn State 20–9 in the Gator Bowl as halfback Al Hunter scored two touchdowns. And in the Peach Bowl, No. 19 North Carolina was upset by unranked Kentucky 21–0 as sophomore tailback Rod Stewart scored all three touchdowns. In their first bowl appearance in 25 years, the Wildcats held the Tar Heels to 108 total yards of offense.

During the 1976 postseason a new bowl game got its start, the Independence Bowl at Shreveport, Louisiana, on December 13. In that contest, McNeese State beat Tulsa, 20–16. One of Tulsa's touchdowns came on defensive end Mel McGowen's 65-yard return of a blocked field goal attempt.

One major unbeaten team, No. 17 Rutgers, 11–0 in its first season without a loss since 1961 and the nation's leader in scoring defense (a 7.4-point average), failed to land a bowl bid.

1977 The only major team to get through the 1977 season unbeaten was No. 1 Texas. On January 2 the Longhorns had a chance to clinch the national championship in the Cotton Bowl. However, the opponent was No. 5 Notre Dame. This was the third time an unbeaten Texas team faced the Fighting Irish in the Cotton Bowl in less than a decade. Texas had won 21–17 to clinch the national crown on New Year's Day 1970, but the following year the Fighting Irish upset the Longhorns 24–11. On January 2, 1978, a record Cotton Bowl crowd of 76,601 saw Notre Dame stun the Longhorns 38–10, taking a 24–10 lead in the first half and extending the margin in the second half. For the Irish, halfback Vegas Ferguson ran for 100 yards and two touchdowns and caught a 17-yard scoring pass from quarterback Joe Montana, and halfback Terry Eurick ran for two touchdowns. Heisman Trophy–winning fullback Earl Campbell, the nation's rushing and scoring leader, had 116 yards rushing for Texas. The victory boosted Notre Dame to No. 1 in the final polls, giving the school its twelfth national title, the seventh since the Associated Press started ranking teams in 1936. Notre Dame also became the first Cotton Bowl participant to receive a $1 million payout.

Two other teams that had a shot at the national championship were No. 2 Oklahoma and No. 4 Michigan. The Wolverines faced No. 13 Washington in the Rose Bowl. The game was the first live satellite telecast of a bowl game to Asia. And on hand to watch the game in person was former president and one-time Michigan center Gerald Ford, who served as Rose parade grand marshal. Leading the Huskies was quarterback Warren Moon, who ran for two touchdowns and passed for 188 yards and a 28-yard score to split end Robert "Spider" Gaines. Quarterback Rick Leach passed for 239 yards and two touchdowns, including a 76-yarder to Curt Stephenson, for Michigan, but Washington hung on for an upset 27–20 win.

In the Orange Bowl, No. 6 Arkansas, in its first year under Lou Holtz, stunned Oklahoma 31–6 behind sophomore running back Roland Sales's 205 yards and two touchdowns rushing. Oklahoma scored only in the last quarter. The margin of victory especially was a surprise because Holtz had suspended his top three scorers from this game for team rule infractions. Sales started as a replacement for one of the suspended players.

In the other major bowl that year, the Sugar Bowl, SEC champion No. 3 Alabama met No. 9 Ohio State. Alabama was led by quarterback Jeff Rutledge, who passed for 109 yards and a touchdown, and fullback Johnny Davis, who ran for 95 yards and two scores, as the Crimson Tide whipped the Buckeyes 35–6. After the game, Ohio State coach Woody Hayes said, "We sure got out-coached here today. They just outplayed us in every department they could have." The victory gave Alabama the No. 2 ranking in the final wire service polls.

The Fiesta Bowl had a good match-up, No. 8 Penn State against No. 15 Arizona State. Penn State defeated the Sun Devils 42–30 to break Arizona State's five-bowl win string as five players scored for the winners. The Gator Bowl also had an excellent pairing, No. 10 Pittsburgh, in Jackie Sherrill's first year, against No. 11 Clemson. The Panthers won with surprising ease, 34–3, as quarterback Matt Cavanaugh passed for 387 yards and four touchdowns, three of them to running back Elliott Walker. Still another good contest took place in the Liberty Bowl, where No. 12 Nebraska came up with a 21–17 win over ACC champion No. 14 North Carolina as Cornhusker reserve quarterback Randy Garcia threw two touchdown passes.

No. 17 Texas A&M was upset 47–28 by No. 20 Southern California in the Bluebonnet Bowl as Trojan quarterback Rob Hertel passed for four touchdowns and sophomore tailback Charles White had 187 yards rushing. In the Tangerine Bowl, No. 19 Florida State rolled over Texas Tech 40–17, highlighted by a 93-yard kickoff return for a touchdown by Seminole running back Larry Key.

The Sun Bowl returned to a December playing date with Stanford, in its first year under Bill Walsh, beating Louisiana State 24–14 on New Year's Eve. All-America quarterback Guy Benjamin passed for 269 yards and three touchdowns for Stanford, while linebacker Gordon Ceresino led the defense with twenty-two tackles. All-America tailback Charles Alexander had 197 yards and a touchdown rushing for LSU.

Added to the bowl lineup this year was the Hall of Fame Classic at Birmingham, Alabama, where Maryland beat Minnesota, 17–7.

Bowl payouts per game averaged $515,714, or $257,857 per team, in this postseason. Over the next two decades, bowl money would increase to enormous sums as corporate sponsorship began to capitalize on the marketing boom of bowl games. For football purists, the movement for a bowl-based Division I-A championship playoff also began taking root.

6 MORE MONEY, MORE BOWLS

By THE LATE 1970S, THE ESTABLISHED BOWLS found themselves either tied to conference contracts to supply at least some of the participants or scrambling to get the best available teams in the latter part of the regular season. Dating back to the 1940s, this had meant sometimes trying to outbid other bowls for desirable teams and sometimes issuing bids a month or so before the season was over. Arranging the best match-ups required money, and by the late 1970s it was becoming obvious that a ready source of money was a corporation looking for a new way to get its name before the public. Corporations could supply not only advertising money but also the clout needed to line up the best broadcasting possibilities. And, for cities seeking new postseason games of their own, what better way than to begin with corporate backing? The bowls began taking advantage of this in the 1980s, and it was a major reason behind the proliferation of postseason contests over the past twenty years. Meanwhile, the number of bowls increased to fifteen in the 1978 postseason, and bowl payouts doubled, reaching an average of $1,110,303 per game or $555,152 per team. This postseason also saw some of the most memorable contests.

Unbeaten No. 1 Penn State had its turn to win a clear national championship after being the only team to complete the 1978 season undefeated. Joe Paterno's fourth undefeated team faced No. 2 Alabama in the Sugar Bowl. Alabama scored first on a 30-yard pass from quarterback Jeff Rutledge to split end Bruce Bolton with eight seconds left in the first half. Penn State's Maxwell Award–winning quarterback Chuck Fusina tied the game after halftime with the lone Penn State touchdown, a 17-yarder to receiver Scott Fitzkee that tied the game 7–7. An 8-yard run by running back Morgan "Major" Ogilvie later in the third quarter put the Crimson Tide up again, 14–7. But it was Alabama's great defensive effort that ended Penn State's dreams, holding the Nittany Lions to just 19 yards rushing and preserving the win with one of the great goal-line stands in football history after Penn State recovered an Alabama fumble on the Crimson Tide 19-yard line with 7:57 left in the game. The Nittany Lions soon had a first down at the 8-yard line and two plays moved the ball just short of the goal line, with Fitzkee driven out of bounds by defensive back Don McNeal just two feet short after a pass reception. On third down, fullback Matt Suhey gained about a foot before being stopped by linebacker Rich Wingo and defensive back Murray Legg. Penn State tried to power across once more, this time with tailback Mike Guman. But he was stopped inches from the goal line by a crushing hit by linebacker Barry Krauss and Legg. The Nittany Lions never got close again, and the game ended 14–7. The win was the first ever in a bowl game by a No. 2 team over a No. 1 team and moved Alabama into the top spot in the final AP poll, the eighth national title for the Crimson Tide.

No. 3 Southern California, winner of the inaugural Pacific-10 title, had defeated Alabama in the regular season, however, and finished No. 1 in the postseason UPI poll after beating No. 5 Michigan in the Rose Bowl. USC All-America tailback Charles White, the nation's rushing leader, ran for 99 yards and scored a disputed touchdown on a 3-yard run that broke a 10–10 tie and turned out to be the winning score. Michigan players claimed to have stripped the ball from White and recovered it before he crossed the goal line, but the officials did not agree, and the touchdown stood for a 17–10 USC victory.

The Orange Bowl was a rematch of No. 4 Oklahoma and No. 6 Nebraska. Oklahoma, the nation's scoring leader (40-point average), lost only to Nebraska, 17–14, in the regular season. Led by Heisman Trophy winner Billy Sims, the nation's scoring leader, who ran for 134 yards and two touchdowns, and quarterback Thomas Lott who scored twice on short runs, the Sooners got revenge with a 31–24 victory. In the Cotton Bowl, No. 10 Notre Dame rallied from a 34–12 deficit in the final quarter to edge No. 9 Houston, 35–34, as time expired. Quarterback Joe Montana, destined for greatness in the NFL, scored two touchdowns and passed for 163 yards and two two-point conversions for the Irish. He finished with an 8-yard scoring toss to split end Kris Haines on the final play of the game. Kicker Joe Unis, a Dallas native, then added the crucial game-winning extra point.

The Gator Bowl had plenty of excitement both on the field and on the sidelines as ACC champion, No. 7 Clemson, which had lost only to Georgia 12–0, squared off with No. 20 Ohio State. On the field, Clemson quarterback Steve Fuller passed for 123 yards and scored on a 4-yard run, freshman tailback Cliff Austin scored on a 1-yard run, and kicker Obed Ariri added a 47-yard field goal and two extra points for a 17-15 victory. Freshman quarterback Art Schlichter passed for 205 yards and ran for 70 yards and two touchdowns for Ohio State. Buckeye Coach Woody Hayes's outstanding career came to a sad end when, in frustration, he slugged a Clemson player who had just intercepted an Ohio State pass late in the game. Hayes, fired after the incident, left a record at Ohio State of 205-61-10 for 1951-78, including thirteen Big 10 titles, six teams unbeaten in regular season, and three national champions. He was named national coach of the year three times.

In other 1978 postseason games, No. 15 UCLA trailed No. 8 Arkansas 10-0 at the half in the Fiesta Bowl, but came back for a 10-10 tie. In the Peach Bowl, No. 17 Purdue beat Georgia Tech 41-21 as Boilermaker quarterback Mark Herrmann passed for two touchdowns and ran for another. Unranked Stanford overcame a 22-0 deficit in the Bluebonnet Bowl on three touchdown passes by quarterback Steve Dils and a field goal by kicker Ken Naber, while linebacker Gordon Ceresino racked up twenty tackles to upset No. 11 Georgia, 25-22. No. 13 Maryland gained only 34 yards rushing and was crushed by Texas 42-0 in the Sun Bowl, while in the Tangerine Bowl, No. 16 Pittsburgh also was upset, losing to North Carolina State 30-17. No. 19 Iowa State lost to Texas A&M 28-12 in the Hall of Fame Classic as Aggie tailback Curtis Dickey ran for 276 yards and a touchdown.

Two new bowls were inaugurated in 1978, the Holiday Bowl at San Diego, California, and the Garden State Bowl at East Rutherford, New Jersey. Trailing 16-10 entering the fourth quarter, Navy defeated Brigham Young, 23-16, on a 65-yard pass from quarterback Bob Leszczynski to end Phil McConkey in the first Holiday Bowl. Sophomore quarterback Jim McMahon passed for one touchdown and scored on a 2-yard run for BYU. In the initial Garden State Bowl, Arizona State overcame an early 10-0 deficit to take a 34-18 win over Rutgers, which was making its first postseason appearance. Arizona State quarterback Mark Malone had a spectacular game, passing for 268 yards and three touchdowns and running for the other two Arizona State scores.

Unbeaten Ohio State, in its first year under Earle Bruce, was ranked No. 1 **1979** going into the 1979 postseason but had a tough Rose Bowl foe in No. 3 Southern California. In the game, USC quarterback Paul McDonald passed

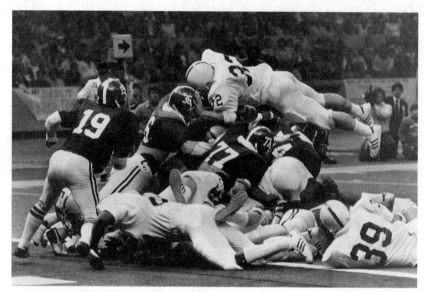

1979 Sugar Bowl—In one of the great goal-line stands in bowl history, Alabama stopped Penn State inches short of the end zone on both third and fourth downs to seize the national championship from the Nittany Lions. On this third-down play, fullback Matt Suhey (32) is stopped by Alabama's Rich Wingo (36), Barry Krauss (77), and Murray Legg (19). (*Collegiate Images*)

for 234 yards, including a 53-yard touchdown to wide receiver Kevin Williams, while the Trojan defense allowed only three field goals and a single touchdown on a 67-yard pass from Buckeye quarterback Art Schlichter, who had 297 yards passing, to freshman split end Gary Williams. But Heisman Trophy– and Maxwell Award–winning tailback Charles White ran for 247 yards and scored a touchdown with only 1:32 left in the game, to give USC a 17–16 upset of the Buckeyes.

Bear Bryant's seventh unbeaten Alabama team, ranked No. 2, hoped to defend its national championship in the Sugar Bowl against No. 6 Arkansas. The Crimson Tide did just that, winning 24–9 to earn a ninth national title, this time finishing No. 1 in both polls. Leading the way was running back Major Ogilvie, who rushed for two touchdowns while fullback Steve Whitman scored on a 12-yard run. For the first time, the Sugar Bowl payout for the two teams topped $2 million—compared with the $15,000 guarantee for the visiting team at the first Sugar Bowl forty-five years earlier.

In the Orange Bowl, No. 5 Oklahoma spoiled a perfect season for No. 4 Florida State. All-America running back Billy Sims, once again the nation's scoring leader, ran for 164 yards and a touchdown, and quarterback J. C. Watts had 127 yards on the ground and scored a key touchdown on a 61-yard run, while defensive back Bud Hebert intercepted three passes, en route to a 24–7 Sooner win.

The Cotton Bowl was the only New Year's Day match-up without an unbeaten team, but it had an exciting game, nonetheless, when No. 8 Houston edged No. 7 Nebraska 17–14. Backup quarterback Terry Elston led the Cougars to victory by running for one touchdown and throwing a game-winning 6-yard scoring strike to Eric Herring with twelve seconds left in the contest.

Two other undefeated teams were active in postseason play, but both lost. McNeese State was thumped 31–7 by Syracuse in the Independence Bowl, while No. 9 Brigham Young lost a heartbreaker 38–37 to Indiana in the Holiday Bowl, a game that saw eight lead changes.

A Garden State Bowl all-time record crowd of 55,493 saw No. 20 Temple make its first bowl appearance in forty-five years a successful one, jumping to a 21–0 lead in the first quarter en route to a 28–17 win over California. Temple quarterback Brian Broomell passed for two touchdowns and running back Kevin Duckett ran for two more scores.

No. 10 Pittsburgh held off unranked Arizona 16–10 in the Fiesta Bowl as freshman quarterback Dan Marino, who later set NFL records for passing touchdowns and yardage, passed for 172 yards and a touchdown, and kicker Mark Schubert booted three field goals, including two 46-yarders. In the Bluebonnet Bowl, No. 12 Purdue got past Tennessee 27–22 as quarterback Mark Herrmann passed for 303 yards and three touchdowns, including the game-winning 17-yard toss to tight end Dave Young in the final moments of the game. No. 13 Washington beat No. 11 Texas 14–7 in the Sun Bowl. In the Peach Bowl, No. 19 Baylor beat No. 18 Clemson 24–18 as freshman quarterback Mike Brannan threw two touchdown passes. Three other nationally ranked teams tasted defeat in 1979 postseason games. No. 14 Michigan was upset by North Carolina 17–15 in the Gator Bowl, No. 15 Tulane lost to Penn State 9–6 in the Liberty Bowl, and No. 16 South Carolina lost to Missouri 24–14 in the Hall of Fame Classic.

No. 1 Georgia was the only Division I-A team to complete the 1980 regular **1980** season undefeated, yet the Bulldogs were a one-point underdog to No. 7 Notre Dame in the Sugar Bowl. The Bulldogs wrapped up their second national championship, however, with a tough 17–10 win over the Fighting Irish. Freshman All-America tailback Herschel Walker ran for 150 yards and both Georgia touchdowns despite suffering a shoulder separation early in the game.

No. 4 Oklahoma, in its second Orange Bowl appearance in a row, squeaked past No. 2 Florida State, 18–17, when quarterback J. C. Watts threw an 11-yard touchdown pass to split end Steve Rhodes with just 1:27 left in the game and then passed to tight end Forrest Valora for the winning two-point conversion. Earlier, kicker Michael Keeling had a 53-yard field goal for the winners. The victory gave the Sooners a No. 3 ranking in the final wire service polls.

In the Rose Bowl, No. 5 Michigan faced No. 16 Washington. Tailback Butch Woolfolk rushed for 182 yards and a touchdown while wide receiver Anthony Carter caught a scoring pass from quarterback John Wangler to help break Michigan's seven-game bowl losing string with a convincing 23–6 win that moved the Wolverines into the No. 4 spot in the final poll.

In the Cotton Bowl, No. 9 Alabama rolled to a 30–2 win over No. 6 Baylor. The Bears lost the ball four times on fumbles and three times on pass interceptions while Alabama scored touchdowns on short runs by running backs Major Ogilvie and Mark Nix and quarterback Donald Jacobs.

No. 3 Pittsburgh trounced No. 18 South Carolina, 37–9, in the Gator Bowl and was rewarded with a No. 2 ranking in both final wire service polls. Fullback Randy McMillan ran for one touchdown and caught a 42-yard scoring pass from quarterback Rick Trocano, who also ran one in from a yard out, while Panther defensive end Rickey Jackson made fourteen solo tackles. Heisman Trophy–winning running back George Rogers, the nation's rushing leader, had 113 yards on the ground for the Gamecocks, but was unable to score. The payout for the Gator Bowl surpassed $900,000 for the first time with this game.

The Fiesta Bowl pitted No. 10 Penn State against No. 11 Ohio State. Buckeye quarterback Art Schlichter passed for 302 yards and three touchdowns, but Penn State won 31–19 as Nittany Lion sophomore running back Curt Warner ran for 155 yards, including a 64-yard scoring jaunt. In the Sun Bow,l No. 8 Nebraska defeated No. 17 Mississippi State, 31–17, as Cornhusker quarterback Jeff Quinn passed for two touchdowns. In the Bluebonnet Bowl, No. 13 North Carolina beat Texas 16–7 on touchdown runs by running back Amos Lawrence and sophomore halfback Kelvin Bryant.

The Holiday Bowl again had one of the more exciting games of the post-season between No. 14 Brigham Young, the nation's scoring leader (46.7-point average), and No. 19 Southern Methodist. BYU trailed 45–25 with only 4:07 left, but pulled out an amazing 46–45 victory on a 41-yard pass from quarterback Jim McMahon to tight end Clay Brown with three seconds left, followed by sophomore kicker Kurt Gunther's winning extra point. McMahon threw for 446 yards and four touchdowns, three of them to Brown, and freshman Vai Sikahema scored on an 83-yard punt return. SMU tailback Craig James scored three touchdowns and his running mate, tail-back Eric Dickerson, ran for 110 yards and two scores.

The Peach Bowl experimented with a January 2 playing date, when No. 20 Miami, paced by sophomore quarterback Jim Kelly, defeated Virginia Tech 20–10.

Following the 1981 season, five bowl games were played on New Year's for **1981** the first time since 1960, as the Fiesta Bowl joined the Rose, Orange, Sugar, and Cotton bowls. For the second year in a row, only one Division I-A team finished the regular season unbeaten, No. 1 Clemson. The Tigers clinched their first national title—and the first by an ACC team since Maryland's 1953 championship—with a 22–15 win over No. 4 Nebraska in the Orange Bowl. Leading Clemson to victory were quarterback Homer Jordan, who passed for 134 yards and a touchdown, and freshman kicker Donald Igwebuike, who had three field goals.

The Sugar Bowl saw an exciting game when Jackie Sherrill's last Pittsburgh team, ranked No. 10, upset SEC co-champion Georgia 24–20 on a fourth down 33-yard scoring strike from quarterback Dan Marino to tight end John Brown with thirty-five seconds left in the game. In the first Sugar Bowl held at night in six years, Marino passed for all three Pittsburgh touch-downs, while All-America tailback Herschel Walker scored twice for Georgia.

In the Cotton Bowl, No. 6 Texas pulled out a 14–12 win over No. 3 Alabama on two fourth period touchdowns, quarterback Robert Brewer scor-ing on a 30-yard run and freshman fullback Terry Orr reaching the end zone on an 8-yard run. Kicker Raul Allegre adding the winning extra points, which broke a six-bowl string of victories for the Crimson Tide.

In the Rose Bowl, Washington, ranked No. 12, whipped No. 13 Iowa, 28–0, as freshman tailback Jacque Robinson ran for 142 yards and two touch-downs, sophomore quarterback Steve Pelluer passed for 142 yards and a two-

1981 Orange Bowl—Oklahoma quarterback J. C. Watts (1) completes a pass to tight end Forrest Valora (82) for a two-point conversion with under 1:30 left in the game to give the Sooners an 18–17 win over Florida State. (*Collegiate Images*)

point conversion, and linebackers Mark Jerue and Ken Driscoll starred on defense. Iowa lost the ball five times on interceptions and fumbles.

A packed Fiesta Bowl stadium saw No. 7 Penn State end No. 8 Southern California's six-bowl winning string with a 26–10 victory. Leading Penn State to the victory were running back Curt Warner, who rushed for 145 yards and two touchdowns, and quarterback Todd Blackledge, who threw for 175 yards, including a 52-yard touchdown to flanker Greg Garrity.

In the Holiday Bowl, No. 14 Brigham Young, the nation's scoring leader with a 38.7-point average, edged No. 20 Washington State—making its first postseason appearance in fifty-one years—38–36 as quarterback Jim McMahon passed for 342 yards and three touchdowns for the winners. No. 19 Southern Mississippi was upset by Missouri 19–17 in the Tangerine Bowl as kicker Bob Lucchesi kicked four field goals for the winners. In the Gator Bowl, No. 11 North Carolina beat Arkansas 31–27 as freshman running back Ethan Horton ran for 144 yards and two touchdowns and running back Kelvin Bryant had 148 yards and a another score rushing. No. 15 Ohio State edged Navy, 31–28, in the Liberty Bowl as Buckeye quarterback Art Schlichter passed for 159 yards and two touchdowns. In the Bluebonnet Bowl, No. 16 Michigan beat No. 19 UCLA 33–14 as sophomore Wolverine quarterback Steve Smith threw a 50-yard scoring strike to wide receiver Anthony Carter, while tailback Butch Woolfolk had 186 yards and a touchdown rushing.

The Garden State Bowl ended its four-year existence with a match between Tennessee and Wisconsin. Volunteer quarterback Steve Alatorre passed for 315 yards and a touchdown while running in another from 6 yards out, and wide receiver Willie Gault scored on a 97-yard kickoff return for a 28–21 Volunteer win. In the Peach Bowl, heavy underdog West Virginia shocked Florida 26–6 as quarterback Oliver Luck passed for a touchdown, freshman kicker Paul Woodside booted four field goals, and a tenacious defense led by linebackers Dennis Fowlkes and Darryl Talley held Florida to a single fourth-quarter score.

In the first California Bowl at Fresno, which brought the number of post-season games to sixteen, Toledo edged San Jose State 27–25.

Two teams made it through the 1982 season unbeaten, although No. 4 **1982** Southern Methodist, completing its first undefeated season since 1947, was tied by Arkansas 17–17 in its final game. The other unbeaten team was No. 1 Georgia, winner of its third straight SEC title behind tailback Herschel Walker, who won the Heisman Trophy and Maxwell Award. The Bulldogs hoped to wrap up their second national championship in three years with a Sugar Bowl win over No. 2 Penn State, loser only to Alabama in a midseason game. Instead, the biggest Sugar Bowl crowd in nine years saw the Nittany Lions grab the national title—their first—by beating Georgia 27–23 in an exciting contest worthy of a title game. Penn State quarterback Todd Blackledge passed for 228 yards and a touchdown to flanker Greg Garrity, running back Curt Warner ran for 117 yards and two scores, and sophomore kicker Nick Gancitano added two field goals. Walker rushed for 103 yards and a touchdown for Georgia, while quarterback John Lastinger passed for two touchdowns.

Meanwhile, Southern Methodist remained undefeated, getting past No. 6 Pittsburgh 7–3 in the Cotton Bowl on a fourth-quarter 9-yard touchdown run by quarterback Lance McIlhenny. Quarterback Dan Marino passed for 181 yards, but Pittsburgh had to settle for only a 43-yard field goal by Eric Schubert. No. 3 Nebraska, the nation's leader in scoring (41.1-point average), overcame a third-quarter 17–7 deficit to win the Orange Bowl 21–20 over No. 13 Louisiana State. Cornhusker quarterback Turner Gill passed for

184 yards and a touchdown and scored on a 1-yard run, and All-America running back Mike Rozier, who caught the scoring pass, had 118 yards rushing. Freshman tailback Dalton Hilliard scored both LSU touchdowns on short runs.

The Rose Bowl was a rematch between No. 5 UCLA and No. 19 Michigan, the Bruins having won 31–27 in regular season. UCLA made it two for two by defeating the Wolverines 24–14 as quarterback Tom Ramsey scored a touchdown and passed for 162 yards and linebacker Blanchard Montgomery scored on an 11-yard pass interception return. Dave Hall, replacing injured quarterback Steve Smith for Michigan in the second quarter, passed for 155 yards and two touchdowns.

In the Fiesta Bowl, No. 11 Arizona State, despite losing its last two regular season games, beat No. 12 Oklahoma 32–21 as quarterback Todd Hons passed for 329 yards and a touchdown, and kicker Luis Zendejas booted three field goals, including a 54-yarder. Freshman running back Marcus Dupree had 239 yards rushing for Oklahoma.

In other notable games involving ranked teams, No. 17 Ohio State rolled over WAC champion Brigham Young 47–17 in the Holiday Bowl as tailback Tim Spencer ran for 167 yards and two touchdowns. Quarterback Steve Young passed for 341 yards and two scores for BYU. The largest Tangerine Bowl crowd ever, 51,296, saw No. 18 Auburn come out a 33–26 winner over Boston College, making its first bowl appearance in forty years. Freshman running back Bo Jackson scored twice for Auburn. Boston College was led by sophomore quarterback Doug Flutie, who threw for 299 yards and two touchdowns, passed for a 2-point conversion, and scored on a 5-yard run. No. 8 Texas was upset by North Carolina 26–10 in the Sun Bowl, while Florida State upended No. 10 West Virginia, 31–12, in the Gator Bowl. And No. 14 Arkansas, the nation's scoring defense leader (10.5-point average), edged Florida 28–24 in the Bluebonnet Bowl as running back Gary Anderson had 161 yards and two touchdowns rushing.

Bear Bryant, who announced his retirement at the end of the 1982 season, made his last bowl appearance a winning one as Alabama beat Illinois 21–15 in the Liberty Bowl. Sophomore fullback Ricky Moore, split end Jesse Bendross, and fullback Craig Turner scored the 'Bama touchdowns on short runs. Bryant died less than a month later, leaving a coaching record of 323–85–17 at Maryland (1945), Kentucky (1946–1953), Texas A&M (1954–1957), and Alabama (1958–1982).

A record crowd of 75,000 turned out at Birmingham, Alabama, to see Air Force meet Vanderbilt in the Hall of Fame Classic. The Falcons overcame a 28–17 deficit in the fourth quarter to win 36–28 despite the efforts of Commodore quarterback Whit Taylor, who passed for 452 yards and four touchdowns, and tailback Norman Jordan, who had twenty pass receptions for 173 yards and three scores. Quarterback Marty Louthan passed for 136 yards and ran for two scores for Air Force.

The number of bowl games remained at sixteen when the defunct Garden State Bowl was replaced by the Aloha Bowl in Honolulu. The fans in Hawaii saw some excellent passing as No. 9 Washington pulled out a 21–20 victory over No. 16 Maryland in its first year under Bobby Ross. Huskies quarterback Tim Cowan passed for 350 yards and three touchdowns, all to wide receiver Anthony Allen, including a 71-yarder, while Maryland quarterback Norman "Boomer" Esaison passed for 251 yards, two touchdowns, and a 2-point conversion.

During the 1983 regular season, in its first unbeaten campaign since 1971, **1983** Big 8 champion Nebraska looked like one of the all-time great college football teams, scoring 624 points behind Heisman Trophy– and Maxwell Award–winning running back Mike Rozier for a nation-leading average of 52 points a game. When No. 1 Nebraska headed into its Orange Bowl date with No. 5 Miami, the only other major unbeaten team, No. 2 Texas, had fallen earlier in the day at the Cotton Bowl. Still, Miami's cocky young squad would be no pushover. The Hurricanes, in their last year under Howard Schnellenberger, won ten in a row after losing their opener to Florida 28–3, and would be playing on their home field in their first Orange Bowl appearance since 1950. The crowd watched in shock as Miami jumped to a 17–0 lead en route to a 31–17 margin heading into the fourth quarter. A furious Nebraska comeback fell just short when the Cornhuskers pulled within 31–30 with forty-eight seconds left in the final quarter—then failed on an attempt to win the game with a 2-point conversion pass when it was batted down by Miami defensive back Ken Calhoun. Freshman quarterback Bernie Kosar led the Miami attack with 300 yards and two touchdowns passing. Rozier had 147 yards rushing for the Cornhuskers, and quarterback Turner Gill passed for 172 yards and ran for a touchdown. Miami leapfrogged into the No. 1 position and its first national championship in the final wire service polls.

Because of the Orange Bowl result, undefeated Texas probably would have won the national championship with a win in the Cotton Bowl, but the Longhorns were upset 10–9 by No. 7 Georgia as Bulldogs quarterback John Lastinger scored on a 17-yard run with 3:22 remaining. Kicker Kevin Butler, who had a 43-yard field goal for Georgia in the first quarter, added the winning extra point. All of the Texas scoring came on three field goals by freshman kicker Jeff Ward.

In the Sugar Bowl, No. 3 ranked SEC champion Auburn nailed down the No. 3 spot in the final wire service rankings with a 9–7 win over No. 8 Michigan. Sophomore All-America running back Bo Jackson had 130 yards rushing for the Tigers and kicker Al Del Greco supplied the scoring with three field goals, including the 19-yard game winner with just twenty-three seconds left.

In Pasadena, unranked UCLA pulled off a shocking 45–9 upset of No. 4 Illinois. The Illini won ten straight after a season-opening loss to Missouri 28–18, but could do little against the Bruins. UCLA quarterback Rick Neuheisel passed for 298 yards and four touchdowns, two to sophomore wide receiver Karl Dorrell. The UCLA victory evened the Rose Bowl series with the Big 10 at 19–19 since the pact began in 1947.

The Fiesta Bowl had an exciting game in which No. 14 Ohio State pulled out a 28–23 win over No. 15 Pittsburgh. The Buckeyes scored one touchdown on Keith Byars's 99-yard kickoff return, but it was quarterback Mike Tomczak's 39-yard touchdown pass to split end Thad Jemison with thirty-nine seconds left that won the game. Pittsburgh freshman quarterback John Congemi passed for 341 yards and two touchdowns.

A good match-up was set in the Gator Bowl, where No. 11 Florida beat No. 10 Iowa 14–6 with the help of four pass interceptions. In other games involving ranked teams, No. 6 SMU was upset by unranked Alabama 28–7 in the Sun Bowl. No. 9 Brigham Young beat Missouri 21–17 in the Holiday Bowl as quarterback Steve Young passed for 314 yards and a touchdown, ran 10 yards for another score, and caught a 15-yard touchdown pass. A wild game in freezing weather in the Liberty Bowl saw Notre Dame come up with a 19–18 win over No. 13 Boston College, although quarterback Doug Flutie passed for 287 yards and three touchdowns for the Eagles. Tailback Allen Pinkett scored twice for the winners. No. 16 Air Force beat Mississippi, 9–3, in the Independence Bowl on three field goals by kicker Sean Pavlich. No. 18 West Virginia edged Kentucky 20–16 in the Hall of Fame contest as quarterback Jeff Hostetler passed for two touchdowns. And No. 20 Baylor lost to Oklahoma State 24–14 in the Bluebonnet Bowl.

The Tangerine Bowl changed its name to Florida Citrus Bowl to represent the Florida citrus industry for its 1983 contest. In the game, Tennessee upset ACC champion No. 16 Maryland 30–23. Tailback Johnnie Jones ran for 154 yards and two touchdowns for the Vols, while quarterback Alan Cockrell passed for 185 yards and another score. Maryland quarterback Frank Reich replaced injured starter Boomer Esiason in the second quarter and passed for 192 yards, and kicker Jess Atkinson had five field goals.

For the first time, average bowl payouts per game topped the $2 million mark. Corporation executives at this time, taking note of the newly named Florida Citrus Bowl, began looking at the possibility of bowl games as being a relatively cheap way to spread corporate names before the public in a highly visible way for weeks leading up to and through the bowl games.

Unbeaten Brigham Young, winner of its ninth straight WAC title in 1984, **1984** headed into the postseason with a No. 1 ranking primarily because the Cougars were the only undefeated Division I-A team in the nation. None of BYU's twelve opponents made the final top-twenty rankings, and the Cougars were not in one of the premier New Year's Day contests. Instead, because of WAC contractual obligations, BYU met unranked Michigan in the Holiday Bowl. Quarterback Robbie Boscoe suffered a severe ankle injury in the first quarter, but still led the Cougars to a 24–17 victory by passing for 343 yards and two touchdowns, including a 13-yarder to back Kelly Smith for the winning score with 1:23 left in the game. On the strength of its unbeaten record, BYU was awarded its first national championship in both final wire service polls.

In the Orange Bowl, No. 4 Washington earned a No. 2 finish in the final rankings with a 28–17 win over No. 2 Oklahoma as Huskies tailback Jacque Robinson ran for 135 yards and a touchdown against the nation's top-ranked rushing defense.

Earlier that day, No. 18 Southern California upset No. 6 Ohio State 20–17 in the Rose Bowl. Stadium capacity was reduced from nearly 106,000 to about 103,500 to widen the field for the 1984 Olympic soccer competition, resulting in a turnout of 102,594, the smallest in that bowl since 1969. USC quarterback Tim Green passed for 128 yards and two touchdowns and kicker Steve Jordan knocked through two 51-yard field goals. Despite giving up

109 yards rushing to All-America tailback Keith Byars, the nation's rushing and scoring leader, the USC defense kept him out of the end zone and forced the Buckeyes to settle for three field goals, including a 52-yarder by kicker Rich Spangler, to go with a single touchdown pass by quarterback Mike Tomczak, who had 290 yards passing on the day.

In the Sugar Bowl, No. 5 Nebraska, the nation's leader in scoring defense (9.5-point average) met No. 11 Louisiana State. Nebraska fell behind 10–0 early in the game, but rallied for a 28–10 victory as quarterback Craig Sundberg scored on a 9-yard touchdown run and passed for three more scores. Television revenue provided a payout for the two teams of more than $4.5 million.

No. 8 Boston College, the national scoring leader (36.7-point average), rolled up even more points in a 45–28 New Year's Day Cotton Bowl victory over Houston. Heisman Trophy– and Maxwell Award–winning quarterback Doug Flutie passed for 180 yards and three touchdowns for the Eagles, including a 63-yarder to sophomore wide receiver Kelvin Martin, while running back Troy Stradford had 196 yards and a touchdown rushing. Houston's scores included a 98-yard kickoff return by Earl Allen and a 25-yard pass interception return by defensive back Audrey McMillian. Boston College became the first Cotton Bowl participant to receive a $2 million payout.

In a game loaded with long scoring plays, No. 14 UCLA squeaked out a 39–37 win over No. 13 Miami in the Fiesta Bowl on a 19-yard field goal by kicker John Lee with fifty-one seconds left. Lee kicked three in the game, including a 51-yarder, while quarterback Steve Bono passed for 243 yards and two touchdowns, and freshman tailback Gaston Green ran for 144 yards and two scores, including a 72-yarder. For Miami, sophomore quarterback Bernie Kosar passed for 292 yards and two touchdowns, and All-America wide receiver Eddie Brown scored on a 68-yard punt return.

In the Gator Bowl, No. 9 Oklahoma State defeated No. 7 South Carolina, 21–14, as quarterback "Rusty" Hilger passed for 205 yards and the winning touchdown, a 25-yarder to tight end Barry Hanna with a minute left. Freshman tailback Thurman Thomas rushed for 155 yards and a score for the winners. In the Aloha Bowl, No. 10 Southern Methodist beat No. 17 Notre Dame 27–20 with a 10-point rally in the final quarter. No. 12 Maryland edged Tennessee 28–27 in the Sun Bowl, sparked by a 57-yard touchdown run by tailback Tommy Neal. No. 15 Florida State, trailing 14–0 at halftime, tied Georgia 17–17 in the Florida Citrus Bowl on a blocked punt return by Joe Wessel with 3:58 left in the game. No. 16 Auburn beat

Arkansas 21–15 in the Liberty Bowl as Tiger running back Bo Jackson scored two touchdowns. And No. 20 Wisconsin was edged by Kentucky 20–19 in the Hall of Fame Classic as sophomore tailback Marc Logan ran 9 yards for one Wildcat score and caught a 27-yard touchdown pass from quarterback Billy Ransdell for another.

Two new bowls were added in this postseason, the Cherry Bowl at Pontiac, Michigan, and the Freedom Bowl at Anaheim, California. Army, in its first winning season since 1977, made the first bowl appearance in its illustrious football history a successful one with a 10–6 win over Michigan State in the Cherry Bowl. Quarterback Nate Sassaman ran for 136 yards, and the Cadets turned two Spartan turnovers into a touchdown and a field goal. In the rainy Freedom Bowl, Iowa clobbered No. 19 Texas 55–17 as Chuck Long put on a passing clinic. The Iowa quarterback completed twenty-nine of thirty-nine passes with no interceptions for 461 yards and set an all-time bowl record with six touchdown tosses.

Three undefeated teams made it to postseason bowls in 1985 but only one, **1985** No. 1 Penn State, appeared in a New Year's Day contest. The largest Orange Bowl crowd in ten years was on hand to see Joe Paterno's fifth unbeaten Penn State team take on No. 3 Oklahoma. Penn State had won five straight bowl games. Sooner running back Lydell Carr had 148 yards rushing, including a 61-yard touchdown run, while freshman quarterback Jamelle Holieway threw a 71-yard touchdown pass to tight end Keith Jackson and kicker Tim Lashar added four field goals, as Oklahoma came away with a 25–10 win— and its sixth national title. The other two undefeated teams, No. 20 Bowling Green and Fresno State, met in the California Bowl, but it was no contest. Fresno State rolled to a 51–7 victory as quarterback Kevin Sweeney threw three touchdown passes and freshman tailback Kelly Skipper ran for two more scores.

No. 2 Miami had a chance to win the national title by beating SEC champion Tennessee in the Sugar Bowl. But the Volunteers crushed the Hurricanes' title hopes with a 35–7 victory despite the efforts of Miami quarterback Vinny Testaverde, who passed for 217 yards and a touchdown. Tennessee touchdowns included a 60-yard run by Jeff Powell and a 6-yard pass from quarterback Daryl Dickey to Jeff Smith.

Shortly after the beginning of the 1985 regular season, on September 26, Sunkist Growers signed a five-year multimillion dollar agreement with the Fiesta Bowl to sponsor a Sunkist Fiesta Bowl game and a Sunkist Fiesta Bowl parade, marking the first title sponsorship of a college football bowl game since the Bacardi Bowl in 1937. The sponsorship allowed the Fiesta Bowl to enter truly major status by increasing its payout to more than $1 million for each team participating. The success of this venture was a harbinger of the trend of corporate sponsorship that would flood the sport in the following years. And for the colleges and universities, it would not be long before huge bowl payouts became an integral part of budget planning for their athletic programs—putting significant pressure on coaches and administrators to make sure their programs provided consistent bowl participants.

The Sunkist Fiesta Bowl title was in effect for the New Year's contest, in which more than 72,000 turned out to see No. 5 Michigan, the nation's leader in scoring defense (6.8-point average), take on No. 7 Nebraska. Running back Jamie Morris had 156 yards rushing and quarterback Jim Harbaugh scored two touchdowns on short runs, as the Wolverines won, 27–23. Cornhusker running back Doug DuBose had 99 yards and a touchdown rushing and caught a 5-yard scoring pass. Michigan finished No. 2 in the final wire service polls.

In the Rose Bowl, No. 13 UCLA came up with a 45–28 upset of No. 4 Iowa. Two players filling in for injured regulars were keys to the UCLA victory. Freshman tailback Eric Ball, replacing regular Gaston Green, had 227 yards and four touchdowns rushing, and quarterback Matt Stevens, replacing regular David Norris, passed for 189 yards and a score and ran for another. Leading Iowa was Maxwell Award winning quarterback Chuck Long, who passed for 319 yards and a touchdown and scored on a 4-yard run.

In the Cotton Bowl, No. 11 Texas A&M, making its first Cotton Bowl appearance in eighteen years, faced No. 16 Auburn. The Aggies won easily, 36–16, as quarterback Kevin Murray passed for 292 yards and a touchdown, fullback Anthony Toney scored twice, and sophomore halfback Keith Woodside caught a touchdown pass and scored on a 22-yard run. Heisman Trophy–winning running back Bo Jackson ran for 129 yards and scored both Tiger touchdowns, one rushing and the other on a 73-yard pass from quarterback Pat Washington.

The Florida Citrus Bowl matched No. 9 Brigham Young against No. 17 Ohio State. The Buckeyes came up with six turnovers and edged the Cougars 10–7. Middle guard Larry Kolic scored the Ohio State touchdown on a 14-yard pass interception return, and kicker Rich Spangler provided the winning margin with a 47-yard field goal. Another match-up of strong teams took place in the Gator Bowl as No. 15 Florida State beat No. 19 Oklahoma State 34–23 as Seminole freshman quarterback Chip Ferguson passed for 338 yards and two touchdowns and scored another himself.

In other bowl games involving ranked teams, No. 10 Air Force beat Texas 24–16 in the Bluebonnet Bowl, No. 12 Louisiana State was upset by Baylor 21–7 in the Liberty Bowl, and No. 14 Arkansas edged Arizona State 18–17 in the Holiday Bowl on a 37-yard field goal by freshman kicker Kendall Trainor with 21 seconds left. No. 15 Alabama beat Southern California 24–3 in the Aloha Bowl, and No. 20 Maryland beat Syracuse 35–18 in the final Cherry Bowl as quarterback Stan Gelbaugh passed for 223 yards and two touchdowns and scored on a 4-yard run.

An all-time Sun Bowl record crowd of 52,203 turned out to see Georgia meet Arizona. The two battled to a 13–13 tie, highlighted by a 52-yard field goal by Arizona kicker Max Zendejas and a 44-yard field goal by Georgia kicker Davis Jacobs.

Only two major teams finished the 1986 season undefeated: No. 1 Miami, **1986** 11–0 in its first unbeaten season since 1950, and No. 2 Penn State, 11–0. Because both teams were independents at the time—and not obligated to any bowl by conference tie-ins—the Sunkist Fiesta Bowl, with the support of NBC Sports, was able to match the two for a true "national championship" contest by doubling its payout ($2.4 million to each team) and moving the game to prime time on Thursday, January 2. It was the first meeting of independents ranked No. 1 and No. 2 since the famous Army–Notre Dame contest in November 1946. Miami, which averaged 38 points a game behind Heisman Trophy– and Maxwell Award–winning quarterback Vinny Testaverde, was the clear favorite. But before a huge Fiesta Bowl crowd, the Nittany Lions came up with five pass interceptions—including one by Pete Giftopoulos in the final seconds of the game—in a 14–10 victory that gave Penn State its second national championship. Penn State's scores came on a 4-yard run by quarterback John Shaffer and a 6-yard run by All-America running back D. J. Dozier. Testaverde passed for 285 yards and tailback Alonzo Highsmith had 119 yards rushing in a losing effort. More than 52 million people watched that Fiesta Bowl contest on television, making it the most-watched college football game of all time.

There were still five bowl games on New Year's, as the Florida Citrus Bowl moved to a January 1 playing date, joining the Rose, Orange, Sugar, and

1986 Rose Bowl—Freshman Eric Ball (21) of UCLA, playing because the starting tail-back was injured, ran for 227 yards and four touchdowns to lead the Bruins to an upset victory over Iowa. (*Pasadena Tournament of Roses*)

Cotton bowls. Although the Orange Bowl was widely watched on television, only 52,717, the smallest crowd since 1947, showed up despite the presence of a powerful Oklahoma team. The No. 3 Sooners rolled over No. 9 Arkansas 42–8. Running back Spencer Tillman scored Sooner touchdowns on runs of 77 and 21 yards, while sophomore quarterback Jamelle Holieway scored twice on short runs.

The Rose Bowl matched No. 7 Arizona State against No. 4 Michigan. The Sun Devils dropped behind 15–3 early in the contest, but came back for a 22–15 victory. Quarterback Jeff Van Raaphorst passed for 193 yards and two short touchdown tosses to flanker Bruce Hill for Arizona State, while kicker Kent Bostrom added three field goals. For Michigan, quarterback Jim Harbaugh scored on a 2-yard run and running back Jamie Morris scored on an 18-yard run. In the Sugar Bowl, in the first of two straight afternoon games for that bowl, No. 6 Nebraska met No. 5 Louisiana State. Husker quarterback Steve Taylor passed for a touchdown and scored on a 2-yard run, and sophomore running back Tyreese Knox ran for two touchdowns in Nebraska's 30–15 victory. The first Big 10 team to appear in the Cotton Bowl, No. 11 Ohio State, faced Texas A&M. Ohio State intercepted five passes, returning two for touchdowns, one of 24 yards by All-America linebacker Chris Spielman and another of 49 yards by linebacker Michael Kee in a 28-12 Buckeye win.

No. 10 Auburn beat unranked Southern California 16–7 in the Florida Citrus Bowl. All-America tailback Brent Fullwood ran for 152 yards and a touchdown for Auburn. USC's only score came on a 24-yard pass interception return by linebacker Marcus Cotton. Two other bowls took on sponsor names this postseason: the Mazda Gator Bowl at Jacksonville, Florida, and the Sea World Holiday Bowl at San Diego, California. No. 20 Stanford was upset by ACC champion Clemson 27–21 in the Gator Bowl after the Cardinal dropped behind 27–0 by halftime. No. 19 Iowa edged San Diego State 39–38 in the Holiday Bowl on a successful 41-yard field goal by kicker Rob Houghtlin in the game's last minute.

In other games involving ranked teams, the Sun Bowl matched No. 12 Washington and No. 13 Alabama. The Crimson Tide won 28–6 as sophomore halfback Bobby Humphrey ran for 159 yards and two touchdowns and caught an 18-yard scoring pass from quarterback Mike Shula. In the Aloha Bowl, No. 16 Arizona beat North Carolina 30–21 for its first postseason win in six tries. An all-time Freedom Bowl record crowd of 55,422 saw No. 15 UCLA take its fifth straight bowl victory with a 31–10 win over Brigham Young. Bruin tailback Gaston Green ran for 266 yards and three touchdowns, including a 79-yarder, and passed for another score, a 13-yard toss to wide receiver Karl Dorrell. No. 14 Baylor beat Colorado 21–9 in the Bluebonnet Bowl as Derrick McAdoo ran for two touchdowns. An exciting Peach Bowl game saw Virginia Tech edge No. 18 North Carolina State 25–24 as sophomore kicker Chris Kinzer booted a 40-yard field goal on the last play of the game.

The total of postseason games remained at eighteen with the addition of the Hall of Fame Bowl at Tampa, Florida, offsetting the absence of the Cherry Bowl. The old Hall of Fame Classic at Birmingham, Alabama, changed its name that year to the All-American Bowl, with Florida State beating Indiana 27–13. Freshman tailback Sammie Smith had 205 yards and two touchdowns rushing for the Seminoles. Freshman running back Anthony Thompson had 127 yards rushing for Indiana. The new Hall of Fame Bowl was a thriller, with Boston College edging No. 17 Georgia 27–24. Leading the Eagles to victory was quarterback Shawn Halloran, who threw for 242 yards and two touchdowns, including the winning 5-yard toss to wide receiver Kelvin Martin with thirty–two seconds left in the game.

Following the 1987 season, unbeaten Miami participated in what turned out **1987** to be the national championship game for the second year in a row, but this time the Hurricanes went in as the No. 2 team. Miami was invited to the Orange Bowl to face unbeaten No. 1 Oklahoma, the nation's leader in both scoring (43.5-point average) and scoring defense (7.5 points per game). In a driving rain, Miami quarterback Steve Walsh passed for 209 yards and two touchdowns—30 yards to running back Melvin Bratton and 23 yards to wide receiver Michael Irvin—and kicker Greg Cox added field goals of 56 and 48 yards. Oklahoma scored on a 1-yard run by halfback Anthony Stafford and a 29-yard "fumblerooskie" run by offensive guard Mark Hutson. The latter was a trick play allowable at the time in which the center pretends to snap the ball but actually leaves it on the ground in front of the quarterback and, during the scramble along the line of scrimmage, another lineman picks up the ball and heads for the goal line. Despite the trick play, Miami upset the Sooners, 20–14, to gain its second national championship. Miami gave Oklahoma its only regular-season defeats in 1985 and 1986, and the string continued in postseason 1987. The game was one of six played on New Year's, with two others, the Peach and Hall of Fame, following on January 2. This postseason also saw additional sponsor names added, the list now including the USF&G Sugar and the John Hancock Sun bowls.

The only unbeaten team in postseason play other than Miami and Oklahoma was No. 4 Syracuse, in its first undefeated season since 1959. The Orangemen, who had only one close game—a 32–31 win over West Virginia in the season finale—met No. 6 Auburn in the USF&G Sugar Bowl. Auburn quarterback Jeff Burger passed for 171 yards and a 17-yard touchdown to wide receiver Lawyer Tillman. Maxwell Award–winning quarterback Don McPherson passed for 140 yards and a 12-yard score to wide receiver Deval Glover for Syracuse, and kicker Tim Vesling added three field goals and an extra point. The game ended in a 16–16 tie when Auburn kicker Win Lyle, who earlier had kicked field goals of 40 and 41 yards, booted a 30-yarder with one second left.

No. 3 Florida State defeated No. 5 Nebraska, 31–28, in the Sunkist Fiesta Bowl. Quarterback Danny McManus passed for 375 yards and three touchdowns for the Seminoles, while Nebraska quarterback Steve Taylor and running back Keith Jones each ran for touchdowns, and wingback Dana Brinson scored on a 52-yard punt return.

During 1987, the Rose Bowl, site of Olympic events in 1932 and 1984, was placed on the National Register of Historic Places by the National Park Service and the U.S. Department of the Interior. That year's postseason bowl saw No. 8 Michigan State face No. 16 Southern California, a team the Spartans had defeated 27–13 in regular season. The contest was the first Rose Bowl covered by a live Spanish-language broadcast. Michigan State made it a sweep of the Trojans with a 20–17 victory behind All-America tailback Lorenzo White, who rushed for 113 yards and two touchdowns. Quarterback Rodney Peete passed for 249 yards and two touchdowns for USC, but the Trojans had five turnovers.

In the Cotton Bowl, No. 13 ranked Southwest Conference champion Texas A&M buried No. 12 Notre Dame 35–10 with a freshman onslaught. Quarterback John "Bucky" Richardson ran for 96 yards and two scores, running back Darren Lewis threw a touchdown pass, and Larry Horton scored on a 2-yard run—freshmen all. Notre Dame quarterback Terry Andrysiak passed for 203 yards and a 17-yard touchdown, to Heisman Trophy–winning split end Tim Brown, who had six pass receptions for 105 yards. And in the Florida Citrus Bowl, No. 14 Clemson beat No. 20 Penn State 35–10 as fullback Tracy Johnson scored three touchdowns for the winners.

Only 23,282—by far the smallest crowd in Bluebonnet Bowl history—turned out on New Year's Eve for the final contest of a bowl that dated to 1959, but they saw a thriller as Texas upset No. 19 Pittsburgh 32–27. Quarterback Bret Stafford passed for 368 yards and two touchdowns, 77 and 60 yards to sophomore wide receiver Tony Jones, for the Longhorns. Pittsburgh was led by reserve quarterback Larry Wanke, who threw for three touchdowns, and All-America fullback Craig "Ironhead" Heyward, who rushed for 136 yards and a score. The Mazda Gator Bowl that same day matched two top teams in No. 7 Louisiana State and No. 9 South Carolina. LSU won easily, 30–13, to keep the Gamecocks winless in seven bowl appearances as Tiger quarterback Tommy Hodson passed for 224 yards and three touchdowns, all to wide receiver Wendell Davis.

In other bowls involving ranked teams, No. 11 Oklahoma State edged West Virginia 35–33 on a rare snowy Christmas Day in El Paso's John Hancock Sun Bowl. Running back Thurman Thomas had 157 yards and four touchdowns rushing for the winners. No. 10 UCLA got by Florida 20–16 in the Aloha Bowl as quarterback Troy Aikman, who would be the first pick in the 1989 NFL draft and go on to an outstanding career with the Dallas Cowboys, passed for 173 yards and a touchdown. In the Liberty Bowl, No. 15 Georgia beat Arkansas 20–17 on a 39-yard field goal by freshman kicker John Kasay on the last play of the game. In the Sea World Holiday Bowl, No. 18

Iowa edged Wyoming 20–19. In the Peach Bowl, No. 17 Tennessee beat Indiana 27–22 as freshman running back Reggie Cobbs had 146 yards and two touchdowns rushing for the Vols.

1988 Following the 1988 regular season, most attention was on the Sunkist Fiesta Bowl and the Federal Express Orange Bowl. The Fiesta Bowl matched the only teams to make it through the season undefeated, No. 1 Notre Dame in its first unbeaten season since 1973, and No. 3 West Virginia, winner of its first Lambert Trophy in its first unbeaten season since 1922. The Orange Bowl matched two other teams with a chance at the national championship, No. 2 Miami, loser only to Notre Dame 31–30 in Jimmy Johnson's last year as coach, and No. 6 Nebraska.

Irish quarterback Tony Rice passed for 213 yards and two touchdowns, including a 29-yarder to freshman split end Raghib "Rocket" Ismail, while fullbacks Anthony Johnson and Rodney Culver each scored on short runs as Notre Dame clinched its thirteenth national title by beating West Virginia 34–21. West Virginia's offense was hampered by early injuries to sophomore quarterback Major Harris and two offensive linemen. In the Orange Bowl, Miami held Nebraska to 135 yards of total offense and beat the Cornhuskers 23–3 to finish No. 2 in the final national polls. All-America quarterback Steve Walsh led the Hurricanes, passing for 277 yards and two touchdowns to sophomore halfback Leonard Conley, and freshman kicker Carlos Huerta added three field goals.

The smallest Sugar Bowl crowd since 1939 saw No. 4 Florida State win a 13–7 defensive battle with No. 7 Auburn, the nation's leader in scoring defense (7.2-point average). Leading the Seminoles to victory were fullback Dayne Williams, who scored on a short run, sophomore kicker Bill Mason with two field goals, and All-America defensive back Deion Sanders, who intercepted an Auburn pass in the end zone on the game's final play. Despite the modest turnout, the payout for the two teams reached a Sugar Bowl high at the time of $6 million. (Bowl payouts reached an average of $3,112,084 per game in this postseason period.) The game also marked the return of that bowl to night contests for the indefinite future.

In the Rose Bowl, No. 11 Michigan squared off with No. 5 Southern California. USC took a 14–3 halftime lead behind quarterback Rodney Peete's two short touchdown runs, but lost the ball five times in the game. Michigan came back behind sophomore fullback Leroy Hoard, who rushed for 142 yards and two touchdowns, and quarterback Demetrius Brown, who passed for 144 yards and a score to pull off a 22–14 upset.

The newly named Mobil Cotton Bowl saw No. 9 UCLA come up with a 17–3 win over No. 8 Arkansas. Quarterback Troy Aikman passed for 172 yards and a touchdown for the Bruins, while freshman tailback Shawn Wills rushed for 120 yards. Arkansas All-America kicker Kendall Trainor had a 49-yard field goal and linebacker LaSalle Harper had twenty tackles, a pass interception, and a fumble recovery in a losing effort. Arkansas Coach Ken Hatfield became the first person to appear in the Cotton Bowl as both player and head coach.

The Mazda Gator Bowl was the only bowl played on Sunday, January 1— the bowl's first non-December playing date since 1971. No. 19 Georgia beat Michigan State 34–27 in Georgia Coach Vince Dooley's last game as quarterback Wayne Johnson passed for 227 yards and three touchdowns, two to tailback Rodney Hampton, who also scored on a 32-yard run.

In other postseason games involving ranked teams, No. 13 Clemson upset No. 10 Oklahoma, Barry Switzer's last team, 13–6 in the Florida Citrus Bowl. In the Hall of Fame game, No. 17 Syracuse beat No. 16 Louisiana State 23–10 as running back Robert Drummond had 122 yards and two touchdowns rushing. No. 20 Alabama beat Army 29–28 in a thrilling John Hancock Sun Bowl. Quarterback David Smith passed for 412 yards and two touchdowns, and kicker Philip Doyle had three field goals for the Crimson Tide, while fullback Ben Barnett had 177 yards rushing and defensive back O'Neal Miller scored on a 57-yard pass interception return for Army. Another great game, the Aloha Bowl, saw No. 18 Washington State upset No. 14 Houston 24–22 as quarterback Timm Rosenbach passed for 306 yards and a touchdown and scored on a 1-yard run for the winners. In the Sea World Holiday Bowl, No. 12 Oklahoma State, the nation's scoring leader with an average of 47.5 points, crushed No. 15 Wyoming 62–14 as Heisman Trophy– and Maxwell Award–winning tailback Barry Sanders, a future NFL record setter, ran for 222 yards and five touchdowns.

No. 1 Colorado, winner of its third Big 8 title in its first unbeaten season since 1937, entered 1989 postseason play as the only undefeated Division I-A team, but seven once-beaten teams also played on New Year's Day, hoping for a shot at the national championship. Colorado faced a tough Federal Express Orange Bowl opponent in No. 4 Notre Dame. Fighting Irish sopho-

1989

more split end Rocket Ismail ran for 108 yards, including a 35-yard touchdown run, and fullback Anthony Johnson scored twice on short runs to dash Colorado's chance at a national title, 21–6. With this game, the Orange Bowl payout reached $4 million per team. Bowls that still had at-large berths had to be prepared to offer competitive payouts with other bowls, as schools by now normally considered the best financial deal, as well as other factors, before accepting a bowl bid. Corporate sponsorship could make a difference in this area.

No. 2 Miami, the nation's scoring defense leader (9.3-point average) in its first year under Dennis Erickson, took advantage of Colorado's loss to seize its third national title with a 33–25 win over No. 7 Alabama in the USF&G Sugar Bowl. Quarterback Craig Erickson led the Hurricanes to victory, passing for 250 yards and three touchdowns, while freshman fullback Steve McGuire and running back Alex Johnson each scored on short runs. Crimson Tide quarterback Gary Hollingsworth passed for 214 yards and three touchdowns.

No. 5 Florida State was matched with No. 6 Nebraska in the Sunkist Fiesta Bowl. And the Seminoles went on to end Nebraska's national title hopes with a 41–17 pounding of the Huskers as quarterback Peter Tom Willis passed for 422 yards and five touchdowns, including two each to wide receiver Terry Anthony and to Reggie Johnson.

No. 3 Michigan's national title hopes ended in the Rose Bowl with a 17–10 loss to No. 12 Southern California. Tailback Ricky Ervins, whose hometown was Pasadena, added special drama to the game when he ran 14 yards for the winning score with 1:10 remaining. Ervins gained 126 yards rushing in the game, while freshman quarterback Todd Marinovich passed for 178 yards and scored a touchdown for USC.

The Mobil Cotton Bowl matched No. 8 Tennessee and No. 10 Arkansas. The Volunteers won 31–27 as freshman running back Chuck Webb ran for 250 yards and two touchdowns, including a 78-yard scoring run, while sophomore quarterback Andy Kelly threw for two touchdowns, including an 84-yarder to wide receiver Anthony Morgan. For the Razorbacks, quarterback Quinn Grovey passed for 207 yards and a touchdown, 67 yards to tight end Billy Winston, while halfback James Rouse ran for 134 yards and a score.

In other games, No. 11 Illinois had a 31–21 victory over No. 15 Virginia in the Florida Citrus Bowl as Illini quarterback Jeff George passed for 321 yards and three touchdowns. And in the Hall of Fame game, No. 9 Auburn

1988 Holiday Bowl—Heisman Trophy winning tailback Barry Sanders (21) of Oklahoma State picks up some of his 222 yards rushing in a December 30 battle of Cowboys. Sanders also scored five touchdowns as Oklahoma State crushed Wyoming. (*Collegiate Images*)

rolled over No. 21 Ohio State 31–14 as quarterback Reggie Slack passed for three touchdowns and scored on a 5-yard run.

An all-time record Mazda Gator Bowl crowd of 82,911 turned out on December 30 to see Danny Ford's last Clemson team, ranked No. 14, meet No. 17 West Virginia. The Tigers intercepted three passes and defeated the Mountaineers 27–7, breaking open a close game with 17 points in the fourth quarter. West Virginia scored first on a 12-yard pass from quarterback Major Harris to freshman wide receiver James Jett, but Clemson came back behind tailback Joe Henderson, who rushed for 92 yards and a touchdown, and freshman defensive tackle Chester McGlockton, who recovered a fumble in end zone for a score.

The Aloha Bowl also had an all-time record crowd, as 50,000 came out to see hometown Hawaii, ranked No. 23, make its first major bowl appearance against Michigan State. (In 1989 the AP poll began selecting the top twenty-five teams, rather than just the top twenty as in previous years.) The apparently nervous Rainbow Warriors turned the ball over eight times and lost to the Spartans 33–13. Michigan State was led by tailback Blake Ezor, who ran for 179 yards and three touchdowns.

In other postseason games involving ranked teams, No. 25 Texas Tech upset No. 20 Duke 49–21 in the All-American Bowl. In Duke's first postseason game in nearly thirty years, Steve Spurrier's last Blue Devil team turned the ball over four times to offset sophomore quarterback David Brown's 268 yards and three touchdowns passing. Running back James Gray had 280 yards and four touchdowns rushing for the winners. A wild game in the Sea World Holiday Bowl saw No. 18 Penn State beat No. 19 Brigham Young 50–39 as quarterback Tony Sacca passed for 206 yards and two touchdowns, linebacker Andre Collins scored a 2-pointer on a 100-yard intercepted conversion play, and Gary Brown scored on a 53-yard fumble return. Quarterback Ty Detmer passed for 576 yards and two scores for BYU and scored two touchdowns on short runs. And No. 16 Texas A&M was upset by No. 24 Pittsburgh 31–28 in the John Hancock Bowl (the first of five straight years in which the Sun Bowl used only its corporate name), as Panther freshman quarterback Alex Van Pelt passed for 354 yards and two touchdowns and scored on a 1-yard run.

The number of postseason games returned to eighteen with the addition of the Copper Bowl at Tucson, Arizona. Arizona's 17–10 victory over North Carolina State was highlighted by an 85-yard pass interception return for a score by Wildcat defensive back Scott Geyer.

1990 Five teams held the No. 1 spot in the Associated Press poll during the 1990 season, with Big 8 champion Colorado—despite an early 23–22 loss to Illinois and a 31–31 tie with Tennessee—holding the position for the last three weeks heading into postseason play. The Buffaloes faced No. 5 Notre Dame in the Federal Express Orange Bowl. Colorado needed a bit of help to come out a 10–9 winner and break a seven-bowl losing string. Ahead by one point late in the final quarter, Colorado was forced to punt. Irish speedster Rocket Ismail, an All-America wide receiver, fielded the punt and raced 91 yards for an apparent touchdown—but officials flagged Notre Dame for a clip, nullifying the score, and Colorado held on to win. The Buffaloes were led by All-America running back Eric Bieniemy, who rushed for 86 yards and a touchdown, and kicker Jim Harper with a 22-yard field goal and an extra point. In the final AP poll on January 2, sportswriters and broadcasters awarded Colorado its first national title.

No. 2 Georgia Tech came away with the UPI share of the national championship, their third, however, following a 45–21 win over No. 19 Nebraska in the Florida Citrus Bowl. Georgia Tech quarterback Shawn Jones scored on a 1-yard run and passed for 277 yards and two touchdowns, while sophomore running back William Bell, who caught one of the scoring passes, also scored on runs of 6 and 57 yards. The UPI board of coaches awarded Georgia Tech the national title by one point, 847–846—the first time the wire service polls declared different champions since Southern California and Alabama shared the title in 1978.

In another major game, No. 4 Miami nailed down the No. 3 spot in the final polls with a 46–3 trouncing of No. 3 Texas in the Mobil Cotton Bowl. Miami quarterback Craig Erickson passed for 272 yards and four touchdowns (two to wide receiver Wesley Carroll), sophomore linebacker Darrin Smith scored on a 34-yard pass interception return, and halfback Leonard Conley ran 26 yards for a touchdown.

In the Rose Bowl, No. 8 Washington jumped to a 33–7 halftime lead and went on to a 46–34 win over No. 17 Iowa. Huskies quarterback Mark Brunell passed for two touchdowns, both to split end Mario Bailey, and scored on runs of 5 and 20 yards, while defensive back Charles Mincy returned a pass interception 37 yards for a touchdown, and defensive back Dana Hall scored on a 27-yard return of a blocked punt.

In the Sugar Bowl, No. 10 Tennessee fell behind unranked Virginia 16–0 at halftime, but came back to beat the Cavaliers 23–22. Volunteer tailback Tony Thompson rushed for 151 yards and two touchdowns, including the winning score on a 1-yard plunge with thirty-one seconds left.

Quarterback Browning Nagle passed for 451 yards and three touchdowns to lead No. 18 Louisville to a 34–7 win over No. 25 Alabama in the Fiesta Bowl. Alabama's only score came on a 49-yard pass interception return by defensive back Charles Gardner.

In other games, No. 12 Michigan beat No. 15 Mississippi 35–3 in the Mazda Gator Bowl as quarterback Elvis Grbac passed for 296 yards and four touchdowns, including tosses of 63 and 50 yards to sophomore wide receiver Desmond Howard. And in the Hall of Fame contest, No. 14 Clemson shut out No. 16 Illinois 30–0 behind quarterback DeChane Cameron's two touchdown passes, defensive back Arlington Nunn's touchdown on a 34-yard pass interception return, and a stout defense that had led the nation in total defense during the regular season.

No. 21 Southern California and No. 22 Michigan State met in the John Hancock Bowl, with the Spartans eking out a 17–16 victory. Quarterback Dan

Enos passed for one score, tailback Hyland Hickson scored on an 18-yard run, and kicker John Langeloh had a 52-yard field goal for the winners.

Several ranked teams were upset in this postseason. No. 25 Ohio State lost to Air Force 23–11 in the Liberty Bowl as Falcon quarterback Rob Perez ran for two touchdowns and sophomore defensive back Carlton McDonald scored on a 40-yard pass interception return. No. 23 Southern Mississippi lost 31–27 to North Carolina State in the All-American Bowl despite an impressive performance by quarterback Brett Favre, a future All-Pro who passed for 341 yards and two touchdowns. Sophomore quarterback Terry Jordan passed for a touchdown and scored on a 10-yard run for the winners. Another upset was Texas A&M's crushing win, 65–14, over No. 13 Brigham Young in the Sea World Holiday Bowl. Aggie quarterback "Bucky" Richardson passed for 203 yards and a touchdown, had 119 yards and two touchdowns rushing, and caught a 22-yard scoring pass.

The number of bowls reached nineteen with the addition of the Blockbuster Bowl at Miami. The inaugural game drew more than 74,000 fans to see No. 6 Florida State and No. 7 Penn State. The Seminoles blocked a field goal attempt and intercepted three passes in a 24–17 win as quarterback Casey Weldon passed for 248 yards and ran for a touchdown, and running back Amp Lee scored twice on the ground. Penn State scored on two long passes, 56 yards from quarterback Tony Sacca to wide receiver David Daniels, and 37 yards from quarterback Tom Bill to wide receiver Terry Smith.

1991   Two Division I-A schools made it through the 1991 season unbeaten, and for the second year in a row the national championship was shared when both won their bowl games. No. 1 Miami led the nation in scoring defense (9.1-point average) and won the inaugural football title in the Big East, a conference that included Pittsburgh, West Virginia, Virginia Tech, and Syracuse. The closest the Hurricanes came to defeat was a 17–16 win over Florida State, when a 34-yard field goal attempt by the Seminoles with twenty-five seconds left sailed wide right. No. 2 Washington won its fourth Pac-10 championship in its first unbeaten season since 1943. At the time, no "championship" contest could be set up between Washington and Miami, even if desired by both schools, because the Huskies and a Big 10 representative were committed to the Rose Bowl by the Pac-10/Big 10 pact.

Washington completed its perfect season with a 34–14 win over No. 4 Big 10 champion Michigan. The Huskies were sparked by sophomore quarterback Billy Joe Hobert, who ran for one score and passed for two touchdowns and a two-point conversion. Quarterback Elvis Grbac, the nation's passing efficiency leader, threw for 130 yards and a touchdown for Michigan, and freshman running back Tyrone Wheatley scored on a 53-yard run, but Heisman Trophy– and Maxwell Award–winning wide receiver Desmond Howard was held to just one pass reception. *USA Today*/ESPN, which took over the coaches' poll from UPI during the regular season, placed Washington No. 1 in its final poll, giving the Huskies their first national title.

On a rainy night in the Federal Express Orange Bowl, Miami also completed its perfect season with a 22–0 win over No. 11 Nebraska, holding the Cornhuskers to 80 yards of total offense and handing them their first shutout since 1973. Miami's offense was led by quarterback Gino Torretta, who passed for 257 yards and a touchdown, freshman fullback Larry Jones, who ran for 144 yards and a score, and All-America kicker Carlos Huerta, who booted three field goals, including a 54-yarder. The win earned the Hurricanes the No. 1 spot in the AP poll, their fourth national title.

In the Fiesta Bowl, No. 6 Penn State, winner of its third straight Lambert Trophy, earned the No. 3 spot in the final polls with a 42–17 win over No. 10 Tennessee. The Nittany Lions trailed 17–7 in the third quarter before breaking the game open and ending Tennessee's five-bowl winning string. Penn State quarterback Tony Sacca passed for 150 yards and four touchdowns, and linebacker Reggie Givens scored on a 23-yard fumble return.

After trailing 16–7 at halftime, No. 18 Notre Dame came up with a 39–28 upset of No. 3 Florida in the USF&G Sugar Bowl. The Fighting Irish were led by sophomore fullback Jerome Bettis, who rushed for 150 yards and three touchdowns, and quarterback Rick Mirer, who passed for 154 yards and two more scores. Quarterback Shane Matthews passed for 370 yards and two touchdowns for the Gators, and kicker Arden Czyzewski made five field goals.

In a rainy, cold Mobil Cotton Bowl, No. 5 Florida State overcame four pass interceptions with six fumble recoveries for a 10–2 win over No. 9 Texas A&M. Seminoles quarterback Casey Weldon scored the only touchdown of the game on a 4-yard run, while the Aggies scored in the first quarter when linebacker Quentin Coryatt tackled Weldon in the end zone for a safety. Sophomore tailback Sean Jackson had 119 yards rushing for the winners.

In other contests, No. 12 East Carolina trailed 34–17 in the final quarter but edged No. 21 North Carolina State 37–34 in the Peach Bowl. Pirate quarterback Jeff Blake passed for 378 yards and four touchdowns, including a 22-yarder to tight end Luke Fisher for the winning score, and ran for another. In the Florida Citrus Bowl, No. 14 California broke a five-bowl winning string by No. 13 Clemson with a 37–13 victory, while in the Hall of Fame game, No. 16 Syracuse beat No. 25 Ohio State 24–17 behind quarterback Marvin Graves, who passed for 309 yards and two touchdowns.

Bobby Ross's last Georgia Tech team upset No. 17 Stanford 18–17 in the Aloha Bowl as quarterback Shawn Jones scored the winning touchdown on a 1-yard run with fourteen seconds remaining. No. 8 Alabama beat No. 15 Colorado 30–25 in the Blockbuster Bowl as quarterback Jay Barker passed for three touchdowns, including one to freshman flanker David Palmer, who also scored on a 52-yard punt return. In the Gator Bowl, No. 20 Oklahoma rolled over No. 19 Virginia, 48–14, as sophomore quarterback Cale Gundy passed for 329 yards and two touchdowns and tailback Mike Gaddis ran for three scores. In the Poulan/Weed Eater Independence Bowl, No. 24 Georgia beat Arkansas 24–15 behind freshman quarterback Eric Zeier, who passed for 228 yards and two touchdowns. In the Thrifty Car Rental Holiday Bowl, No. 7 Iowa tied Brigham Young 13–13 as running back Mike Saunders ran for both Hawkeye touchdowns and Quarterback Ty Detmer passed for 350 yards and both scores for the Cougars.

In the Freedom Bowl, No. 23 Tulsa beat San Diego State 28–17 behind tailback Ron Jackson, who ran for 211 yards and all four Tulsa touchdowns. And in the John Hancock Bowl, No. 22 UCLA won a defensive game over Illinois 6–3 on two field goals by kicker Louis Perez. An all-time Liberty Bowl record crowd of 61,497 was on hand to see Air Force beat Mississippi State 38–15, sparked by quarterback Rob Perez, who ran for 114 yards and a touchdown, defensive back Shannon Yates, who scored on a 35-yard fumble return, and linebacker Vergil Simpson, who recovered a fumble in end zone for 6 points. The final California Bowl also had an all-time record crowd, 34,825, as Bowling Green met Fresno State, the nation's scoring leader (44.2-point average). Bowling Green won 28–21, snapping Fresno State's five-bowl winning string.

1992   Discussion of the possibility of a playoff system to determine the national football champion among Division I-A members was widespread enough by the 1990s that bowl organizers and sponsors began to see it as a threat that might destroy the bowl system that had gradually developed over the preceding fifty years. NCAA Division II and III schools had begun a playoff system for the national championship in 1973, and Division I-AA began playoffs in 1978 when schools in that classification split from Division I-A status. Thus, four of the major bowls—the Orange, Sugar, Cotton, and Fiesta—agreed in 1992 to form a Bowl Coalition aimed at staging a national championship game between the teams ranked No. 1 and No. 2 in the AP and *USA Today*/ESPN polls at the end of the regular season. Even with the Rose Bowl still tied into the agreements with the Big 10 and Pacific-10, the new system worked well enough the first year when No. 1 Miami and No. 2 Alabama were selected to meet in the USF&G Sugar Bowl on New Year's 1993. Miami won its second straight Big East championship behind Heisman Trophy– and Maxwell Award–winning quarterback Gino Torretta, while Alabama, completing its first unbeaten season since 1979, defeated Florida 28–21 in the first SEC championship playoff game. Miami had won twenty-nine consecutive games and five straight bowl contests.

Alabama proved that thirteen was not an unlucky number. The Tide held Miami to 13 points in a 34–13 win that nailed down Alabama's tenth national title—its first in thirteen years, or since the days of the immortal Bear Bryant—and Alabama's defensive back George Teague (who wore jersey number 13), returned a pass interception 31 yards for a touchdown and also stripped Miami flanker Lamar Thomas of the ball on Alabama's 15-yard line as he was headed for an apparent score. Torretta passed for 278 yards for Miami, but was intercepted three times. The combined payout for the two teams in the Sugar Bowl by now had reached almost $8.5 million, more than two hundred times the initial payout in 1935.

Two other teams were undefeated in 1992, but only one was victorious in postseason play. No. 7 Michigan won the Rose Bowl 38–31 over No. 9 Washington. The smallest Rose Bowl crowd since 1955 watched the Wolverines win as 225-pound running back Tyrone Wheatley ran for 235 yards and three touchdowns, including scoring runs of 56 and 88 yards, and quarterback Elvis Grbac passed for 175 yards and two scores, both to tight end Tony McGee. Quarterback Mark Brunell passed for 308 yards and two touchdowns, including a 64-yarder to freshman split end Jason Shelley, for the Huskies. The other unbeaten team, No. 4 Texas A&M, lost 28–3 to No. 5 Notre Dame in the Mobil Cotton Bowl. Notre Dame won easily as quarterback Rick Mirer passed for 119 yards and two touchdowns, including one of 26 yards to fullback Jerome Bettis, who also ran for two scores.

No. 3 Florida State finished second in both final polls after a 27–14 victory in the Federal Express Orange Bowl over No. 11 Nebraska. The Seminoles won their eighth straight bowl contest under Coach Bobby Bowden as quarterback Charlie Ward passed for 187 yards and two touchdowns, and tailback Sean Jackson ran for 101 yards and a score. Freshman quarterback Tommie Frazier threw two touchdown passes for the Cornhuskers.

In the IBM OS/2 Fiesta Bowl, No. 6 Syracuse defeated No. 10 Colorado 26–22 for its fifth straight bowl victory. Sophomore running back Kirby Dar Dar scored on a 100-yard kickoff return for Syracuse, running back David Walker had 80 yards and a touchdown rushing, and quarterback Marvin Graves scored on a 28-yard run. Sophomore quarterback Kordell Stewart passed for 217 yards and two touchdowns for the Buffaloes.

In other games, No. 8 Georgia beat No. 15 Ohio State 21–14 in the Florida Citrus Bowl as quarterback Eric Zeier passed for 242 yards and tailback Garrison Hearst, the nation's scoring leader, ran for 163 yards and two touchdowns. In the Hall of Fame Bowl, No. 17 Tennessee beat No. 16 Boston College 38–23 as sophomore quarterback Heath Shuler ran for two scores and passed for 245 yards and two more touchdowns for the Volunteers. No. 13 Stanford beat No. 21 Penn State 24–3 in the Blockbuster Bowl as quarterback Steve Stenstrom passed for 210 yards and two touchdowns. In the Outback Steak House Gator Bowl, No. 14 Florida beat No. 12 North Carolina State 27–10 as quarterback Shane Matthews passed for 247 yards and two touchdowns and scored on a 1-yard run, and running back Errict Rhett had 182 yards rushing.

Several ranked teams lost in postseason games. Kansas upset No. 25 Brigham Young 23–20 in the Aloha Bowl. Highlights included a 94-yard kickoff return for a score by Cougar freshman running back Hema Heimuli and a 74-yard touchdown pass from Kansas wide receiver Matt Gay to sophomore tight end Rodney Harris. Unranked Fresno State beat No. 23 Southern California, the nation's scoring leader (40.5-point average), 24–7 in the Freedom Bowl. And No. 22 Arizona lost to Baylor 20–15 in the John Hancock Bowl.

No. 18 Washington State, sparked by quarterback Drew Bledsoe's sensational passing, did win its postseason game, 31–28 over Utah in the Weiser Lock Copper Bowl. Bledsoe threw for 476 yards and two touchdowns, 87 and 48 yards, to wide receiver Philip Bobo, who had seven pass receptions for 212 yards. And No. 20 Mississippi also won, defeating Air Force 13–0 in the Liberty Bowl.

The number of bowls remained at eighteen despite the demise of the California Bowl. The inaugural Las Vegas Bowl kicked off the bowl season on December 18 as MAC champion Bowling Green met Nevada, winner of the Big West title in its first year in Division I-A competition. It was Nevada's first bowl appearance since the Harbor Bowl of January 1, 1949, but the Wolf Pack lost a 35–34 heartbreaker when Bowling Green quarterback Erik White completed a fourth-down 2-yard touchdown pass to Dave Hankins with just twenty-two seconds left.

After eight New Year's Day games, the season was wrapped up on January 2 at the Peach Bowl, where No. 19 North Carolina finished with a 21–17 win over No. 24 Mississippi State.

The Bowl Coalition, with a bit of luck, worked again following the 1993 sea- **1993** son. Auburn finished its first unbeaten season since 1958 in its first year under Terry Bowden, but was on NCAA probation for recruiting violations and could not play in the SEC championship game or a bowl contest. Only two bowl-eligible Division I-A teams, Nebraska and West Virginia, made it through the season undefeated. Both were eligible to play in Coalition bowls, but did not meet face to face because once-beaten Florida State was ranked No. 1. This time the Federal Express Orange Bowl played host to the title game between Florida State and No. 2 Nebraska. No. 3 West Virginia would meet No. 8 Florida in the USF&G Sugar Bowl the same night. New Year's Day, 1994 would be the last time that all four of the traditional major bowls, the Rose, Sugar, Cotton, and Orange, were played on the same day.

Florida State led the nation in scoring (43.2-point average) behind Heisman Trophy– and Maxwell Award–winning quarterback Charlie Ward and also led in scoring defense (9.4-point average). Before a huge Orange Bowl crowd of 81,536, the Seminoles squeaked past Nebraska 18–16 on a 22-yard field goal by Scott Bentley with twenty-one seconds left. Nebraska was unsuccessful on a 45-yard field goal attempt moments later on the last play of the game. Bentley kicked four field goals in the contest, Ward passed for 286 yards, and fullback William Floyd scored on a 1-yard run. Nebraska quarterback Tommie Frazier passed for 206 yards and a touchdown, 34 yards to sophomore split end Reggie Baul, and had 77 yards rushing.

In the Sugar Bowl, West Virginia faced a speedy Florida team that had won its second SEC title by defeating Alabama 28-13 in the league's championship game. West Virginia scored first on a 32-yard pass from quarterback Jake Kelchner to wide receiver Jay Kearney. But it was all Florida after that as quarterback Terry Dean passed for 255 yards and a touchdown, 39 yards to wide receiver Willie Jackson, running back Errict Rhett ran for 105 yards and three scores, and freshman defensive back Lawrence Wright scored on a 52-yard pass interception return for a 41–7 victory.

Florida State was voted the No. 1 team in the final polls, a decision criticized by Notre Dame coach Lou Holtz, whose team defeated Florida State in the regular season and came away with a 24–21 victory over No. 7 Texas A&M in the Mobil Cotton Bowl, ending the season with a record of 11–1. In the newly renovated Cotton Bowl stadium—a $14 million project that included the replacement of artificial turf with natural grass—the No. 4 ranked Fighting Irish upended Texas A&M on a 31-yard field goal by kicker Kevin Pendergast with 2:17 left. Notre Dame's touchdowns came on a 19-yard run by quarterback Kevin McDougal, and short runs by fullbacks Ray Zellars and freshman Marc Edwards. Quarterback Corey Pullig passed for 238 yards and a touchdown for the Aggies. Although Notre Dame had a late-season win over Florida State as justification for a No. 1 ranking for the Irish, Notre Dame's record had been blemished by a 41–39 loss to Boston College on a last-second 41-yard field goal by David Gordon in its last game just a week after the win over the Seminoles. All of this simply added more fuel to the burning debate over the need for a national championship playoff system for Division I-A teams.

In the Rose Bowl, No. 9 Wisconsin played No. 14 UCLA. Wisconsin took advantage of six turnovers in a 21–16 win, breaking an eight-game bowl winning string by UCLA and giving the Badgers their first Rose Bowl win in four tries. Wisconsin was paced by fullback Brent Moss, who ran for 158 yards and two touchdowns, and quarterback Darrell Bevell, who scored what turned out to be the game winner on a 21-yard run in the final quarter.

In the IBM OS/2 Fiesta Bowl, No. 16 Arizona shut out No. 10 Miami, 29–0. Arizona's victory was sparked by sophomore quarterback Dan White, who passed for two touchdowns, both to wide receiver Troy Dickey, and running back Charles Levy, who ran for 142 yards and scored on a 68-yard run. No. 6 Tennessee was upset by No. 13 Penn State 31–13 in the CompUSA Florida Citrus Bowl as quarterback Kerry Collins passed for two touchdowns and tailback Ki-Jana Carter ran for two more. In the Carquest Bowl, No. 15 Boston College beat Virginia 31–13 as quarterback Glenn Foley passed for 391 yards and three touchdowns, including a 78-yarder to wide receiver Clarence Cannon. And in the Hall of Fame Bowl, No. 23 Michigan rolled over North Carolina State 42–7 as running back Tyrone Wheatley ran for two touchdowns, wide receiver Derrick Alexander scored on a 79-yard punt return, and freshman defensive back Clarence Thompson scored on a 43-yard pass interception return.

In other bowls, No. 19 Oklahoma romped over Texas Tech, 41–10, in the John Hancock Bowl as quarterback Cale Gundy passed for 215 yards and three scores. No. 17 Colorado beat Fresno State, 41–30, in the Aloha Bowl as sophomore tailback Rashaan Salaam had 135 yards and three touchdowns rushing. No. 25 Louisville defeated Michigan State in the Liberty Bowl, 18–7, behind quarterback Jeff Brohm, who threw for 197 yards and a touchdown. No. 20 Kansas State crushed Wyoming, 52–17, in the Weiser Lock Copper Bowl as quarterback Chad May passed for 275 yards and two touchdowns, and wide receiver Andre Coleman scored on a 61-yard pass reception and a 68-yard punt return. In the Thrifty Car Rental Holiday Bowl, No. 11 Ohio State defeated Brigham Young, 28–21, behind tailback Raymont Harris, who had 235 yards and three touchdowns rushing, while BYU sophomore quarterback John Walsh passed for 389 yards and three scores. No. 18 Alabama upset No. 12 North Carolina, 24–10, in the Outback Steak House Gator Bowl as sophomore quarterback Brian Burgdorf passed for two touchdowns and scored on a 33-yard run. In the Peach Bowl, No. 24 Clemson defeated Kentucky, 14–13, on two extra points by kicker Nelson Welch. No. 22 Virginia Tech beat No. 21 Indiana, 45–20, in the Poulan/Weed Eater Independence Bowl as freshman defensive back Antonio Banks scored on an 80-yard blocked field goal return, had a pass interception, and recovered a fumble.

The number of bowls reached nineteen with the addition of the Builders Square Alamo Bowl at San Antonio, Texas. A crowd of 45,716 turned out for the inaugural contest, in which quarterback Dave Barr passed for 266 yards and three touchdowns, and linebacker Jerrott Willard scored on a 61-yard pass interception return, in a 37–3 California victory over Iowa.

1994

For the first time in its three-year existence, the Bowl Coalition was unable to match the No. 1 and No. 2 teams for a national championship game after the 1994 season because No. 2 Penn State, as Big 10 champion, was obligated to play in the non-Coalition Rose Bowl. Nebraska again went through the regular season unbeaten—no opponent came closer than ten points—and again ended up in the FedEx Orange Bowl, but this time the Cornhuskers entered the contest as No. 1, having held that spot in the AP poll since November 1. Nebraska, which had lost seven straight bowl games, would meet No. 3 Miami, which lost only to Washington 38–20, ending the Hurricanes' fifty-eight-game home winning string, but had led the nation in scoring defense (10.8-point average). An all-time Orange Bowl record crowd of 81,753 was on hand as Nebraska won 24–17 to clinch its third national title, its first since 1971 and first under Coach Tom Osborne. Fullback Cory Schlesinger ran for two touchdowns and quarterback Brooks Berringer threw a 19-yard scoring pass to tight end Mark Gilman to lead the Cornhusker attack. Quarterback Frank Costa passed for 248 yards and two touchdowns, 35 yards to wide receiver Chris T. Jones and 44 yards to wide receiver Jonathan Harris, for Miami, and kicker Dane Prewitt added a 44-yard field goal. Since the Orange Bowl was the only major bowl game played on New Year's Day, a Sunday, the national championship was determined before the other principal games were played, on January 2.

The other unbeaten Division I-A team, Penn State, the nation's scoring leader (47.8-point average), earned a trip to Pasadena for its first Rose Bowl appearance in seventy-two years by winning the Big 10 title in its second year of eligibility. The Nittany Lions wrapped up the perfect season with a 38–20 win over No. 12 Oregon. But Penn State would finish second to Nebraska in the final polls. Maxwell Award–winning quarterback Kerry Collins (nation's passing efficiency leader) passed for 200 yards for the Nittany Lions, while All-America tailback Ki-Jana Carter had 156 yards and three touchdowns rushing, including an 83-yard scoring run on Penn State's first offensive play of the game. Oregon got an extraordinary performance from quarterback Danny O'Neil, who passed for 456 yards and two touchdowns. The consensus was that Nebraska deserved the national title with its bowl win over Miami, despite Penn State's perfect season. Yet the fact that the No. 1 and No. 2 teams were not able to meet in a bowl game added pressure for a modification of the Bowl Coalition.

In the Sugar Bowl, No. 7 Florida State had a rematch with No. 5 Florida, having played to a 31–31 tie in the final game of the regular season. Florida State won the rematch 23–17 for its tenth straight bowl victory under Bobby Bowden. Quarterback Danny Kanell passed for 252 yards and a touchdown for the Seminoles, tailback Warrick Dunn threw a 73-yard touchdown pass to flanker Omar Ellison, and kicker Dan Mowrey added three field goals. Quarterback Danny Wuerfel passed for 394 yards, including an 82-yard scoring toss to freshman wide receiver Ike Hilliard, and scored on a 1-yard run for Florida.

In the IBM OS/2 Fiesta Bowl, No. 4 Colorado easily defeated unranked Notre Dame, 41–24. Quarterback Kordell Stewart passed for 205 yards and a touchdown and ran for 143 yards and another score for the Buffaloes, while Heisman Trophy–winning tailback Rashaan Salaam, nation's leader in rushing and scoring, ran for three touchdowns. Freshman quarterback Ron Powlus passed for 259 yards and three touchdowns for the Irish.

The Mobil Cotton Bowl was host to a 55–14 romp by No. 21 Southern California over Texas Tech. For USC, quarterback Rob Johnson passed for 289 yards and three touchdowns, two to future NFL star wide receiver Keyshawn Johnson, who had eight pass receptions for 222 yards and three scores, including an 86-yarder from sophomore quarterback Brad Otton. This was the final year for the Cotton Bowl agreement with the Southwest Conference that began with the 1941 bowl, as the conference was dissolved after the 1995 season.

In other contests, No. 6 Alabama beat No. 13 Ohio State 24–17 in the CompUSA Florida Citrus Bowl as Crimson Tide quarterback Jay Barker passed for 317 yards, including a 50-yard scoring toss to running back Sherman Williams, who also ran for 166 yards and a touchdown. In the Hall of Fame Bowl, No. 25 Duke was upset by Wisconsin 34–20 as Badger running back Terrell Fletcher had 241 yards and two touchdowns rushing. And South Carolina won its first bowl game in nine tries, beating West Virginia 24–21 in the Carquest Bowl as quarterback Steve Taneyhill passed for 227 yards and a touchdown and scored on a 4-yard run. In the Peach Bowl, No. 23 North Carolina State upset No. 16 Mississippi State 28–24 as five Wolfpack players scored.

The Freedom Bowl bowed out with one last game. The final contest saw the first meeting since 1983 of one-time conference rivals No. 14 Utah and No. 15 Arizona. The Utes won, 16–13.

No. 11 Kansas State was upset by Boston College 12–7 in a defensive battle in the Aloha Bowl. In the Poulan/Weed Eater Independence Bowl, No. 18 Virginia beat Texas Christian 20–10 as quarterback Mike Groh passed for 199 yards and a touchdown. In the Weiser Lock Copper Bowl, No. 22 Brigham Young defeated Oklahoma 31–6 to break a five-bowl winless string as quarterback John Walsh passed for 454 yards and four touchdowns. In the Sun Bowl, Southwest Conference co-champion Texas upset No. 19 North

Carolina 35–31 as running back Anthony Holmes had 161 yards and four touchdowns rushing. The same day No. 17 Virginia Tech was upended by Tennessee 45–23 in the Outback Steakhouse Gator Bowl as Vols freshman quarterback Peyton Manning, destined for NFL stardom, passed for 189 yards and a touchdown. No. 10 Colorado State lost to No. 20 Michigan 24–14 in the Thrifty Car Rental Holiday Bowl, and in the Builders Square Alamo Bowl, No. 24 Washington State got by Southwest Conference co-champion Baylor 10–3.

Although the Bowl Coalition had worked reasonably well twice in its three-year existence, it was obvious that there were still major flaws in the system if the top two Division I-A football teams were to meet annually in the postseason to determine a national champion. Thus, a new system would be tried with the 1995 season.

7 A NATIONAL CHAMPIONSHIP?

SPORTSWRITERS, BROADCASTERS, AND MANY FANS complained about the Bowl Coalition being unable to match the No. 1 and No. 2 teams in the 1994 postseason, and by the time the 1995 season rolled around, the Coalition had been replaced by a new Bowl Alliance. On the surface, there was little difference between the two. Under the Coalition, there still had been conference tie-ins with the Orange, Sugar, and Cotton bowls, but the final match-ups were based on the combined standings of teams in the final regular season wire service polls. Thus, it had been possible to select the No. 1 and No. 2 teams to meet in any of the Coalition bowls—as long as it did not involve the Big 10 or Pac-10 champion. The Rose Bowl still adhered only to its Pac-10/Big 10 pact and would not be involved with the Alliance, either. In addition, the Cotton Bowl this time was not a participant because of the imminent demise of the Southwest Conference, leaving only the Orange, Sugar, and Fiesta bowls in the new agreement. Under the Alliance, a predetermined rotation system allowed a different bowl each year to make the first two selections of participants, with elimination of the conference tie-ins that had been in existence for years. This made it easier to match the top two teams in the AP and USAToday/ESPN polls.

A packed Fiesta Bowl on January 2, 1996, watched Tom Osborne's fourth unbeaten Cornhusker team complete the drive to its second consecutive national championship by smashing Florida 62–24. All-America quarterback Tommie Frazier of the Cornhuskers ran for 199 yards and two touchdowns and passed for 105 yards, including a 16-yard scoring toss to running back Lawrence Phillips. Phillips added 165 yards and two touchdowns rushing, and defensive back Michael Booker scored on a 42-yard pass interception return. Gator quarterback Danny Wuerffel, the nation's passing efficiency leader, managed 255 yards and one touchdown passing, and wide receiver Reidel Anthony scored on a 93-yard kickoff return.

The only other undefeated Division I-A team, No. 25 Toledo, met Nevada in the Las Vegas Bowl in a rematch of their earlier regular season game that Toledo won, 49–35. Despite the small turnout for the game, the fans were rewarded with the first overtime game ever in bowl history. Toledo came out ahead, 40–37, as running back Wasean Tait scored four touchdowns—the final one a 3-yard run in overtime to win the game. The tiebreaker system, which had been in effect for NCAA Division II and III playoff games since 1973, was added for Division I-A bowl games for the first time in the 1995 postseason and would be extended to regular season games in 1996.

The smallest Sugar Bowl crowd in nine years turned out for the meeting of No. 13 Virginia Tech and No. 9 Texas. Because of broadcast contracts and other income, however, the combined payout for the participants nearly doubled from the previous year to more than $15.5 million. The Hokies won the game 28–10 as quarterback Jim Druckenmiller passed for 266 yards and a touchdown, 54 yards to flanker Bryan Still, who also scored on a 60-yard punt return. Quarterback James Brown passed for a touchdown for Texas, and kicker Phil Dawson had a 52-yard field goal.

A half-dozen games were played on January 1, including the Toyota Gator Bowl, which had been played in December the previous four years, the CompUSA Florida Citrus Bowl, and the Outback Bowl, formerly the Hall of Fame Bowl. The Florida Citrus Bowl had an unusual circumstance when it matched two teams tied for No. 4, Tennessee and Ohio State. Volunteer quarterback Peyton Manning passed for 182 yards and a touchdown, while tailback Jay Graham had 154 yards rushing and scored on a 69-yard run in a 20–14 Volunteer win. Quarterback Bobby Hoying passed for 246 yards and a touchdown for Ohio State, and Heisman Trophy– and Maxwell Award–winning tailback Eddie George ran for 101 yards and a score. The combined payout for this bowl was $6 million.

In the Gator Bowl, Syracuse embarrassed No. 23 Clemson 41–0 as freshman quarterback Donovan McNabb, a future NFL star, passed for 309 yards and three touchdowns, including 38 and 56 yards to wide receiver Marvin Harrison, and scored on a 5-yard run. It was the sixth straight bowl win for the Orangemen. Despite rain and mud, a large crowd turned out for the newly named Outback Bowl in Tampa, where No. 15 Penn State trounced No. 16 Auburn 43–14. Quarterback Wally Richardson passed for 217 yards and four touchdowns, two to wide receiver Bobby Engram, and tailback Stephen Pitts rushed for 118 yards and caught a touchdown pass.

In the Rose Bowl, No. 17 Southern California, which won a share of its eighth Pac-10 title, ended No. 3 Northwestern's Cinderella season. The Wildcats won their first Big 10 title since 1936 and led the nation in scoring defense (12.7-point average) in their first winning season since 1971. Despite excellent performances by quarterback Steve Schnur, who passed for 336 yards and ran for a touchdown, and running back Darnell Autry, who had 110 yards and three scores rushing,the Wildcats lost to the Trojans 41–32. For USC, quarterback Brad Otton passed for 391 yards and two touchdowns, 21 yards to fullback Terry Barnum and 56 yards to All-America wide receiver Keyshawn Johnson, who had twelve pass receptions for 216 yards, while sophomore running backs LaVale Woods and Delon Washington each scored on short runs.

In rain and a twenty-six-degree wind chill at the Cotton Bowl, No. 7 Colorado rolled over No. 12 Oregon 38–6. Sophomore quarterback John Hessler passed for 115 yards and two touchdowns and scored on a 1-yard run for the Buffaloes, while tailback Herchell Troutman rushed for 100 yards and another touchdown. Perhaps the most exciting play was a 95-yard pass interception return for a score by Colorado freshman defensive back Marcus Washington, the longest interception return ever in any bowl.

In the FedEx Orange Bowl, No. 8 Florida State met No. 6 Notre Dame on a cloudy, humid night. Quarterback Danny Kanell passed for 290 yards, four touchdowns—three to wide receiver Andre Cooper—and a 2-point conversion (also to Cooper) for the Seminoles, and tailback Warrick Dunn had 151 yards rushing. Reserve quarterback Tom Krug, subbing for starter Ron Powlus who was injured in a late-season game, passed for 140 yards and three touchdowns, including tosses of 39 and 33 yards to wide receiver Derrick Mayes, for Notre Dame. The Seminoles won, 31–26, for their fourteenth consecutive bowl game without a loss.

In other bowls, No. 11 Kansas defeated UCLA 51–30 in the Aloha Bowl as quarterback Mark Williams passed for 288 yards and three touchdowns, including a 77-yarder to wide receiver Isaac Byrd, and scored on a 6-yard run. Freshman quarterback Cade McNown threw three touchdown passes for UCLA. In the Builders Square Alamo Bowl, No. 19 Texas A&M upset No. 14 Michigan 22–20 as kicker Kyle Bryant booted five field goals and freshman running back Eric Bernard scored on a 9-yard run. Sophomore quarterback Brian Griese threw two touchdown passes, 39 and 44 yards to wide receiver Amani Toomer, for the Wolverines. The Sun Bowl also saw an upset, with

1995 Las Vegas Bowl—Wasean Tait of Toledo downs the ball in the end zone after one of his four touchdowns against Nevada in the first overtime game in bowl history. Tait led the Rockets to an exciting 40-37 win on December 14 to finish undefeated. Toledo had beaten the Wolf Pack 49-35 in an early regular-season game. (*Collegiate Images*)

Iowa beating No. 20 Washington 38–18 with the help of five field goals, including a 50-yarder, by kicker Brion Hurley. In the Plymouth Holiday Bowl, No. 10 Kansas State smashed Colorado State 54–21 behind quarterback Brian Kavanagh, who passed for 242 yards and four touchdowns. In the Peach Bowl, No. 18-ranked ACC co-champion Virginia beat Georgia 34–27, while in the Carquest Bowl, No. 24 Arkansas was upset by North Carolina 20–10. Bowl payouts leaped to an average of $5,632,778 per game this postseason.

1996   Under the Bowl Alliance rotation agreement, the newly named Nokia Sugar Bowl was the site for the 1996 postseason championship game, but it could not match the top two teams because No. 2 Arizona State was committed to play in the Rose Bowl. Instead, the Sugar Bowl matched intrastate rivals No. 1 Florida State and No. 3 Florida. The two met in the Sugar Bowl two years previously, with Florida State winning 23–17. They met again in the last game of the 1996 regular season with a 24–21 win by the Seminoles, knocking Florida out of the top spot in the national polls, a position it had held for the previous ten weeks. But Steve Spurrier's Gators, the nation's top scoring team with an average of 46.6 points per game, then defeated Alabama 45–30 in the title game to win their fourth straight SEC crown. Florida State, winner of its fifth straight ACC title in its first undefeated season since 1979, held the No. 1 spot in the last two polls of the regular season. Bobby Bowden's Seminoles were winners of eleven straight bowl games and were unbeaten in their last fourteen postseason contests.

The largest Sugar Bowl crowd in more than twenty years saw Heisman Trophy– and Maxwell Award–winning quarterback Danny Wuerffel pass for 306 yards and three touchdowns, all to All-America wide receiver Ike Hilliard, and score on a 16-yard run for the Gators, and sophomore running back Terry Jackson rushed for 118 yards and two scores, including one on a 42-yard run, as No. 3 Florida avenged its regular season loss, with a 52–20 thumping of the Seminoles, to take its first national championship.

Arizona State might well have taken the national title with Florida State's loss, but the Sun Devils lost a heartbreaker to No. 4 Ohio State in the Rose Bowl. Quarterback Jake Plummer, who threw for 201 yards and a touchdown, scored on an 11-yard run with just 1:40 left to give the Sun Devils a 17–14 lead and an apparent victory. However, Buckeye sophomore quarterback Joe Germaine, who grew up just a few miles from the Arizona State campus, drove his team 65 yards—with the help of two pass interference penalties—and threw a 5-yard scoring pass to freshman wide receiver David Boston with just nineteen seconds left to pull out a 20–17 victory.

In the Fiesta Bowl, No. 7 Penn State faced No. 20 Texas. Only one of the Longhorns' regular-season defeats had been by more than four points, and they upset Nebraska 37–27 in the first Big 12 championship contest. But they had little success against the Nittany Lions, despite quarterback James Brown's 254 yards passing. Running back Curtis Enis led Penn State, running for two scores and catching a touchdown pass and a 2-point conversion pass from quarterback Wally Richardson en route to a 38–15 victory. Penn State's other touchdowns came on a 5-yard run by freshman fullback Aaron Harris and a 1-yard run by sophomore fullback Anthony Cleary.

The Southwestern Bell Cotton Bowl played host to a thrilling game between No. 5 Brigham Young and No. 14 Kansas State. Behind by 10 points with eleven minutes left, Cougar quarterback Steve Sarkisian, the nation's passing efficiency leader, connected on two touchdown passes, including a 28-yarder to wide receiver K. O. Kealaluhi with 3:39 remaining to pull out a 19–15 victory. Linebacker Shay Muirbrook had an amazing six quarterback sacks for the winners. Quarterback Brian Kavanagh passed for 233 yards and two scores, 41 yards to wide receiver Andre Anderson and 72 yards to wide receiver Kevin Lockett, for the Wildcats. But BYU intercepted a Kansas State pass near the Cougar goal line with just seconds left to preserve the victory.

In the Gator Bowl, No. 12 North Carolina, the nation's leader in scoring defense (10-point average), had a 20–13 win over No. 25 West Virginia, the nation's leader in total defense. Sophomore quarterback Oscar Davenport, subbing for injured regular Chris Keldorf, passed for 175 yards and a touchdown for the Tar Heels and scored on a 5-yard run, and freshman kicker Josh McGee added two field goals. Quarterback Chad Johnston passed for 197 yards, including a 34-yard scoring toss to wide receiver David Saunders, and freshman kicker Jay Taylor added two 47-yard field goals, but the Mountaineers came up short.

No. 6 Nebraska met No. 10 Virginia Tech in the FedEx Orange Bowl, where Cornhusker quarterback Scott Frost scored on runs of 5 and 22 yards, running back Damon Benning ran in two more, and defensive tackle Jason Peter scored on a 31-yard fumble return in a 41–21 triumph. Virginia Tech quarterback Jim Druckenmiller passed for 214 yards and all three Hokie touchdowns.

In other bowls involving ranked teams, No. 9 Tennessee defeated No. 11 Northwestern 48–28 in the CompUSA Florida Citrus Bowl as quarterback Peyton Manning passed for 408 yards and four touchdowns and scored on a 10-yard run for the Volunteers. In the Outback Bowl, No. 16 Alabama beat No. 15 Michigan 17–14 as freshman running back Shaun Alexander ran 46 yards for a score and linebacker Dwayne Rudd scored on an 88-yard interception return. Quarterback Brian Griese passed for 287 yards and a touchdown for Michigan. No. 19 Miami beat Virginia 31–21 in the Carquest Bowl as quarterback Ryan Clement passed for 274 yards, including a 70-yard touchdown pass to wide receiver Yatil Green, and defensive back Tremain Mack scored on a 79-yard fumble return and a 42-yard pass interception return. No. 23 Syracuse beat Houston 30–17 in the St. Jude Liberty Bowl for its seventh straight bowl victory as running back Malcolm Thomas ran for 201 yards and a touchdown and quarterback Donovan McNabb scored twice on short runs. In the Peach Bowl, No. 17 Louisiana State edged Clemson 10–7, while No. 21 Iowa had an easy 27–0 win over Texas Tech in the Builders Square Alamo Bowl. In the Plymouth Holiday Bowl, No. 8 Colorado beat

No. 13 Washington 33–21 as quarterback Koy Detmer passed for 371 yards and three touchdowns, including a 76-yarder to wide receiver Rae Curruth. Wide receiver Jerome Pathon scored on an 86-yard kickoff return for Washington. No. 24 Army had a tough 32–29 loss to Auburn in the Poulan/Weed Eater Independence Bowl after rallying for 22 points in the fourth quarter. Quarterback Dameyune Craig passed for 372 yards and two touchdowns and scored on a 33-yard run for the Tigers.

The annual expansion of the number of bowls continued following the 1997   **1997**
season with an increase to twenty postseason contests. Added to the list were the Motor City Bowl at Pontiac, Michigan, and the Sports Humanitarian Bowl at Boise, Idaho. Attendance was down at a couple of the major bowls, but all-time record high attendance was recorded at some of the smaller bowls—the Insight.com (formerly the Copper) Bowl and the Poulan/Weed Eater Independence Bowl, as well as at the Chick-Fil-A Peach and Florida Citrus bowls. Most eyes in this postseason, however, were focused on the Rose and Orange bowls.

Under the Bowl Alliance agreement, it was the FedEx Orange Bowl's turn to host a national championship game after the 1997 season. It was able to line up No. 2 Nebraska, but the team ranked No. 1 in both major polls was Michigan, the nation's scoring defense leader (8.9 points per game), which was obligated to play in the Rose Bowl. So Nebraska faced No. 3 Tennessee in the Orange Bowl. Unless Michigan lost in the Rose Bowl, neither Nebraska nor Tennessee would have much chance of becoming No. 1 even with a victory, or would they?

In Pasadena, Michigan met No. 8 Washington State, winner of its first conference title since 1930. Michigan completed its perfect season with a 21–16 victory as quarterback Brian Griese passed for 251 yards and all three Wolverine touchdowns. Quarterback Ryan Leaf passed for 331 yards and a touchdown for the Cougars and wide receiver Shawn Tims scored on a 14-yard run. The victory kept the Wolverines in the No. 1 position in the final AP poll, giving them a share of their seventh national title—the first since 1948.

The following night in the Orange Bowl, Nebraska met Tennessee with its national title hopes still a possibility if the Cornhuskers could achieve an impressive win. Nebraska, the nation's scoring leader (47.1 points a game) in Tom Osborne's last season, ended up trouncing Tennessee 42–17 as tailback

Ahman Green had 206 yards and two touchdowns rushing, quarterback Scott Frost passed for 125 yards and ran for three touchdowns, and the Cornhuskers' defense held Maxwell Award–winning Tennessee quarterback Peyton Manning to 134 yards and a single touchdown passing. The victory impressed the coaches voting in the *USA Today*/ESPN poll enough to declare Nebraska the national champion, the fifth national title for the Cornhuskers and Osborne's third in four years.

In the Chick-Fil-A Peach Bowl, No. 13 Auburn pulled out a 21–17 win over Clemson after trailing 17–6 at the end of the third quarter. In the fourth quarter, War Eagle quarterback Dameyune Craig, who passed for 228 yards in the game, scored on a 22-yard run and running back Rusty Williams added another score with a 7-yard run, but both 2-point conversion attempts failed. Auburn intercepted a pass near the end of the contest and converted it into a game-winning field goal by Jaret Holmes, who had three for the day, including a 54-yarder.

No. 4 Florida State got back on the winning side in postseason play with a 31–14 win over No. 9 Ohio State in the Nokia Sugar Bowl. Seminole quarterback Thad Busby passed for 334 yards and a touchdown, 27 yards to wide receiver E. G. Green, and scored on a 9-yard run, while freshman fullback William McCray scored twice on 1-yard runs. In the Southwestern Bell Cotton Bowl, No. 5 UCLA ended its season successfully with a 29–23 win over No. 20 Texas A&M. Leading the Bruins were quarterback Cade McNown, the nation's passing efficiency leader, who threw for 239 yards and two touchdowns and ran 20 yards for a touchdown and for a 2-point conversion. The Aggies scored on a 64-yard lateral play from linebacker Dat Nguyen to sophomore defensive back Brandon Jennings, a 74-yard run by running back Dante Hall, and a 43-yard run by sophomore wide receiver Chris Cole. In the Toyota Gator Bowl, No. 7 North Carolina rolled to an easy 42–3 win over Virginia Tech as quarterback Chris Keldorf passed for 290 yards and three touchdowns, All-America defensive back Dré Bly scored on a 6-yard return of a blocked punt, and All-America defensive end Greg Ellis recovered a fumble in the end zone for another score. In the Outback Bowl, No. 12 Georgia whipped Wisconsin 33–6 as running back Robert Edwards had 110 yards and three touchdowns rushing.

No. 6 Florida broke the four-bowl winning string of No. 11 Penn State with a 21–6 victory before an all-time record Florida Citrus Bowl crowd of 72,940. Running back Fred Taylor had 234 yards rushing for the Gators and

All-America wide receiver Jaquez Green caught two touchdown passes. Penn State scored only on field goals of 42 and 30 yards by sophomore kicker Travis Forney.

In other games, No. 23 Air Force fell to Oregon 41–13 in the Las Vegas Bowl as quarterback Jason Maas passed for three touchdowns and also caught a 69-yard scoring pass from alternate quarterback Akili Smith. In the Aloha Bowl, No. 21 Washington beat No. 25 Michigan State 51–23, highlighted by two touchdown passes by quarterback Brock Huard, a 64-yard scoring run by fullback Mike Reed, a 56-yard pass interception return by defensive back Tony Parrish, and a 66-yard pass interception return by sophomore linebacker Lester Towns. In the Plymouth Holiday Bowl, No. 19 Missouri fell to No. 18 Colorado State 35–24. In the Builders Square Alamo Bowl, No. 17 Purdue beat No. 24 Oklahoma State 33–20 behind quarterback Billy Dicken, who passed for 325 yards and two touchdowns, including a 69-yarder to sophomore wide receiver Chris Daniels, and scored on a 1-yard run. No. 16 Arizona State beat Iowa 17–7 in the Norwest Sun Bowl as running back Michael Martin had 169 yards and a touchdown rushing. Conference USA champion Southern Mississippi, ranked No. 22, routed Pittsburgh 41–7 in the AXA Liberty Bowl as quarterback Lee Roberts passed for 227 yards and three touchdowns, all to wide receiver Sherrod Gideon.

The Tostitos Fiesta Bowl saw No. 10 Kansas State end Syracuse's seven-bowl winning string as Wildcat quarterback Michael Bishop passed for 317 yards and four touchdowns, three to wide receiver Darnell McDonald, and ran for 73 yards and a score in a 35–18 victory. Quarterback Donovan McNabb passed for 271 yards and ran for 81 yards in a losing effort.

An all-time record crowd of 49,385 in the Insight.com Bowl, the former Copper Bowl, saw Arizona come out a 20–14 winner over New Mexico. Sophomore tailback Trung Canidate ran for 97 yards and a touchdown for the Wildcats, and running back Kelvin Eafon ran for 75 yards and two more scores. An all-time record Poulan/Weed Eater Independence Bowl crowd of 50,459 turned out for a rematch of No. 15 Louisiana State and Notre Dame. The Fighting Irish had won in the regular season, 24–6, but the Tigers got revenge with a 27–9 victory as sophomore running back Rondell Mealey ran for 222 yards and two touchdowns, and freshman wide receiver Abram Booty scored on a 12-yard pass from quarterback Herb Tyler.

In the inaugural Motor City Bowl, Mississippi faced Marshall. It was the first year of Division I-A competition for Marshall, which won Division I-AA national titles in 1992 and 1996. Mississippi edged the Thundering Herd 34–31 despite three touchdown passes by Marshall quarterback Chad Pennington, including an 80-yarder to All-America wide receiver Randy Moss. Quarterback Stewart Patridge passed for 332 yards and three touchdowns for the Rebels, and running back John Avery rushed for 110 yards and another score. On the distinctive blue artificial turf at the field in Boise, Idaho, in the inaugural Sportsman Humanitarian Bowl, Cincinnati took a 35–19 victory over Utah State.

1998 The 1998 postseason saw yet another agreement put into place in an attempt to determine a Division I-A national football champion. This time it was the Bowl Championship Series (BCS), which included the Rose Bowl along with the Orange Bowl, Sugar Bowl, and Fiesta Bowl, and an agreement for ABC-TV to televise all four of the BCS contests. Teams in the Atlantic Coast, Big East, Big 12, Big Ten, Pacific-10, and Southeastern conferences along with the University of Notre Dame all were provided access to automatic berths in BCS bowls, but independents (other than Notre Dame) and members of other conferences were not likely to be chosen. Selection of the teams to meet in the BCS series was based on a complex formula including: average standing in the AP media poll and the *USA Today*/ESPN coaches poll; computer average of seven computer systems used; rank of schedule strength compared to other Division I-A teams in actual games played; one point for each loss during the season; a subtotal of the values from the previous four factors listed; quality win component (with BCS standings at the end of a season determining final quality of win points); total (in which value of the quality win component is subtracted from the subtotal). After all that, the top two teams as determined under the BCS formula were to be matched in the bowl whose turn it was to host the "championship" game.

Although the NCAA has sponsored Division II and III playoffs since 1973 and a Division I-AA playoff system since 1978, it never has had a role in devising or supervising a playoff for Division I-A teams. The BCS agreement, modified over succeeding years, is scheduled to last through the 2005 season—after which it could undergo major changes, or even be thrown out. In the meantime, controversy continues annually over the teams selected for the BCS contests and whether the criteria are fair ones.

In the first year of competition under the BCS, the Tostitos Fiesta Bowl drew the title game, which matched No. 1 Tennessee against No. 2 Florida

State on January 4, two days after the other postseason games had been completed. The delay was partly to accommodate ABC's agreement to broadcast all four BCS bowls. Before an all-time record Fiesta Bowl crowd of 80,470 on the mild night of January 4, Tennessee nailed down its fourth national championship—first since 1951—with a 23–16 win over the Seminoles. Quarterback Tamaurice "Tee" Martin passed for 278 yards and two touchdowns, defensive back Dwayne Goodrich scored on a 54-yard pass interception return, and kicker Jeff Hall added a field goal and two extra points for the winners. Reserve quarterback Marcus Outzen passed for 145 yards and scored on a 7-yard run for Florida State, while sophomore fullback William McCray scored on a 1-yard run, and All-America kicker Sebastian Janikowski had a 34-yard field goal.

No. 3 Ohio State received the Nokia Sugar Bowl bid to play No. 8 Texas A&M, winner of its first Big 12 title with a double overtime 36–33 win over previously unbeaten Kansas State in the league's championship game. Buckeye quarterback Joe Germaine passed for 222 yards and a touchdown, while running back Joe Montgomery rushed for 96 yards and scored on a 10-yard run, and Kevin Griffin returned a blocked punt 16 yards to score, in a 24–14 Ohio State victory. Afterwards, the Buckeyes were voted the No. 2 team in the nation in both major polls. Quarterback Branndon Stewart passed for 187 yards and a touchdown for Texas A&M. Sponsorship and broadcast contributions allowed another quantum leap in combined payouts to the participants—a staggering $25 million.

The other BCS game was the Rose Bowl, which was taking part for the first time in the championship arrangement. Pressure from ABC-TV also led to sponsorship of the Rose contest for the first time—but in a different form from other corporate-sponsored bowls. In keeping with the tradition and dignity of the event, Rose officials would not allow a sponsor to be part of the Rose Bowl's name. However, they would allow a "presenting sponsor," which would act in much the same capacity as sponsors of other bowls, to be mentioned by ABC announcers covering the game. Thus, AT&T became the first Rose Bowl "presenting sponsor" in 1999, followed by PlayStation 2 in 2003 and Citi for the 2004 contest. The game featured No. 9 Wisconsin, the nation's leader in scoring defense (10.2-point average), and No. 6 UCLA. Wisconsin running back Ron Dayne ran for 246 yards and four touchdowns, including a 54-yarder, and freshman defensive back Jamar Fletcher scored on a 46-yard pass interception return to lead the Badgers to a tough 38–31

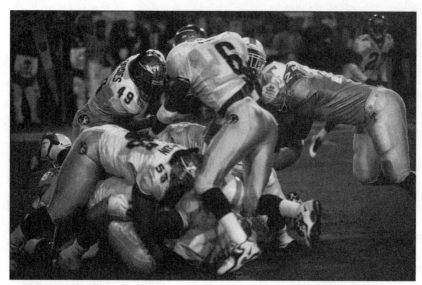

1999 Fiesta Bowl—Florida State defenders stop Tennessee on this play, but the Volunteers won an exciting game over the No. 2 Seminoles to nail down their first national championship since 1951 and fourth overall. (Collegiate Images)

win. All-America quarterback Cade McNown passed for 340 yards and two touchdowns for UCLA, and fullback Durell Price scored on a 61-yard pass from freshman wide receiver Freddie Mitchell.

Tulane fans felt their team deserved a BCS berth after its first unbeaten season since 1939 and its first perfect season since 1931. Tulane won its first Conference USA title—also its first title since taking an SEC championship in 1949—and only one opponent, Louisville, had come within a touchdown. But Tulane had to settle for the Liberty Bowl, where it completed a perfect season and broke a four-bowl losing string with a convincing 41–27 win over Brigham Young. Quarterback Shaun King, the nation's passing efficiency leader, threw for 276 yards and two touchdowns, including a 60-yarder to sophomore wide receiver Kerwin Cook, and had 109 yards and another score rushing for Tulane, while defensive back Michael Jordan added a score on a 79-yard interception return. For BYU, quarterback Kevin Feterik passed for 267 yards and two touchdowns.

The Chick-Fil-A Peach Bowl matched No. 19 Georgia and No. 13 Virginia. In a game full of offense, the Bulldogs came out on top, 35–33, as freshman quarterback Quincy Carter passed for 222 yards and two touchdowns, including a 14-yarder to All-America defensive back Champ Bailey, and scored on a 1-yard run, while running back Olandis Gary ran for 110 yards and two scores. Virginia quarterback Aaron Brooks accounted for four Cavalier touchdowns, passing for 226 yards and three scores, including 43 and 67 yards to wide receiver Terrence Wilkins, and running for 112 yards, including a 30-yard touchdown sprint.

In the Southwestern Bell Cotton Bowl, No. 20 Texas faced No. 25 Mississippi State. Freshman quarterback Major Applewhite passed for 225 yards and three touchdowns, including 59 and 52 yards to wide receiver Wane McGarity, for the Longhorns, and Heisman Trophy– and Maxwell Award–winning running back Ricky Williams ran for 203 yards and two more scores for a 38–11 win. No. 12 Georgia Tech took on No. 17 Notre Dame in the Toyota Gator Bowl. The Yellow Jackets won 35–28, their fifth straight postseason victory, as quarterback Joe Hamilton passed for 237 yards and three touchdowns, including tosses of 44 and 55 yards to wide receiver Dez White, and scored on a 5-yard pass from freshman running back Joe Burns. Running back Autry Denson had 130 yards and three touchdowns rushing for the Irish. By now, the minimum payout for the Gator Bowl had reached $3.3 million per team.

In the CompUSA Florida Citrus Bowl, future Super Bowl star quarterback Tom Brady passed for 209 yards and a touchdown and running back Anthony Thomas had 132 yards and three scores rushing, as No. 15 Michigan upset No. 11 Arkansas 45–31. Quarterback Clint Stoerner passed for 232 yards and two touchdowns for the Razorbacks. In the Outback Bowl, No. 22 Penn State beat Kentucky 26–14 as quarterback Kevin Thompson threw a 56-yard touchdown pass to split end Joe Nastasi, split end Chafie Fields scored on a 19-yard run, and kicker Travis Forney added four field goals. Quarterback Tim Couch passed for 336 yards and both touchdowns for the Wildcats.

In the FedEx Orange Bowl, No. 7 Florida met No. 18 Syracuse, as Gator quarterback Doug Johnson, before being injured, passed for 195 yards and two touchdowns, while his replacement, sophomore Jesse Palmer, passed for 113 yards and a touchdown and scored on a 1-yard run in a 31–10 victory. Quarterback Donovan McNabb passed for 192 yards and a touchdown for Syracuse and had 72 yards rushing in a losing effort.

An all-time Culligan Holiday Bowl record crowd of 65,354 turned out as No. 5 Arizona beat No. 14 Nebraska 23–20 to break a four-bowl winning string by the Cornhuskers. Quarterback Keith Smith passed for 143 yards and a touchdown for the Wildcats, and kicker Mark McDonald kicked three field goals, one of 48 yards, and two extra points. Cornhusker freshman quarterback Eric Crouch passed for 193 yards and two touchdowns.

The number of bowls reached twenty-two in the 1998 postseason with the addition of the Oahu Classic, as part of a doubleheader with the newly named Jeep Aloha Classic, and the Music City Bowl at Nashville, Tennessee. In addition, the Carquest Bowl at Miami underwent another name change, to the Micronpc.com Bowl. Bowl payouts also reached an all-time record high average of $6,632,909 per game in this postseason.

In Honolulu, more than 46,000 turned out for the inaugural Oahu Classic to watch No. 16 Air Force play Washington. The Falcons won 45–25 as quarterback Blane Morgan passed for 267 yards and two touchdowns, 79 yards to wide receiver Matt Farmer and 30 yards to sophomore halfback Scott McKay, who also scored on a 15-yard run. Quarterback Brock Huard passed for 267 yards for the Huskies. In the other half of the Christmas doubleheader, No. 21 Oregon lost a high-scoring game to Colorado 51–43 in the Jeep Aloha Classic for the Buffaloes' fifth straight postseason win. Defensive back Ben Kelly returned the opening kickoff 93 yards for Colorado's first score, while Quarterback Mike Moschetti passed for four touchdowns for the winners, and defensive back Damon Wheeler scored on a 52-yard pass interception return. Quarterback Akili Smith passed for 456 yards and two touchdowns for the Ducks.

Sophomore quarterback Drew Brees passed for 230 yards and three touchdowns and freshman kicker Travis Dorsch had three field goals, as unranked Purdue upset No. 4 Kansas State, the nation's scoring leader (48-point average), 37–34 in the Builders Square Alamo Bowl. Wildcats quarterback Michael Bishop threw for three scores, including an 88-yarder to wide receiver Darnell McDonald. On the same day, in the Micronpc.com Bowl, No. 24 Miami beat North Carolina State 46–23 as quarterback Scott Covington passed for 320 yards and two touchdowns, including an 80-yarder to sophomore wide receiver Santana Moss, for the Hurricanes, and running back Edgerrin James ran for 156 yards and two scores.

The first Music City Bowl was played at Vanderbilt's stadium, where Virginia Tech broke a five-bowl winning string by Alabama with a 38–7 win— the first victory by the Hokies over the Crimson Tide in an eleven-game series dating to 1932. The two had not met since 1979. Highlights for

Virginia Tech were a 43-yard scoring run by quarterback Al Clark and a 27-yard pass interception return for a score by defensive back Anthony Midget.

Upon completion of the 1999 regular season, it was the turn of the Nokia **1999** Sugar Bowl to host the championship game, which matched two major teams that had completed the season undefeated, Florida State and Virginia Tech. Again, the title game was set for January 4, two days after the rest of postseason play was completed. The other major unbeaten team, MAC champion Marshall, was matched against Brigham Young in the Motor City Bowl. The number of bowl games increased to twenty-three, with the addition of the Mobile Alabama Bowl. Yet this season saw the highest average attendance, 55,655 per contest, more than 1.25 million people, since the establishment of as many as twenty bowl games in one season.

No. 1 Florida State was the first team since Nebraska in 1983 to lead the AP poll every week of the regular season, and led the *USA Today*/ESPN poll every week as well, while No. 2 Virginia Tech led the nation in both scoring (41.4-point average) and scoring defense (10.5-point average) in its first unbeaten season since 1954 and its first perfect regular season since 1918. Chris Weinke passed for 329 yards and four touchdowns, 64 and 43 yards to All-America flanker Peter Warrick, and 63 and 14 yards to split end Ron Dugans, and a two-point conversion, while Warrick also scored on a 59-yard punt return and Jeff Chaney scored on a blocked punt return, as Florida State clinched its second national championship with a 46–29 win. Virginia Tech freshman quarterback Michael Vick, the nation's passing efficiency leader, threw for 225 yards and a touchdown, 49 yards to sophomore flanker Andre Davis, and ran for 97 yards and another score, but the breakdown of special teams sealed the Hokies' fate.

For the second straight year, BYU would serve as the opponent for Marshall, ranked No. 11, which completed its perfect season with a 21–3 win in the Motor City Bowl. Tailback Doug Chapman scored all three touchdowns for the Thundering Herd on a 30-yard pass from quarterback Chad Pennington, an 87-yard run, and a 1-yard run after BYU took an early 3–0 lead on a 28-yard field goal by kicker Owen Pochman.

In the Fiesta Bowl No. 3 Nebraska faced No. 6 Tennessee. Nebraska won 31–21 as sophomore quarterback Eric Crouch passed for 148 yards and a touchdown, running back Dan Alexander had 108 yards and a touchdown rushing, and Bobby Newcombe scored on a 60-yard punt return. In the Rose

Bowl, No. 4 Wisconsin became the first Big 10 school to win the Rose Bowl two years in a row with a 17–9 victory over No. 22 Stanford. Heisman Trophy– and Maxwell Award–winning tailback Ron Dayne ran for 200 yards and a touchdown for the Badgers, and freshman quarterback Brooks Bollinger passed for 103 yards and scored on a 1-yard run. Quarterback Todd Husak passed for 261 yards for Stanford.

In the FedEx Orange Bowl, No. 8 Michigan faced No. 5 Alabama. Quarterback Tom Brady passed for 369 yards and four touchdowns, three to sophomore flanker Dave Terrell, while Alabama tailback Shaun Alexander ran for 161 yards and three scores and sophomore flanker Freddie Milons scored on a 62-yard punt return. The game went to overtime with the score tied 28–28. Michigan scored first in overtime on a 25-yard strike from Brady to sophomore tight end Shawn Thompson and sophomore kicker Hayden Epstein booted the last of his five extra points. Alabama then put the ball in the end zone but missed the extra point wide right and the Wolverines came away with an exciting 35–34 victory.

Another contest that went into overtime was the Outback Bowl, where No. 21 Georgia beat No. 19 Purdue 28–25 after trailing 25–0 in the second quarter. The comeback was sparked by sophomore quarterback Quincy Carter, who passed for 243 yards and a touchdown and scored on an 8-yard run. Kicker Hap Hines made two field goals, including a 21-yarder to win the game in overtime. Purdue quarterback Drew Brees passed for 378 yards and four touchdowns, two to wide receiver Chris Daniels.

In the Southwestern Bell Cotton Bowl, No. 24 Arkansas, after a 3–3 first half standoff, broke a seven-bowl losing string with a 27–6 win over No. 14 Texas, holding the Longhorns to minus 27 yards rushing. In the OurHouse.com Florida Citrus Bowl, No. 9 Michigan State beat No. 10 Florida 37–34 as quarterback Bill Burke passed for three touchdowns, all to split end Plaxico Burress, and linebacker T. J. Turner scored on a 24-yard fumble return. In the Toyota Gator Bowl, No. 23 Miami ended No. 17 Georgia Tech's five-bowl winning string with a 28–13 victory. Sophomore quarterback Kenny Kelly threw a 15-yard scoring pass to split end Andre King, freshman running back Clinton Portis scored on a 73-yard run, tailback James Jackson had 107 yards and a touchdown rushing, and split end Reggie Wayne scored on a 17-yard pass from freshman quarterback Ken Dorsey for the Hurricanes. In the AXA Liberty Bowl, No. 16 Southern Mississippi defeated Colorado State, 23–17, as sophomore defensive back Chad Williams scored on a 5-yard fumble return, Brandon Francis recovered a blocked punt in the end zone for a touchdown, and running back Derrick Nix scored on a 3-yard run.

An all-time record Sylvania Alamo Bowl crowd of 65,380 saw No. 13 Penn State blank No. 18 Texas A&M 24–0. Quarterback Rashard Casey threw a 45-yard touchdown pass to sophomore wide receiver Eddie Drummond and scored on a 4-yard run for the Nittany Lions, defensive back Derek Fox scored on a 34-yard pass interception return, and kicker Travis Forney added a 39-yard field goal. And an all-time record crowd of 59,221 attended the HomePoint.com Music City Bowl, where Syracuse beat Kentucky 20–13 after trailing 10–0 in the first quarter. Sophomore running back James Mungro ran for 162 yards and two touchdowns for Syracuse, and sophomore quarterback Dusty Bonner passed for 308 yards for Kentucky. In the Crucial.com Humanitarian Bowl, Boise State beat Louisville, 34–31, behind quarterback Bart Hendricks, who had 361 yards of total offense, including a touchdown pass to Shay Swan and a 3-yard scoring run, freshman running back Brock Forsey, who ran for 152 yards and had 269 all-purpose yards, and defensive back Shaunard Harts with a touchdown on an 80-yard pass interception return. Quarterback Chris Redman passed for 314 yards and two touchdowns, including a 54-yarder to wide receiver Arnold Jackson, for Louisville, while Zek Parker scored on a 91-yard kickoff return.

In the inaugural Mobile Alabama Bowl, Texas Christian came out a 28–14 winner over No. 20 East Carolina as running back LaDainian Tomlinson, the nation's rushing leader, ran for 124 yards and two scores for the Horned Frogs. No. 7 Kansas State beat Washington 24–20 in the Culligan Holiday Bowl as quarterback Jonathan Beasley passed for 216 yards and ran for three touchdowns. In the Chick-Fil-A Peach Bowl, No. 15 Mississippi State broke a four-bowl losing string with a 17–7 win over Clemson. No. 12 Minnesota was upset by Oregon 24–20 in the Norwest Sun Bowl as sophomore quarterback Joey Harrington passed for 252 yards and a touchdown and ran for two scores for the Ducks. No. 25 Boston College lost a wild 62–28 game to unranked Colorado in the Insight.com Bowl as sophomore running back Cortlen Johnson had 201 yards and two touchdowns rushing, defensive back Ben Kelly scored on an 88-yard punt return, and the Buffaloes scored twice on pass interception returns.

Following the 2000 season, it was the FedEx Orange Bowl's turn to host the **2000** "championship" game on January 3. All in all, twenty-five postseason games were scheduled between December 20 and January 3, with the galleryfurniture.com Bowl at Houston, Texas, and the Silicon Valley Classic at San Jose, California, added to the slate.

The FedEx Orange Bowl matched undefeated No. 1 Oklahoma and No. 3 Florida State. Although Miami was ranked No. 2 in the AP poll, the BSC formula chose Florida State for the championship game. Oklahoma's defense stymied the Florida State offense, holding the Seminoles to only 27 yards rushing. Oklahoma stars included All-America quarterback Josh Heupel, who had 214 yards passing, including twenty-five completions to eight receivers, running back Quentin Griffin, whose 10-yard touchdown run in the fourth quarter sealed the game, and kicker Tim Duncan, with field goals of 27 and 42 yards and an extra point. Heisman Trophy–winning quarterback Chris Weinke passed for 274 yards for Florida State and flanker Atrews Bell had seven pass receptions for 137 yards, but the Seminoles scored only on a safety near the end of the game. The 13–2 victory handed the Sooners their seventh national title, the first since 1985, and their first perfect season since 1974.

In the Sugar Bowl the previous night, No. 2 Miami had kept its national championship hopes alive with a 37–20 win over No. 7 Florida. Miami cruised to victory as sophomore quarterback Ken Dorsey passed for 270 yards and three touchdowns and sophomore kicker Todd Sievers added three field goals and four extra points. Freshman quarterback Rex Grossman passed for 252 yards and a score for Florida.

No. 4 Washington met No. 14 Purdue in the Rose Bowl, and quarterback Marques Tuiasosopo passed for 138 yards and a touchdown and ran for 75 yards and another score, as the Huskies won 34–24. Maxwell Award–winning quarterback Drew Brees passed for 275 yards and two touchdowns, both to wide receiver Vinny Sutherland, for the Boilermakers. In the Fiesta Bowl No. 5 Oregon State played No. 10 Notre Dame, and the Beavers romped to a 41–9 win as quarterback Jonathan Smith passed for 305 yards and three touchdowns, including a 74-yarder to wide receiver Chad Johnson, while sophomore defensive back Terrell Roberts scored on a 45-yard fumble return. It was the fifth straight bowl defeat for the Fighting Irish.

No. 11 Kansas State, which lost twice to unbeaten Oklahoma, including 27–24 in the Big 12 championship game, beat No. 21 Tennessee in the SBC Cotton Bowl Classic, 35–21, as quarterback Jonathan Beasley passed for 210 yards and two touchdowns, including a 56-yarder to wide receiver Quincy Morgan, and ran for 98 yards and another score, while running back Josh

Scobey ran for 147 yards and two touchdowns. Running back Travis Henry scored on an 81-yard run for the Vols, and freshman defensive back Jabari Greer scored on a 78-yard pass interception return. In the Gator Bowl, No. 6 Virginia Tech beat No. 16 Clemson, 41–20, as sophomore quarterback Michael Vick passed for 205 yards and a touchdown, and scored on a 6-yard run, while sophomore tailback Lee Suggs had 73 yards and three touchdowns rushing.

No. 17 Michigan beat No. 20 Auburn 31–28 in the Capital One/Florida Citrus Bowl. Michigan won behind quarterback Drew Henson, who passed for 294 yards and two touchdowns, and running back Anthony Thomas, who had 182 yards and two touchdowns rushing. Quarterback Ben Leard passed for 394 yards and three scores for Auburn. In the Outback Bowl, No. 19 Ohio State was upset by unranked South Carolina 24–7.

The biggest AXA Liberty Bowl crowd in nine years turned out to see No. 23 Colorado State meet No. 22 Louisville. Despite Louisville quarterback Dave Ragone's 321 yards passing and two touchdowns, including a 58-yarder to sophomore wide receiver Damien Dorsey, Colorado State won 22–17 behind running back Cecil Sapp's 160 yards and a touchdown rushing, wide receiver Frank Rice's 16-yard scoring run, and kicker C. W. Hurst's three field goals.

All-time record crowds attended several bowls, including the first contest of the postseason—the Mobile Alabama Bowl, where 40,300 saw Southern Mississippi pull off a 28–21 upset of No. 13 Texas Christian. Quarterback Jeff Kelly passed for 159 yards and three touchdowns, including a 56-yarder to sophomore wide receiver LeRoy Handy, for the winners, and defensive back Leo Barnes scored on a 50-yard pass interception return. All-America running back LaDainian Tomlinson, nation's leader in yards rushing per game, ran for 118 yards and two scores for TCU. An all-time Motor City Bowl record crowd of 52,911 saw Marshall beat Cincinnati 25–14 behind sophomore quarterback Byron Leftwich and rover back Michael Owens. And an all-time record Chick-Fil-A Peach Bowl crowd of 73,614 turned out as Louisiana State was a 28–14 upset winner over No. 15 Georgia Tech. LSU was led by quarterback Rohan Davey, who passed for 174 yards and three touchdowns, two short tosses to fullback Tommy Banks and a 9-yarder to wide receiver Josh Reed.

In the final Jeep Aloha Classic, Boston College beat Arizona State, 31–17, as quarterback Tim Hasselback passed for 209 yards and two touchdowns, 58 yards to wide receiver Dedrick Dewalt and 40 yards to wide receiver Ryan Read, running back Cedric Washington had 109 yards and two touchdowns rushing, and kicker Mike Sutphin made a 50-yard field goal.

In other games, No. 24 Georgia beat George Welsh's last Virginia team 37–14 in the Oahu Classic as sophomore quarterback Cory Phillips passed for 213 yards and a touchdown. In the Culligan Holiday Bowl, No. 8 Oregon outscored No. 12 Texas as quarterback Joey Harrington passed for 273 yards and two touchdowns, including a 55-yarder to tailback Maurice Morris, caught an 18-yard touchdown pass from wide receiver Keenan Howry, and scored on a 9-yard run in a 35–30 victory. Sophomore quarterback Chris Simms passed for 245 yards and scored on a 4-yard run for Texas, and running back Victor Ike scored on a 93-yard kickoff return. And in the Sylvania Alamo Bowl, No. 9 Nebraska crushed No. 18 Northwestern 66–17, the highest total ever by one team in any bowl game. Cornhusker quarterback Eric Crouch ran for two touchdowns and threw for two more, and running back Dan Alexander rushed for 240 yards and two scores.

In the new bowl games, East Carolina met Texas Tech in Houston in the galleryfurniture.com Bowl. East Carolina won 40–27 as quarterback David Garrard passed for 229 yards and a touchdown, and scored on a 6-yard run, running back Leonard Henry had two touchdowns rushing, and wingback Keith Stokes scored on 71-yard punt return. For the Red Raiders, sophomore quarterback Kliff Kingsbury passed for 307 yards and four touchdowns, including a 65-yarder to wide receiver Darrell Jones. In the Silicon Valley Classic, Air Force hung on to beat Fresno State 37–34 after leading 34–7 at halftime. Quarterback Mike Thiessen passed for two touchdowns, both to halfback Scotty McKay, and ran for two more for the Falcons in the first half. Fresno State quarterback David Carr passed for 391 yards and five touchdowns, four during a furious second half rally, including a 73-yarder to running back Paris Gaines and tosses of 47 and 51 yards to sophomore wide receiver Bernard Berrian. But the Bulldogs fell short.

2001   The 2001 season was affected by the brutal terrorist attacks of September 11. Division I-A games scheduled for the following Thursday and Saturday (September 13 and 15) were postponed or canceled. And patriotic themes were a mainstay in pre-game and halftime shows in the postseason bowls.

The number of bowls following the 2001 season remained at twenty-five despite the demise of the Aloha Classic, the Oahu Classic, and the Micron.com Bowl. The combined Aloha and Oahu Classics became the

Seattle Bowl played in that Washington city, while the other spots were filled by the New Orleans Bowl in Louisiana's Superdome kicking off the postseason, and a new Tangerine Bowl in Orlando, Florida. Meanwhile, the Mobile Alabama Bowl was renamed the GMAC Bowl.

January 3 again was set for the "championship" contest, this time in the Rose Bowl, the first time in fifty-five years the Big 10 and Pacific-10 (or its forerunners) had not been involved in the "granddaddy of them all." Lined up instead were top-ranked Miami, the only undefeated Division I-A team, and No. 4 Nebraska. Nebraska was a controversial selection, as the Cornhuskers had not even made the Big 12 championship contest because of a 62–36 loss to Colorado in their final regular-season game. Yet they still were the No. 2 team in the complex BCS ratings formula. Miami clinched its fifth national title with a 37–14 romp over the Cornhuskers after leading 34–0 at halftime. Larry Coker of the Hurricanes became only the second coach to win the national title in his first season as a head coach, the first being Bennie Oosterbaan of Michigan in 1948. Leading the Hurricanes to their fifth straight bowl victory were Maxwell Award–winning quarterback Ken Dorsey, who passed for 362 yards and three touchdowns, 49 and 8 yards to sophomore wide receiver Andre Johnson and 21 yards to tight end Jeremy Shockey, while running back Clinton Portis scored on a 39-yard run, and defensive back James Lewis had a touchdown on a 47-yard pass interception return. Heisman Trophy–winning quarterback Eric Crouch had 114 yards rushing and 62 yards passing for the Cornhuskers, who scored only on a 16-yard run by sophomore fullback Judd Davies and a 71-yard punt return by defensive back DeJuan Groce.

The FedEx Orange Bowl was played between No. 6 Maryland, still with national title hopes at the time, and No. 5 Florida. The Terrapins, taking their first ACC title since 1985, ended Florida State's eight-year grip on the conference crown, even though Maryland lost to the Seminoles 52–31. It also was the first bowl trip for the Terps in eleven years. Florida demolished Maryland's title hopes with a 56–23 thrashing as sophomore All-America quarterback Rex Grossman, the nation's passing efficiency leader, threw for 248 yards and four touchdowns, two to All-America wide receiver Jabar Gaffney, wide receiver Taylor Jacobs scored on two pass receptions, including a 46-yarder from quarterback Brock Berlin, and tailback Earnest Graham rushed for 149 yards and two scores. Quarterback Shaun Hill passed for 257 yards, including a 64-yard scoring toss to sophomore wide receiver Jafar Williams, for Maryland.

In the Nokia Sugar Bowl, No. 7 Illinois met No. 12 Louisiana State, and the Tigers outscored the Illini 47–34 as quarterback Rohan Davey passed for 444 yards and three touchdowns, two to All-America wide receiver Josh Reed, who caught fourteen passes for 239 yards, while running back Domanick Davis ran for 122 yards and four more scores. Illinois quarterback Kurt Kittner passed for 262 yards and four touchdowns, two to sophomore wide receiver Brandon Lloyd. In the Fiesta Bowl, No. 2 Oregon played No. 3 Colorado, and Oregon broke Colorado's six-bowl winning string with a 38–16 victory as quarterback Joey Harrington passed for 350 yards and four touchdowns, including a 79-yarder to sophomore wide receiver Samie Parker.

In the Florida Citrus Bowl, No. 8 Tennessee broke No. 17 Michigan's four-bowl winning string with a 45–17 victory as quarterback Casey Clausen passed for 393 yards and three touchdowns, including a 64-yarder to sophomore tight end Jason Witten, and also scored twice on 1-yard runs. No. 10 Oklahoma, in its first Cotton Bowl appearance ever, won a 10–3 defensive struggle over unranked Arkansas. Quarterback Nate Hybl passed for 175 yards and scored on a 1-yard run for the winners, and kicker Tim Duncan added a 32-yard field goal. The Sooners' defense held Arkansas to 50 yards total offense. The biggest Gator Bowl crowd in twelve years watched No. 24 Florida State defeat No. 15 Virginia Tech 30–17 as freshman quarterback Chris Rix passed for 326 yards and two touchdowns, 77 and 23 yards to wide receiver Javon Walker, and scored on a 1-yard run, while freshman kicker Xavier Beitia had field goals of 50, 47, and 35 yards.

An all-time Outback Bowl record crowd of 66,249 saw a thriller between No. 14 South Carolina and No. 22 Ohio State. With South Carolina leading 28-0 in the third-quarter, Buckeye quarterback Steve Bellisari, who passed for 320 yards on the day, engineered a remarkable four-touchdown comeback, passing for two and running in another himself, but a late interception led to sophomore kicker Daniel Weaver's 42-yard field goal on the last play of the game to win it for the Gamecocks 31–28. Quarterback Phil Petty passed for 227 yards and two touchdowns for South Carolina, and fullback Andrew Pinnock ran for two scores.

In the AXA Liberty Bowl, No. 19 Brigham Young faced No. 23 Louisville. BYU, loser only at Hawaii 72–45 in its final regular-season game, led the nation in scoring (46.8-point average) while winning its second Mountain West title. But the Cougars had been without multitalented All-America running back Luke Staley, the nation's scoring leader, in the Hawaii game and would be without him again in the Liberty Bowl. The Cardinals won the game, 28–10, as quarterback Dave Ragone passed for 228 yards and three touchdowns, and running back Henry Miller scored on a 1-yard run.

Postseason records fell in the GMAC Bowl as Marshall overcame a 38–8 halftime deficit to beat East Carolina 64–61 in two overtimes. Quarterback Byron Leftwich passed for 576 yards and four touchdowns and ran in a score as well to lead the Thundering Herd to victory. He directed an 80-yard drive in just fifty seconds to tie the game in regulation time. Wide receiver Denero Marriott had fifteen pass receptions for 234 yards for Marshall, while running back Leonard Henry had 195 yards and three touchdowns rushing for the Pirates.

Colorado State won the inaugural New Orleans Bowl by defeating North Texas 45–20. Seven players scored for the Rams, with sophomore quarterback Bradlee Van Pelt passing for one touchdown and running for another, and kicker Kent Naughton booting a 46-yard field goal and six extra points. Pittsburgh won the first Tangerine Bowl played since 1982 by defeating North Carolina State 34–19. Panther quarterback David Priestley passed for 271 yards and two touchdowns to wide receiver Antonio Bryant, while freshman defensive back Gregory Golden scored on a 90-yard kickoff return for the Wolfpack. Georgia Tech won the first Seattle Bowl with a 24–14 upset of No. 11 Stanford. Quarterback George Godsey passed for 266 yards and a touchdown, 34 yards to wide receiver Kelly Campbell, and also scored on a 2-yard run for the winners. Utah beat Southern California 10–6 before an all-time record Sega Sports Las Vegas Bowl crowd of 30,894. Running back Adam Tate rushed for 103 yards and a touchdown for Utah and kicker Ryan Kaneshiro added a 26-yard field goal.

No. 9 Texas outlasted No. 21 Washington 47–43 in the Culligan Holiday Bowl. Texas quarterback Major Applewhite passed for 473 yards and four touchdowns, and sophomore running back Ivan Williams ran for two more scores. Sophomore quarterback Cody Pickett passed for 293 yards and two touchdowns for Washington, tailback Willie Hurst rushed for 137 yards and two scores, sophomore defensive tackle Terry Johnson scored on a 38-yard interception return, and kicker John Anderson added field goals of 43, 43, and 40 yards.

Texas A&M broke a four-bowl losing string by defeating Texas Christian 28–9 in the galleryfurniture.com Bowl. Quarterback Mark Farris passed for

191 yards, including an 82-yard scoring toss to wide receiver Mickey Jones, and scored on a 1-yard run for the Aggies, and running back Joe Weber ran for two more scores. Defensive back Charlie Owens scored the only Horned Frog touchdown on an 89-yard fumble return. No. 16 Georgia's four-bowl winning string was ended by Boston College in the Music City Bowl, as running back William Green had 149 yards and a touchdown rushing in a 20–16 Eagles victory. In the Insight.com Bowl, No. 18 Syracuse rolled over Kansas State 26–3 as running back James Mungro scored three touchdowns, one on a 65-yard run. In the Motor City Bowl, No. 25 Toledo beat Cincinnati 23–16 despite an excellent performance by Cincinnati freshman quarterback Gino Guidugli, who passed for 283 yards and a touchdown. In the Wells Fargo Sun Bowl, No. 13 Washington State edged Purdue as quarterback Jason Gesser passed for 281 yards and a touchdown and scored on a 1-yard run, defensive back Jason David scored on a 45-yard pass interception return, and kicker Drew Dunning had four field goals for in the Cougars' 33–27 win. Freshman quarterback Kyle Orton passed for 419 yards and two scores for Purdue. In the Silicon Valley Classic, No. 20 Fresno State fell to Michigan State 44–35 as quarterback Jeff Smoker threw for 376 yards and three touchdowns, including scoring tosses of 72 and 69 yards to sophomore wide receiver Charles Rogers, and tailback T. J. Duckett had 184 yards and two touchdowns rushing. Quarterback David Carr passed for 531 yards and four touchdowns, including a 79-yarder to wide receiver Rodney Wright, in a losing effort.

2002   Three more bowls were added for the 2002 postseason, bringing the total number to twenty-eight. This meant almost half of the Division I-A teams would have the opportunity to play in a bowl game. The new ones were the ConAgra Foods Hawaii Bowl in Honolulu, the Continental Tire Bowl at Charlotte, North Carolina, and the Diamond Walnut San Francisco Bowl. In addition, the Tangerine took on a sponsor as the Mazda Tangerine Bowl, the Culligan Holiday changed to the Pacific Life Holiday Bowl, the galleryfurniture.com Bowl became simply the Houston Bowl, the Music City became the Gaylord Hotels Music City Bowl, and the Florida Citrus became the Capital One Bowl.

   This time the BCS "championship" contest, scheduled for January 3 in the Tostitos Fiesta Bowl, generated little controversy as it matched the only two undefeated Division I-A teams, defending national champion Miami and

2001 GMAC Bowl—Marshall quarterback Byron Leftwich (7) passed for 576 yards and four touchdowns on December 19 as the Thundering Herd overcame a 38–8 halftime deficit to defeat East Carolina in two overtimes. The combined 64–61 score was the highest ever in postseason play. (*Collegiate Images*)

opportunistic Ohio State. The crowd of more than 77,000 saw a game worthy of a national title contest. Ohio State ended Miami's 34-game winning streak and five-bowl victory string with a double overtime 31–24 win to take its fifth national title and complete the Buckeyes' first perfect season since their last national championship season in 1968. But it took a controversial pass interference call in the second overtime to give Ohio State another shot—a successful one—at scoring the winning points. Leading the Buckeyes to victory were quarterback Craig Krenzel, who had 122 yards passing and 80 yards and two touchdowns rushing, the second a 1-yard score in the first overtime, and freshman tailback Maurice Clarett, who scored two touchdowns on short runs, the second a 5-yard dash in the second overtime for the game winner. Sophomore All-America kicker Mike Nugent added a 44-yard field goal and four extra points for Ohio State. Miami quarterback Ken Dorsey passed for 296 yards and two touchdowns, 25 yards to freshman wide receiver Roscoe Parrish and, in the first overtime, 7 yards to sophomore tight end Kellen Winslow. Sophomore All-America running back Willis McGahee scored on a 9-yard run before being injured, and kicker Todd Sievers added a 40-yard field goal and three extra points for the Hurricanes.

The FedEx Orange Bowl matched No. 3 Iowa and No. 5 Southern California and their outstanding quarterbacks, Heisman Trophy–winner

Carson Palmer of USC and Iowa's Brad Banks, the nation's passing efficiency leader. Despite an auspicious start for Iowa, with wide receiver C. J. Jones returning the opening kickoff 100 yards for a touchdown, Palmer and USC prevailed 38–17. Palmer passed for 303 yards and a touchdown, tailback Justin Fargas ran for 122 yards and two scores, and backs Sultan McCullough and Sunny Byrd each scored on the ground. For Iowa, Banks ended up with 204 yards and a touchdown passing.

In the Sugar Bowl, No. 4 Georgia beat No. 16 Florida State, 26–13, as tailback Musa Smith ran for 145 yards, defensive back Bruce Thornton scored on a 71-yard pass interception return, split end Terrence Edwards scored on a 37-yard pass from freshman quarterback D. J. Shockley, and kicker Billy Bennett added four field goals. Florida State wide receiver Anquan Boldin caught a touchdown pass and also threw one, a 40-yarder to sophomore wide receiver Craphonso Thorpe. A disappointing crowd of only 86,848, the smallest Rose Bowl attendance since 1944, was on hand for the hundredth anniversary of the first Tournament of Roses game. The reason for the smaller turnout may have been dissatisfaction with the traditional Big 10–Pacific 10 pairings had been interrupted by the Rose Bowl's inclusion in the BCS matchups for the second year in a row. When that occurred the previous year, the Rose at least had the national championship game between Miami and Nebraska, and a capacity crowd was on hand. In 2003, however, Big 10 co-champion Ohio State was playing for the national title in the Fiesta Bowl, and conference co-champion Iowa was assigned by the BCS to the Orange Bowl to meet Pac-10 co-champion Southern California. Assigned to play Pac-10 co-champion Washington State in the Rose Bowl was Big 12 champion Oklahoma. No. 8 Oklahoma rolled to a 34–14 win over No. 7 Washington State as quarterback Nate Hybl passed for 240 yards and two touchdowns, running back Quentin Griffin ran for 144 yards and a score, and sophomore defensive back Antonio Perkins returned a punt 51 yards for a touchdown. Quarterback Jason Gesser, though hobbled with an injury, passed for 239 yards and a touchdown for Washington State, and wide receiver Sammy Moore scored on an 89-yard kickoff return.

In the SBC Cotton Bowl, No. 9 Texas beat unranked LSU, 35–20, as quarterback Chris Simms passed for 269 yards and two touchdowns, including a 51-yarder to wide receiver Roy Williams, who also scored on a 39-yard run, and linebacker Lee Jackson scored on 46-yard fumble return. Sophomore quarterback Marcus Randall passed for 193 yards and a touchdown for LSU.

The largest crowd in the Gator Bowl in thirteen years saw No. 17 North Carolina State roll to a surprisingly easy 28–6 win over No. 11 Notre Dame as quarterback Philip Rivers passed for 228 yards and two touchdowns, and freshman tailback T. A. McLendon scored a pair of touchdowns on short runs. Notre Dame lost quarterback Carlyle Holiday to an injury in the first half and managed to score only on two field goals. In the Capital One Bowl, No. 19 Auburn beat No. 10 Penn State 13–9 in a defensive battle as sophomore running back Ronnie Brown ran for 184 yards and both Auburn touchdowns. And in the Outback Bowl, No. 12 Michigan won a high-scoring 38–30 game over No. 22 Florida as quarterback John Navarre passed for 319 yards and a touchdown, and running back Chris Perry ran for four scores.

Attendance records were set at the GMAC Bowl and at the Crucial.com Humanitarian Bowl. In the GMAC Bowl, before 40,646, Marshall rolled to a 38–15 win over Louisville. Quarterback Byron Leftwich passed for four touchdowns, two to wide receiver Denero Marriott and a pair to wide receiver Demetrius Doss, for the Thundering Herd. Quarterback Dave Ragone passed for 193 yards and a score for the Cardinals. Before 30,446 at the Crucial.com Humanitarian Bowl, No. 18 Boise State came out the 34–16 victor over Iowa State. Running back Brock Forsey, the nation's scoring leader, ran for three touchdowns for the Broncos, and quarterback Ryan Dinwiddie passed for 160 yards and a touchdown and scored on a 1-yard run.

A capacity crowd of 73,535 turned out for the inaugural Continental Tire Bowl at Charlotte, North Carolina, between Virginia and No. 15 West Virginia in the first meeting of these neighbor state rivals since 1985. Freshman tailback Wali Lundy sparked the Cavaliers with 127 yards and two touchdowns rushing, and two more scores on pass receptions, while quarterback Matt Schaub passed for 182 yards and a touchdown and scored on a 1-yard run, as Virginia snapped a four-bowl losing string with a 48–22 upset win. Sophomore quarterback Rasheed Marshall passed for 215 yards and scored on a 1-yard run for West Virginia, and running back Avon Cobourne had 117 yards and two touchdowns rushing. In the other new bowls, Tulane beat Hawaii 36–28 in the ConAgra Foods Hawaii Bowl and No. 21 Virginia Tech had a 20–13 win over Air Force in the Diamond Walnut San Francisco Bowl.

The Sylvania Alamo Bowl was a thriller as Wisconsin engineered a 31–28 overtime upset win over No. 14 Colorado on a 37-yard field goal by sophomore kicker Mike Allen. Quarterback Brooks Bollinger passed for 163 yards and two touchdowns and ran for 82 yards and another score for Wisconsin, while wide receiver D. J. Hackett caught two scoring passes for Colorado and defensive back Donald Strickland scored on a 91-yard pass interception return.

In other bowls, No. 24 Pittsburgh beat Oregon State 38–13 in the Insight.com Bowl as quarterback Rod Rutherford threw a 40-yard touchdown pass to freshman wide receiver Larry Fitzgerald and scored on a 1-yard run, and defensive back Shawn Robinson scored on a 66-yard punt return. In the Pacific Life Holiday Bowl, No. 6 Kansas State got by Arizona State 34–27 as quarterback Ell Roberson passed for 215 yards and a touchdown and ran for three scores. In the Gaylord Hotels Music City Bowl, No. 25 Arkansas was upset by Minnesota 29–14 as quarterback Asad Abdul-Khaliq passed for 216 yards and a touchdown, and kicker Dan Nystrom had five field goals. In the AXA Liberty Bowl, No. 23 Colorado State fell 17–3 to Texas Christian. Quarterback Sean Stilley passed for one Horned Frog touchdown and tailback Ricky Madison ran in the other. No. 20 Maryland rolled over Tennessee 30–3 in the Chick-Fil-A Peach Bowl as quarterback Scott McBrien ran for two touchdowns, defensive back Curome Cox scored on a 54-yard pass interception return, and kicker Nick Novak added three field goals.

The total bowl payout for this postseason was a record high $172,710,000, but the per game average ($6,168,214) and per team average ($3,084,107) were a few hundred thousand dollars below the all-time averages set in the 1998 postseason. Bowl total attendance also reached a record high of 1,416,103, although the per game average of 50,575 was the lowest in twenty-three years given the greater number of bowls.

2003   Total number of bowl games for the 2003 postseason remained at twenty-eight, when the Seattle Bowl was dropped but was replaced by the Plains Capital Fort Worth Bowl in Texas. A few name changes also were made because of different sponsors, but for the most part the lineup remained little different from the 2002 postseason.

This time the Nokia Sugar Bowl was the site for the national "championship" game on January 4, but the complex BCS formula's selections led to unprecedented controversy about the whole system. Pac-10 champion Southern California, loser only to California 34–31 in triple overtime and ranked No. 1 in both the AP and *USA Today*/ESPN rankings, was not even selected to participate at New Orleans. Instead, the berths were awarded to

No. 2 Louisiana State, loser only to Florida 19–7 and victor over Georgia 34–13 in the SEC title game, and No. 3 Oklahoma, which had been embarrassed by Kansas State 35–7 in the Big 12 championship game after winning all twelve of its regular-season contests. Instead, USC was invited to the Rose Bowl to play No. 4-ranked Big 10 champion Michigan. This led to the possibility of the selection of national co-champions, just the sort of result that the various bowl arrangements had tried to avoid since the formation of the Bowl Coalition in 1992.

Southern California proved to a capacity crowd that it was worthy of its claim, defeating Michigan 28–14 as sophomore quarterback Matt Leinart passed for 327 yards and three touchdowns, 25 and 47 yards to wide receiver Keary Colbert and 6 yards to freshman tailback Lendale White, and scored on a 15-yard pass from sophomore All-America wide receiver Mike Williams. Quarterback John Navarre passed for 271 yards and a score for Michigan, and All-America running back Chris Perry had 85 yards and a touchdown rushing, but the Wolverines never posed a serious threat. In the final AP poll, USC was awarded its ninth national title, its first since 1978.

When LSU met Oklahoma in the Sugar Bowl three nights later, most of those in the sold-out stadium knew that the winner was playing for a share of the national championship, not for sole possession. LSU won 21–14, holding Oklahoma to only 154 total yards while freshman running back Justin Vincent had 117 yards rushing, including an 18-yard scoring run, quarterback Matt Mauck passed for 124 yards, sophomore wide receiver Skyler Green scored on a 24-yard run, and defensive end Marcus Spears scored on a 20-yard interception return. Heisman Trophy–winning quarterback Jason White had only 102 yards passing for Oklahoma, and sophomore running back Kejuan Jones scored both Sooner touchdowns on 1-yard runs. In the final coaches' poll, which by contract with the BCS allowed championship votes only for the winner of the BCS title game, LSU was awarded its second national championship, first since 1958.

In the other BCS games, No. 10 Miami edged No. 9 Florida State 16–14 in the Orange Bowl on a 51-yard third-quarter field goal by freshman kicker Jon Peattie. Miami, which had defeated the Seminoles 22–14 in the regular-season finale, won as quarterback Brock Berlin passed for 157 yards, running back Jarrett Payton rushed for 131 yards, freshman running back Tyrone Moss scored on a 3-yard run, and Peattie booted field goals of 32 and 44 yards as well as his game winner. Florida State led 14–13 at halftime on a touchdown run by freshman running back Lorenzo Booker and a pass from quarterback Chris Rix to sophomore quarterback Matt Henshaw. In the Tostitos Fiesta Bowl, No. 7 Ohio State led 35–14 after three quarters, then withstood a final-quarter rally by No. 8 Kansas State for a 35–28 win. Buckeye quarterback Craig Krenzel passed for 189 yards and four touchdowns, two each to freshman flanker Santonio Holmes and split end Michael Jenkins, and split end John Hollins scored on a blocked punt return. For Kansas State, quarterback Ell Roberson passed for 294 yards and ran for two touchdowns.

No. 11 Georgia outscored No. 12 Purdue 34–27 in overtime in the Capital One Bowl as quarterback David Greene passed for 327 yards and three touchdowns, two to flanker Fred Gibson, and freshman running back Kregg Lumpkin had 90 yards rushing and scored the winning touchdown in overtime on a 1-yard run. Kicker Billy Bennett added two field goals and four extra points for the winners. Boilermaker quarterback Kyle Orton passed for 230 yards and a touchdown and ran for two scores. In the Outback Bowl, No. 13 Iowa beat No. 17 Florida 37–17 as quarterback Nathan Chandler passed for 170 yards and a touchdown and scored on a 5-yard run, running back Fred Russell had 150 yards rushing and scored on a 34-yard run, and All-America kicker Nate Kaeding added three field goals and four extra points. Florida freshman quarterback Chris Leak passed for 268 yards and two touchdowns, 70 yards to wide receiver Kelvin Kight and 25 yards to sophomore wide receiver Dallas Baker. And in a Toyota Gator Bowl rematch, No. 23 Maryland upended No. 20 West Virginia 41–7 behind quarterback Scott McBrien, who passed for 381 yards and three touchdowns, and wide receiver Steve Suter scored on a 76-yard punt return. The Terps beat the Mountaineers 34–7 in regular season.

The SBC Cotton Bowl Classic saw an exciting contest between No. 16 Mississippi and No. 21 Oklahoma State. Mississippi quarterback Eli Manning, son of Archie and brother of Peyton Manning, quarterback stars in earlier bowls, passed for 259 yards and two touchdowns and scored on a 1-yard run, while running back Tremaine Turner rushed for 133 yards and a score and caught a 16-yard touchdown pass, and kicker Jonathan Nichols added a 33-yard field goal in a 31–28 victory. Quarterback Josh Fields threw for 307 yards and a touchdown for the Cowboys, wide receiver Rashaun Woods caught eleven passes for 223 yards and a score, and freshman running back Vernand Morency scored two touchdowns on short runs. No. 6

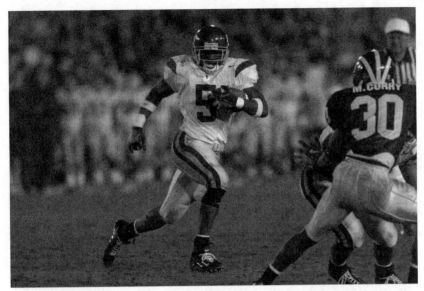

2004 Rose Bowl—Southern California freshman tailback Reggie Bush (5) gains yardage against Michigan in a victory that earned the Trojans a tie with LSU for the 2003 national championship. (*Pasadena Tournament of Roses*)

Tennessee was upset 27–14 by unranked Clemson in the Chick-Fil-A Peach Bowl as sophomore quarterback Charlie Whitehurst passed for 246 yards, running back Chad Jasmin rushed for 130 yards and a touchdown, and sophomore tailbacks Duane Coleman and Kyle Browning scored on 8-yard runs. In a losing effort, quarterback Casey Clausen passed for 384 yards and both Tennessee touchdowns.

In the new Plains Capital Fort Worth Bowl, No. 18 ranked WAC champion Boise State pulled out an exciting 34–31 win over No. 18 Texas Christian as quarterback Ryan Dinwiddie passed for 325 yards and three touchdowns, including a 54-yarder to freshman running back Jeff Carpenter. Freshman tailback Lonta Hobbs ran for 117 yards and a touchdown for TCU, and freshman wide receiver Cory Rodgers caught a 22-yard scoring toss from sophomore quarterback Brandon Hassell.

In other bowls involving ranked teams, No. 13 Miami (Ohio) rolled over Louisville 49–28 in the GMAC Bowl as quarterback Ben Roethlisberger passed for 376 yards and four touchdowns, two to wide receiver Michael Larkin, running back Calvin Murray rushed for 142 yards and a score, and defensive back Matt Pusateri scored on a 35-yard interception return. In the

Alamo Bowl, No. 22 Nebraska beat Michigan State 17–3 as sophomore running back Cory Ross ran for 138 yards and two touchdowns and the Cornhuskers held the Spartans to 18 yards rushing. On December 30 in the Pacific Life Holiday Bowl, No. 5 Texas was upset 28–20 by No. 15 Washington State as Cougar quarterback Matt Kegel passed for 203 yards and two touchdowns, both to wide receiver Sammy Moore, including a 54-yarder, and running back Jonathan Smith had 110 yards and a score rushing. In the Wells Fargo Sun Bowl, No. 24 Minnesota edged Oregon 31–30 in the only bowl in this postseason decided by one point. Running back Laurence Maroney had 131 yards and a touchdown rushing for the Gophers, while quarterback Asad Abdul-Khaliq passed for 172 yards, Thomas Tapeh scored three touchdowns on short runs, and kicker Rhys Lloyd added a 42-yard field goal. Oregon sophomore quarterback Kellen Clemens threw for 363 yards and three touchdowns, two to wide receiver Samie Parker, and sophomore kicker Jared Siegel had three field goals. In the AXA Liberty Bowl, No. 25 Utah blanked Southern Mississippi 17–0 in the first bowl shutout in four years. Defensive back Morgan Scalley clinched the game with a fourth quarter score on a 74-yard fumble return.

After all was said and done, the 2003 postseason left Division I-A with national co-champions for the first time since 1997, five years after the Bowl Coalition went into effect in an attempt to prevent just such an occurrence. And the BCS, controversial from the beginning, received unprecedented criticism from fans, coaches, sportswriters, and broadcasters for the postseason 2003 selections. Could the BCS become effective with just modest tweaking, or is a major reorganization needed? Is it possible, or even desirable, for the traditional bowl system to be used as a satisfactory playoff system for Division I-A college football teams? And is it truly necessary to name one team the national champion every season in any case? No quick or easy solutions appear in sight.

REFLECTIONS

MY FIRST ACQUAINTANCE WITH BOWL GAMES came on January 1, 1947, when I settled in close to the big living room radio set and listened to the CBS broadcast of Rice's 8-0 win over Tennessee in the Orange Bowl and the NBC broadcast of Illinois' 45-14 romp over undefeated UCLA in the Rose Bowl in the first contest under the Big 10-Pacific Coast Conference pact. Ten bowl games that day were subsequently recognized by the NCAA, and there would have been one more had not the Alamo Bowl been postponed for three days because the field was covered with a thick layer of ice. Every bowl for big college teams was scheduled on New Year's Day. None was televised, and most were not even heard on radio by much of the nation. One could see highlights of the major bowls a few days later in the newsreels at movie theaters.

A lot of bowls in that 1946 postseason involved small college teams: three in November, nearly a dozen in December, and nearly ten more on New Year's Day. But most of these drew little note except by followers of the teams involved. Most attracted fewer than 12,000 fans, except for the Pineapple Bowl in Honolulu, where 20,000 turned out to see Hawaii defeat Utah 19-16, and the Little Rose Bowl game in Pasadena in December, which drew 51,000 to see what in effect was a battle for the junior college national championship. Compton Junior College of California beat Kilgore Junior College of Texas 10-0 in that one. In addition, there were two popular all-star contests. The South beat the North 20-13 before 22,500 in the Blue and Gray game at Montgomery, Alabama, in December, and the West defeated the East 13-9 in the Shrine game at San Francisco on New Year's Day before 62,000—a crowd exceeded only by the Rose and Sugar Bowls in that postseason. Among teams that played in these smaller bowls, only two currently are classified as Division I-A by the NCAA. They are North Texas State, which defeated College of Pacific 14-13 in the Optimist Bowl at Houston, Texas, and Toledo, which beat Bates 21-12 in the Glass Bowl at Toledo, Ohio. Both were December games.

The situation was similar for the first decade of my acquaintance with bowl games: a dozen or fewer bowl games for the bigger schools, most or all played on New Year's Day. There was a special aura about the twenty or so teams selected to participate in those games, and New Year's Day and college football were synonymous. Even as major changes took place in the structure of postseason play in succeeding decades, the tradition of bowl games gave a distinctive flavor to college football that remained unique for Division I-A after the NCAA divided its membership into classifications in the 1970s and went to playoff systems in Division I-AA, Division II, and Division III.

Yet this particular distinction is in danger of falling by the wayside because of the proliferation of bowl games in recent decades and the demand for a playoff system to determine a single national champion annually. Even if some of the traditional bowl games were retained in a playoff system, it would not be the same. That already has been seen in the "playoff" attempts in the past dozen years under the Bowl Coalition of 1992-1994, the Bowl Alliance of 1995-1997, and the Bowl Championship Series in effect since 1998. In the 2003 postseason, especially, the crescendo of criticism was deafening after Southern California, ranked No.1 in both the AP and *USA Today*/ESPN polls, was left out of the BCS playoff game on January 4 in the Nokia Sugar Bowl in favor of teams ranked No. 2 and No. 3 in the wire service polls, but rated first and second under the complex BCS formula. No. 2 Louisiana State beat No. 3 Oklahoma 21-14 in the Sugar Bowl to win the national championship—or did it? Yes, according to the coaches poll of *USA Today*/ESPN, in which by contract the voters are required to cast national championship votes only for the winner of the BCS title game. No, according to the sportswriters and sports broadcasters who voted in the AP poll. They chose USC as the national champion after the Trojans defeated Michigan 28-14 in the Rose Bowl.

Thus, for the first time since 1997, when Michigan was named national champion by AP and Nebraska by *USA Today*/ESPN, the selectors could not settle on one team as national champion. And the 1997 split was five years after various bowl "playoff" systems had first been instituted in postseason 1992. Arguments could be made that at least one of the best teams in the land did not have a chance to win the title in several of the years since the playoff systems have been tried. In 1994, for example, in the last year of the Bowl Coalition, No. 2 Penn State was committed to the Rose Bowl (which was not a part of the Coalition), so the national title went to No. 1 Nebraska, which beat No. 3 Miami in the FedEx Orange Bowl. Under the Bowl Alliance in 1996, the situation was similar. No. 2 Arizona State was committed to the Rose Bowl (still not in the "playoff" system), and the national title went to No. 3 Florida, which upset No. 1 Florida State in the Nokia Sugar Bowl. Arizona State was defeated by Ohio State in the Rose Bowl, however, in effect forfeiting its claim to the national crown. In 1997, No. 1 Michigan was left out of the championship game by its commitment to the Rose Bowl. Michigan completed a perfect season with a bowl victory over Washington State, and was voted national champion in the AP poll, but the coaches chose No. 2 Nebraska, which defeated No. 3 Tennessee in the FedEx Orange Bowl.

The first two years of the BCS system did match the No. 1 and No. 2 teams (the Rose Bowl finally was included in the system), but in the 2000 postseason No. 1 Oklahoma was awarded the national championship with a win over No. 3 Florida State in the FedEx Orange Bowl, while No.2 Miami beat Florida in the Nokia Sugar Bowl. In the 2001 postseason, the BCS got serious criticism for matching No. 4 Nebraska, which had not even won the Big 12 title, against No. 1 Miami in the Rose Bowl. Miami won easily to annex the national championship, while No. 2 Oregon beat No. 3 Colorado in the Tostitos Fiesta Bowl. The No. 1- and No. 2-ranked teams were matched following the 2002 season. Then came the deluge of criticism in connection with the postseason 2003 selections.

Dissatisfaction even showed up in the television ratings for the "championship" game. The Sugar Bowl had a 14.5 national rating, barely higher than the 14.4 of the Rose Bowl played on a day in which four other bowl games took place. And it was down considerably from an 18.6 rating for the "championship" game the previous year in the Fiesta Bowl. Each rating point represents about one million households.

Not content with two teams sharing national honors after the 2003 postseason, a proposal was made for one further game to be played. Ted Waitt, chairman and CEO of the Gateway computer firm, offered both USC and LSU $10 million in scholarships for disadvantaged students if they would play on the weekend of January 24-25. The winner not only would be recognized as the true national champion, but would receive another $10 million in scholarships and $1 million in Gateway products. The proposal was made in letters to LSU Chancellor Mark Emmert, USC President Steven Sample, and NCAA President Myles Brand. But the NCAA ruled that such a game would not be possible under its current bylaws.

Many possible changes in the BCS system were discussed in the months preceding the 2004 regular season, with agreement reached between February and July on a number of modifications. Discarded were proposals to make it imperative for a team to win its conference championship before being considered for the title game and to drop all computer rankings from the selection formula. Instead, the "human" polls were brought back into prominence, which should eliminate the chance of a No. 1 team being denied a spot in the title game, as was the case with USC last season. Under the formula announced on July 15, the Associated Press poll of sportswriters/broadcasters will count for one-third of each team's ranking, one-third will be based on the rankings in the USA Today/ESPN coaches poll, and the final one-third will be from a combination of six computer rankings. This will go into effect during the 2004 season.

Earlier, it was decided that a fifth BCS bowl would be added, starting in 2006, opening up two more spots for members of conferences not currently tied in automatically to the BCS system. The extra game would be the championship contest played at the site of one of the current BCS bowls—Rose, Orange, Sugar, or Fiesta—on a rotating basis. It would take place a week or more after the regular bowl is played at that site. Discussions also were begun on proposals to eventually include all Division I-A members in the BCS structure.

Even if possible to match the No. 1 and No. 2 teams annually in the revised BCS system, can it or any other system preserve the uniqueness of the bowl system? Not likely. Already, the focus on a championship contest normally scheduled two or three days after New Year's Day diminishes the aura of the special holiday games. It has become much more like a Super Bowl atmosphere, with similar buildup and hype, and much less like a traditional bowl game—whether played in the Rose, Orange, Sugar, or Fiesta. And the 2006 plan for a championship game at an even later date gives the bowl system still more of a Super Bowl-type atmosphere.

Is it such a bad thing for Division I-A college football to be different from the other NCAA classifications, anyway? Does it really cheapen the sport when more than one school can claim to be national champion? The wire service polls disagreed on which school should be named national champion in all three of the first years after the UP coaches poll was instituted, in 1950-1952. It happened three more times in the decade ending in 1960 and six times in the decade of 1961-1970. But co-champions were named only three times in the 1971-1980 decade, and since then only three times more—in 1990, 1991 and 1997—before the 2003 BCS fiasco. And, whenever co-champions have been named, it has extended bragging rights while leading to heated discussions between the regular college football seasons. Thus, college football remains a topic of lively debate in what normally are slow periods of coverage of the sport by sportswriters and broadcasters.

The college atmosphere of the bowls has been eroding since the latter decades of the twentieth century. Halftime—especially in the larger bowls—is taken up on television with endless rehashing and analysis of action on the field that the viewer already has seen in dozens of instant replays, or by showing rock stars or other ubiquitous celebrities taking the spotlight. Members of the marching bands of the participating schools, who normally put in long hours of rehearsal for a few minutes of entertainment for bowl crowds, are fortunate if they get any television exposure on game day.

The plethora of bowl games also takes away from the traditional aura of the postseason. With twenty-eight bowl games following the past two seasons, and the same number expected following the 2004 regular season, receiving a bid nowadays seems less of a reward for an outstanding season and a challenge to prove yourself against another quality team, and more of a necessity to fill in the holes in the athletic budgets for many schools. Most coaches these days are happy enough to receive any bowl bid. It gives them extra practice days, almost like an extra spring training period, and sometimes their contracts contain provisions sweetening their income through bowl participation. And with only five bowl games actually played on the January 1 traditional date in 2004, the enchantment of New Year's Day being synonymous with college football also is on the wane. One who experienced the mystique of college football bowl games in the mid-twentieth century cannot help but wish for those simpler and, in some ways, more magical times.

Yet, it is unlikely that the number of bowl games will be pared back any time in the foreseeable future. Too much is at stake financially for the bowls, for broadcasters and the accompanying revenue from commercials, and for university athletic departments that rely on income from frequent bowl appearances. Whereas bowl games used to be covered by a half-dozen or more networks, syndicates, and individual television stations, in recent years they have become almost a monopoly of ABC-TV and ESPN, both of which are part of the Walt Disney conglomerate. In the 2003 postseason, ABC-TV telecast the four BCS games in the Rose, Orange, Sugar, and Fiesta Bowls, as well as the Capital One Bowl, while ESPN or ESPN2 covered most of the rest. There are still a few exceptions. The Cotton Bowl was televised by Fox Sports, the Gator Bowl by NBC, and the Sun Bowl by CBS. But ESPN covered the Alamo, Continental Tire, Fort Worth, Hawaii, Holiday, Houston, Humanitarian, Independence, Insight, Las Vegas, Liberty, Motor City, Music City, Outback, Peach, and Tangerine bowls, and ESPN2 televised the GMAC, New Orleans, San Francisco, and Silicon Valley bowls.

In addition, America's apparent obsession with having a No.1 in almost everything seems fated ultimately to lead to some sort of playoff system in Division I-A college football as well. It is sad to see a further erosion of the unique traditions formed by a century of college football bowl contests. The consolation is that as long as the contests are documented, past games will not be forgotten, nor are such traditions likely to completely disappear in the future. Under whatever format, the holiday periods following college football's regular seasons will continue to produce dramatic games, superlative individual performances, and enduring memories.

APPENDIX 1

Major bowls recognized by the NCAA, 1902-2004

Regular season records follow each team name. Teams are listed in alphabetical order where there is a tie game. An asterisk indicates an overtime game, multiple asterisks indicate the number of overtimes. Boldface indicates national champion(s) and all-time attendance records.

Date	Bowl	Winner	Score	Loser	Atten.
Jan. 1, 1902	Rose	**Michigan** (10-0)	49-0	Stanford (3-1-2)	8,000
Jan. 1, 1916	Rose	Washington State (6-0)	14-0	Brown (5-3-1)	7,000
Jan. 1, 1917	Rose	Oregon (6-0-1)	14-0	Pennsylvania (7-2-1)	26,000
Jan. 1, 1918	Rose	Mare Island (5-0)	19-7	Camp Lewis (5-1-1)	25,000
Jan. 1, 1919	Rose	Great Lakes (6-2)	17-0	Mare Island (10-0)	NA
Jan. 1, 1920	Rose	**Harvard** (8-0-1)	7-6	Oregon (5-1)	30,000
Jan. 1, 1921	Rose	**California** (8-0)	28-0	Ohio St. (7-0)	42,000
Jan. 1, 1921	Ft. Worth Cl.	Centre (7-2)	63-7	Texas Christian (9-0)	9,000
Dec. 26, 1921	San Diego Cl.	Centre (9-0)	38-0	Arizona (7-1)	5,000
Jan. 2, 1922	Rose	**California** (9-0)	0-0	Wash. & Jeff. (10-0)	40,000
Jan. 2, 1922	Dixie Classic	Texas A&M (5-1-2)	22-14	Centre (10-0)	12,000
Dec. 25, 1922	San Diego Cl.	West Virginia (9-0-1)	21-13	Gonzaga (5-2)	5,000
Jan. 1, 1923	Rose	Sou. California (9-1)	14-3	Penn St. (6-3-1)	43,000
Jan. 1, 1924	Rose	Navy (5-1-2)	14-14	Washington (10-1)	40,000
Dec. 25, 1924	L.A. Chr. Fest.	Sou. California (8-2)	20-7	Missouri (7-1)	47,000
Jan. 1, 1925	Rose	**Notre Dame** (9-0)	27-10	Stanford (7-0-1)	53,000
Jan. 1, 1925	Dixie Classic	W. V. Wesleyan (8-2)	9-7	Sou. Methodist (5-0-4)	7,000
Jan. 1, 1926	Rose	**Alabama** (9-0)	20-19	Washington (10-0-1)	50,000
Jan. 1, 1927	Rose	**Alabama** (9-0)	7-7	Stanford (10-0)	57,417
Date	Bowl	Winner	Score	Loser	Atten.
Jan. 2, 1928	Rose	Stanford (7-2-1)	7-6	Pittsburgh (8-0-1)	65,000
Jan. 1, 1929	Rose	**Georgia Tech** (9-0)	8-7	California (6-1-2)	66,604
Jan. 1, 1930	Rose	Sou. California (9-2)	47-14	Pittsburgh (9-0)	72,000
Jan. 1, 1931	Rose	**Alabama** (9-0)	24-0	Washington St. (9-0)	60,000

Date	Bowl	Winner	Score	Loser	Atten.
Jan. 1, 1932	Rose	**Sou. California** (9-1)	21-12	Tulane (11-0)	75,562
Jan. 1, 1933	Rose	**Sou. California** (9-0)	35-0	Pittsburgh (8-0-2)	78,874
Jan. 1, 1934	Rose	Columbia (7-1)	7-0	Stanford (8-1-1)	35,000
Jan. 1, 1934	Dixie Classic	Arkansas (7-3)	7-7	Centenary (8-0-3)	12,000
Jan. 1, 1935	Rose	**Alabama** (9-0)	29-13	Stanford (10-0)	84,474
Jan. 1, 1935	Orange	Bucknell (5-2-2)	26-0	Miami (5-2-1)	5,134
Jan. 1, 1935	Sugar	Tulane (10-1)	20-14	Temple (7-0-2)	22,026
Jan. 1, 1936	Rose	Stanford (7-1)	7-0	**Sou. Methodist** (12-0)	84,474
Jan. 1, 1936	Orange	Catholic University (7-1)	20-19	Mississippi (9-2)	6,568
Jan. 1, 1936	Sugar	Texas Christian (11-1)	3-2	Louisiana St. (9-1)	35,000
Jan. 1, 1936	Sun	Hardin-Simmons (7-3)	14-14	N. Mex. A&M (7-1-1)	11,000
Jan. 1, 1937	Rose	Pittsburgh (7-1-1)	21-0	Washington (7-1-1)	87,196
Jan. 1, 1937	Orange	Duquesne (7-2)	13-12	Mississippi St. (7-2-1)	9,210
Jan. 1, 1937	Sugar	Santa Clara (8-1)	21-14	Louisiana St. (9-0-1)	41,000
Jan. 1, 1937	Sun	Hardin-Simmons (8-2)	34-6	Texas Mines (5-2-1)	10,000
Jan. 1, 1937	Cotton	Texas Christian (8-2-2)	16-6	Marquette (7-1)	17,000
Jan. 1, 1937	Bacardi	Auburn (7-2-1)	7-7	Villanova (7-2)	12,000
Jan. 1, 1938	Rose	California (9-0-1)	13-0	Alabama (9-0)	90,000
Jan. 1, 1938	Orange	Auburn (5-2-3)	6-0	Michigan St. (8-2)	18,972
Jan. 1, 1938	Sugar	Santa Clara (8-0)	6-0	Louisiana St. (9-1)	45,000
Jan. 1, 1938	Sun	West Virginia (7-1-1)	7-6	Texas Tech (8-3)	12,000
Jan. 1, 1938	Cotton	Rice (5-3-2)	28-14	Colorado (8-0)	37,000
Jan. 2, 1939	Rose	Sou. California (8-2)	7-3	Duke (9-0)	89,452
Jan. 2, 1939	Orange	Tennessee (10-0)	17-0	Oklahoma (10-0)	32,191
Jan. 2, 1939	Sugar	**Texas Christian** (10-0)	15-7	Carnegie Tech (7-1)	50,000
Jan. 2, 1939	Sun	Utah (7-1-2)	26-0	New Mexico (8-2)	13,000
Jan. 2, 1939	Cotton	St. Mary's (6-2)	20-13	Texas Tech (10-0)	40,000
Jan. 1, 1940	Rose	Sou. California (7-0-2)	14-0	Tennessee (10-0)	92,200
Jan. 1, 1940	Orange	Georgia Tech (7-2)	21-7	Missouri (9-1)	29,278
Jan. 1, 1940	Sugar	**Texas A&M** (10-0)	14-13	Tulane (8-1-1)	73,000
Jan. 1, 1940	Sun	Arizona St. (8-2)	0-0	Catholic U. (8-1)	12,000
Jan. 1, 1940	Cotton	Clemson (8-1)	6-3	Boston College (9-1)	20,000
Jan. 1, 1941	Rose	Stanford (9-0)	21-13	Nebraska (8-1)	91,500
Jan. 1, 1941	Orange	Mississippi St. (9-0-1)	14-7	Georgetown (8-1)	29,554
Jan. 1, 1941	Sugar	Boston College (10-0)	19-13	Tennessee (10-0)	73,181
Jan. 1, 1941	Sun	Western Reserve (7-1)	26-13	Arizona St. (7-1-2)	14,000
Jan. 1, 1941	Cotton	Texas A&M (8-1)	13-12	Fordham (7-1)	45,500
Jan. 1, 1942	Rose	Oregon St. (7-2)	20-16	Duke (9-0)	56,000
Jan. 1, 1942	Orange	Georgia (8-1-1)	40-26	Texas Christian (7-3)	35,786
Jan. 1, 1942	Sugar	Fordham (7-1)	2-0	Missouri (8-1)	72,000
Jan. 1, 1942	Sun	Tulsa (7-2)	6-0	Texas Tech (9-1)	14,000
Jan. 1, 1942	Cotton	Alabama (8-2)	29-21	Texas A&M (9-2)	38,000

Date	Bowl	Winner	Score	Loser	Atten.
Jan. 1, 1943	Rose	Georgia (10-1)	9-0	UCLA (7-3)	93,000
Jan. 1, 1943	Orange	Alabama (7-3)	37-21	Boston College (8-1)	25,166
Jan. 1, 1943	Sugar	Tennessee (8-1-1)	14-7	Tulsa (10-0)	70,000
Jan. 1, 1943	Sun	Second Air Force (10-0-1)	13-7	Hardin-Simmons (8-0-1)	16,000
Jan. 1, 1943	Cotton	Texas (8-2)	14-7	Georgia Tech (9-1)	36,000
Jan. 1, 1944	Rose	Sou. California (7-2)	29-0	Washington (4-0)	68,000
Jan. 1, 1944	Orange	Louisiana St. (5-3)	19-14	Texas A&M (7-1-1)	25,203
Jan. 1, 1944	Sugar	Georgia Tech (7-3)	20-18	Tulsa (6-0-1)	69,000
Jan. 1, 1944	Sun	Southwestern (9-1-1)	7-0	New Mexico (3-1)	18,000
Jan. 1, 1944	Cotton	Randolph Field (9-1)	7-7	Texas (7-1)	15,000
Jan. 1, 1945	Rose	Sou. California (7-0-2)	25-0	Tennessee (7-0-1)	91,000
Jan. 1, 1945	Orange	Tulsa (7-2)	26-12	Georgia Tech (8-2)	23,279
Jan. 1, 1945	Sugar	Duke (5-4)	29-26	Alabama (5-1-2)	72,000
Jan. 1, 1945	Sun	Southwestern (6-5)	35-0	U. of Mexico	13,000
Jan. 1, 1945	Cotton	Oklahoma A&M (7-1)	34-0	Texas Christian (7-2-1)	37,000
Jan. 1, 1946	Rose	Alabama (9-0)	34-14	Sou. California (7-3)	93,000
Jan. 1, 1946	Orange	Miami (8-1-1)	13-6	Holy Cross (8-1)	35,709
Jan. 1, 1946	Sugar	Oklahoma (8-0)	33-13	St. Mary's (7-1)	75,000
Jan. 1, 1946	Sun	New Mexico (5-1-1)	34-24	Denver (4-4-1)	15,000
Jan. 1, 1946	Cotton	Texas (9-1)	40-27	Missouri (6-3)	45,000
Jan. 1, 1946	Gator	Wake Forest (4-3-1)	26-14	South Carolina (2-3-3)	7,362
Jan. 1, 1946	Oil	Georgia (8-2)	20-6	Tulsa (8-2)	27,000
Jan. 1, 1946	Raisin	Drake (4-4-1)	13-12	Fresno St. (4-5-2)	10,000
Jan. 1, 1947	Rose	Illinois (7-2)	45-14	UCLA (10-0)	90,000
Jan. 1, 1947	Orange	Rice (8-2)	8-0	Tennessee (9-1)	36,152
Jan. 1, 1947	Sugar	Georgia (10-0)	20-10	North Carolina (8-1-1)	73,300
Jan. 1, 1947	Sun	Cincinnati (8-2)	18-6	Virginia Tech (3-3-3)	10,000
Jan. 1, 1947	Cotton	Arkansas (6-3-1)	0-0	Louisiana St. (9-1)	38,000
Jan. 1, 1947	Gator	Oklahoma (7-3)	34-13	N. Carolina St. (8-2)	10,134
Jan. 1, 1947	Oil	Georgia Tech (8-2)	41-19	St. Mary's (6-2)	23,000
Jan. 1, 1947	Raisin	San Jose St. (8-1-1)	20-0	Utah St. (7-1-1)	13,000
Jan. 1, 1947	Tangerine	Catawba (9-1)	31-6	Maryville (Tenn.) (9-0)	9,000
Jan. 1, 1947	Harbor	Montana St. (5-3-1)	13-13	New Mexico (5-5-1)	7,000
Jan. 4, 1947	Alamo	Hardin-Simmons (10-0)	20-0	Denver (5-4-1)	3,730
Dec. 6, 1947	Great Lakes	Kentucky (7-3)	24-14	Villanova (6-2-1)	14,908
Jan. 1, 1948	Rose	Michigan (9-0)	49-0	Sou. California (7-1-1)	93,000
Jan. 1, 1948	Orange	Georgia Tech (9-1)	20-14	Kansas (8-0-2)	59,578
Jan. 1, 1948	Sugar	Texas (9-1)	27-7	Alabama (8-2)	72,000
Jan. 1, 1948	Sun	Miami (Ohio) (8-0-1)	13-12	Texas Tech (6-4)	18,000
Jan. 1, 1948	Cotton	Penn St. (9-0)	13-13	Sou. Methodist (9-0-1)	43,000
Jan. 1, 1948	Gator	Georgia (7-4)	20-20	Maryland (7-2-1)	16,666
Jan. 1, 1948	Raisin	Pacific (9-1)	26-14	Wichita (7-3)	13,000
Jan. 1, 1948	Tangerine	Catawba (10-1)	7-0	Marshall (9-2)	9,000
Jan. 1, 1948	Harbor	Hardin-Simmons (7-3)	53-0	San Diego St. (7-2-1)	12,000
Jan. 1, 1948	Salad	Nevada (8-2)	13-6	North Texas St. (10-1)	12,500
Jan. 1, 1948	Delta	Mississippi (8-2)	13-9	Texas Christian (4-4-2)	28,120
Jan. 1, 1948	Dixie	Arkansas (5-4-1)	21-19	William & Mary (9-1)	22,000

Date	Bowl	Winner	Score	Loser	Atten.
Dec. 18, 1948	Shrine	Hardin-Simmons (4-4-3)	40-12	Ouachita Baptist (9-3)	5,000
Dec. 30, 1948	Camellia	Hardin-Simmons (5-4-3)	49-12	Wichita (5-3-1)	4,500
Jan. 1, 1949	Rose	Northwestern (7-2)	20-14	California (10-0)	93,000
Jan. 1, 1949	Orange	Texas (6-3-1)	41-28	Georgia (9-1)	60,523
Jan. 1, 1949	Sugar	Oklahoma (9-1)	14-6	North Carolina (9-0-1)	82,000
Jan. 1, 1949	Sun	West Virginia (8-3)	21-12	Texas Western (8-1-1)	13,000
Jan. 1, 1949	Cotton	Sou. Methodist (8-1-1)	21-13	Oregon (9-1)	69,000
Jan. 1, 1949	Gator	Clemson (10-0)	24-23	Missouri (8-2)	32,939
Jan. 1, 1949	Raisin	Occidental (8-0)	21-20	Colorado A&M (8-2)	10,000
Jan. 1, 1949	Tangerine	Murray St.	21-21	Sul Ross St.	9,000
Jan. 1, 1949	Harbor	Villanova (7-2-1)	27-7	Nevada (8-2)	20,000
Jan. 1, 1949	Salad	Drake (6-3)	14-13	Arizona (6-4)	17,500
Jan. 1, 1949	Delta	William & Mary (6-2-2)	20-0	Oklahoma A&M (6-3)	15,069
Jan. 1, 1949	Dixie	Baylor (5-3-2)	20-7	Wake Forest (6-3)	20,000
Dec. 31, 1949	Raisin	San Jose St. (8-4)	20-13	Texas Tech (7-4)	9,000
Jan. 1, 1950	Salad	Xavier (Ohio) (9-1)	33-21	Arizona St. (7-2)	18,500
Jan. 2, 1950	Rose	Ohio St. (6-1-2)	17-14	California (10-0)	100,963
Jan. 2, 1950	Orange	Santa Clara (7-2-1)	21-13	Kentucky (9-2)	64,816
Jan. 2, 1950	Sugar	Oklahoma (10-0)	35-0	Louisiana St. (8-2)	82,470
Jan. 2, 1950	Sun	Texas Western (7-2-1)	33-20	Georgetown (5-4)	15,000
Jan. 2, 1950	Cotton	Rice (9-1)	27-13	North Carolina (7-3)	75,347
Jan. 2, 1950	Gator	Maryland (8-1)	20-7	Missouri (7-3)	18,409
Jan. 2, 1950	Tangerine	St. Vincent (9-0)	7-6	Emory & Henry (11-0)	10,000
Dec. 9, 1950	Pres. Cup	Texas A&M (6-4)	40-20	Georgia (6-2-3)	12,245
Jan. 1, 1951	Rose	Michigan (5-3-1)	14-6	California (9-0-1)	98,939
Jan. 1, 1951	Orange	Clemson (8-0-1)	15-14	Miami (9-0-1)	65,181
Jan. 1, 1951	Sugar	Kentucky (10-1)	13-7	**Oklahoma** (10-0)	82,000
Jan. 1, 1951	Sun	West Texas St. (9-1)	14-13	Cincinnati (8-3)	16,000
Jan. 1, 1951	Cotton	Tennessee (10-1)	20-14	Texas (9-1)	75,349
Jan. 1, 1951	Gator	Wyoming (9-0)	20-7	Washington & Lee (8-2)	19,834
Jan. 1, 1951	Tangerine	Morris Harvey (9-0)	35-14	Emory & Henry (10-1)	10,000
Jan. 1, 1951	Salad	Miami (Ohio) (8-1)	34-21	Arizona St. (9-1)	23,000
Jan. 1, 1952	Rose	Illinois (8-0-1)	40-7	Stanford (9-1)	96,825
Jan. 1, 1952	Orange	Georgia Tech (10-0-1)	17-14	Baylor (8-1-1)	65,839
Jan. 1, 1952	Sugar	Maryland (9-0)	28-13	**Tennessee** (10-0)	82,000
Jan. 1, 1952	Sun	Texas Tech (6-4)	25-14	Pacific (6-4)	17,000
Jan. 1, 1952	Cotton	Kentucky (7-4)	20-7	Texas Christian (6-4)	75,347
Jan. 1, 1952	Gator	Miami (7-3)	14-0	Clemson (7-2)	34,577
Jan. 1, 1952	Tangerine	Stetson (6-1-2)	35-20	Arkansas St. (10-1)	12,500
Jan. 1, 1952	Salad	Houston (5-5)	26-21	Dayton (7-2)	17,000
Jan. 1, 1953	Rose	Sou. California (9-1)	7-0	Wisconsin (6-2-1)	101,500
Jan. 1, 1953	Orange	Alabama (9-2)	61-6	Syracuse (7-2)	66,280
Jan. 1, 1953	Sugar	Georgia Tech (11-0)	24-7	Mississippi (8-0-2)	82,000
Jan. 1, 1953	Sun	Pacific (6-3-1)	26-7	Mississippi Sou. (10-1)	11,000
Jan. 1, 1953	Cotton	Texas (8-2)	16-0	Tennessee (8-1-1)	75,504
Jan. 1, 1953	Gator	Florida (7-3)	14-13	Tulsa (8-1-1)	30,015
Jan. 1, 1953	Tangerine	East Texas St. (10-0)	33-0	Tennessee Tech (9-1)	12,340

Date	Bowl	Winner	Score	Loser	Atten.
Jan. 1, 1954	Rose	Michigan St. (8-1)	28-20	UCLA (8-1)	101,000
Jan. 1, 1954	Orange	Oklahoma (8-1-1)	7-0	**Maryland** (10-0)	68,640
Jan. 1, 1954	Sugar	Georgia Tech (8-2-1)	42-19	West Virginia (8-1)	76,000
Jan. 1, 1954	Sun	Texas Western (7-2)	37-14	Mississippi Sou. (9-1)	9,500
Jan. 1, 1954	Cotton	Rice (8-2)	28-6	Alabama (6-2-3)	75,504
Jan. 1, 1954	Gator	Texas Tech (10-1)	35-13	Auburn (7-2-1)	28,641
Jan. 1, 1954	Tangerine	Arkansas St. (8-0-1)	7-7	East Texas St. (10-0)	12,967
Dec. 31, 1954	Gator	Auburn (7-3)	33-13	Baylor (7-3)	28,426
Jan. 1, 1955	Rose	**Ohio St.** (9-0)	20-7	Sou. California (8-3)	89,191
Jan. 1, 1955	Orange	Duke (7-2-1)	34-7	Nebraska (6-4)	68,750
Jan. 1, 1955	Sugar	Navy (7-2)	21-0	Mississippi (9-1)	82,000
Jan. 1, 1955	Sun	Texas Western (7-3)	47-20	Florida St. (8-3)	14,000
Jan. 1, 1955	Cotton	Georgia Tech (7-3)	14-6	Arkansas (8-2)	75,504
Jan. 1, 1955	Tangerine	Omaha (10-0)	7-6	East. Kentucky (8-0-1)	12,759
Dec. 31, 1955	Gator	Vanderbilt (7-3)	25-13	Auburn (8-1-1)	32,174
Jan. 2, 1956	Rose	Michigan St. (8-1)	17-14	UCLA (9-1)	100,809
Jan. 2, 1956	Orange	**Oklahoma** (10-0)	20-6	Maryland (10-0)	76,561
Jan. 2, 1956	Sugar	Georgia Tech (8-1-1)	7-0	Pittsburgh (7-3)	80,175
Jan. 2, 1956	Sun	Wyoming (7-3)	21-14	Texas Tech (7-2-1)	14,500
Jan. 2, 1956	Cotton	Mississippi (9-1)	14-13	Texas Christian (9-1)	75,504
Jan. 2, 1956	Tangerine	Juniata (8-0)	6-6	Missouri Valley (9-1)	10,000
Dec. 29, 1956	Gator	Georgia Tech (9-1)	21-14	Pittsburgh (7-2-1)	36,256
Jan. 1, 1957	Rose	Iowa (8-1)	35-19	Oregon St. (7-2-1)	97,126
Jan. 1, 1957	Orange	Colorado (7-2-1)	27-21	Clemson (7-1-2)	73,280
Jan. 1, 1957	Sugar	Baylor (8-2)	13-7	Tennessee (10-0)	81,000
Jan. 1, 1957	Sun	George Washington (7-1-1)	13-0	Texas Western (9-1)	13,500
Jan. 1, 1957	Cotton	Texas Christian (7-3)	28-27	Syracuse (7-1)	68,000
Jan. 1, 1957	Tangerine	West Texas St. (7-2)	20-13	Miss. Southern (7-1-1)	11,000
Dec. 28, 1957	Gator	Tennessee (7-3)	3-0	Texas A&M (8-2)	41,160
Jan. 1, 1958	Rose	**Ohio St.** (8-1)	10-7	Oregon (7-3)	98,202
Jan. 1, 1958	Orange	Oklahoma (9-1)	48-21	Duke (6-2-2)	76,561
Jan. 1, 1958	Sugar	Mississippi (8-1-1)	39-7	Texas (6-3-1)	82,000
Jan. 1, 1958	Sun	Louisville (8-1)	34-20	Drake (7-1)	13,000
Jan. 1, 1958	Cotton	Navy (8-1-1)	20-7	Rice (7-3)	75,504
Jan. 1, 1958	Tangerine	East Texas St. (8-1)	10-9	Miss. Southern (8-2)	11,000
Dec. 13, 1958	Bluegrass	Oklahoma St. (7-3)	15-6	Florida St. (7-3)	7,000
Dec. 27, 1958	Tangerine	East Texas St. (9-1)	26-7	Missouri Valley (8-0)	4,000
Dec. 27, 1958	Gator	Mississippi (8-2)	7-3	Florida (6-3-1)	41,312
Dec. 31, 1958	Sun	Wyoming (7-3)	14-6	Hardin-Simmons (6-4)	13,000
Jan. 1, 1959	Rose	Iowa (7-1-1)	38-12	California (7-3)	98,297
Jan. 1, 1959	Orange	Oklahoma (9-1)	21-6	Syracuse (8-1)	75,281
Jan. 1, 1959	Sugar	**Louisiana St.** (10-0)	7-0	Clemson (8-2)	82,000
Jan. 1, 1959	Cotton	Air Force (9-0-1)	0-0	Texas Christian (8-2)	75,504
Dec. 19, 1959	Liberty	Penn St. (8-2)	7-0	Alabama (7-1-2)	36,211
Dec. 19, 1959	Bluebonnet	Clemson (8-2)	23-7	Texas Christian (8-2)	55,000
Dec. 31, 1959	Sun	New Mexico St. (7-3)	28-8	North Texas St. (9-1)	14,000
Jan. 1, 1960	Rose	Washington (9-1)	44-8	Wisconsin (7-2)	100,809

Date	Bowl	Winner	Score	Loser	Atten.
Jan. 1, 1960	Orange	Georgia (9-1)	14-0	Missouri (6-4)	72,186
Jan. 1, 1960	Sugar	Mississippi (9-1)	21-0	Louisiana St. (9-1)	83,000
Jan. 1, 1960	Cotton	**Syracuse** (10-0)	23-14	Texas (9-1)	75,504
Jan. 1, 1960	Tangerine	Middle Tenn. St. (9-0-1)	21-12	Presbyterian (9-1)	12,500
Jan. 2, 1960	Gator	Arkansas (8-2)	14-7	Georgia Tech (6-4)	45,104
Dec. 17, 1960	Liberty	Penn St. (6-3)	41-12	Oregon (7-2-1)	16,624
Dec. 17, 1960	Bluebonnet	Alabama (8-1-1)	3-3	Texas (7-3)	68,000
Dec. 30, 1960	Tangerine	The Citadel (7-2-1)	27-0	Tennessee Tech (8-2)	13,000
Dec. 31, 1960	Sun	New Mexico St. (10-0)	20-13	Utah St. (9-1)	16,000
Dec. 31. 1960	Gator	Florida (8-2)	13-12	Baylor (8-2)	50,112
Jan. 2, 1961	Rose	Washington (9-1)	17-7	**Minnesota** (8-1)	97,314
Jan. 2, 1961	Orange	Missouri (9-1)	21-14	Navy (9-1)	72,212
Jan. 2, 1961	Sugar	Mississippi (9-0-1)	14-6	Rice (7-3)	82,851
Jan. 2, 1961	Cotton	Duke (7-3)	7-6	Arkansas (8-2)	74,000
Nov. 23, 1961	Mercy	Fresno St. (9-0)	36-6	Bowling Green (8-1)	33,145
Dec. 9, 1961	Gotham	Baylor (5-5)	24-9	Utah St. (9-0-1)	15,123
Dec. 9, 1961	Aviation	New Mexico (6-4)	28-12	West. Michigan (5-3-1)	3,694
Dec. 16, 1961	Liberty	Syracuse (7-3)	15-14	Miami (7-3)	15,712
Dec. 16, 1961	Bluebonnet	Kansas (6-3-1)	33-7	Rice (7-3)	52,000
Dec. 29, 1961	Tangerine	Lamar Tech (7-2-1)	21-14	Middle Tenn. St. (7-3)	6,000
Dec. 30, 1961	Sun	Villanova (7-2)	17-9	Wichita (8-2)	15,000
Dec. 30, 1961	Gator	Penn St. (7-3)	30-15	Georgia Tech (7-3)	50,202
Jan. 1, 1962	Rose	Minnesota (7-2)	21-3	UCLA (7-3)	98,214
Jan. 1, 1962	Orange	Louisiana St. (9-1)	25-7	Colorado (9-1)	68,150
Jan. 1, 1962	Sugar	**Alabama** (10-0)	10-3	Arkansas (8-2)	82,910
Jan. 1, 1962	Cotton	Texas (9-1)	12-7	Mississippi (9-1)	75,504
Dec. 15, 1962	Liberty	Oregon St. (8-2)	6-0	Villanova (7-2)	17,048
Dec. 15, 1962	Gotham	Nebraska (8-2)	36-34	Miami (7-3)	6,166
Dec. 22, 1962	Tangerine	Houston (6-4)	49-21	Miami (Ohio) (8-1-1)	7,500
Dec. 22, 1962	Bluebonnet	Missouri (7-1-2)	14-10	Georgia Tech (7-2-1)	55,000
Dec. 29, 1962	Gator	Florida (6-4)	17-7	Penn St. (9-1)	50,026
Dec. 31, 1962	Sun	West Texas St. (8-2)	15-14	Ohio University (8-2)	16,000
Jan. 1, 1963	Rose	**Sou. California** (10-0)	42-37	Wisconsin (8-1)	98,698
Jan. 1, 1963	Orange	Alabama (9-1)	17-0	Oklahoma (8-2)	72,880
Jan. 1, 1963	Sugar	Mississippi (9-0)	17-13	Arkansas (9-1)	82,900
Jan. 1, 1963	Cotton	Louisiana St. (8-1-1)	13-0	Texas (9-0-1)	75,504
Dec. 21, 1963	Liberty	Mississippi St. (6-2-2)	16-12	N. Carolina St. (8-2)	8,309
Dec. 21, 1963	Bluebonnet	Baylor (7-3)	14-7	Louisiana St. (7-3)	50,000
Dec. 28, 1963	Tangerine	Western Kentucky (9-0-1)	27-0	Coast Guard (8-0)	7,500
Dec. 28, 1963	Gator	North Carolina (8-2)	35-0	Air Force (7-3)	50,018
Dec. 31, 1963	Sun	Oregon (7-3)	21-14	Sou. Methodist (4-6)	26,500
Jan. 1, 1964	Rose	Illinois (7-1-1)	17-7	Washington (6-4)	96,957
Jan. 1, 1964	Orange	Nebraska (9-1)	13-7	Auburn (9-1)	72,647
Jan. 1, 1964	Sugar	Alabama (8-2)	12-7	Mississippi (7-0-2)	80,785
Jan. 1, 1964	Cotton	**Texas** (10-0)	28-6	Navy (9-1)	75,504
Dec. 12, 1964	Tangerine	East Carolina (8-1)	14-13	Massachusetts (8-1)	8,000
Dec. 19, 1964	Liberty	Utah (8-2)	32-6	West Virginia (7-3)	6,059
Dec. 19, 1964	Bluebonnet	Tulsa (8-2)	14-7	Mississippi (5-4-1)	50,000
Dec. 26, 1964	Sun	Georgia (6-3-1)	7-0	Texas Tech (6-3-1)	28,500

Date	Bowl	Winner	Score	Loser	Atten.
Jan. 1, 1965	Rose	Michigan (8-1)	34-7	Oregon St. (8-2)	100,423
Jan. 1, 1965	Orange	Texas (9-1)	21-17	**Alabama** (10-0)	72,647
Jan. 1, 1965	Sugar	Louisiana St. (7-2-1)	13-10	Syracuse (7-3)	65,000
Jan. 1, 1965	Cotton	Arkansas (10-0)	10-7	Nebraska (9-1)	75,504
Jan. 2, 1965	Gator	Florida St. (8-1-1)	36-19	Oklahoma (6-3-1)	50,408
Dec. 11, 1965	Tangerine	East Carolina (8-1)	31-0	Maine (8-1)	8,350
Dec. 18, 1965	Liberty	Mississippi (6-4)	13-7	Auburn (5-4-1)	38,607
Dec. 18, 1965	Bluebonnet	Tennessee (7-1-2)	27-6	Tulsa (8-2)	40,000
Dec. 31, 1965	Sun	Texas Western (7-3)	13-12	Texas Christian (6-4)	27,450
Dec. 31, 1965	Gator	Georgia Tech (6-3-1)	31-21	Texas Tech (8-2)	60,127
Jan. 1, 1966	Rose	UCLA (7-2-1)	14-12	**Michigan St.** (10-0)	100,087
Jan. 1, 1966	Orange	**Alabama** (8-1-1)	39-28	Nebraska (10-0)	72,214
Jan. 1, 1966	Sugar	Missouri (7-2-1)	20-18	Florida (7-3)	67,421
Jan. 1, 1966	Cotton	Louisiana St. (7-3)	14-7	Arkansas (10-0)	76,200
Dec. 10, 1966	Tangerine	Morgan St. (8-0)	14-6	West Chester St. (8-2)	7,138
Dec. 10, 1966	Liberty	Miami (7-2-1)	14-7	Virginia Tech (8-1-1)	39,101
Dec. 17, 1966	Bluebonnet	Texas (6-4)	19-0	Mississippi (8-2)	67,000
Dec. 24, 1966	Sun	Wyoming (9-1)	28-20	Florida St. (6-4)	24,381
Dec. 31, 1966	Cotton	Georgia (9-1)	24-9	Sou. Methodist (8-2)	75,400
Dec. 31, 1966	Gator	Tennessee (7-3)	18-12	Syracuse (8-2)	60,312
Jan. 2, 1967	Rose	Purdue (8-2)	14-13	Sou. California (7-3)	100,807
Jan. 2, 1967	Orange	Florida (8-2)	27-12	Georgia Tech (9-1)	72,426
Jan. 2, 1967	Sugar	Alabama (10-0)	34-7	Nebraska (9-1)	82,000
Dec. 2, 1967	Junior Rose	West Texas St. (7-3)	35-13	San Fernando St. (6-3)	28,802
Dec. 16, 1967	Tangerine	Tennessee-Martin (9-1)	25-8	West Chester St. (10-0)	5,500
Dec. 16, 1967	Liberty	North Carolina St. (8-2)	14-7	Georgia (7-3)	35,045
Dec. 23, 1967	Bluebonnet	Colorado (8-2)	31-21	Miami (7-3)	30,156
Dec. 30, 1967	Sun	Texas-El Paso (6-2-1)	14-7	Mississippi (6-3-1)	34,685
Dec. 30, 1967	Gator	Florida St. (7-2-1)	17-17	Penn St. (8-2)	68,019
Jan. 1, 1968	Rose	**Sou. California** (9-1)	14-3	Indiana (9-1)	102,946
Jan. 1, 1968	Orange	Oklahoma (9-1)	26-24	Tennessee (9-1)	77,993
Jan. 1, 1968	Sugar	Louisiana St. (6-3-1)	20-13	Wyoming (10-0)	78,963
Jan. 1, 1968	Cotton	Texas A&M (6-4)	20-16	Alabama (8-1-1)	75,504
Dec. 14, 1968	Liberty	Mississippi (6-3-1)	34-17	Virginia Tech (7-3)	46,206
Dec. 27, 1968	Tangerine	Richmond (7-3)	49-42	Ohio U. (10-0)	16,144
Dec. 28, 1968	Sun	Auburn (6-4)	34-10	Arizona (8-2)	32,307
Dec. 28, 1968	Gator	Missouri (7-3)	35-10	Alabama (8-2)	68,011
Dec. 30, 1968	Peach	Louisiana St. (7-3)	31-27	Florida St. (8-2)	35,545
Dec. 31, 1968	Bluebonnet	Sou. Methodist (7-3)	28-27	Oklahoma (7-3)	53,543
Jan. 1, 1969	Rose	**Ohio St.** (9-0)	27-16	Sou. California (9-0-1)	102,063
Jan. 1, 1969	Orange	Penn St. (10-0)	15-14	Kansas (9-1)	77,719
Jan. 1, 1969	Sugar	Arkansas (9-1)	16-2	Georgia (8-0-2)	82,113
Jan. 1, 1969	Cotton	Texas (8-1-1)	36-13	Tennessee (8-1-1)	72,000
Dec. 6, 1969	Pasadena	San Diego St. (10-0)	28-7	Boston U. (9-1)	41,276
Dec. 13, 1969	Liberty	Colorado (7-3)	47-33	Alabama (6-4)	50,042
Dec. 20, 1969	Sun	Nebraska (8-2)	45-6	Georgia (5-4-1)	29,723
Dec. 26, 1969	Tangerine	Toledo (10-0)	56-33	Davidson (7-3)	16,311
Dec. 27, 1969	Gator	Florida (8-1-1)	14-13	Tennessee (9-1)	72,248
Dec. 30, 1969	Peach	West Virginia (9-1)	14-3	South Carolina (7-3)	48,452

Date	Bowl	Winner	Score	Loser	Atten.
Dec. 31, 1969	Bluebonnet	Houston (8-2)	36-7	Auburn (8-2)	55,203
Jan. 1, 1970	Rose	Sou. California (9-0-1)	10-3	Michigan (8-2)	103,878
Jan. 1, 1970	Orange	Penn St. (10-0)	10-3	Missouri (9-1)	77,282
Jan. 1, 1970	Sugar	Mississippi (7-3)	27-22	Arkansas (9-1)	82,500
Jan. 1, 1970	Cotton	**Texas** (10-0)	21-17	Notre Dame (8-1-1)	73,000
Dec. 12, 1970	Liberty	Tulane (7-4)	17-3	Colorado (6-4)	44,640
Dec. 19, 1970	Sun	Georgia Tech (8-3)	17-9	Texas Tech (8-3)	30,512
Dec. 19, 1970	Pasadena	Long Beach St. (9-2)	24-24	Louisville (8-3)	20,472
Dec. 28, 1970	Tangerine	Toledo (11-0)	40-12	William & Mary (5-6)	15,164
Dec. 30, 1970	Peach	Arizona St. (10-0)	48-26	North Carolina (8-3)	52,126
Dec. 31, 1970	Bluebonnet	Alabama (6-5)	24-24	Oklahoma (7-4)	53,829
Jan. 1, 1971	Rose	Stanford (8-3)	27-17	Ohio St. (9-0)	103,839
Jan. 1, 1971	Orange	**Nebraska** (10-0-1)	17-12	Louisiana St. (9-2)	80,699
Jan. 1, 1971	Sugar	Tennessee (10-1)	34-13	Air Force (9-2)	78,655
Jan. 1, 1971	Cotton	Notre Dame (9-1)	24-11	**Texas** (10-0)	72,000
Jan. 2, 1971	Gator	Auburn (8-2)	35-28	Mississippi (7-3)	71,136
Dec. 18, 1971	Sun	Louisiana St. (8-3)	33-15	Iowa St. (8-3)	33,503
Dec. 18, 1971	Pasadena	Memphis St. (4-6)	28-9	San Jose St. (5-5-1)	15,244
Dec. 20, 1971	Liberty	Tennessee (9-2)	14-13	Arkansas (8-2-1)	51,410
Dec. 27, 1971	Fiesta	Arizona St. (10-1)	45-38	Florida St. (8-3)	51,089
Dec. 28, 1971	Tangerine	Toledo (11-0)	28-3	Richmond (5-5)	16,750
Dec. 30, 1971	Peach	Mississippi (9-2)	41-18	Georgia Tech (6-5)	36,771
Dec. 31, 1971	Gator	Georgia (10-1)	7-3	North Carolina (9-2)	71,208
Dec. 31, 1971	Bluebonnet	Colorado (9-2)	29-17	Houston (9-2)	54,720
Jan. 1, 1972	Rose	Stanford (8-3)	13-12	Michigan (11-0)	103,154
Jan. 1, 1972	Orange	**Nebraska** (12-0)	38-6	Alabama (11-0)	78,151
Jan. 1, 1972	Sugar	Oklahoma (10-1)	40-22	Auburn (9-1)	84,031
Jan. 1, 1972	Cotton	Penn St. (10-1)	30-6	Texas (8-2)	72,000
Dec. 18, 1972	Liberty	Georgia Tech (6-4-1)	31-30	Iowa St. (5-5-1)	50,021
Dec. 23, 1972	Fiesta	Arizona St. (9-2)	49-35	Missouri (6-5)	51,318
Dec. 29, 1972	Tangerine	Tampa (9-2)	21-18	Kent St. (6-4-1)	20,062
Dec. 29, 1972	Peach	North Carolina. St. (7-3-1)	49-13	West Virginia (8-3)	52,671
Dec. 30, 1972	Sun	North Carolina (10-1)	32-28	Texas Tech (8-3)	31,312
Dec. 30, 1972	Gator	Auburn (9-1)	24-3	Colorado (8-3)	71,114
Dec. 30, 1972	Bluebonnet	Tennessee (9-2)	24-17	Louisiana St. (9-1-1)	52,961
Dec. 31, 1972	Sugar	Oklahoma (10-1)	14-0	Penn St. (10-1)	80,123
Jan. 1, 1973	**Rose**	**Sou. California** (11-0)	42-17	Ohio St. (9-1)	**106,869**
Jan. 1, 1973	Orange	Nebraska (8-2-1)	40-6	Notre Dame (8-2)	80,010
Jan. 1, 1973	Cotton	Texas (9-1)	17-13	Alabama (10-1)	72,000
Dec. 17, 1973	Liberty	North Carolina St. (8-3)	31-18	Kansas (7-3-1)	50,011
Dec. 21, 1973	Fiesta	Arizona St. (10-1)	28-7	Pittsburgh (6-4-1)	50,878
Dec. 22, 1973	Tangerine	Miami (Ohio) (10-0)	16-7	Florida (7-4)	37,234
Dec. 28, 1973	Peach	Georgia (6-4-1)	17-16	Maryland (8-3)	38,107
Dec. 29, 1973	Sun	Missouri (7-4)	34-17	Auburn (6-5)	30,127
Dec. 29, 1973	Gator	Texas Tech (10-1)	28-19	Tennessee (8-3)	62,109
Dec. 29, 1973	Bluebonnet	Houston (10-1)	47-7	Tulane (9-2)	44,358
Dec. 31, 1973	**Sugar**	**Notre Dame** (10-0)	24-23	**Alabama** (11-0)	**85,161**
Jan. 1, 1974	Rose	Ohio St. (9-0-1)	42-21	Sou. California (9-1-1)	105,267
Jan. 1, 1974	Orange	Penn St. (11-0)	16-9	Louisiana St. (9-2)	60,477
Jan. 1, 1974	Cotton	Nebraska (8-2-1)	19-3	Texas (8-2)	67,500

Date	Bowl	Winner	Score	Loser	Atten.
Dec. 16, 1974	Liberty	Tennessee (6-3-2)	7-3	Maryland (8-3)	51,284
Dec. 21, 1974	Tangerine	Miami (Ohio) (9-0-1)	21-10	Georgia (6-5)	15,895
Dec. 23, 1974	Bluebonnet	Houston (8-3)	31-31	N. Carolina St. (9-2)	35,122
Dec. 28, 1974	Peach	Texas Tech (6-4-1)	6-6	Vanderbilt (7-3-1)	31,695
Dec. 28, 1974	Sun	Mississippi St. (8-3)	26-24	North Carolina (7-4)	30,131
Dec. 28, 1974	Fiesta	Oklahoma St. (6-5)	16-6	Brigham Young (7-3-1)	50,878
Dec. 30, 1974	Gator	Auburn (9-2)	27-3	Texas (8-3)	63,811
Dec. 31, 1974	Sugar	Nebraska (8-3)	13-10	Florida (8-3)	67,890
Jan. 1, 1975	Rose	**Sou. California** (9-1-1)	18-17	Ohio St. (10-1)	106,721
Jan. 1, 1975	Orange	Notre Dame (9-2)	13-11	Alabama (11-0)	71,801
Jan. 1, 1975	Cotton	Penn St. (9-2)	41-20	Baylor (8-3)	67,500
Dec. 20, 1975	Tangerine	Miami (Ohio) (10-1)	20-7	South Carolina (7-4)	20,247
Dec. 22, 1975	Liberty	Sou. California (7-4)	20-0	Texas A&M (10-1)	52,129
Dec. 26, 1975	Sun	Pittsburgh (7-4)	33-19	Kansas (7-4)	33,240
Dec. 26, 1975	Fiesta	Arizona St. (11-0)	17-14	Nebraska (10-1)	51,396
Dec. 27, 1975	Bluebonnet	Texas (9-2)	38-21	Colorado (9-2)	52,748
Dec. 29, 1975	Gator	Maryland (8-2-1)	13-0	Florida (9-2)	64,012
Dec. 31, 1975	Sugar	Alabama (10-1)	13-6	Penn St. (9-2)	75,212
Dec. 31, 1975	Peach	West Virginia (8-3)	13-10	N. Carolina St. (7-3-1)	45,134
Jan. 1, 1976	Rose	UCLA (8-2-1)	23-10	Ohio St. (11-0)	105,464
Jan. 1, 1976	Orange	**Oklahoma** (10-1)	14-6	Michigan (8-1-2)	76,799
Jan. 1, 1976	Cotton	Arkansas (9-2)	31-10	Georgia (9-2)	74,500
Dec. 13, 1976	Independence	McNeese St. (9-2)	20-16	Tulsa (7-3-1)	15,542
Dec. 18, 1976	Tangerine	Oklahoma St. (8-3)	49-21	Brigham Young (9-2)	31,048
Dec. 20, 1976	Liberty	Alabama (8-3)	36-6	UCLA (9-1-1)	52,736
Dec. 25, 1976	Fiesta	Oklahoma (8-2-1)	41-7	Wyoming (8-3)	48,174
Dec. 27, 1976	Gator	Notre Dame (8-3)	20-9	Penn St. (7-4)	67,827
Dec. 31, 1976	Bluebonnet	Nebraska (7-3-1)	27-24	Texas Tech (10-1)	48,618
Dec. 31, 1976	Peach	Kentucky (7-4)	21-0	North Carolina (9-2)	54,132
Jan. 1, 1977	Rose	Sou. California (10-1)	14-6	Michigan (10-1)	106,182
Jan. 1, 1977	Orange	Ohio St. (8-2-1)	27-10	Colorado (8-3)	65,537
Jan. 1, 1977	Sugar	**Pittsburgh** (11-0)	27-3	Georgia (10-1)	76,117
Jan. 1, 1977	Cotton	Houston (9-2)	30-21	Maryland (11-0)	54,500
Jan. 2, 1977	Sun	Texas A&M (9-2)	37-14	Florida (8-3)	33,252
Dec. 17, 1977	Independence	Louisiana Tech (8-1-2)	24-14	Louisville (7-3-1)	18,500
Dec. 19, 1977	Liberty	Nebraska (8-3)	21-17	North Carolina (8-2-1)	49,456
Dec. 22, 1977	Hall of Fame	Maryland (7-4)	17-7	Minnesota (7-4)	47,000
Dec. 23, 1977	Tangerine	Florida St. (9-2)	40-17	Texas Tech (7-4)	44,502
Dec. 25, 1977	Fiesta	Penn St. (10-1)	42-30	Arizona St. (9-2)	57,727
Dec. 30, 1977	Gator	Pittsburgh (8-2-1)	34-3	Clemson (8-2-1)	72,289
Dec. 31, 1977	Sun	Stanford (8-3)	24-14	Louisiana St. (8-3)	31,318
Dec. 31, 1977	Bluebonnet	Sou. California (7-4)	47-28	Texas A&M (8-3)	52,842
Dec. 31, 1977	Peach	North Carolina St. (7-4)	24-14	Iowa St. (8-3)	36,733
Jan. 2, 1978	Rose	Washington (7-4)	27-20	Michigan (10-1)	105,312
Jan. 2, 1978	Orange	Arkansas (10-1)	31-6	Oklahoma (10-1)	60,987
Jan. 2, 1978	Sugar	Alabama (10-1)	35-6	Ohio St. (9-2)	76,811
Jan. 2, 1978	**Cotton**	**Notre Dame** (10-1)	38-10	Texas (11-0)	**76,601**
Dec. 16, 1978	Independence	East Carolina (8-3)	35-13	Louisiana Tech (6-4)	18,200
Dec. 16, 1978	Garden St.	Arizona St. (8-3)	34-18	Rutgers (9-2)	33,402
Dec. 20, 1978	Hall of Fame	Texas A&M (7-4)	28-12	Iowa St. (8-3)	41,500

BOWL GAMES

Date	Bowl	Winner	Score	Loser	Atten.
Dec. 22, 1978	Holiday	Navy (8-3)	23-16	Brigham Young (9-3)	52,500
Dec. 23, 1978	Sun	Texas (8-3)	42-0	Maryland (9-2)	33,122
Dec. 23, 1978	Tangerine	North Carolina St. (8-3)	30-17	Pittsburgh (8-3)	31,356
Dec. 23, 1978	Liberty	Missouri (7-4)	20-15	Louisiana St. (8-3)	53,064
Dec. 25, 1978	Peach	Purdue (8-2-1)	41-21	Georgia Tech (7-4)	20,277
Dec. 25, 1978	Fiesta	Arkansas (9-2)	10-10	UCLA (8-3)	55,227
Dec. 29, 1978	Gator	Clemson (10-1)	17-15	Ohio St. (7-3-1)	72,011
Dec. 31, 1978	Bluebonnet	Stanford (7-4)	25-22	Georgia (9-1-1)	34,084
Jan. 1, 1979	Rose	**Sou. California** (11-1)	17-10	Michigan (10-1)	105,629
Jan. 1, 1979	Orange	Oklahoma (10-1)	31-24	Nebraska (9-2)	66,365
Jan. 1, 1979	Sugar	**Alabama** (10-1)	14-7	Penn St. (11-0)	76,824
Jan. 1, 1979	Cotton	Notre Dame (8-3)	35-34	Houston (9-2)	32,500
Dec. 15, 1979	Independence	Syracuse (6-5)	31-7	McNeese St. (11-0)	27,234
Dec. 15, 1979	Garden St.	Temple (9-2)	28-17	California (6-5)	55,493
Dec. 21, 1979	Holiday	Indiana (7-4)	38-37	Brigham Young (11-0)	52,200
Dec. 22, 1979	Sun	Washington (9-2)	14-7	Texas (9-2)	33,412
Dec. 22, 1979	Tangerine	Louisiana St. (6-5)	34-10	Wake Forest (8-3)	38,142
Dec. 22, 1979	Liberty	Penn St. (7-4)	9-6	Tulane (9-2)	50,021
Dec. 25, 1979	Fiesta	Pittsburgh (10-1)	16-10	Arizona (6-4-1)	55,347
Dec. 28, 1979	Gator	North Carolina (7-3-1)	17-15	Michigan (8-3)	70,407
Dec. 29, 1979	Hall of Fame	Missouri (6-5)	24-14	South Carolina (8-3)	62,785
Dec. 31, 1979	Bluebonnet	Purdue (9-2)	27-22	Tennessee (7-4)	40,542
Dec. 31, 1979	Peach	Baylor (7-4)	24-18	Clemson (8-3)	57,371
Jan. 1, 1980	Rose	Sou. California (10-0-1)	17-16	Ohio St. (11-0)	105,526
Jan. 1, 1980	Orange	Oklahoma (10-1)	24-7	Florida St. (11-0)	66,714
Jan. 1, 1980	Sugar	**Alabama** (11-0)	24-9	Arkansas (10-1)	77,486
Jan. 1, 1980	Cotton	Houston (10-1)	17-14	Nebraska (10-1)	72,032
Dec. 13, 1980	Independence	Sou. Mississippi (8-3)	16-14	McNeese St. (10-1)	45,000
Dec. 14, 1980	Garden St.	Houston (6-5)	35-0	Navy (8-3)	41,417
Dec. 19, 1980	Holiday	Brigham Young (11-1)	46-45	Sou. Methodist (8-3)	50,214
Dec. 20, 1980	**Tangerine**	Florida (7-4)	35-20	Maryland (8-3)	**52,541**
Dec. 26, 1980	Fiesta	Penn St. (9-2)	31-19	Ohio St. (9-2)	66,738
Dec. 27, 1980	Sun	Nebraska (9-2)	31-17	Mississippi St. (9-2)	34,723
Dec. 27, 1980	Liberty	Purdue (8-3)	28-25	Missouri (8-3)	53,667
Dec. 27, 1980	Hall of Fame	Arkansas (6-5)	34-15	Tulane (7-4)	30,000
Dec. 29, 1980	Gator	Pittsburgh (10-1)	37-9	South Carolina (8-3)	72,297
Dec. 31, 1980	Bluebonnet	North Carolina (10-1)	16-7	Texas (7-4)	36,667
Jan. 1, 1981	Rose	Michigan (9-2)	23-6	Washington (9-2)	104,863
Jan. 1, 1981	Orange	Oklahoma (9-2)	18-17	Florida St. (10-1)	71,043
Jan. 1, 1981	Sugar	**Georgia** (11-0)	17-10	Notre Dame (9-1-1)	77,895
Jan. 1, 1981	Cotton	Alabama (9-2)	30-2	Baylor (10-1)	74,281
Jan. 2, 1981	Peach	Miami (8-3)	20-10	Virginia Tech (8-3)	45,384
Dec. 12, 1981	Independence	Texas A&M (6-5)	33-16	Oklahoma St. (7-4)	47,300
Dec. 13, 1981	Garden St.	Tennessee (7-4)	28-21	Wisconsin (7-4)	38,782
Dec. 18, 1981	Holiday	Brigham Young (10-2)	38-36	Washington St. (8-2-1)	52,419
Dec. 19, 1981	Tangerine	Missouri (7-4)	19-17	Southern Miss. (9-1-1)	50,466
Dec. 19, 1981	California	Toledo (8-3)	27-25	San Jose St. (9-2)	15,565
Dec. 26, 1981	Sun	Oklahoma (6-4-1)	40-14	Houston (7-3-1)	33,816
Dec. 28, 1981	Gator	North Carolina (9-2)	31-27	Arkansas (8-3)	71,009
Dec. 30, 1981	Liberty	Ohio St. (8-3)	31-28	Navy (7-3-1)	43,216
Dec. 31, 1981	Bluebonnet	Michigan (8-3)	33-14	UCLA (7-3-1)	40,309

Appendix 1 221

Date	Bowl	Winner	Score	Loser	Atten.
Dec. 31, 1981	Peach	West Virginia (8-3)	26-6	Florida (7-4)	37,582
Dec. 31, 1981	Hall of Fame	Mississippi St. (7-4)	10-0	Kansas (8-3)	41,672
Jan. 1, 1982	Rose	Washington (9-2)	28-0	Iowa (8-3)	105,611
Jan. 1, 1982	Orange	**Clemson** (11-0)	22-15	Nebraska (9-2)	72,748
Jan. 1, 1982	Sugar	Pittsburgh (10-1)	24-20	Georgia (10-1)	77,224
Jan. 1, 1982	Cotton	Texas (9-1-1)	14-12	Alabama (9-1-1)	73,243
Jan. 1, 1982	Fiesta	Penn St. (9-2)	26-10	Sou. California (9-2)	71,053
Dec. 11, 1982	Independence	Wisconsin (6-5)	14-3	Kansas St. (6-4-1)	49,503
Dec. 17, 1982	Holiday	Ohio St. (8-3)	47-17	Brigham Young (8-3)	52,533
Dec. 18, 1982	Tangerine	Auburn (8-3)	33-26	Boston College (8-2-1)	51,296
Dec. 18, 1982	California	Fresno St. (10-1)	29-28	Bowling Green (7-4)	30,000
Dec. 25, 1982	Sun	North Carolina (7-4)	26-10	Texas (9-2)	31,359
Dec. 25, 1982	Aloha	Washington (9-2)	21-20	Maryland (8-3)	30,055
Dec. 29, 1982	Liberty	Alabama (7-4)	21-15	Illinois (7-4)	54,123
Dec. 30, 1982	Gator	Florida St. (8-3)	31-12	West Virginia (9-2)	80,913
Dec. 31, 1982	Bluebonnet	Arkansas (8-2-1)	28-24	Florida (8-3)	31,557
Dec. 31, 1982	Peach	Iowa (7-4)	28-22	Tennessee (6-4-1)	50,134
Dec. 31, 1982	Hall of Fame	Air Force (7-5)	36-28	Vanderbilt (8-3)	75,000
Jan. 1, 1983	Rose	UCLA (9-1-1)	24-14	Michigan (8-3)	104,991
Jan. 1, 1983	Orange	Nebraska (11-1)	21-20	Louisiana St. (8-2-1)	68,713
Jan. 1, 1983	Sugar	**Penn St.** (10-1)	27-23	Georgia (11-0)	78,124
Jan. 1, 1983	Cotton	Sou. Methodist (10-0-1)	7-3	Pittsburgh (9-2)	60,359
Jan. 1, 1983	Fiesta	Arizona St. (9-2)	32-21	Oklahoma (8-3)	70,533
Dec. 10, 1983	Independence	Air Force (9-2)	9-3	Mississippi (6-5)	41,274
Dec. 17, 1983	California	Northern Illinois (9-2)	20-13	Cal-St. Fullerton (7-4)	20,464
Dec. 17, 1983	Florida Citrus	Tennessee (8-3)	30-23	Maryland (8-3)	50,183
Dec. 22, 1983	Hall of Fame	West Virginia (8-3)	20-16	Kentucky (6-4-1)	42,000
Dec. 23, 1983	Holiday	Brigham Young (10-1)	21-17	Missouri (7-4)	51,480
Dec. 24, 1983	Sun	Alabama (7-4)	28-7	Sou. Methodist (10-1)	41,412
Dec. 26, 1983	Aloha	Penn St. (7-4-1)	13-10	Washington (8-3)	37,212
Dec. 29, 1983	Liberty	Notre Dame (6-5)	19-18	Boston College (9-2)	38,229
Dec. 30, 1983	Gator	Florida (8-2-1)	14-6	Iowa (9-2)	81,293
Dec. 30, 1983	Peach	Florida St. (6-5)	28-3	North Carolina (8-3)	25,648
Dec. 31, 1983	Bluebonnet	Oklahoma St. (7-4)	24-14	Baylor (7-3-1)	50,090
Jan. 2, 1984	Rose	UCLA (6-4-1)	45-9	Illinois (10-1)	103,217
Jan. 2, 1984	Orange	**Miami** (10-1)	31-30	Nebraska (12-0)	75,549
Jan. 2, 1984	Sugar	Auburn (10-1)	9-7	Michigan (9-2)	77,893
Jan. 2, 1984	Cotton	Georgia (9-1-1)	10-9	Texas (11-0)	67,891
Jan. 2, 1984	Fiesta	Ohio St. (8-3)	28-23	Pittsburgh (8-2-1)	66,484
Dec. 15, 1984	Independence	Air Force (7-4)	23-7	Virginia Tech (8-3)	41,000
Dec. 15, 1984	California	UNLV (10-2)	30-13	Toledo (8-2-1) (won*)	21,741
Dec. 21, 1984	Holiday	**Brigham Young** (12-0)	24-17	Michigan (6-5)	61,243
Dec. 22, 1984	Sun	Maryland (8-3)	28-27	Tennessee (7-3-1)	50,126
Dec. 22, 1984	Florida Citrus	Florida St. (7-3-1)	17-17	Georgia (7-4)	51,821
Dec. 22, 1984	Cherry	Army (7-3-1)	10-6	Michigan St. (6-5)	70,332
Dec. 26, 1984	Freedom	Iowa (7-4-1)	55-17	Texas (7-3-1)	24,093
Dec. 27, 1984	Liberty	Auburn (8-4)	21-15	Arkansas (7-3-1)	50,108
Dec. 28, 1984	Gator	Oklahoma St. (9-2)	21-14	South Carolina (10-1)	82,138
Dec. 29, 1984	Hall of Fame	Kentucky (8-3)	20-19	Wisconsin (7-3-1)	47,300
Dec. 29, 1984	Aloha	Sou. Methodist (9-2)	27-20	Notre Dame (7-4)	41,777
Dec. 31, 1984	Bluebonnet	West Virginia (7-4)	31-14	Texas Christian (8-3)	43,260

Date	Bowl	Winner	Score	Loser	Atten.
Dec. 31, 1984	Peach	Virginia (7-2-2)	27-24	Purdue (7-4)	41,107
Jan. 1, 1985	Rose	Sou. California (8-3)	20-17	Ohio St. (9-2)	102,594
Jan. 1, 1985	Orange	Washington (10-1)	28-17	Oklahoma (9-1-1)	56,294
Jan. 1, 1985	Sugar	Nebraska (9-2)	28-10	Louisiana St. (8-2-1)	75,608
Jan. 1, 1985	Cotton	Boston College (9-2)	45-28	Houston (7-4)	56,522
Jan. 1, 1985	Fiesta	UCLA (8-3)	39-37	Miami (8-4)	60,310
Dec. 14, 1985	California	Fresno St. (10-0-1)	51-7	Bowling Green (11-0)	32,554
Dec. 21, 1985	Independence	Minnesota (6-5)	20-13	Clemson (6-5)	42,800
Dec. 21, 1985	Cherry	Maryland (8-3)	35-18	Syracuse (7-4)	51,858
Dec. 22, 1985	Holiday	Arkansas (9-2)	18-17	Arizona St. (8-3)	42,324
Dec. 27, 1985	Liberty	Baylor (8-3)	21-7	Louisiana St. (9-1-1)	40,186
Dec. 28, 1985	**Sun**	Arizona (8-3)	13-13	Georgia (7-3-1)	**52,203**
Dec. 28, 1985	Aloha	Alabama (8-2-1)	24-3	Sou. California (6-5)	35,183
Dec. 28, 1985	Florida Citrus	Ohio St. (8-3)	10-7	Brigham Young (11-2)	50,920
Dec. 30, 1985	Gator	Florida St. (8-3)	34-23	Oklahoma St. (8-3)	79,417
Dec. 30, 1985	Freedom	Washington (6-5)	20-17	Colorado (7-4)	30,961
Dec. 31, 1985	Bluebonnet	Air Force (11-1)	24-16	Texas (8-3)	42,000
Dec. 31, 1985	Peach	Army (8-3)	31-29	Illinois (6-4-1)	29,857
Dec. 31, 1985	Hall of Fame	Georgia Tech (8-2-1)	17-14	Michigan St. (7-4)	45,000
Jan. 1, 1986	Rose	UCLA (8-2-1)	45-28	Iowa (10-1)	103,292
Jan. 1, 1986	Orange	**Oklahoma** (10-1)	25-10	Penn St. (11-0)	74,178
Jan. 1, 1986	Sugar	Tennessee (8-1-2)	35-7	Miami (10-1)	77,432
Jan. 1, 1986	Cotton	Texas A&M (9-2)	36-16	Auburn (8-3)	73,137
Jan. 1, 1986	Sunkist Fiesta	Michigan (9-1-1)	27-23	Nebraska (9-2)	72,454
Dec. 13, 1986	California	San Jose St. (9-2)	37-7	Miami (Ohio) (8-3)	10,743
Dec. 20, 1986	Independence	Mississippi (7-3-1)	20-17	Texas Tech (7-4)	46,369
Dec. 23, 1986	Hall of Fame	Boston College (8-3)	27-24	Georgia (8-3)	30,000
Dec. 25, 1986	Sun	Alabama (8-2-1)	28-6	Washington (8-2-1)	48,722
Dec. 27, 1986	Mazda Gator	Clemson (7-2-2)	27-21	Stanford (8-3)	80,104
Dec. 27, 1986	Aloha	Arizona (8-3)	30-21	North Carolina (7-3-1)	26,743
Dec. 29, 1986	Liberty	Tennessee (6-5)	21-14	Minnesota (6-5)	51,327
Dec. 30, 1986	S. W. Holiday	Iowa (8-3)	39-38	San Diego St. (8-3)	59,473
Dec. 30, 1986	Freedom	UCLA (7-3-1)	31-10	Brigham Young (8-4)	55,422
Dec. 31, 1986	Bluebonnet	Baylor (8-3)	21-9	Colorado (6-5)	40,476
Dec. 31, 1986	Peach	Virginia Tech (8-2-1)	25-24	N. Carolina St. (8-2-1)	53,668
Dec. 31, 1986	All-American	Florida St. (6-4-1)	27-13	Indiana (6-5)	30,000
Jan. 1, 1987	Rose	Arizona St. (9-1-1)	22-15	Michigan (11-1)	103,168
Jan. 1, 1987	Orange	Oklahoma (10-1)	42-8	Arkansas (9-2)	52,717
Jan. 1, 1987	Sugar	Nebraska (9-2)	30-15	Louisiana St. (9-2)	76,234
Jan. 1, 1987	Cotton	Ohio St. (9-3)	28-12	Texas A&M (9-2)	74,188
Jan. 1, 1987	Florida Citrus	Auburn (9-2)	16-7	Sou. California (7-4)	51,113
Jan. 2, 1987	Sunkist Fiesta	**Penn St.** (11-0)	14-10	Miami (11-0)	73,098
Dec. 12, 1987	California	Eastern Michigan (9-2)	30-27	San Jose St. (10-1)	24,000
Dec. 19, 1987	Independence	Washington (6-4-1)	24-12	Tulane (6-5)	41,683
Dec. 22, 1987	All-American	Virginia (7-4)	22-16	Brigham Young (9-3)	37,000
Dec. 25, 1987	J. Hancock Sun	Oklahoma St. (9-2)	35-33	West Virginia (6-5)	43,240
Dec. 25, 1987	Aloha	UCLA (9-2)	20-16	Florida (6-5)	24,839
Dec. 29, 1987	Liberty	Georgia (8-3)	20-17	Arkansas (9-3)	53,249
Dec. 30, 1987	S.W. Holiday	Iowa (9-3)	20-19	Wyoming (10-2)	61,892
Dec. 30, 1987	Freedom	Arizona St. (6-4-1)	33-28	Air Force (9-3)	33,261
Dec. 31, 1987	Mazda Gator	Louisiana St. (9-1-1)	30-13	South Carolina (8-3)	82,119

Date	Bowl	Winner	Score	Loser	Atten.
Dec. 31, 1987	Bluebonnet	Texas (6-5)	32-27	Pittsburgh (8-3)	23,282
Jan. 1, 1988	Rose	Michigan St. (8-2-1)	20-17	Sou. California (8-3)	103,847
Jan. 1, 1988	Orange	**Miami** (11-0)	20-14	Oklahoma (11-0)	74,760
Jan. 1, 1988	USF&G Sugar	Auburn (9-1-1)	16-16	Syracuse (11-0)	75,495
Jan. 1, 1988	Cotton	Texas A&M (9-2)	35-10	Notre Dame (8-3)	73,006
Jan. 1, 1988	Sunkist Fiesta	Florida St. (10-1)	31-28	Nebraska (10-1)	72,112
Jan. 1, 1988	Florida Citrus	Clemson (9-2)	35-10	Penn St. (8-3)	53,152
Jan. 2, 1988	Peach	Tennessee (9-2-1)	27-22	Indiana (8-3)	58,737
Jan. 2, 1988	Hall of Fame	Michigan (7-4)	28-24	Alabama (7-4)	60,156
Dec. 10, 1988	California	Fresno St. (9-2)	35-30	West. Michigan (9-2)	31,272
Dec. 23, 1988	Independence	Sou. Mississippi (9-2)	38-18	Texas-El Paso (10-2)	20,242
Dec. 24, 1988	J. Hancock Sun	Alabama (8-3)	29-28	Army (9-2)	48,719
Dec. 25, 1988	Aloha	Washington St. (8-3)	24-22	Houston (9-2)	35,132
Dec. 28, 1988	Liberty	Indiana (7-3-1)	34-10	South Carolina (8-3)	39,210
Dec. 29, 1988	All-American	Florida (6-5)	14-10	Illinois (6-4-1)	48,218
Dec. 29, 1988	Freedom	Brigham Young (8-4)	20-17	Colorado (8-3)	35,941
Dec. 30, 1988	S.W. Holiday	Oklahoma St. (9-2)	62-14	Wyoming (11-1)	60,718
Dec. 31, 1988	Peach	North Carolina St. (7-3-1)	28-23	Iowa (6-3-3)	44,635
Jan. 1, 1989	Mazda Gator	Georgia (8-3)	34-27	Michigan St. (6-4-1)	76,236
Jan. 2, 1989	Rose	Michigan (8-2-1)	22-14	Sou. California (10-1)	101,688
Jan. 2, 1989	FedEx Orange	Miami (10-1)	23-3	Nebraska (11-1)	79,480
Jan. 2, 1989	USF&G Sugar	Florida St. (10-1)	13-7	Auburn (10-1)	61,934
Jan. 2, 1989	Mobil Cotton	UCLA (9-2)	17-3	Arkansas (10-1)	74,304
Jan. 2, 1989	Sunkist Fiesta	**Notre Dame** (11-0)	34-21	West Virginia (11-0)	74,911
Jan. 2, 1989	Florida Citrus	Clemson (9-2)	13-6	Oklahoma (9-2)	53,571
Jan. 2, 1989	Hall of Fame	Syracuse (9-2)	23-10	Louisiana St. (8-3)	51,112
Dec. 9, 1989	California	Fresno St. (10-1)	27-6	Ball St. (7-2-2)	31,610
Dec. 16, 1989	Independence	Oregon (7-4)	27-14	Tulsa (6-5)	30,333
Dec. 25, 1989	Aloha	Michigan St. (7-4)	33-13	Hawaii (9-2-1)	50,000
Dec. 28, 1989	Liberty	Mississippi (8-3)	42-29	Air Force (8-3-1)	60,128
Dec. 28, 1989	All-American	Texas Tech (8-3)	49-21	Duke (8-3)	47,750
Dec. 29, 1989	S.W. Holiday	Penn St. (7-3-1)	50-39	Brigham Young (10-2)	61,113
Dec. 30, 1989	John Hancock	Pittsburgh (7-3-1)	31-28	Texas A&M (8-3)	44,887
Dec. 30, 1989	**Mazda Gator**	Clemson (9-2)	27-7	West Virginia (8-2-1)	**82,911**
Dec. 30, 1989	Peach	Syracuse (7-4)	19-18	Georgia (6-5)	44,991
Dec. 30, 1989	Freedom	Washington (7-4)	34-7	Florida (7-4)	33,858
Dec. 31, 1989	Copper	Arizona (7-4)	17-10	N. Carolina St. (7-4)	37,237
Jan. 1, 1990	Rose	Sou. California (8-2-1)	17-10	Michigan (10-1)	103,450
Jan. 1,1990	FedEx Orange	Notre Dame (11-1)	21-6	Colorado (11-0)	81,190
Jan. 1, 1990	USF&G Sugar	**Miami** (10-1)	33-25	Alabama (10-1)	77,452
Jan. 1, 1990	Mobil Cotton	Tennessee (10-1)	31-27	Arkansas (10-1)	74,358
Jan. 1, 1990	Sunkist Fiesta	Florida St. (9-2)	41-17	Nebraska (10-1)	73,953
Jan. 1, 1990	Florida Citrus	Illinois (9-2)	31-21	Virginia (10-2)	60,016
Jan.1, 1990	Hall of Fame	Auburn (9-2)	31-14	Ohio St. (8-3)	52,535
Dec. 8, 1990	California	San Jose St. (8-2-1)	48-24	Cen. Michigan (8-2-1)	25,431
Dec. 15, 1990	Independence	Louisiana Tech (8-3)	34-34	Maryland (6-5)	48,325
Dec. 25, 1990	Aloha	Syracuse (6-4-2)	28-0	Arizona (7-4)	14,185
Dec. 27, 1990	Liberty	Air Force (6-5)	23-11	Ohio St. (7-3-1)	13,144
Dec. 28, 1990	All-American	North Carolina St. (6-5)	31-27	Sou. Mississippi (8-3)	44,000
Dec. 28, 1990	Blockbuster	Florida St. (9-2)	24-17	Penn St. (9-2)	74,021
Dec. 29, 1990	Peach	Auburn (7-3-1)	27-23	Indiana (6-4-1)	38,912

Date	Bowl	Winner	Score	Loser	Atten.
Dec. 29, 1990	S.W. Holiday	Texas A&M (8-3-1)	65-14	Brigham Young (10-2)	61,441
Dec. 29, 1990	Freedom	Colorado St. (8-4)	32-31	Oregon (8-3)	41,450
Dec. 31, 1990	John Hancock	Michigan St. (7-3-1)	17-16	Sou. California (8-3-1)	50,562
Dec. 31, 1990	Dom.'s Copper	California (6-4-1)	17-15	Wyoming (9-3)	36,340
Jan. 1, 1991	Rose	Washington (9-2)	46-34	Iowa (8-3)	101,273
Jan. 1, 1991	FedEx Orange	**Colorado** (10-1-1)	10-9	Notre Dame (9-2)	77,062
Jan. 1, 1991	USF&G Sugar	Tennessee (8-2-2)	23-22	Virginia (8-3)	75,132
Jan. 1, 1991	Mobil Cotton	Miami (9-2)	46-3	Texas (10-1)	73,521
Jan. 1, 1991	Mazda Gator	Michigan (8-3)	35-3	Mississippi (9-2)	68,927
Jan. 1, 1991	Fiesta	Louisville (9-1-1)	34-7	Alabama (7-4)	69,098
Jan. 1, 1991	Hall of Fame	Clemson (9-2)	30-0	Illinois (8-3)	63,154
Jan. 1, 1991	Florida Citrus	**Georgia Tech** (10-0-1)	45-21	Nebraska (9-2)	72,328
Dec.14, 1991	California	Bowling Green (10-1)	28-21	Fresno St. (10-1)	34,825
Dec. 25, 1991	Aloha	Georgia Tech (7-5)	18-17	Stanford (8-3)	34,433
Dec. 28, 1991	Blockbuster	Alabama (10-1)	30-25	Colorado (8-2-1)	52,644
Dec. 29, 1991	Gator	Oklahoma (8-3)	48-14	Virginia (8-2-1)	62,003
Dec. 29, 1991	Liberty	Air Force (9-3)	38-15	Mississippi St. (7-4)	61,497
Dec. 29, 1991	Independence	Georgia (8-3)	24-15	Arkansas (6-5)	46,932
Dec. 30, 1991	Thrif. Holiday	Brigham Young (8-3-1)	13-13	Iowa (10-1)	60,646
Dec. 30, 1991	Freedom	Tulsa (9-2)	28-17	San Diego St. (8-3-1)	34,217
Dec. 31, 1991	John Hancock	UCLA (8-3)	6-3	Illinois (6-5)	42,821
Dec. 31, 1991	Dom.'s Copper	Indiana (6-4-1)	24-0	Baylor (8-3)	35,752
Jan. 1, 1992	Rose	**Washington** (11-0)	34-14	Michigan (10-1)	103,566
Jan. 1, 1992	FedEx Orange	**Miami** (11-0)	22-0	Nebraska (9-1-1)	77,747
Jan. 1, 1992	USF&G Sugar	Notre Dame (9-3)	39-28	Florida (10-1)	75,132
Jan. 1, 1992	Mobil Cotton	Florida St. (10-2)	10-2	Texas A&M (10-1)	73,728
Jan. 1, 1992	Fiesta	Penn St. (10-2)	42-17	Tennessee (9-2)	71,133
Jan. 1, 1992	Peach	East Carolina (10-1)	37-34	N. Carolina St. (9-2)	59,322
Jan. 1, 1992	Florida Citrus	California (9-2)	37-13	Clemson (9-1-1)	64,192
Jan. 1, 1992	Hall of Fame	Syracuse (9-2)	24-17	Ohio St. (8-3)	57,789
Dec. 18, 1992	Las Vegas	Bowling Green (9-2)	35-34	Nevada (7-4)	15,476
Dec. 25, 1992	Aloha	Kansas (7-4)	23-20	Brigham Young (8-4)	42,933
Dec. 29, 1992	Freedom	Fresno St. (8-4)	24-7	Sou. California (6-4-1)	50,745
Dec. 29, 1992	Weiser Copper	Washington St. (8-3)	31-28	Utah (6-5)	40,876
Dec. 30, 1992	Thrif. Holiday	Hawaii (10-2)	27-17	Illinois (6-4-1)	44,457
Dec. 31, 1992	John Hancock	Baylor (6-5)	20-15	Arizona (6-4-1)	41,622
Dec. 31, 1992	O.S.H. Gator	Florida (8-4)	27-10	N. Carolina St. (9-2-1)	71,233
Dec. 31, 1992	Liberty	Mississippi (8-3)	13-0	Air Force (7-4)	32,107
Dec. 31, 1992	Independence	Wake Forest (7-4)	39-35	Oregon (6-5)	31,337
Jan. 1, 1993	Rose	Michigan (8-0-3)	38-31	Washington (9-2)	94,236
Jan. 1, 1993	FedEx Orange	Florida St. (11-1)	27-14	Nebraska (9-2)	57,324
Jan. 1, 1993	USF&G Sugar	**Alabama** (12-0)	34-13	Miami (11-0)	76,789
Jan. 1, 1993	Mobil Cotton	Notre Dame (9-1-1)	28-3	Texas A&M (12-0)	71,615
Jan. 1, 1993	IBM Fiesta	Syracuse (9-2)	26-22	Colorado (9-1-1)	70,224
Jan. 1, 1993	Florida Citrus	Georgia (9-2)	21-14	Ohio St. (8-2-1)	65,861
Jan. 1, 1993	Hall of Fame	Tennessee (8-3)	38-23	Boston College (8-2-1)	52,056
Jan. 1, 1993	Blockbuster	Stanford (9-3)	24-3	Penn St. (7-4)	45,554
Jan. 2, 1993	Peach	North Carolina (8-3)	21-17	Mississippi St. (7-4)	69,125
Dec. 17, 1993	Las Vegas	Utah St. (6-5)	42-33	Ball St. (8-2-1)	15,508
Dec. 24, 1993	John Hancock	Oklahoma (8-3)	41-10	Texas Tech (6-5)	43,848
Dec. 25, 1993	Aloha	Colorado (7-3-1)	41-30	Fresno St. (8-3)	44,009

Date	Bowl	Winner	Score	Loser	Atten.
Dec. 28, 1993	St. Jude Liberty	Louisville (8-3)	18-7	Michigan St. (6-5)	21,097
Dec. 29, 1993	Weiser Copper	Kansas St. (8-2-1)	52-17	Wyoming (8-3)	49,075
Dec. 30, 1993	Thrif. Holiday	Ohio St. (9-1-1)	28-21	Brigham Young (6-5)	52,108
Dec. 30, 1993	Freedom	Sou. California (7-5)	28-21	Utah (7-5)	37,203
Dec. 31, 1993	O.S.H. Gator	Alabama (8-3-1)	24-10	North Carolina (10-2)	67,205
Dec. 31, 1993	Peach	Clemson (8-3)	14-13	Kentucky (6-5)	63,416
Dec. 31, 1993	Independence	Virginia Tech (8-3)	45-20	Indiana (8-3)	33,819
Dec. 31, 1993	Buil. Sq. Alamo	California (8-4)	37-3	Iowa (6-5)	45,716
Jan. 1, 1994	Rose	Wisconsin (9-1-1)	21-16	UCLA (8-3)	101,237
Jan. 1, 1994	FedEx Orange	**Florida St.** (11-1)	18-16	Nebraska (11-0)	81,536
Jan. 1, 1994	USF&G Sugar	Florida (10-2)	41-7	West Virginia (11-0)	75,437
Jan. 1, 1994	Mobil Cotton	Notre Dame (10-1)	24-21	Texas A&M (10-1)	69,855
Jan. 1, 1994	IBM Fiesta	Arizona (9-2)	29-0	Miami (9-2)	72,260
Jan. 1, 1994	Florida Citrus	Penn St. (9-2)	31-13	Tennessee (9-1-1)	72,456
Jan. 1, 1994	Hall of Fame	Michigan (7-4)	42-7	N. Carolina St. (7-4)	52,649
Jan. 1, 1994	Carquest	Boston College (8-3)	31-13	Virginia (7-4)	38,516
Dec. 15, 1994	Las Vegas	UNLV (6-5)	52-24	Cen. Michigan (9-2)	17,562
Dec. 25, 1994	Aloha	Boston College (6-4-1)	12-7	Kansas St. (9-2)	44,862
Dec. 27, 1994	Freedom	Utah (9-2)	16-13	Arizona (8-3)	27,477
Dec. 28, 1994	Independence	Virginia (8-3)	20-10	Texas Christian (7-4)	27,242
Dec. 29, 1994	Weiser Copper	Brigham Young (9-3)	31-6	Oklahoma (6-5)	45,122
Dec. 30, 1994	Sun	Texas (7-4)	35-31	North Carolina (8-3)	50,612
Dec. 30, 1994	O.S.H. Gator	Tennessee (7-4)	45-23	Virginia Tech (8-3)	62,200
Dec. 30, 1994	Thrif. Holiday	Michigan (7-4)	24-14	Colorado St. (10-1)	59,453
Dec. 31, 1994	St. Jude Liberty	Illinois (6-5)	30-0	East Carolina (7-4)	33,280
Dec. 31, 1994	Buil. Sq. Alamo	Washington St. (7-4)	10-3	Baylor (7-4)	44,106
Jan. 1, 1995	**FedEx Orange**	**Nebraska** (12-0)	24-17	Miami (10-1)	**81,753**
Jan. 1, 1995	Peach	North Carolina St. (8-3)	28-24	Mississippi St. (8-3)	64,902
Jan. 2, 1995	Rose	Penn St. (11-0)	38-20	Oregon (9-3)	102,247
Jan. 2, 1995	USF&G Sugar	Florida St. (9-1-1)	23-17	Florida (10-1-1)	76,224
Jan. 2, 1995	Mobil Cotton	Sou. California (7-3-1)	55-14	Texas Tech (6-5)	70,218
Jan. 2, 1995	IBM Fiesta	Colorado (10-1)	41-24	Notre Dame (6-4-1)	73,968
Jan. 2, 1995	Florida Citrus	Alabama (11-1)	24-17	Ohio St. (9-3)	71,195
Jan. 2, 1995	Hall of Fame	Wisconsin (6-4-1)	34-20	Duke (8-3)	61,384
Jan. 2, 1995	Carquest	South Carolina (6-5)	24-21	West Virginia (7-5)	50,833
Dec. 14, 1995	Las Vegas	Toledo (10-0-1)	40-37*	Nevada (9-2)	11,127
Dec. 25, 1995	Aloha	Kansas (9-2)	51-30	UCLA (7-4)	41,111
Dec. 27, 1995	Weiser Copper	Texas Tech (8-3)	55-41	Air Force (8-4)	41,004
Dec. 28, 1995	Buil. Sq. Alamo	Texas A&M (8-3)	22-20	Michigan (9-3)	64,597
Dec. 29, 1995	Sun	Iowa (7-4)	38-18	Washington (7-3-1)	49,116
Dec. 29, 1995	Independence	Louisiana St. (6-4-1)	45-26	Michigan St. (6-4-1)	48,835
Dec. 29, 1995	Plym. Holiday	Kansas St. (9-2)	54-21	Colorado St. (8-3)	51,051
Dec. 30, 1995	St. Jude Liberty	East Carolina (8-3)	19-13	Stanford (7-3-1)	47,398
Dec. 30, 1995	Peach	Virginia (8-4)	34-27	Georgia (6-5)	70,825
Dec. 30, 1995	Carquest	North Carolina (6-5)	20-10	Arkansas (8-4)	34,428
Dec. 31, 1995	USF&G Sugar	Virginia Tech (9-2)	28-10	Texas (10-1-1)	70,283
Jan. 1, 1996	Rose	Sou. California (8-2-1)	41-32	Northwestern (10-1)	100,102
Jan. 1, 1996	FedEx Orange	Florida St. (9-2)	31-26	Notre Dame (9-2)	72,198
Jan. 1, 1996	Cotton	Colorado (9-2)	38-6	Oregon (9-2)	58,214
Jan. 1, 1996	Toyota Gator	Syracuse (8-3)	41-0	Clemson (8-3)	45,202
Jan. 1, 1996	Florida Citrus	Tennessee (10-1)	20-14	Ohio St. (11-1)	70,797
Jan. 1, 1996	Outback	Penn St. (8-3)	43-14	Auburn (8-3)	65,313

Date	Bowl	Winner	Score	Loser	Atten.
Jan. 2, 1996	Tostitos Fiesta	**Nebraska** (11-0)	62-24	Florida (12-0)	79,864
Dec. 19,1996	Las Vegas	Nevada (8-3)	18-15	Ball St. (8-3)	10,118
Dec. 25, 1996	Aloha	Navy (8-3)	42-38	California (6-5)	43,380
Dec. 27, 1996	St. Jude Liberty	Syracuse (8-3)	30-17	Houston (7-4)	49,163
Dec. 27, 1996	Copper	Wisconsin (7-5)	38-10	Utah (8-3)	42,122
Dec. 27, 1996	Carquest	Miami (8-3)	31-21	Virginia (7-4)	46,418
Dec. 28, 1996	Peach	Louisiana St. (9-2)	10-7	Clemson (7-4)	63,622
Dec. 29, 1996	Buil. Sq. Alamo	Iowa (8-3)	27-0	Texas Tech (7-4)	55,677
Dec. 30, 1996	Plym. Holiday	Colorado (9-2)	33-21	Washington (9-2)	54,749
Dec. 31, 1996	FedEx Orange	Nebraska (10-2)	41-21	Virginia Tech (10-1)	63,297
Dec. 31, 1996	Norwest Sun	Stanford (6-5)	38-0	Michigan St. (6-5)	42,721
Dec. 31, 1996	Independence	Auburn (7-4)	32-29	Army (10-1)	41,366
Jan. 1, 1997	Rose	Ohio St. (10-1)	20-17	Arizona St. (11-0)	100,635
Jan. 1, 1997	SW Bell Cotton	Brigham Young (13-1)	19-15	Kansas St. (9-2)	71,928
Jan. 1, 1997	Toyota Gator	North Carolina (9-2)	20-13	West Virginia (8-3)	52,103
Jan. 1, 1997	Tostitos Fiesta	Penn St. (10-2)	38-15	Texas (8-4)	65,106
Jan. 1, 1997	Florida Citrus	Tennessee (9-2)	48-28	Northwestern (9-2)	63,467
Jan. 1, 1997	Outback	Alabama (9-3)	17-14	Michigan (8-3)	53,161
Jan. 2, 1997	Nokia Sugar	**Florida** (11-1)	52-20	Florida St. (11-0)	78,344
Dec.20, 1997	Las Vegas	Oregon (6-5)	41-13	Air Force (10-2)	21,514
Dec. 25, 1997	Aloha	Washington (7-4)	51-23	Michigan St. (7-4)	44,598
Dec. 26, 1997	Motor City	Mississippi (7-4)	34-31	Marshall (10-2)	43,340
Dec. 27, 1997	Insight.com	Arizona (6-5)	20-14	New Mexico (9-3)	49,385
Dec. 28, 1997	Independence	Louisiana St. (8-3)	27-9	Notre Dame (7-5)	50,459
Dec. 29, 1997	Plym. Holiday	Colorado St. (10-2)	35-24	Missouri (7-4)	50,761
Dec. 29, 1997	Carquest	Georgia Tech (6-5)	35-30	West Virginia (7-4)	28,262
Dec. 29, 1997	Sports Hum.	Cincinnati (7-4)	35-19	Utah St. (6-5)	16,131
Dec. 30, 1997	Buil. Sq. Alamo	Purdue (8-3)	33-20	Oklahoma St. (8-3)	55,552
Dec. 31, 1997	Norwest Sun	Arizona St. (8-3)	17-7	Iowa (7-4)	49,104
Dec. 31, 1997	AXA Liberty	Sou. Mississippi (8-3)	41-7	Pittsburgh (6-5)	50,209
Dec. 31, 1997	Tostitos Fiesta	Kansas St. (10-1)	35-18	Syracuse (9-3)	69,367
Jan. 1, 1998	Rose	**Michigan** (11-0)	21-16	Washington St. (10-1)	101,219
Jan. 1, 1998	Nokia Sugar	Florida St. (10-1)	31-14	Ohio St. (10-2)	67,289
Jan. 1, 1998	SW Bell Cotton	UCLA (9-2)	29-23	Texas A&M (9-3)	59,215
Jan. 1, 1998	Toyota Gator	North Carolina (10-1)	42-3	Virginia Tech (7-4)	54,116
Jan. 1, 1998	Florida Citrus	Florida (9-2)	21-6	Penn St. (9-2)	72,940
Jan. 1, 1998	Outback	Georgia (9-2)	33-6	Wisconsin (8-4)	56,186
Jan. 2, 1998	FedEx Orange	**Nebraska** (12-0)	42-17	Tennessee (11-1)	74,002
Jan. 2, 1998	Ch-Fil-A Peach	Auburn (9-3)	21-17	Clemson (7-4)	71,212
Dec. 19, 1998	Las Vegas	North Carolina (6-5)	20-13	San Diego St. (7-4)	21,429
Dec. 23, 1998	Motor City	Marshall (11-1)	48-29	Louisville (7-4)	32,206
Dec. 25, 1998	Jeep Aloha Cl.	Colorado (7-4)	51-43	Oregon (8-3)	46,451
Dec. 25, 1998	Oahu Classic	Air Force (11-1)	45-25	Washington (6-5)	46,451
Dec. 26, 1998	Insight.com	Missouri (7-4)	34-31	West Virginia (8-3)	36,147
Dec. 29, 1998	Buil. Sq. Alamo	Purdue (8-4)	37-34	Kansas St. (11-1)	60,780
Dec. 29, 1998	Micronpc.com	Miami (8-3)	46-23	North Carolina St. (7-4)	44,387
Dec. 29, 1998	Music City	Virginia Tech (8-3)	38-7	Alabama (7-4)	41,248
Dec. 30, 1998	**Cull. Holiday**	Arizona (11-1)	23-20	Nebraska (9-3)	**65,354**
Dec. 30, 1998	Humanitarian	Idaho (8-3)	42-35	Sou. Mississippi (7-4)	19,664
Dec. 31, 1998	Norwest Sun	Texas Christian (6-5)	28-19	Sou. California (8-4)	46,612
Dec. 31, 1998	AXA Liberty	Tulane (11-0)	41-27	Brigham Young (9-4)	52,192

Date	Bowl	Winner	Score	Loser	Atten.
Dec. 31, 1998	Ch-Fil-A Peach	Georgia (8-3)	35-33	Virginia (9-2)	72,876
Dec. 31, 1998	Independence	Mississippi (6-5)	35-18	Texas Tech (7-4)	46,862
Jan. 1, 1999	Rose	Wisconsin (10-1)	38-31	UCLA (10-1)	93,872
Jan. 1, 1999	Nokia Sugar	Ohio St. (10-1)	24-14	Texas A&M (11-2)	76,503
Jan. 1, 1999	SW Bell Cotton	Texas (8-3)	38-11	Mississippi St. (8-4)	72,611
Jan. 1, 1999	Toyota Gator	Georgia Tech (9-2)	35-28	Notre Dame (9-2)	70,791
Jan. 1, 1999	Outback	Penn St. (8-3)	26-14	Kentucky (7-4)	66,005
Jan. 1, 1999	Florida Citrus	Michigan (9-3)	45-31	Arkansas (9-2)	63,584
Jan. 2, 1999	FedEx Orange	Florida (9-2)	31-10	Syracuse (8-3)	67,919
Jan. 4, 1999	**Tostitos Fiesta**	**Tennessee (12-0)**	23-16	Florida St. (11-1)	**80,470**
Dec. 18, 1999	EAS Las Vegas	Utah (8-3)	17-16	Fresno St. (8-4)	28,227
Dec. 22, 1999	Mobile Ala.	Texas Christian (7-4)	28-14	East Carolina (9-2)	34,200
Dec. 25, 1999	Jeep Aloha Cl.	Wake Forest (6-5)	23-3	Arizona St. (6-5)	40,974
Dec. 25, 1999	Oahu Classic	Hawaii (8-4)	23-17	Oregon St. (7-4)	40,974
Dec. 27, 1999	Motor City	Marshall (12-0)	21-3	Brigham Young (8-3)	44,863
Dec. 28, 1999	Sylvania Alamo	Penn St. (9-3)	24-0	Texas A&M (8-3)	65,380
Dec. 29, 1999	Cull. Holiday	Kansas St. (10-1)	24-20	Washington (7-4)	57,118
Dec. 29, 1999	.Music City	Syracuse (6-5)	20-13	Kentucky (6-5)	59,221
Dec. 30, 1999	Ch-Fil-A Peach	Mississippi St. (9-2)	17-7	Clemson (6-5)	73,315
Dec. 30, 1999	Humanitarian	Boise St. (9-3)	34-31	Louisville (7-4)	29,283
Dec. 30, 1999	Micron.com	Illinois (7-4)	63-21	Virginia (7-4)	31,089
Dec. 31, 1999	Norwest Sun	Oregon (8-3)	24-20	Minnesota (8-3)	48,757
Dec. 31, 1999	AXA Liberty	Sou. Mississippi (8-3)	23-17	Colorado St. (8-3)	54,866
Dec. 31, 1999	Independence	Mississippi (7-4)	27-25	Oklahoma (7-4)	49,873
Dec. 31, 1999	Insight.com	Colorado (6-5)	62-28	Boston College (8-3)	35,762
Jan. 1, 2000	Rose	Wisconsin (9-2)	17-9	Stanford (8-3)	93,731
Jan. 1, 2000	FedEx Orange	Michigan (9-2)	35-34*	Alabama (10-2)	70,461
Jan. 1, 2000	SW Bell Cotton	Arkansas (7-4)	27-6	Texas (9-4)	72,723
Jan. 1, 2000	Toyota Gator	Miami (8-4)	28-13	Georgia Tech (8-3)	43,416
Jan. 1, 2000	Florida Citrus	Michigan St. (9-2)	37-34	Florida (9-3)	62,011
Jan. 1, 2000	Outback	Georgia (7-4)	28-25*	Purdue (7-4)	54,059
Jan. 2, 2000	Tostitos Fiesta	Nebraska (11-1)	31-21	Tennessee (9-2)	71,526
Jan. 4, 2000	Nokia Sugar	**Florida St. (11-0)**	46-29	Virginia Tech (11-0)	79,280
Dec. 20, 2000	GMAC Ala.	Sou. Mississippi (7-4)	28-21	Texas Christian (10-1)	40,300
Dec. 21, 2000	Las Vegas	UNLV (7-5)	31-14	Arkansas (6-5)	29,113
Dec. 24, 2000	Oahu Classic	Georgia (7-4)	37-14	Virginia (6-5)	24,187
Dec. 25, 2000	Jeep Aloha Cl.	Boston College (6-5)	31-17	Arizona St. (6-5)	24,397
Dec. 27, 2000	Motor City	Marshall (7-5)	25-14	Cincinnati (7-4)	52,911
Dec. 27, 2000	g-furniture.com	East Carolina (7-4)	40-27	Texas Tech (7-5)	33,899
Dec. 28, 2000	Insight.com	Iowa St. (8-3)	37-29	Pittsburgh (7-4)	41,813
Dec. 28, 2000	Humanitarian	Boise St. (9-2)	38-23	Texas-El Paso (8-3)	26,203
Dec. 28, 2000	Music City	West Virginia (6-5)	49-38	Mississippi (7-4)	47,119
Dec. 28, 2000	Micron.com	North Carolina St. (7-4)	38-30	Minnesota (6-5)	28,359
Dec. 29, 2000	Wells Fargo Sun	Wisconsin (8-4)	21-20	UCLA (6-5)	49,093
Dec. 29, 2000	AXA Liberty	Colorado St. (9-2)	22-17	Louisville (9-2)	58,302
Dec. 29, 2000	Ch-Fil-A Peach	Louisiana St. (7-4)	28-14	Georgia Tech (9-2)	73,614
Dec. 29, 2000	Cull. Holiday	Oregon (9-2)	35-30	Texas (9-2)	63,278
Dec. 30, 2000	Sylvania Alamo	Nebraska (9-2)	66-17	Northwestern (8-3)	60,028
Dec. 31, 2000	Independence	Mississippi St. (7-4)	43-41*	Texas A&M (7-4)	36,974
Dec. 31, 2000	Silicon Vall. Cl.	Air Force (8-3)	37-34	Fresno St. (7-4)	26,542
Jan. 1, 2001	Rose	Washington (10-1)	34-24	Purdue (8-3)	94,392
Jan. 1, 2001	SBC Cotton	Kansas St. (10-3)	35-21	Tennessee (8-3)	63,465

BOWL GAMES

Date	Bowl	Winner	Score	Loser	Atten.
Jan. 1, 2001	Toyota Gator	Virginia Tech (10-1)	41-20	Clemson (9-2)	68,741
Jan. 1, 2001	Tostitos Fiesta	Oregon St. (10-1)	41-9	Notre Dame (9-2)	75,428
Jan. 1, 2001	CapOne/Citrus	Michigan (8-3)	31-28	Auburn (9-3)	66,928
Jan. 1, 2001	Outback	South Carolina (7-4)	24-7	Ohio St. (8-3)	65,229
Jan. 2, 2001	Nokia Sugar	Miami (10-1)	37-20	Florida (10-2)	64,407
Jan. 3, 2001	FedEx Orange	**Oklahoma** (12-0)	13-2	Florida St. (11-1)	76,835
Dec. 18, 2001	New Orleans	Colorado St. (6-5)	45-20	North Texas (5-6)	27,004
Dec. 19, 2001	GMAC	Marshall (10-2)	64-61**	East Carolina (6-5)	40,139
Dec. 20, 2001	Tangerine	Pittsburgh (6-5)	34-19	N. Carolina St. (7-4)	28,562
Dec. 25, 2001	Sega Las Vegas	Utah (7-4)	10-6	Sou. California (6-5)	30,894
Dec. 27, 2001	Independence	Alabama (6-5)	14-13	Iowa St. (7-4)	45,627
Dec. 27, 2001	Seattle	Georgia Tech (7-5)	24-14	Stanford (9-2)	30,144
Dec. 28, 2001	Cull. Holiday	Texas (10-2)	47-43	Washington (8-3)	60,548
Dec. 28, 2001	Music City	Boston College (7-4)	20-16	Georgia (8-3)	46,125
Dec. 28, 2001	g-furniture.com	Texas A&M (7-4)	28-9	Texas Christian (6-5)	53,480
Dec. 29, 2001	Insight.com	Syracuse (9-3)	26-3	Kansas St. (6-5)	40,028
Dec. 29, 2001	Sylvania Alamo	Iowa (6-5)	19-16	Texas Tech (7-4)	65,232
Dec. 29, 2001	Motor City	Toledo (9-2)	23-16	Cincinnati (7-4)	44,164
Dec. 31, 2001	Wells Far. Sun	Washington St. (9-2)	33-27	Purdue (6-5)	47,812
Dec. 31, 2001	AXA Liberty	Louisville (10-2)	28-10	Brigham Young (12-1)	58,968
Dec. 31, 2001	Ch-Fil-A Peach	North Carolina (7-5)	16-10	Auburn (7-4)	71,827
Dec. 31, 2001	Humanitarian	Clemson (6-5)	49-24	Louisiana Tech (7-4)	23,472
Dec. 31, 2001	Silicon Vall. Cl.	Michigan St. (6-5)	44-35	Fresno St. (11-2)	30,456
Jan. 1, 2002	Nokia Sugar	Louisiana St. (9-3)	47-34	Illinois (10-1)	77,688
Jan. 1, 2002	SBC Cotton	Oklahoma (10-2)	10-3	Arkansas (7-4)	72,955
Jan. 1, 2002	Toyota Gator	Florida St. (7-4)	30-17	Virginia Tech (8-3)	72,202
Jan. 1, 2002	Tostitos Fiesta	Oregon (10-1)	38-16	Colorado (10-2)	74,118
Jan. 1, 2002	Florida Citrus	Tennessee (10-2)	45-17	Michigan (8-3)	59,693
Jan. 1, 2002	Outback	South Carolina (8-3)	31-28	Ohio St. (7-4)	66,249
Jan. 2, 2002	FedEx Orange	Florida (9-2)	56-23	Maryland (10-1)	73,640
Jan. 3, 2002	Rose	**Miami** (11-0)	37-14	Nebraska (11-1)	93,781
Dec. 17, 2002	New Orleans	North Texas (7-5)	24-19	Cincinnati (7-6)	19,024
Dec. 18, 2002	GMAC	Marshall (10-2)	38-15	Louisville (7-5)	40,646
Dec. 23, 2002	Maz.Tangerine	Texas Tech (8-5)	55-15	Clemson (7-5)	21,689
Dec. 25, 2002	Sega Las Vegas	UCLA (7-5)	27-13	New Mexico (7-6)	30,324
Dec. 25, 2002	ConAg. Hawaii	Tulane (7-5)	36-28	Hawaii (10-3)	31,535
Dec. 26, 2002	Insight.com	Pittsburgh (8-4)	38-13	Oregon St. (8-4)	40,533
Dec. 26, 2002	Motor City	Boston College (8-4)	51-25	Toledo (9-4)	51,872
Dec. 27, 2002	Independence	Mississippi (6-6)	27-23	Nebraska (7-6)	46,096
Dec. 27, 2002	PacLife Holiday	Kansas St. (10-2)	34-27	Arizona St. (8-5)	58,717
Dec. 27, 2002	Houston	Oklahoma St. (7-5)	33-23	Sou. Mississippi (7-5)	44,687
Dec. 28, 2002	Sylvania Alamo	Wisconsin (7-6)	31-28*	Colorado (9-4)	50,690
Dec. 28, 2002	Contin. Tire	Virginia (8-5)	48-22	West Virginia (9-3)	73,535
Dec. 30, 2002	Music City	Minnesota (7-5)	29-14	Arkansas (9-4)	39,183
Dec. 30, 2002	Seattle	Wake Forest (6-6)	38-17	Oregon (7-5)	38,241
Dec. 31, 2002	Wells Far. Sun	Purdue (6-6)	34-24	Washington (7-5)	48,917
Dec. 31, 2002	AXA Liberty	Texas Christian (9-2)	17-3	Colorado St. (10-3)	55,207
Dec. 31, 2002	Ch-Fil-A Peach	Maryland (10-3)	30-3	Tennessee (8-4)	68,330
Dec. 31, 2002	Humanitarian	Boise St. (11-1)	34-16	Iowa St. (7-6)	30,446
Dec. 31, 2002	Silicon Vall. Cl.	Fresno St. (8-5)	30-21	Georgia Tech (7-5)	10,132
Dec. 31, 2002	San Francisco	Virginia Tech (9-4)	20-13	Air Force (8-4)	25,966
Jan. 1, 2003	Rose	Oklahoma (11-2)	34-14	Washington St. (10-2)	86,848

Date	Bowl	Winner	Score	Loser	Atten.
Jan. 1, 2003	Nokia Sugar	Georgia (12-1)	26-13	Florida St. (9-4)	74,269
Jan. 1, 2003	SBC Cotton	Texas (10-2)	35-20	Louisiana St. (8-4)	70,817
Jan. 1, 2003	Toyota Gator	North Carolina St. (10-3)	28-6	Notre Dame (10-2)	73,491
Jan. 1, 2003	Capital One	Auburn (8-4)	13-9	Penn St. (9-3)	66,334
Jan. 1, 2003	Outback	Michigan (9-3)	38-30	Florida (8-4)	65,101
Jan. 2, 2003	FedEx Orange	Sou. California (10-2)	38-17	Iowa (11-1)	75,971
Jan. 3, 2003	Tostitos Fiesta	**Ohio St.** (13-0)	31-24**	Miami (12-0)	77,502
Dec. 16, 2003	New Orleans	Memphis (8-4)	27-17	North Texas (9-3)	25,184
Dec. 18, 2003	GMAC	Miami (Ohio) (12-1)	49-28	Louisville (9-3)	40,620
Dec. 22, 2003	Maz. Tangerine	North Carolina St. (7-5)	56-26	Kansas (6-6)	26,482
Dec. 23, 2003	Fort Worth	Boise St. (12-1)	34-31	Texas Christian (11-1)	38,028
Dec. 24, 2003	Sega Las Vegas	Oregon St. (7-5)	55-14	New Mexico (8-4)	25,437
Dec. 25, 2003	Shera. Hawaii	Hawaii (8-5)	54-48***	Houston (7-5)	29,005
Dec. 26, 2003	Insight	California (7-6)	52-49	Virginia Tech (8-4)	42,364
Dec. 26, 2003	Motor City	Bowling Green (10-3)	28-24	Northwestern (6-6)	51,286
Dec. 27, 2003	Contin. Tire	Virginia (7-5)	23-16	Pittsburgh (8-4)	51,236
Dec. 29, 2003	Alamo	Nebraska (9-3)	17-3	Michigan St. (8-4)	56,226
Dec. 30, 2003	PacLife Holiday	Washington St. (9-3)	28-20	Texas (10-2)	61,102
Dec. 30, 2003	Silicon Vall. Cl.	Fresno St. (8-5)	17-9	UCLA (6-6)	20,126
Dec. 30, 2003	Houston	Texas Tech (7-5)	38-14	Navy (8-4)	51,068
Dec. 31, 2003	Wells Far. Sun	Minnesota (9-3)	31-30	Oregon (8-4)	49,894
Dec. 31, 2003	AXA Liberty	Utah (9-2)	17-0	Sou. Mississippi (9-3)	55,989
Dec. 31, 2003	Independence	Arkansas (8-4)	27-14	Missouri (8-4)	49,625
Dec. 31, 2003	Music City	Auburn (7-5)	28-14	Wisconsin (7-5)	55,219
Dec. 31, 2003	San Francisco	Boston College (7-5)	35-21	Colorado St. (7-5)	25,621
Jan. 1, 2004	Rose	**Sou. California** (11-1)	28-14	Michigan (10-2)	93,849
Jan. 1, 2004	FedEx Orange	Miami (10-2)	16-14	Florida St. (10-2)	76,739
Jan. 1, 2004	Toyota Gator	Maryland (9-3)	41-7	West Virginia (8-4)	78,892
Jan. 1, 2004	Capital One	Georgia (10-3)	34-27	Purdue (9-3)	64,565
Jan. 1, 2004	Outback	Iowa (9-3)	37-17	Florida (8-4)	65,372
Jan. 2, 2004	SBC Cotton	Mississippi (9-3)	31-28	Oklahoma St. (9-3)	73,928
Jan. 2, 2004	**Ch-Fil-A Peach**	Clemson (8-4)	27-14	Tennessee (10-2)	**75,125**
Jan. 2, 2004	Tostitos Fiesta	Ohio St. (10-2)	35-28	Kansas St. (11-3)	73,425
Jan. 3, 2004	Humanitarian	Georgia Tech (6-6)	52-10	Tulsa (8-4)	23,118
Jan. 4, 2004	Nokia Sugar	**Louisiana St.** (12-1)	21-14	Oklahoma (12-1)	79,342

APPENDIX 2

Bowl Game Records

Individual records, one game

Most points: 30
Barry Sanders, Oklahoma State, vs. Wyoming (Holiday 1988)
Sheldon Canley, San Jose State, vs. Central Michigan (California 1990)
Steven Jackson, Oregon State, vs. New Mexico (Sega Sports Las Vegas 2003)

Most points responsible for: 40
Bobby Layne, Texas (18 rushing, 12 passing, 6 receiving, 4 PATs), vs. Missouri (Cotton 1946)

Most total yardage: 594
Ty Detmer, Brigham Young (18 rushing, 576 passing) vs. Penn State (Holiday 1989)

Most net passing yardage: 576
Ty Detmer, Brigham Young, vs. Penn State (Holiday 1989)
Byron Leftwich, Marshall, vs. East Carolina (2 overtimes) (GMAC 2001)

Most touchdown passes thrown: 6
Chuck Long, Iowa, vs. Texas (Freedom 1984)

Most pass receptions: 20
Walker Gillette, Richmond, vs. Ohio (Tangerine 1968)
Norman Jordan, Vanderbilt, vs. Air Force (Hall of Fame 1982)

Most touchdown passes caught: 4
Bob McChesney, Hardin-Simmons, vs. Wichita State (Camellia 1948)
Fred Biletnikoff, Florida State, vs. Oklahoma (Gator 1965)

Most pass reception yardage: 299
Rodney Wright, Fresno State, vs. Michigan State (Silicon Valley 2001)

Longest touchdown pass play: 95 yards
Ronnie Fletcher to Ben Hart, Oklahoma, vs. Florida State (Gator 1965)

Most net rushing yards: 280
James Gray, Texas Tech, vs. Duke (All-American 1989)

Most rushing touchdowns: 5
Neil Snow, Michigan, vs. Stanford (Rose 1902. Note: touchdowns counted as only 5 points)
Barry Sanders, Oklahoma State, vs. Wyoming (Holiday 1988)
Sheldon Canley, San Jose State, vs. Central Michigan (California 1990)

Longest run from scrimmage: 99 yards (TD)
Terry Baker, Oregon State, vs. Villanova (Liberty 1962)

Most all-purpose yards: 359
Sherman Williams, Alabama, vs. Ohio State (Florida Citrus 1995)

Longest field goal: 62 yards
Tony Franklin, Texas A&M, vs. Florida (Sun 1977)

Most field goals made: 5
Jess Atkinson, Maryland, vs. Tennessee (Florida Citrus 1983)
Arden Czyzewski, Florida, vs. Notre Dame (Sugar 1992)
Kyle Bryant, Texas A&M, vs. Michigan (Alamo 1995)
Tim Rogers, Mississippi, vs. North Carolina State (Peach 1995)
Dan Nystrom, Minnesota, vs. Arkansas (Music City 2002)

Most extra points made: 7
James Weaver, Centre, vs.Texas Christian (Fort Worth Classic 1921)
Layne Talbot, Texas A&M, vs. Brigham Young (Holiday 1990)
Neil Rackers, Illinois, vs. Virginia (Micronpc.com 1999)
Josh Brown, Nebraska, vs. Northwestern (Alamo 2000)

Longest punt (regular punt): 82 yards
Ike Pickle, Mississippi State, vs. Duquesne (Orange 1937)

Longest punt (quick kick): 84 yards
Kyle Rote, Southern Methodist, vs. Oregon (Cotton 1949)

Highest average per punt (minimum 5): 53.8 yards
Mat McBriar, Hawaii, 5 punts, vs. Tulane (Hawaii 2002)

Longest punt return: 88 yards (TD)
Ben Kelly, Colorado, vs. Boston College (Insight.com 1999)

Longest kickoff return: 100 yards
Al Hoisch, UCLA, vs. Illinois (Rose 1947)
Bob Smith, Texas A&M, vs. Georgia (Presidential Cup 1950)
Mike Fink, Missouri, vs. Arizona State (Fiesta 1972)
Dave Lowery, Brigham Young, vs. Oklahoma State (Tangerine 1976)
Pete Panuska, Tennessee, vs. Maryland (Sun 1984)
Kirby Dar Dar, Syracuse, vs. Colorado (Fiesta 1993)
Derrick Mason, Michigan State, vs. Louisiana State (Independence 1995)
Deltha O'Neal, California, vs. Navy (Aloha 1996)
C. J. Jones, Iowa, vs. Southern California (Orange 2003)

Most pass interceptions: 4
Manuel Aja, Arizona State, vs. Xavier (Ohio) (Salad 1950)
Jim Dooley, Miami, vs. Clemson (Gator 1952)

Longest pass interception return: 95 yards (TD)
Marcus Washington, Colorado, vs. Oregon (Cotton 1996)

Longest lateral interception return: 98 yards (TD)
Greg Mather, Navy, vs. Missouri (Orange 1961)

Most total tackles (including assists): 31
Lee Roy Jordan, Alabama, vs. Oklahoma (Orange 1963)

Most tackles for losses: 6
LaMarcus McDonald, TCU, vs. Texas A&M (galleryfurniture.com 2001)

Most quarterback sacks: 6
Shay Muirbrook, Brigham Young, vs. Kansas State (Cotton 1997)

Most fumbles recovered: 2
Rod Kirby, Pittsburgh, vs. Arizona State (Fiesta 1973)
Michael Stewart, Fresno State, vs. Bowling Green (California 1985)
Randall Brown, Ohio State, vs. Alabama (Florida Citrus 1995)

Most kicks blocked: 2
Carlton Williams, Pittsburgh, vs. Arizona State (Fiesta 1973)
Bracey Walker, North Carolina, vs. Mississippi State (Peach 1993)

Team records, one game

Most total yards gained: 718
Arizona State, vs. Missouri (Fiesta 1972)

Fewest total yards allowed: -21
Southwestern (Texas), vs. University of Mexico (Sun 1945)

Most net rushing yards: 524
Nebraska, vs. Florida (Fiesta 1996)

Fewest rushing yards allowed: -61
Boston College, vs. Kansas State (Aloha 1994)

Most passing yards: 576
Brigham Young, vs. Penn State (Holiday 1989)
Marshall, vs. East Carolina (2 overtimes) (GMAC 2001)

Fewest passing yards allowed: -50
Southwestern (Texas), vs. University of Mexico (Sun 1945)

Most touchdowns scored: 10
Nebraska, vs. Northwestern (Alamo 2000)

Most fumbles: 11
Mississippi (lost 6), vs. Alabama (Sugar 1964)

Most penalties: 21
Mississippi State (188 yards), vs. Clemson (Peach 1999)

Most yards penalized: 202
Miami (16 penalties), vs. Texas (Cotton 1991)

Fewest penalties: 0
Alabama, vs. Washington (Rose 1926)
Texas, vs. Randolph Field (Cotton 1944)
Clemson, vs. Miami (Gator 1952)
Pittsburgh, vs. Georgia Tech (Gator 1956)
Rice, vs. Kansas (Bluebonnet 1961)
Texas, vs. Alabama (Cotton 1973)
Louisiana Tech, vs. East Carolina (Independence 1978)
Southern Methodist, vs. Alabama (Sun 1983)

Most points scored by an individual team: 66
Nebraska, vs. Northwestern (Alamo 2000)

Most points scored, both teams combined (regulation): 101
California 52, Virginia Tech 49 (Insight 2003)

Most points scored, both teams combined (overtime): 125
Marshall 64, East Carolina 61 (GMAC 2001)

Largest margin of victory: 55 points
Alabama 61, Syracuse 6 (Orange 1953)

Fewest points scored by a winning team: 2
Fordham 2, Missouri 0 (Sugar 1942)

Fewest points scored, both teams combined: 0
California 0, Washington & Jefferson 0 (Rose 1922)
Arizona State 0, Catholic University 0 (Sun 1940)
Arkansas 0, Louisiana State 0 (Cotton 1947)
Air Force 0, Texas Christian 0 (Cotton 1959)

Team and coaching records, multiple games

Top ten teams: most bowl appearances

Team	Appearances	W–L–T
1. Alabama	51	29–19–3
2. Tennessee	44	23–21–0
3. Texas	43	20–21–2
4. Nebraska	42	21–21–0
4. USC	42	27–15–0
6. Georgia	39	21–15–3
7. Oklahoma	37	23–13–1
7. Penn State	37	23–12–2
9. LSU	35	17–17–1
9. Michigan	35	18–17–0
9. Ohio State	35	16–19–0
10. Arkansas	34	11–20–3

Top ten teams: most bowl victories

Team	Wins	W–L–T
1. Alabama	29	29–19–3
2. USC	27	27–15–0
3. Oklahoma	23	23–13–1
3. Penn State	23	23–12–2
3. Tennessee	23	23–21–0
6. Georgia	21	21–15–3
6. Georgia Tech	21	21–11–0
6. Nebraska	21	21–21–0
9. Texas	20	20–21–2
10. Mississippi	19	19–12–0

Top ten teams: best winning percentage (minimum 15 appearances)

Team	Percentage	W–L–T
1. Oklahoma St.	.667	10–5–0
2. Georgia Tech	.656	21–11–0
3. Penn State	.649	23–12–2
4. USC	.643	27–15–0
5. Oklahoma	.635	23–13–1
6. Mississippi	.613	19–12–0
7. Boston C.	.600	9–6–0
8. Florida State	.594	18–12–2
9. Alabama	.598	29–19–3
10. Syracuse	.595	12–8–1

Top ten coaches: most bowl victories

Coach	Wins	W–L–T
1. Joe Paterno	20	20–10–1
2. Bobby Bowden	18	18–8–1
3. Bear Bryant	15	15–12–2
4. Lou Holtz	12	12–8–2
4. Tom Osborne	12	12–13–0
6. Don James	10	10–5–0
6. John Vaught	10	10–8–0
8. Bobby Dodd	9	9–4–0
8. Johnny Majors	9	9–7–0

Coach	Wins	W–L–T
10. Terry Donahue	8	8–4–1
10. Vince Dooley	8	8–10–2
10. John Robinson	8	8–1–0
10. Darrell Royal	8	8–7–1
10. Jackie Sherrill	8	8–6–0
10. Barry Switzer	8	8–5–0

Top ten coaches: best winning percentage (minimum ten games)

Coach	Percentage	W–L–T
1. Bobby Dodd	.692	9–4–0
2. Bobby Bowden	.685	18–8–1
3. Don James	.667	10–5–0
4. Joe Paterno	.661	20–10–1
5. Terry Donahue	.654	8–4–1
6. Barry Switzer	.615	8–5–0
7. Lou Holtz	.591	12–8–2
7. Bill Yeoman	.591	6–4–1
9. Earle Bruce	.583	7–5–0
10. Jackie Sherrill	.571	8–6–0

Top ten coaches: total bowl appearances

Coach	Bowls	W–L–T
1. Joe Paterno	31	20–10–1
2. Bear Bryant	29	15–12–2
3. Bobby Bowden	27	18–8–1
4. Tom Osborne	25	12–13
5. Lou Holtz	22	12–8–2
5. LaVell Edwards	22	7–14–1
7. Vince Dooley	20	8–10–2
8. John Vaught	18	10–8–0
9. Hayden Fry	17	7–9–1
9. Bo Schembechler	17	5–12–0
10. Johnny Majors	16	9–7–0
10. Darrell Royal	16	8–7–1

SOURCES

Principal sources include newspaper and magazine articles, and correspondence with current and former coaches, players, and sports information directors over many years and, more recently, Web sites of bowls and schools noted in the text along with other Internet sources. Among the more useful books and magazines were:

Baker, Dr. L. H. *Football: Facts and Figures*. New York, 1945.
Bernstein, Mark F. *Football: The Ivy League Origins of an American Obsession*. Philadelphia, 2001.
Boda, Steve Jr., compiler. *College Football All-Time Record Book*. New York, 1969.
Brondfield, Jerry. *Great Moments in American Sports*. New York, 1974.
Clark, Kristine Setting. *Undefeated, Untied, and Uninvited: A Documentary of the 1951 University of San Francisco Dons Football Team*. Irvine, Calif., 2002.
College Football Illustrated. 1948 and 1949 issues.
Football Illustrated Annual. Various issues, 1933–1949.
Football Media Guides. 125 colleges and universities, various years.
"G.I. All-American Team—1944." *Yank: The Army Weekly*, Dec. 22, 1944.
Grange, Red. *My Favorite Football Stories*. New York, 1955.
Hendrickson, Joe. *Tournament of Roses: The First 100 Years*. Los Angeles, 1989.
Intercollegiate and Professional Football. New York, 1949.
Mulé, Marty. *Sugar Bowl: The First Fifty Years*. Birmingham, 1983.
National Collegiate Sports Service, producer. *College Football Modern Record Book*. New York, 1973.
NCAA Football's Finest. Overland Park, Kan., 1990.
NCAA Football's Finest. Indianapolis, 2002.
NCAA Official Football Guide and Football Records. Annually, 1943–2003.
Nelson, David M. *Anatomy of a Game: Football, the Rules, and the Men who*

Made the Game. Newark, Del., 1994.

Ours, Robert M. *College Football Almanac*. New York, 1984.

_____ *College Football Encyclopedia*. Rocklin, Calif., 1994.

_____ *College Football Encyclopedia*. CD. Volumes 2–4. 1999–2002.

Russell, Fred. "The Best Game I Ever Saw." *Football Digest*, 1949.

Smith, Loran. *Fifty Years on the Fifty: The Orange Bowl Story*. Charlotte, N.C., 1983.

Stern, Bill. *Bill Stern's Favorite Football Stories*. New York, 1948.

Street & Smith. *Football Pictorial Year Book*. Various issues, 1945–2003.

Waldorf, John. *NCAA Football Rules Committee Chronology of 100 Years 1876 to 1976*. Shawnee Mission, Kan., 1975.

INDEX